Cambridge Studies in Cultural Systems

The Lumbee problem:
The making of an American Indian people

Cambridge Studies in Cultural Systems

Clifford Geertz, Editor

The Lumbee problem: The making of an American Indian people

Karen I. Blu

New York University

Cambridge University Press

Cambridge
London   New York   New Rochelle
Melbourne   Sydney

Published by the Press Syndicate of the University of Cambridge
The Pitt Building, Trumpington Street, Cambridge CB2 1RP
32 East 57th Street, New York, NY 10022, USA
296 Beaconsfield Parade, Middle Park, Melbourne 3206, Australia

© Cambridge University Press 1980

First published 1980

Printed in the United States of America
Typeset by David E. Seham Assoc., Inc., Metuchen, N.J.
Printed and bound by The Murray Printing Co., Westford, Mass.

Library of Congress Cataloging in Publication Data
Blu, Karen I
The Lumbee problem.

Bibliography: p.
Includes index.
1. Lumbee Indians. 2. Ethnicity. I. Title.
E99.C91B57   970.004'97   79-12908
ISBN 0 521 22525 6   hard covers
ISBN 0 521 29542 4   paperback

For Harriet I. Arzt, Franz Arzt, Sr., and Hertha J. Schiele and to the memory of Marshall A. Blu, Edwin H. Johnson, and Arthur F. Schiele

Contents

Preface

After a wiltingly hot, humid summer of living and working in Robeson County, North Carolina, I found myself confronted by a nagging, insistent question: How is the rather colorful career of the numerous, feisty people known as the Lumbee Indians to be understood? Although I had come to Robeson County to work with the Indians, by the end of that first summer I knew that if I were ever to comprehend them and their way of life, much broader understandings were needed – of the South, of Lumbee history, of Eastern Indians, and of ethnicity.

First, it was necessary to know Robeson County Whites and Blacks as well as Indians, which meant understanding something about the South and the all-pervasive consciousness of race and the past with which all its people are imbued. Second, the history of the area and of the relations between Indians and others needed to be traced and placed in the perspective of larger events in the state and nation. Third, because the Lumbee were active in pan-Indian enterprises and in federal affairs, it became important to consider their Indianness in the light of others' ideas about Indianness generally. And finally, because the entire nation was, at that time (1967–68), vividly witnessing the full impact of the civil rights movement and the beginnings of a popular emphasis on ethnicity, the issue of how the Lumbee are related to these national concerns emerged.

This work, then, traces the political and legal history of the Indians of Robeson County, arguing that Lumbee political activities have been powerfully affected by the interplay between their own and others' conceptions of who they are. In so doing, it offers insights into the workings of racial ideology and practice in both the past and present South. These insights in turn shed light on the nature of Indianness as it is widely experienced by nonreservation Southeastern Indians, of whom it is too often mistakenly asserted, "They would rather be White, but they can't, so they'll settle for Indian." Race and ethnicity, as concepts and as elements guiding action, are seen to be at the heart of the matter. These issues and their implications as they are worked

ix

out in the United States must be understood before the concepts can be applied to circumstances in other nations. That too-ready cross-cultural application has led to confusion and error is patent: what to do about it is less clear, though some suggestions are offered in the final chapter.

The notion of "understanding" is a crucial one throughout. What is it to "understand"? As used here, it is to learn not only of the "outside" forces that impinge upon a people – in this case, the Lumbee – but to learn how these forces are conceived and how they are affected by other notions, orientations, and emotions. It is to have a sense of what it must have meant to be an Indian in Robeson County at one period or another. In order for a non-Lumbee to have any sense of what it is to be a Lumbee, there must be a translation from the insider's experiences, ideas, and sentiments into terms intelligible to an outsider. It is this translation, providing a bridge by which the insider's sensibilities can meet the outsider's somewhat different ones, that has been called "interpretation" (Geertz 1973). A comprehension is sought of others' moods and motivations, of their perceptions of the world, of their ethos. Only then can people's actions and reactions to either "outside" or "inside" forces and events "make sense."

Creating "understanding" in this special sense, one which derives, of course, from Max Weber, is a task well suited to the anthropological enterprise. The prolonged on-site residence and the daily observation and participation in local life demanded by anthropological fieldwork facilitate the creation of this kind of understanding as survey research alone can never do. Concretely, the anthropologist seeks "understanding" by paying particular attention to the things people say or do not say, the way they say them or do not, and what they are doing with whom when they say them. The words that are chosen, the emphasis placed on them, the mood of the moment, the flavor of an encounter are all significant clues to "understanding." Because this is the case, from time to time in this work I have cited long passages from my fieldnotes and other pertinent documents in order to allow the reader to judge for himself something of the tone and quality of statements and events.

Anthropology has often been wrongly thought to be the study of exotic, out-of-the-way people, a discipline unsuited to dealing with the problems and complexities of modern life. In fact, the insights and techniques gained through the study of small-scale societies can usefully be applied in large, industrialized and industrializing areas (see, e.g., Fallers 1974). Such skills can be especially useful in studying one's own society, for many years an anthropological taboo because, it was feared, one's objectivity would be compromised. Precisely because training in anthropology exposes one to the welter of social and

cultural variation in the world, an anthropologist studying his own society is more aware of his possible cultural blinders and is likely to take
for granted much less about his own society than those without that
training. At the same time, the anthropologist studying his own culture
is a "familiar stranger," one somewhat apart, yet at least partially versed
in the sensibilities and outlook of those he desires to understand and
potentially able to delve deeply into their nuances because he is so
versed. Further, a finely tuned attention to matters usually overlooked
– to the everyday, the quietly unobvious – is the anthropologist's special talent, one that stands him in especially good stead in his own
society, where these subtleties tend to go unremarked.

Although promoting "understanding" is not exclusively the prov-
ince of anthropology, the fact remains that today it is usually anthropologists who adopt this kind of approach. W. Lloyd Warner and
his associates conveyed it rather unintentionally in their study of
"Yankee City" in the 1930s and 1940s, but since the early 1950s and
the growing dissatisfaction with the study of single communities there
have been few works based on extensive fieldwork in the United States
that are, like this one, neither "community studies" nor "subculture
studies" (the study of a single group more or less in isolation from its
neighbors and nation). And despite the election of Georgia's Jimmy
Carter to the Presidency and the emergence of the "Sun Belt" into
national awareness, up-to-date published studies that increase our
grasp of the South's diversity, complexity, and cultural flexibility remain exceedingly rare. The work presented here is in part an attempt to
redress the peculiar neglect of the South as an appropriate area of study
for anthropologists and others concerned with the study of meaning.

Few sociologists today are concerned with "understanding" in their
study of the United States, however much their fellows may have been
in earlier decades. The kind of study offered here enhances and com-
plements the statistical profiles and macro-views now more generally
available. Historians of the South have not ordinarily attempted to
convey "understanding" as it is meant here, either, though there are a
few very notable exceptions. Those who have often provided the most
vivid accounts of the Southern insider's point of view have been
novelists and autobiographers, but they do not trace the structure or
the implications of that point of view, a task for social scientists. What
interpretive anthropology can offer to other approaches is a sense of
how the actors in events see themselves and what might motivate them
to act as they do, thereby embodying statistics and making human the
scale of eventful change.

Unlike most historical and sociological works, anthropological
studies of American Indians have traditionally been concerned with

"world view" – the insiders' notions of what their world is all about. Rarely, however, have these world views been discussed as they confront, synthesize, intrude into, or conflict with the views of those around them. To judge from the existing literature, a Native American world view can be maintained, threatened, or destroyed, can adapt and change, but almost never is to be seen as it coexists with others in a dynamic way (for an exception see Braroe 1975). The focus here is on the way certain aspects of Lumbee world view are enmeshed with their neighbors' views and what has happened as a result of the way they are enmeshed. This study is the first full-scale, documented, scholarly work to employ both past and present circumstances in the analysis of what has happened to a nonreservation Eastern Indian people, of how they have survived and managed to thrive despite strong efforts to discourage and disband them.

It should be evident, then, that this study is intended to speak to those interested in the American South, in ethnicity, in change, in American Indians, and in group identity, be they anthropologists, sociologists, historians, or interested laymen. The Lumbee seem altogether a timely people, perforce interested in their "roots" before it became a fashionable nationwide passion, articulating for themselves an identity essentially "ethnic" (rather than "racial") at a time when only a few social scientists used the term, and holding fast and occasionally fiercely to an identity denigrated by others when it would have been easy for many of them to take a materially more comfortable route of "passing" for White.

A look at the Lumbee as both Southerners and Native Americans shows that some common notions about the South, about Indians, and about what it takes to make a viable society must be altered. If Southern racial ideology appears rigid and unyielding, its workings are far more flexible and complicated than has generally been acknowledged. The evidence of the Lumbee and many other "interstitial" peoples neither Black nor White is compelling on this point.

The Lumbee also suggest, by lacking what are thought to be "traditional" Indian customs and traits, that Indianness is based in an orientation toward life, a sense of the past, "a state of mind," as one Lumbee put it. It is the *way* of doing and being that is "Indian," not what is done or the blood quantum of the doer. Indians from many different groups have, of course, said something like this before, but never before has a whole group been seen to exemplify the point so forcefully. Treating the Lumbee as both Indian and Southern emphasizes the extent to which Indians are influenced by their local milieu, which leads to the conclusion that some differences among Native Americans may, today, be attributable to their having become in varying degrees Westerners, or Northeasterners, or Californians, or whatever. The regional factor in Indian studies has been largely ignored or glossed over, as has the amount of influence Indians have on their localities.

Finally, the Lumbee can be seen as an "indigenous" ethnic group – a group that has developed its identity from within the United States and does not look to an immigrant past as the core of its distinctiveness. The development of this kind of ethnic identity has been slighted in favor of the study of more traditional, immigrant-based groups. The Lumbee, unlike some Native American peoples, have chosen to mix in rather than withdraw from the larger society, and therefore cannot be considered an isolated enclave. Indeed, they see themselves and are seen by others as structurally similar, for certain purposes, to Italian-Americans, Black Americans, or Greek-Americans as well as to other Native Americans. At the same time, they claim and have been accorded indigenous status. Their history exemplifies the complicated intertwining of race and ethnicity, as those concepts have been used in the United States by laymen and social scientists. Further, the concept of "the ethnic group" as it is thought of today is a peculiarly American phenomenon, which is one of the reasons attempts to generalize it to other areas of the world have encountered problems.

With the general rise of "ethnic consciousness" in America, native Americans have lately come to be considered "ethnics," although most of the literature on Indians treats them either in substantial isolation from the surrounding nation or as victims of it. Hopefully, this work will be just one of a number of studies concerned with Indian sources of resiliency, their integration into the local and national economy and polity, and their impact on their neighbors. The Lumbee are never simply acted upon – they are quite definitely actors acting.

K. I. B.

New York, New York
November 1979

Acknowledgments

Any enterprise that extends over a period of more than ten years, evolving slowly throughout and changing form substantially several times, inevitably owes its final form to the contributions, knowing and unknowing, of many people, and to the support of several institutions and granting agencies. The project began as dissertation fieldwork, which was carried out in 1967–68 under a Predoctoral Research Fellowship from the National Institute of Mental Health, U.S. Public Health Service (5-Fl-MH-24, 135-03 and -04). During my tenure in 1971–72 as a National Endowment for the Humanities Postdoctoral Research Fellow in American Indian Studies at the Department of Anthropology, Smithsonian Institution, I revisited Robeson County and obtained much of the historical documentation used in this work. The manuscript took final form and was typed in 1976–77 at the Institute for Advanced Study, Princeton, New Jersey.

The search for unpublished documents or rare published ones is always time consuming and frequently frustrating. Among those who have substantially helped to minimize the difficulties of my search for such documents are Margaret Blaker, then head archivist of the National Anthropological Archives, and Barbara Tucker, who is responsible for interlibrary loans at the Institute for Advanced Study. Also at the Institute for Advanced Study, Peggy A. Clarke efficiently supervised the final typing of the manuscript, and she, Jamye Edwards, Portia Edwards, Amy Jackson, and Catharine Rhubart typed it with unfailing patience, good humor, and exceptional care.

My work with the Lumbee began while I was a graduate student at the University of Chicago and I am indebted to a number of those who were then on the faculty: Fred Eggan, the late Lloyd A. Fallers, Raymond D. Fogelson, Paul Friedrich, Clifford Geertz, and David M. Schneider. Their intellectual influences permeate this volume. I am particularly indebted to Fogelson and Schneider who provided, each in his own way, invaluable advice and encouragement. At the Smithsonian Institution, William C. Sturtevant provided me with an important introduction to the

xiv

Lumbee; he and Sam Stanley have consistently helped me to view the Lumbee in the larger context of Eastern Indians. Harold W. Scheffler's constructive comments and insistence on clarity have aided me immeasurably since I was an undergraduate and have improved several of my manuscripts on the Lumbee. At the Institute for Advanced Study, Clifford Geertz's incisive questions pushed me further toward an interdisciplinary approach. He, Thomas O. Beidelman, Sam Stanley, and Robert Thomas read this manuscript and offered valuable suggestions for its improvement. I am also indebted to those who have discussed, read, and commented on other manuscripts I have done on the Lumbee or on parts of this one: Raymond J. DeMallie, Fred Eggan, Dale F. Eickelman, Raymond D. Fogelson, Nancy Foner, Loretta Fowler, Enrique Gildemeister, Susan James, Julius Moshinsky, Sherry B. Ortner, Robert A. Paul, Lawrence Rosen, Liane Rosenblatt, Ellen and William Sewell, Philip Silverman, Quentin Skinner, and Martin Trow. My co-fieldworker and ex-husband, Gerald M. Sider, participated with me in common early field experiences and countless discussions, I believe to our mutual benefit.

Finally, I am deeply indebted to the many people of Robeson County who contributed in various and important ways to this enterprise, and especially to the Indians who accepted, tentatively at first, warmly later, two Northern White anthropologists when they had no particular reason to do so. I am saddened by the deaths of several Indian friends who would, I hope, have liked to see the fruits of their generously given time. I have deliberately mentioned no names when I could have mentioned many, for fear that to identify individuals might be to jeopardize their privacy and in so doing to cause embarrassment, distress, and perhaps even hardship. My gratitude for their anonymous help is correspondingly the greater.

1. Why the Lumbee?

How do a group of people who are legally designated "free persons of color" and who have Indian ancestry but no records of treaties, reservations, an Indian language, or peculiarly "Indian" customs become accepted socially and legally as Indians?

To uncover just how this remarkable transition has been made by the Lumbee Indians of Robeson County, North Carolina, is the task of this enterprise. What makes the transition particularly remarkable is that by many traditional standards the Lumbee should either have ceased to exist or should currently be a thoroughly disordered, discordant, and disconsolate lot, hardly deserving designation as "a people." For the past 180 years, the Lumbee have apparently lacked any formal political organization, have had no obviously "Indian" cultural appurtenances, and have been prone to a factionalism that has sometimes been intense. Yet they flourish in a sometimes hostile environment. They have improved their social and legal status, their standard of living and educational attainments, and have become the largest Indian group east of the Mississippi, a group increasingly active in pan-Indian affairs.

In short, the Lumbee have been quite successful, in their own terms and in others' as well. Just how they did it remains the central question. It is my argument that their success is strongly related to (1) their continuing ability to incorporate outsiders into their community and to foster creativity from the resultant heterogeneity; (2) their pervasive factionalism, usually considered a destructive force, but in this case a constructive one in the absence of formal arenas of competition and in the presence of strong orientations in individuals to work for the benefit of the group; and (3) their effective exploitation of economic opportunities, first in establishing a firm and ongoing agricultural land base, later in developing a pattern of temporary out-migration for employment, and most recently in moving into manufacturing industries, small businesses, and professions. Finally, the key to all these, the driving force behind each of them, is the ideas Lumbees have about who they are as a people – what Isaacs (1974) has called "basic group identity."

1

Lumbee ideas about their Indianness have allowed for the incorporation of outsiders, have given direction to the efforts of factions, and
have provided an impetus to find economic opportunities that will
allow Indians to stay or return "home."

Their accomplishments have not come easily to the Lumbee. They
have had to struggle continuously against the White-dominated racial
system in which they live and for the identity they insist they have (cf.
Wallace and Fogelson 1965). I have sought to portray something of the
saga of this struggle from the middle of the nineteenth century to the
last quarter of the twentieth, highlighting now one set of figures and
their particular circumstances and then another. In doing this, I have
tried to tease out the meaning of their group identity to the Lumbee and
how this identity has affected and been affected by political activity.

Why should the Lumbee be of any general interest?

By doing what they have done, the Lumbee present problems for several sociological and anthropological assumptions about the way
groups maintain themselves. First, they challenge anthropological
postulates about the need for obviously distinctive "cultural" differences, such as customs, crafts, language, arts, or even symbols used by
and in reference to one group only. Such differences, it has been argued, are required if a group is to maintain itself as an entity vis-à-vis
its neighbors, particularly if the group lacks formal political organization. Second, the Lumbee challenge sociological and social anthropological ideas that formal organization of some kind is necessary
to hold together large groups, which cannot operate on a face-to-face
basis. The Lumbee community maintains no membership lists and easily absorbs the children of in-married outsiders, a difficulty for research-
ers who seek for neatly defined boundaries and rules for crossing them.
Finally, factionalism, which has apparently pervaded the Indian community for as long as we know anything about it, has not had the disor-
ganizing effects so often ascribed to it and so often witnessed in other
groups, thereby raising the question "Why not?"

If the Lumbee lack the traditional mechanisms for holding themselves together – formal organization, explicit membership criteria, distinctive cultural paraphernalia – then what does hold them together?
My answer is, again, their shared ideas about themselves as a people.
Coming to an understanding of just what those ideas are is a major part
of this undertaking. And in gaining that understanding, other theoretical issues are raised about how symbols work and how they change.
For example, it may be asked in what ways do the Lumbee assert their

distinctiveness as a people, and how do their neighbors perceive their differentness? Wherein can a distinct Lumbee Indian identity be said to lie? And how has this identity been forged and maintained for more than 180 years, despite great pressures to merge with Blacks and persistent temptations to assimilate with Whites? It appears that the Lumbee and their Black and White neighbors draw upon a pool of symbols shared by all of them, but they use the symbols differently, or attach different meanings to them, in creating and maintaining their distinctiveness. Further, the interpretive frameworks into which the symbols fit differ from group to group and must also be analyzed in order to understand what the symbols mean.

Aside from these theoretical considerations, an investigation of the Lumbee contributes both to research on the American South and to American Indian studies. The Lumbee, an influential population in both county and state since about 1860, were originally classified as "free persons of color" and later as "free Negroes." Historians have lumped the Lumbee and other groups like them scattered throughout the Southeast (and, to a degree, throughout the East) with Blacks who were freed before the end of the Civil War, terming them all "free Negroes" (e.g., Berlin 1974, Franklin 1943, Genovese 1974). If groups that maintained a distinction (one recognized by their neighbors) between themselves and freed Blacks were considered separately, a different picture of the dynamics of the 1800s might emerge. In any event, the present picture would become richer and more complicated.

A growing literature on groups that have at some time received a "third race" classification, whether as "Indians," "Chinese," or "Turk-Americans," forces a reconsideration of views of the South based on an oversimplified Black–White dichotomy (see, for example, Price 1950, Loewen 1971, Kim 1977, Woods 1972, Fischer 1970, Stanton 1971, Blu n.d.). Throughout the South, the prevalence of pockets in which three, or sometimes more, "races" are recognized presents an opportunity for comparative study on how groups developed the different identities they now have, how they accomplished their ends, and what kind of resistance they encountered (all encountered some). Some of the groups, at least, are not as isolated as they once appeared. It is clear, for example, that the Lumbee have had ongoing relationships with the Haliwa, the Waccamaw, the Coharie, and the Person County Indians in North Carolina for a number of years. Further study on the nature, extent, and influences of such contacts is needed.

Work on American Indian groups has neglected nonreservation Indians who have no ties or claims on services through the Bureau of Indian Affairs (BIA). Reservation groups and nonreservation Indians in Oklahoma who retain some services from the BIA have been widely studied, but relatively little attention has been given to Indians who have had to "make it on their own," as one Lumbee put it. The Lumbee today are the fifth largest Indian people in the United States, according to the 1970 U.S. census (U.S. Bureau of the Census–Population, 1973b), in which they are underreported.[1] Despite their size and impact on Southeastern nonreservation Indian affairs, there is a relative dearth of published scholarly information about the group.

The Lumbee and groups like them have begun to try to coordinate their efforts at self-betterment through agencies such as the newly established North Carolina Commission on Indian Affairs, which includes several non-BIA affiliated nonreservation Indian groups in North Carolina. Most nontreaty groups of this sort are located in the Eastern United States (and in consequence have had the longest and most intense contact with non-Indians), and have had to struggle to assert their identities in a cultural milieu where a dark skin suggests to many Whites the presence of at least one or two drops of Black "blood," all that is needed for many Whites to consider a person "Black." In such a context, "Indianness" is easy to lose and "Blackness" easy to gain. Most of these groups today exhibit a wide range of physical characteristics, with great variation in skin color, hair texture, and facial features. Among the Southeastern nonreservation, non-BIA affiliated Indians, the Lumbee have always been in the forefront, leading the struggle for legal recognition and improved educational opportunities. Their accomplishments have frequently made the way easier for other groups, and Lumbee teachers and preachers working in other groups have often encouraged and aided them.

As nonreservation groups such as the Lumbee have become more active and influential in pan-Indian affairs, some reservation Indians have begun to oppose, for example, Lumbee access to benefits from federal programs for Indians. In 1975, the National Congress of American Indians barred the Lumbee from renewing their membership of long standing.

The Lumbee must be viewed in two contexts – as American Indians and as Southerners – for both these larger settings have an impact on the way Indians present themselves and on the way others respond to them. On the one hand, Lumbees increasingly have come to deal directly with other Indians in pan-Indian activities, and in these they stress their kinship with other Indians in the form of facing similar discrimination, of possessing a similar past in which the main theme is loss of independence and land to Whites, and of sharing common problems (e.g., Dial and Barton comments in *Indian Voices* 1970: 117–22, 323–4). At the same time, Lumbees are quite well aware of the differences between their own situation as nonreservation and nontreaty Indians and the situation of reservation and treaty groups, and these differences give rise to Lumbee expressions both of superiority ("For us to get a reservation would set us back a hundred years") and of inferiority ("We've lost our culture").[2] On the other hand, Lumbees have to present themselves to Whites, who, they know, have images of "real Indians" as feather-wearing, bead-working, jewelry-making, and horse-riding people like the Dakota in the Old West (V. Deloria 1969). Lumbees have to cope with the images that Whites have about Indians in general in such a way that Lumbees can be included in the category "Indian" (by changing the characteristics of the category, or by making their own characteristics appear to fit, or both). As Lumbee awareness of national Indian affairs has increased, Lumbee strategies have altered. At the same time, by thrusting themselves into the national arena as they did by routing the Ku Klux Klan in 1958, by participating in the Trail of Broken Treaties with the American Indian Movement (AIM) in 1972, and by filling prominent positions on the federal Indian Claims Commission and the Indian Policy Review Board, they are beginning to have an impact on Indian affairs and ultimately, perhaps, on the nation's image of Indians.

As Southerners, the Lumbee have participated in the great events of Southern history, from the Revolutionary War, when a few Indian men fought beside Whites for independence, to the Civil War and Reconstruction, during which a guerrilla band led by a young Indian named Henry Berry Lowry held local Whites at bay for several years. The Indians share with Whites and Blacks the memory of ancestors' stories about these events, if not the same interpretations of them. But of all aspects of Southern experience, the most pervasive is the system of racial classification and the institutionalized segregation of races based on it. It is within this system that the Lumbee have had to work to establish their identity. The Lumbee struggle for a separate Indian identity has had to be fought in terms of racial ideology and its institutionalization. At the same time, by steadfastly refusing to accept the classification assigned them by Whites, the Indians changed the course of events in Robeson County and paved the way for the legal recognition of other "third race" groups in North Carolina. As they have responded to changing racial and economic conditions in the state, the Lumbee have managed to exert political influence far greater than their numbers alone would suggest.

What kind of evidence is cited?

Given that the Lumbee and, to a smaller degree, their Black and White neighbors are the focus of this study, it may be asked what kinds of data are to be presented here. They are derived from two sources – anthropological fieldwork and documentary materials. My field research was carried out between 1966 and 1975 during periods ranging from a few days' visit to seventeen months of continuous participant-observation as a resident of Robeson County in 1967–68. These years were particularly interesting for fieldwork, as they represented a critical period for the Lumbee. The first large-scale voter registration projects following the passage of the 1965 federal Voting Rights Act were being launched, and the first election with a potential for electing non-Whites to public offices was held. It was also a time when federal Office of Economic Opportunity (OEO) funds were beginning to provide employment in the county and state for a few college-educated Indians and Blacks. Such employment was significant because it was not vulnerable to local pressures in the way that other, more traditional employment for the better educated, such as teaching, was. In short, it was a period of excitement and hope for Indians and Blacks, of uncertainty and anxiety for many Whites, and an ideal one for the anthropologist.

Although during most of my shorter visits and in my initial encounters with Robeson County I was alone, I shared the prolonged field experience with my then husband, Gerald M. Sider, who is also an anthropologist. Both of us are, in Southern parlance, Yankee Whites. We pooled our information and shared countless discussions about the meaning of events. Each of us had access to somewhat different aspects of social life, and by combining our impressions, we both achieved a fuller understanding of a complicated situation. We resided in Pembroke, the one Indian town in the county, and had both Indian and White next-door neighbors. Although we knew many Pembroke people, we also met, interviewed, and attended meetings with people from other areas of the county in towns and the countryside. Further, we gathered information from members of all three "races" in the county – Black, Indian, and White.

"Race," particularly in the Southern United States, is an emotionally laden term used to designate various categories of people. Those who are assigned to one category are assumed to be biologically different from those of another in important ways. Very often the assumed biological differences, which are said to be evident from physical appearance, are thought to produce moral, intellectual, and psychological differences that can then be evaluated as inferior or superior. People are often treated differently according to their racial classification. This is a kind of "folk" or everyday, common use of the term "race" in the United States, and it merges unscientific ideas about biology with observed and sometimes enforced social differentiation and discrimination.

For biologists, however, a race is a relatively isolated breeding population within a given species. The isolation of the breeding population, whether geographic or social, has resulted in the development of genes and/or gene frequencies that distinguish it in minor ways from other populations of the same species. Even biologists disagree about just which populations constitute races and how the boundaries between them are to be drawn. There is no widely accepted taxonomy of biologically defined races of humans, and some physical anthropologists maintain that there is *no* acceptable biological taxonomy of human races. By contrast, many sociologists and anthropologists have viewed race as a social classification that does not necessarily mirror biological divisions. From this point of view – which is taken in this work – what is significant and more readily knowable is the way people assign one another to racial categories (in Robeson County, to the categories of Black, White, and Indian) and how they behave in terms of these socially defined categories. Here, the social facts of the matter must not be confused with the biological or genetic facts. For example, someone who is socially classified as "Black" may be genetically far more similar to those classified socially as "White" than to others designated socially as "Black." It cannot be assumed, as so many people do, that every individual's physical appearance importantly reveals either his genetic heritage or his social classification.

Because most of my work in Robeson County was with Indians, the material on Indian life is the most comprehensive and richest. Such unevenness is an unavoidable consequence of working in a situation where three "races" exist in three separate, but intertwined communities among which mutual suspicion and hostility exist, though in varying degrees. In this kind of situation, commitment to one group, a necessity if depth of material is to be gained, creates distance from other groups (cf. Dollard 1937, Powdermaker 1939 and 1966).

Because I was interested in the elusive subject of identity, a subject that tended to disappear when direct inquiries were made, I concentrated more heavily on people who were highly articulate and less on those who were not. Information was gathered principally from informal interviews, conversations, political meetings, church services, and informal gatherings. I took notes during large political gatherings and in formal interviews. Otherwise, I made notes as soon after conversations as possible and checked these against the memories of other participants. I have tried to make statements from these qualitative data that have, in Coles's phrase, "the ring of truth to them" (Coles 1971:42).[3] In presenting material from my fieldnotes, I have changed or deleted names and occasionally places and have altered or omitted details that might betray the privacy and anonymity promised to those who made this book possible.

In addition to fieldwork, I have relied on research conducted in the National Anthropological Archives, the National Archives, the Library of Congress, the University of North Carolina's North Carolina Collection, the Lumberton, North Carolina, library and the files of several Lumberton-based organizations and agencies.[4] Throughout, I have sought to gain an historical perspective on the Lumbee and the changes that have occurred in Robeson County. Indeed, this perspective has changed my interpretation of events in 1967–68 considerably. When I left the field in August, 1968, the prospect for future cooperation between Blacks and Indians appeared dismal and the likelihood of electing, in the near future, Indians and Blacks who were not strongly beholden to Whites seemed slight. When the political victories resulting from Black and Indian cooperation began to be won in the 1970s, it seemed inexplicable until a pattern of political activity, with its factionalism, changing leadership, and multiplex tactics emerged from historical analysis.

If the analysis presented here is to be developmental, it must trace the changes between then and now. "Then" is, essentially, the first period for which there is substantial, qualitative information about the people who were to become Lumbee Indians and their relations with their neighbors, namely, the 1860s and 1870s. "Now" is 1967–68 unless otherwise specified. Because the next chapter outlines what is known about the origins of the group and what can be inferred about its life in the middle 1800s, the remainder of this chapter will be devoted to a brief sketch of Robeson County today, with special emphasis on the racial situation so that the contrast with earlier conditions can be kept firmly in mind.

Robeson County today

Robeson County, the largest county in North Carolina, covers 949 square miles. Located on the inner edge of the Coastal Plain, it is flat, sandy, and humid.[5] Most of the county is farmland intersected by swamps and streams that used to be far more extensive and once predominated in the center of the county where the majority of Indians have always lived. The county is cut through by important highways, railroad lines, and a river (see Maps 1 and 2).

The Lumber, or Lumbee, River, which runs across the county from northwest to southeast and flows eastward, is not navigable by large craft because of its uneven depth, shifting sandbars, and fallen trees and brush. In 1918, William Haynes published an account of a canoe trip down the river that makes clear the difficulties heavier craft would

Map 1. Robeson County, North Carolina, and major cities to which Lumbees migrate

encounter (1918:5–7, 48). A number of "swamps" or "pocosins" drain into the river, in effect segmenting the county. Many areas of the county are named for the swamps that run through them, such as "Back Swamp," "Burnt Swamp," and "Raft Swamp."

In addition to the river, two railroad lines, one running east and west (the Seaboard Air Line) and the other north and south (the Atlantic

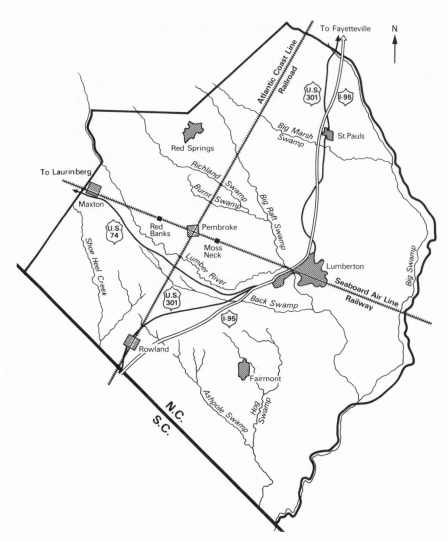

Map 2. Robeson County, North Carolina

Coast Line), intersect at what is now the Indian town of Pembroke. Railroads have long provided the Indians with access to the outside world, and Indians were reported as frequent travelers on the east–west line during the 1860s and 1870s. At that time, there was a station located in the heart of the Indian settlement at Moss Neck (a station that no longer exists). This ready access and their use of railway transportation indicates that the Indians of Robeson County have not been nearly so isolated as has sometimes been supposed. In 1968, at a Pembroke town council meeting, the proposal of the Atlantic Coast Line to discontinue passenger service to Pembroke town by canceling the scheduled stop of local trains was discussed and rather reluctantly agreed upon, so the town and the county do not currently have access to passenger trains traveling north or south. Passenger rail traffic has been diverted to Hamlet, North Carolina, in Richmond County, about thirty-five miles west of Pembroke, and to Fayetteville, in Cumberland County, about forty miles north.

Finally, major highways traverse Robeson County. Nearly bisecting the county from north to south is one of the nation's major interstate highways, I-95, the main auto route from Maine to Florida. Before the building of the interstate, U.S. Route 301, which roughly parallels I-95 through the county, was one of the important national north–south thoroughfares. From near Lumberton, the county seat, U.S. Route 74 works its way westward across the state to Asheville in the mountains.

To a Northerner, the Robeson County climate seems warm most of the year. Aside from one or two ice storms, winters usually produce little snow, and the heavy winter coats considered a necessity to those living as far south as Washington, D.C., are almost never needed. The ice storms, when they come, wreak havoc on the roads because motorists are unaccustomed to driving on ice and snow, and accidents result. Many houses are not insulated or heated with such unusual conditions in mind, and their inhabitants, particularly the poor, suffer terribly from the exceptional cold. Although these severe storms are unusual, the fifty-degree (Fahrenheit) "normal" winter temperature is augmented by penetrating dampness to produce a strong chilling effect. In summer, the not infrequent ninety-degree (Fahrenheit) and higher temperatures combine with high humidity to produce a feeling of pervasive hot stickiness, particularly on windless days. Because the land is low lying, summer nights are frequently nearly as warm as the days. The high humidity, winter and summer, is maintained by the swamps and streams still prevalent in the county and by the numerous drainage ditches that have, especially since about 1900, been constructed to increase land available for farming.

Because of its flatness, perhaps the most striking physical feature of Robeson County is the sky, with its richly colored sunsets spreading across the horizon and its dramatic dark storms rolling overhead. In winter, the landscape is rather bleak, with empty or stubble-filled fields interrupted by leafless trees and dried brown shrubbery relieved by straggly, long-needled loblolly pines, waxy-leafed magnolias, and a few other evergreens. By contrast, spring and summer vegetation is colorful and luxuriant, with honeysuckle vines curling through the undergrowth and along roadways, fields rich with growing crops, and such flowering trees as crepe myrtle, "acacia," and sweet, lemony-scented magnolias. To one who has never before seen tobacco growing, the sight of the broad-leafed tobacco plants reaching above one's head and growing in neat rows is especially impressive when the plants are surmounted, briefly, by a spray of pink and white flowers. The flowers are quickly cut off ("topped") by the farmers so that they will not sap the growth from the leaves and so that wind storms are less likely to blow down the plants. Later in the summer, the by-then-brown cotton bolls burst open to reveal their fluffy white interiors, and the fields take on a snow-touched appearance. The few cotton fields that have been picked clean by hand stand out from those picked by machine. As one Indian remarked, "Those machine-picked fields are still white."

Making a living

In 1967, Robeson County was one of the most densely populated rural counties in the United States.[6] It also ranked among the twenty or so poorest counties in the nation. Although primarily rural in character, Robeson County has one city – Lumberton, the county seat, with a population of about 17,000 in 1970 – and six small incorporated towns with populations between 1,358 and 3,383 (see Map 2 and Table 1). There are no major urban centers of North or South Carolina nearby. Charlotte, North Carolina, is roughly a two-hour drive from the center of Robeson County, and Raleigh–Durham–Chapel Hill are about two and one-half hours by car. Winston-Salem is farther. The nearest largish city is Fayetteville, North Carolina (population 53,510 in 1970), about thirty-five miles north of Lumberton. Fayetteville is the nearby center for two huge military installations – Fort Bragg, an army base, and Pope Air Force Base. In the late 1960s, during the Vietnam War, these bases were filled with military personnel who spent off-duty time in Fayetteville. At that time, it was also the nearest place where a major national newspaper, such as the *New York Times,* could be purchased.

Immediately south of Robeson County is Dillon County, South Carolina, site of a large motel and tourist center. This motel, with its satellite liquor, bath towel, fireworks, and souvenir stores, has become a well-known stopping place for many tourists who travel north and south on Interstate Highway 95. Indians frequently proclaimed, whether correctly or not, "You can get *anything* there." When it was illegal to sell beer, wine, and liquor in Robeson (as it was in 1967), Indians seeking to purchase any of these items legally often drove to this South Carolina tourist center, where they could also be entertained by the passing parade of, to them, strange people with strange ways.

Table 1. *Characteristics of Robeson County*

	1970	1960	1950	1940
Size in square miles	949 (next largest, Sampson Co., is 945 sq. mi.)	944		
Population				
Total	84,842	89,102	87,769	76,860
Whites	36,262	36,552		
Blacks	21,876	26,256		
Indians	26,486	26,278		
Other	218	16		
Towns and cities (population)				
Towns				
Fairmont town[a]	2,827	2,286	2,319	1,993
Maxton town[a]	1,885	1,755	1,974	1,656
Pembroke town (Indian)	1,982	1,372	1,212	783
Midstate Mill (unincorporated)	(N.A.)[b]	1,090		
Red Springs town[a]	3,383	2,767	2,245	1,559
Rowland town	1,358	1,408	1,293	999
Saint Pauls[a]	2,011	2,249	2,251	1,923
City				
Lumberton city (county seat)[a]	16,961	15,305	9,186	5,803
Whites	11,505	10,835		
Blacks	4,010	4,128		
Indians	1,427	342		
Other	29	(N.A.)		

[a]These towns have annexed parts of their surrounding townships of the same name.
[b]N.A. = not available.
Sources: For size in square miles: *Census of Population: 1970* (Washington, D.C.: U.S. Government Printing Office), Table 9, and 1960 census, Table 6. For population by race: 1970 census, Table 34, and 1960 census, Table 28. For population of towns and cities: 1970 census, Table 10, and 1960 census, Tables 7 and 8.

This, then, is one observer's account of the look and feel of the more obvious physical features of Robeson County. But to further an understanding of the county that is the background against which the political activities of Indians, Whites, and Blacks take place, Robeson's place in the state and the state's position in the nation must be made clear. In 1966, North Carolina ranked forty-third among the fifty states in per capita income. Between 1950 and 1965, North Carolina employment in agriculture dropped from one-quarter to less than one-tenth of total civilian employment. During the same period in the United States as a whole, employment in agriculture dropped less dramatically from about one-eighth to one-twentieth of total employment. While the number of agricultural workers was declining, the number of North Carolina workers in manufacturing increased. By 1966, almost one-third of the workers in North Carolina were employed in manufacturing, whereas only about one-quarter of the national labor force was so employed (Van Alstyne 1967:6, 12–15).

One of the reasons for the increase in North Carolina manufacturing jobs is that manufacturing wages there were the lowest in the nation in 1965. North Carolina and Mississippi ranked together at the bottom of the scale of average hourly wages paid per state – $1.82 (the national average was $2.61). At that time, not only was more than 80 percent of the state's manufacturing employment in industries paying *less* than the national average wage, but, worse, two-thirds of the new manufacturing jobs created in the state between 1960 and 1965 were in industries paying less than the average wage *for the state.* In 1966, new employment opportunities came primarily in the textile, apparel, and furniture industries, all of which paid below the 1965 North Carolina average hourly earnings. Further, four of six industries that were declining in employment nationally (textiles, lumber, tobacco, and food) were major employers in North Carolina (Van Alstyne 1967:17–27). Amid such grim statistics, the economic growth of the Sunbelt in the 1970s was not foreseen.

It must be asked how Robeson County fit into this economic picture of the state in the late 1960s. Like workers throughout the state, Robeson County workers were shifting gradually from agriculture to manufacturing between 1960 and 1970 (see Table 2). During the 1960s, the economy of the county was heavily dependent upon flue-cured tobacco, the major cash crop, although there were a few textile factories, a sand bag factory, and a rubber-soled sport shoe factory manufacturing "sneakers" or "tennis shoes," among a few others. Since 1967–68, several new factories have gone into operation manufacturing such diverse products as chemicals, glass, and sportswear. It has been estimated that these new factories have created roughly 10,000 new jobs,

Table 2. Robeson County employment by industry

Industries of employed persons	1970	1960
Total employed[a]	29,050	27,330
Agriculture, forestry, and fisheries	4,000	11,178
Mining	12	5
Construction	2,625	1,406
Manufacturing	9,604	3,851
Railroads and railway express service	64	79
Trucking service and warehousing	197	173
Other transportation	81	103
Communications	135	118
Utilities and sanitary services	412	211
Wholesale trade	625	408
Food, bakery, and dairy stores	683	669
Eating and drinking places	435	262
Other retail trade	2,697	2,204
Bank, real estate, and finance	700	410
Business and repair services	517	491
Private households	902	1,350
Other personal services	814	616
Entertainment and recreation services	58	53
Hospitals	564	379
Health services except hospitals	265	(N.A.)[b]
Education–elementary, secondary, college, and other	2,308	1,515
Welfare, religious, and nonprofit membership organizations	294	194
Other professional and related services	352	296
Public administration	706	686
Experienced unemployed	1,086	1,481

[a] In the 1960 census, employed persons were 14 years old and over; in the 1970 census, employed persons were 16 years old and over. In 1970, there were 287 employed persons 14 and 15 years old, 222 in nonagricultural industries.

[b] N.A. = not available.

Sources: Census of Population: 1970 (Washington, D.C.: U.S. Government Printing Office), Table 123, and 1960 census, Table 85.

which have provided more employment opportunities for everyone, if not yet equally.[7]

During the decade of the 1960s, median family income in Robeson County increased by $3,428, but the increase was not evenly distributed. It has been reported that 72 percent of Indians, but only 22 percent of Whites, had incomes of less than $7,000.[8] The level of education in the county also rose. The population of the county as a whole had completed more years of high school in 1970 than in 1960, the percentage of high school graduates increasing by about 4 percent (see Table 3). Fewer people had no school years completed.

Despite these improvements, Robeson remains a poor county in a relatively poor state. In 1970, 32 percent of all Robeson families had incomes below the poverty level, and 40 percent had incomes of less than 25 percent above the poverty level. Only 9 of North Carolina's 100 counties had higher percentages of families with incomes less than 25 percent above the poverty level (U.S. Bureau of the Census– Population 1973a:Table 124).

In Robeson, the burden of poverty falls disproportionately on Blacks and Indians, a legacy of the system of racial discrimination. Thus, in 1970, 56 percent of all Black families had incomes below the poverty level, and 65 percent had incomes of less than 25 percent above the poverty level (U.S. Bureau of the Census– Population 1973a:Table 128; no separate figures are available for Indians). There also remains a discrepancy between White and non-White educational levels. Whereas the median number of years of school completed in 1970 was 8.8 for all males and 9.7 for all females, it was only 6.9 for Black males and 8.4 for Black females. Similarly, of all Robesonians twenty-five years and older, 28.2 percent were high school graduates, but only 16 percent of Blacks the same ages were high school graduates. In median years of school completed, Robeson ranked in the bottom quarter of North Carolina counties (U.S. Bureau of the Census– Population 1973a:Tables 120 and 125).

With the increasing importance of manufacturing, which by 1970 was the largest employer in Robeson, and the decreasing importance of agriculture came a shift in the number and size of farms. Fewer and larger farms, given increasing mechanization, mean fewer farm operators and laborers. The large, corporate farms eliminate and absorb the small, singly owned marginal farms. In this respect, the decrease in numbers of Black farm operators is especially dramatic (see Tables 4 and 5).

In 1967–68, the trend toward large-scale farming and increased mechanization, both requiring large capital expenditures, was impressionistically evident as sharecroppers were being converted into day laborers (see Blu 1972 and Sider 1971). Day laborers made less money

Table 3. Income and education in Robeson County

	1970		1960	
Income Median family income–all families	$5,675 $3,552 (Black families)		$2,247 $1,242 (non-White families)	
Education (persons 25 years old and over)	All persons	Black persons	All persons	Non-White persons
No school years completed	1,312	385	2,011	1,444
Elementary: 1–4 years	4,859	1,775	7,642	5,575
5–7 years	8,401	2,489	10,015	5,793
8 years	4,092	860	3,385	1,633
High school: 1–3 years	9,502	2,108	5,871	2,565
4 years	6,079	992	5,046	1,209
College: 1–3 years	2,439	203	2,250	413
4 years or more	2,543	257	1,986	668
Number	39,227	9,069	38,206	19,300
Percent of high school graduates	28.2%	16.0%	24.3%	11.9%

Sources: For income: *Census of Population: 1970* (Washington, D.C.: U.S. Government Printing Office), Tables 124 and 128, and 1960 census, Tables 86 and 88. For education: 1970 census, Tables 120 and 125, and 1960 census, Tables 83 and 87.

Table 4. *Agriculture in Robeson County: farm income and crops*

	1969	1969 rank in state	1964
Number of farms	3,227		4,669
Land in farms (acres)	345,725		357,795
Average size of farm (acres)	107.1		76.6
Farm income and sales			
Market value of all agricultural products sold	$34,191,279	6th(13% decline)	$39,274,500
Average per farm	$10,595	42nd	$8,412
Farm production expenses, average per farm	$7,135		(N.A.)[a]
Crops, including nursery products and hay	$28,380,408		$35,053,961
Forest products	$256,298		$91,457
Livestock, poultry and their products	$5,554,573		$4,122,126
Principal crops and farm products			
Tobacco (pounds)[b]	31,430,515	3rd(5% of state production)	
Cotton (bales)	13,767	2nd(12% of state production)	
Field corn (acreage)	69,981	1st	
Soybeans (acreage)	34,683	2nd	
Vegetables, sweet corn, and melons	1,567	6th	
Improved pecans (pounds)	40,579	1st(24% of state production on farms with sales of $2,500 and over)	
Hogs and pigs (number)	45,643 (75,038 sold)	7th (7th)	

[a] N.A. = not available.

[b] Of farms with sales of $2,500 and more, the value of tobacco sold ($19,545,122) in 1969 was 57% of the market value of all agricultural products sold in Robeson County.

Sources: For number of farms and land in farms: *Census of Agriculture: 1969* (Washington, D.C.: U.S. Government Printing Office), Robeson County Table 1 (p. 617). For farm income and sales: 1969 census of agriculture, Robeson Conty, Table 4 (p. 617); summary data, selected items, Table 6 (p. 292). Principal crops: 1969 census of agriculture, summary data, pp. 293–304, 316–17.

Table 5. *Agriculture in Robeson County: operators, owners, and laborers*

	1969		1964	
	All farms	Black-operated farms	All farms	Black-operated farms
Farm operators farms	3,227	391	4,669	2,802
acres	345,725	16,400	357,795	135,035
Full owners farms	1,654	187	1,377	675
acres	145,847	7,956	97,116	28,952
Part owners farms	755	84	842	365
acres	142,317	3,924	116,525	26,618
Tenants farms	818	120	2,435	1,759
acres	57,561	4,520	132,695	78,704
Percent of tenancy	25.3	30.6	52.2	62.8
Hired farm laborers by numbr of days worked				
150 days or more	570		701	
less than 150 days	18,009		(N.A.)	

Source: Census of Agriculture: 1969 (Washington, D.C.: U.S. Government Printing Office), Robeson County Tables 3 and 14 (pp. 617 and 621).

and had lower status and prestige than sharecroppers, in addition to not being free to organize their own schedule of work. Although the creation of new manufacturing jobs has apparently eased unemployment somewhat (see Table 2), it is far from clear that the out-of-work sharecroppers or day laborers are those who now hold manufacturing jobs.

As a part of the state of North Carolina, Robeson must be viewed not only as an important county in the "flue-cured tobacco belt" but also as the site of one of the branches of what is now the state university system, Pembroke State University. Robeson has even had a moment or two of special prominence in the history of the state. One period of prominence came at the end of the Civil War and the beginning of Reconstruction, when a small Indian-led band of outlaws, apparently initially bent on vengeance, killed and robbed Whites virtually at will, to the outrage of Whites in many areas of the state.

Another moment came at the close of Reconstruction. In 1874, a Conservative (Democratic) majority was elected in both branches of the bicameral state legislature, confirming Conservative control, which had first been gained in 1870 when Conservatives held two-thirds of the General Assembly seats. In Southern White Conservative terms, this "redeemed" the state from the rule of "carpetbaggers, scalawags, and niggers."[9] In 1875, the Democratically dominated legislature called for the election of delegates to a constitutional convention. The election was closely contested across the state, and it became clear that the outcome would be very close. During these elections, the state Democratic chairman sent a telegram to the Democratic chairman of Robeson County containing the message, "As you love your State hold Robeson" (Lawrence 1939:94–5). In the county, Democratic candidates were elected by a slight majority, thereby "holding" Robeson and giving rise to the expression, "Hold Robeson and Save the State," a phrase "once known from the mountains to the sea" (Lawrence 1939:94). The final results of the state election left the Democrats and Republicans tied, after the death of one elected Democrat, and three Independents held the balance of power. In the end, the Democrats converted an Independent or two and pushed through part of their "reform" program. They established the principle of separate schools for separate races, banned miscegenation, and took the control of county governments out of local hands.

Robeson also achieved prominence when one of its leading White citizens, Angus W. McLean, was elected governor of North Carolina in 1925 and served a full term of four years (North Carolina governors may not succeed themselves). Earlier, under President Woodrow Wilson, McLean had become Assistant Secretary of the U.S. Treasury (Lawrence 1939:131–2). Since that time, Robeson has been less prominent in state affairs, although Robeson politicians have often taken active and leading roles in state politics.

For the Indians in the county, Robeson is the heartland or homeland of "our people," some 30,000–40,000 individuals legally designated as Lumbee Indians. Although a number of Lumbees live in surrounding North and South Carolina counties and clustered in a few urban areas of the United States, such as Baltimore; Richmond, Virginia; Detroit; High Point, and Greensboro, North Carolina; and Philadelphia, most reside in Robeson County, where they constitute nearly a third of the population (see Map 1). The roughly 90,000 inhabitants of Robeson County are about evenly divided into three culturally or socially defined "races" – Blacks, Indians, and Whites (see Table 1). In 1790, the ancestors of those who were later to be classified as Indians made up only about one-twentieth of the population, having increased to about one-third today (U.S. Bureau of the Census–Population 1908, 1961, 1973a, 1973b). Although between 1960 and 1970, Robeson County lost population, principally among Blacks, Blacks and Indians together continue to outnumber Whites, a fact of which everyone in the county is well aware.

Part of the Indian population in Robeson County is a group Lumbees call "the Smilings," or, more politely, "the Independent Indians." This is a relatively small group of people who originated in Sumter County, South Carolina, and who moved to Robeson County en masse during the opening decades of this century. There are no accurate population figures for this group, and reasonable estimates range between 150 and 500. The status of the Smilings is mostly of concern to them and to Lumbees, who tend to accept the Smilings as Indians, but to rank them below Lumbees and above Blacks. At first, the Lumbee refused to accept Smiling children in their schools, and for a time the Independent Indians had separate schools, thereby making Robeson a county with four separate school systems. During the 1950s, the Independent Indians' school was merged with the regular Lumbee schools, and Lumbees' concern over such status differences seems now to be fading. Where I have used the term "Indian" in this work, except where specifically noted otherwise, I mean it to apply to those legally designated as "Lumbee Indians" and not to the Smilings, about whom little is known. In general, however, it appears that the relation between the Independent Indians and their Black and White neighbors more or less parallels that observed between Lumbees and their neighbors.

Whites and Blacks live mainly in the scattered towns of Robeson County. Most of the Indians, except for those in Pembroke and, increasingly, in Lumberton, live in the rural areas of the county as farmers or as workers in local factories. Despite the lack of a reservation, the Lumbee form a distinct community within Robeson County. The ties among the members of this community are informal ones based on kinship, friendship, common interests, and shared perceptions. There are no officials who are appointed or elected to represent the Indian community exclusively.

Within the county, the town of Pembroke is the symbolic and social center for Lumbee Indian life.

> In a conversation with an Indian woman and another "Yankee" White woman about an article on the Lumbee written by a Vista volunteer, I mentioned that the volunteer hadn't even been to Pembroke. The Indian woman, who was annoyed about the article because it said unflattering things about the Lumbee, said, "No, just to Lumberton, and we don't really even think of them as part of here." The other White woman protested, "But there are a lot of Indians over there," to which the Indian replied, "Yes, but everyone thinks of Pembroke as the cultural center and the educational center of the Indian people."

Although the Indian woman in this conversation was herself from Pembroke, she reflects the general Indian view. Indians who come from areas outside Pembroke sometimes express bitterness that Pembroke is regarded as the center of Indian life, but they do not deny its position. Lumberton, the county seat, is classified by Indians as a "White town."

Pembroke is the only town in the county controlled by non-Whites. A majority of the townspeople are Indian, as are a majority of the governing officials and civil servants (the mayor, town councilmen, town clerk, and police chief). Pembroke also contains many Indian-owned and Indian-managed businesses, a large segment of the Indian middle-class, and Pembroke State University, a branch of the state university system that originated as an Indian normal school in 1887. Until the middle 1950s, this school served only Indians. Then, after the *Brown* v. *Board of Education* Supreme Court decision of 1954, the school was formally open to both Blacks and Whites. Relatively few Blacks have attended, however. Now the student body is largely White and at most 20 percent Indian. Indians are both proud of the school's improvements and disgruntled at their loss of control over it. The school's president is an Indian, although less than 10 percent of the faculty is Indian. Educational matters have long been an important focus of Indian political activity.

Living with "race"

As I have already indicated, race consciousness is pervasive in Robeson County. The effects of it, though often obvious, are sometimes quite subtle, and at least the outlines of it must be understood because it is a critical part of the milieu in which all people in Robeson operate. It is a commonplace to note that just as there have been great changes in the South since the landmark Supreme Court decisions of the 1950s, there are also strong continuities. I went to North Carolina in 1966 as a "Yankee," that is, a Northerner, with no prior experience in the South except driving through it on the way to somewhere else. I had read anthropological and sociological works of the 1930s and 1940s (Dollard 1937; Powdermaker 1939; Davis, Gardner, and Gardner 1941) and expected to find a new New South greatly changed. I did find changes, but often not the ones I had most expected – the outward signs of segregation were disappearing, and I was surprised at the number of concerned and liberal-thinking White Southerners I encountered. On the other hand, the tenacity with which some Whites clung to remarkably traditional racial perspectives and stereotypes was also unexpected. The most conspicuous evidence of segregation had disappeared after legal segregation was declared unconstitutional. Gone were the three separate seating areas in a Robeson movie theater, the three sets of drinking fountains and rest rooms, and the separate waiting areas in bus and train stations. On the other hand, there was still de facto three-way segregation in most churches, schools, voluntary organizations, restaurants, and personal service businesses. Barber shops, beauty salons, and funeral parlors still rarely had clients of more than one race, and even bootleggers (those who make and/or sell non-tax-paid alcoholic beverages) generally sold their products to people of a single race. Much of the racial etiquette reported in the older ethnographies and studies of the South could still be observed, particularly between Blacks and Whites.

However, several Indians remarked during the election campaigns of 1968 that White politicians had for the first time been willing to shake hands with them or to address them with a title such as "Mister." Said one Indian, "It's the first time they've put a handle to your name." And one of my first experiences in Robeson, in 1966, suggested that some of the old barriers were breaking down. Having arrived for my first visit to the county, I asked the White manager of my Lumberton motel, who knew nothing of my interest in Indians, where I could get a good meal. She readily suggested a nearby restaurant and explained how to get to it.[10] Then she added "It's run by an Indian, but 90 percent of his customers are White." When I entered the restaurant, there were indeed a number of Whites as well as Indians eating dinner there. When I later recounted this incident to Indians, most expressed surprise that a Lumberton White had directed me to an Indian restaurant, however many of its customers were White.

Indians spoke with enthusiasm about the demise of the most notice-able signs of segregation, but they still rarely ate in "White" restau-rants. Some establishments were too expensive for the majority of In-dians, but even middle-class Indians who could clearly afford to go avoided such places because, they said, they didn't "feel comfortable" in them.

If the obvious forms of institutionalized segregation are changing, the racial dogma that supports segregation has changed less. It may be that the number of people who espouse a rigid formulation of racial ideology and the encapsulation of the races has grown smaller. Still, a number of important and influential Whites express themselves, at least privately, in terms familiar to students of American racial ideology, and these people have influenced the course of development in Robeson County. For believers in racial dogma, it explains physical and behavioral differ-ences among human beings, and classifies and ranks them on that basis. The differences among human beings categorized into the "races" are thought to be both "natural" and God-given. Religious justifications range from the simple, "If God had intended men to be all alike, he wouldn't have made them different colors" to the sophisticated citation of the biblical story of Ham (Gen. 9:20–7).[11] Ham was one of Noah's sons, the one who looked upon his father's nakedness when he should have averted his eyes as the others did. Noah cursed Ham's descen-dants, declaring, "a servant of servants shall he be unto his brethren" (Gen. 9:24). For Whites who cite this passage, Blackness is the visible evidence of the curse, as is the social position of Blacks. In any event, for those who invoke religious justifications for their racial ideology, the moral rightness of their position is affirmed.

But it is in popular or folk notions of biology that racial dogma is most deeply embedded (see Schneider 1965a). "Blood" is the mystical medium that transfers from parent to child physical characteristics and the moral, intellectual, and psychological qualities linked to them. This notion has not been appreciably affected by scientific evidence from modern genetics and evolutionary biology. Evolutionary biology was not taught in Robeson County public schools as late as 1967–68. Indeed, a "belief" in evolution was frequently contrasted with belief in God in a way that assumed one could not "believe" in both. For fundamentalist Christians of all races (and even for those Jews who tended toward fundamentalism), evolution and religion were seen as being in direct conflict with one another.

Because in folk biology "blood" links parent and child, it is used as an idiom with which to talk about kinship as well as about race. "Blood will tell," it is said, in families as well as in races. If "blood" can bear with it mental capacities, moral sense, and character along with physical characteristics, it can be evaluated as better and worse when the qualities and characteristics it bears are judged. Whites who hold to racial dogma assert that "White blood" is superior on every count – it confers higher intelligence, a stronger sense of responsibility, higher moral standards, and potentially more beauty than any other type of blood. Conversely, "Black blood" is inferior to any other blood on all these counts. Thus, Whites consider Blacks to be physically unattractive, possessed of an offensive odor, lazy, stupid, lacking in initiative, uncaring about other Blacks, musical, and good at sports. They are said to be passionate and loose in their sexual behavior. It is this passion, presumably, that White men seek in Black women, despite their assertion that Black women are ugly. It is also this passion in Black men from which White women, with their "finer sensibilities," must be protected.[12]

For Whites, blood is a substance that can be either racially pure or racially polluted. Black blood pollutes White blood absolutely, so that, in the logical extreme, one drop of Black blood makes an otherwise White man Black. On the other hand, White blood tends to upgrade Black blood, if not, today, to purify it entirely.[13] Black blood pollutes both Indian and White blood, but because White blood is, according to Whites, the most pure, it is worse for Black and White blood to mix *in* a White woman (actually, in her child who is in her womb) than in a Black woman. Black and White mixing of blood is considered by Whites to be worse than Indian and Black mixing. Of course, these ideas about purity and pollution add to the horror, disgust, and anxieties about Black sexuality with which some Whites discuss miscegenation.[14]

White ideas about "Indian blood" are less formalized and clear-cut. Indian blood, if it entered a White family in a much earlier generation and if it did not come from Robeson County Indians, is apparently not polluting and can be rather enhancing. A "Cherokee princess" is perhaps the most frequently mentioned Indian ancestor. It may only take one drop of Black blood to make a person a Negro, but it takes a lot of Indian blood to make a person a "real" Indian, as White comments such as the following suggest: "He's not a real Indian – he doesn't have enough Indian blood," or "He doesn't have any more Indian blood than I do."

White views of Indians are disparate. Most Whites seem to agree that Indians are a proud people, a characteristic that often engenders respect from Whites. But this pride is too often linked, say many Whites, to "meanness," a tendency toward sensitivity to insult and toward violent response. For Whites, meanness is a negative quality, whereas for Indians it is a positive one. It is noteworthy that although Whites are outspoken about their fear of Indian violence, they do not regard Indians as sexually dangerous, whereas they do consider Blacks to be sexually dangerous. One of the positive qualities attached to Henry Berry Lowry, an outlawed Indian leader in the 1860s and 1870s, even by his most implacable foes, was that he was never known to molest White women.[15]

Aside from these general qualities, Whites often do not agree about the nature of Indians. Some Whites say that Indians are honest and hardworking; others that they are lazy or dishonest. Some Whites say that Indians "stick together" and "act clannish"; others that they never agree on anything, are never united. Some Indians are considered to be "good-looking" by Whites, although their beauty presumably cannot match that of a beautiful White. In short, a few Whites have stereotypes of Indians, but the stereotypes differ from one White to another. Other Whites seem not to have developed a stereotype at all. The fact that Whites do not have a single widely agreed-upon view of Indians has allowed Indians more flexibility than Blacks have, and a greater range of behavior that can be defined by Whites as acceptable. The lack of agreement has also meant that Whites have not presented a united front against Indians, and Indians have been able to play off one segment of the White community against another to achieve their own ends.

There is far more agreement among Whites about what Blacks are like. For Whites who subscribe to racial dogma, Blacks are patient, childlike, and happy with very little in their "natural" state, but they are temperamentally unstable, easily led astray, and may exhibit vicious, "unreasonable" tempers. Whites distinguish between "good ones," who are pleasant, smiling, joking, servile, and polite, and "bad ones," who have become "uppity," assertive, and demanding of the same privileges granted Whites.

Whites have developed a notion of why Blacks behave as they do – namely, that Blacks are like children and as such undisciplined, unstable, concerned with the immediate, and requiring supervision for their own good. This notion is a powerful explanatory device for those who believe it, and it appears to be highly resistant to change (see Blu 1977 for further elaboration on stereotyping). Because many Whites are more or less agreed about the nature of Blacks and about the kind of behavior to expect from them, Whites can easily act concertedly, even without formal organization, to pressure a Black who is behaving in a way that they find unacceptable. Blacks, of course, know quite well what kind of behavior Whites prefer, and they can choose to conform to the expectations or to violate them. They also know that violating the expectations can bring "trouble" from Whites.

On the basis of their ideas about "blood" and "racial purity," Whites have constructed rules for assigning racial identity through parentage. These rules seem to be accepted by all the races, both for themselves and for the others. A child with two White parents is considered White. A child with one White parent and one Indian parent is considered Indian. A child with one Black parent is considered Black, whatever the race of the other parent. Although these rules are supposed to assure the racial purity of White blood by accepting children as White only if both parents are White, the fact is that the rules are based in practice on the social identity of parents rather than on the identity of genitor and genetrix. It is a truism that one can identify the genetic mother of a child more easily than the genetic father, and usually the social father of a child is assumed to be the child's genitor unless there is strong evidence to the contrary. In the absence of a socially recognized father, a child generally takes the racial identity of the mother.[16]

It is assumed by Whites that a child's appearance is determined by the blood passed on to him by his parents. This blood carries the racial characteristics of each parent and is thought to be especially manifest in skin color, nose shape, and hair texture. For Whites, these physical characteristics have come to represent, to symbolize different races. Blacks are identified with dark skin, a flat, short nose, and kinky hair; Indians with coppery skin, straight or wavy hair, and straight, long noses; and Whites with light skin, straight or curly hair, and a nose that is not flat.

Of these physical characteristics, which at once stand as symbols for race and are features that people sometimes talk about as actual indicators of race, skin color is by far the most important. Skin color has come to stand powerfully for racial differences. It is a part-for-whole symbol fraught with emotional intensity. For Whites, it stands for White biological superiority (which carries with it moral, aesthetic, and intellectual superiority) and Black and Indian inferiority. The darker the skin, the more inferior the race. Problems arise, however, when Whites actually try to identify an individual's race on the basis of how he looks.

Anyone attempting to identify racial affiliation in Robeson County solely on the basis of physical appearance is faced with an enormous variety of physical types in all races, particularly among Indians. Indians may vary in skin color from very light to quite dark, and other features considered to be racial markers also vary widely. Eye color ranges from blue to hazel to dark brown; hair texture from straight to wavy to very curly or even kinky; hair color from blond to brown to black; and nose shape from aquiline to relatively flat and broad. These features occur in dozens of different combinations. Although Whites frequently assert that they can tell a person's race by looking at his physical appearance, in fact, they often cannot. A White teacher, in an incident recounted to me by an Indian friend, made incorrect assumptions about race by looking at a classroom of children:

> During a summer session of a special preschool program for children, a White teacher complained to an Indian teacher that she thought the Indian teacher had been assigned all the White children. The Indian teacher replied with some asperity that there were only two White children in her class, but the rest were all Indian. She said that the children's birth certificates might say "White" (if the children were born away from Robeson County), but their mothers were Indian, so the children were Indian. The White teacher, who had not seen the birth certificates, apparently accepted this and made no further complaint.[17]

Indians recognize that Whites have difficulty using physical appearance as an accurate indicator of race, and they often joke about it. For example, in a car on the way to a political meeting, an Indian man remarked wryly, "To look at John Smith [the White "high sheriff"], you could go out in the street and find Indians who look more White than he does, but they still go for Indians." And after a political gathering in the county seat that had been organized by Whites and was attended by people of all three races, I was leaving with the group of Indians I had arrived with, sat with, and talked with during the gathering. We had met and spoken to several Whites. Then one of the Indians grinned and said to the group of us, "Didn't Miz Sider make a nice Indian girl tonight?" This was humorous play on the Indians' knowledge that the Whites, whom I did not know personally, had assumed that I was an Indian because I had been associating with Indians and not because I "looked Indian." In fact, Whites who met me when I was with Indians did frequently assume that I was Indian. Occasionally, Indians who did not know me assumed the same thing, until it became clear one way or another that I was not. Indians also have difficulty determining the racial classification of people whom they do not know, but Indians tend not to assume that they can readily determine someone's race, whereas Whites often assume that they, as Whites with superior knowledge, can.

A lack of correspondence between actual skin color and the racial status it presumably indicates causes widespread confusion and is a more general Southern problem. Anne Moody, a Black woman who grew up in Mississippi, recounts the confusion she experienced as a child learning about racial distinctions and how to make them:

I remember the day I had seen my two uncles Sam and Walter. They were just as White as Katie them. But Grandma Winnie was darker than Mama, so how could Sam and Walter be white? . . .

"Mama," I said, "why ain't Sam and Walter white?"

"'Cause they mama ain't white," she answered.

"But you say a long time ago they daddy is white."

"If the daddy is white and the mama is colored, then that don't make the children white."

"But they got the same hair and color like Bill and Katie them got," I said.

"That still don't make them white! Now git out of that tub!" she snapped.

Every time I tried to talk to Mama about white people she got mad. Now I was more confused than before. If it wasn't the straight hair and the white skin that made you white, then what was it [Moody 1968:27–8]?

People of all races try to reduce the confusion produced by variations in skin color and other physical features in a number of ways. One obvious way is to "know" someone – that is, to know their parentage and hence their social identity on a personal basis. Another way is to ask a person's race outright:

> An Indian said that he and a Black friend were present at court during the trial of a man whose surname did not indicate his race. The surname is one possessed by Blacks and Whites and Indians. After the White judge had heard the testimony and before sentencing the man, he leaned forward over the bench and said to the defendant, "You have quite a suntan, are you Indian or White?" The man said he was Indian and was thereupon sentenced.[18]

Asking a person about his race directly, however, is generally considered indelicate at best and, as a first question, rude. Whites, Indians, or Blacks who are trying to be polite usually prefer to rely on other information in determining racial identity.

Surnames are sometimes indicators of racial identity. Certain surnames, such as Oxendine, Lowry, and Locklear, are found only among Indians in Robeson County. The bearers of such surnames, if they originate from Robeson, will invariably be Indians. Except for a few Greek or "Jewish" surnames, there are no distinctive White (or Black) surnames. Other indicators of racial identity are behavioral – dialect, mannerisms, bearing, carriage, gestures. Where a person comes from in the county or where he is living can also be suggestive of racial identity, particularly taken in conjunction with other clues. There is also an element of "birds of a feather flock together," as can be seen from people assuming that I was an Indian because I associated with Indians. Most people in all three races tend to assume that people prefer the company of those who are racially like themselves, so that for leisure activities, groups are assumed to (and usually do) contain people of only one race. I was often told, by both Whites and Indians, that people "naturally" prefer to be with those of their own race because they are "more comfortable among their own people."

Blacks and Indians resist the implications of racial dogma partly through reinterpretation of the ranking assigned them by Whites, through an avoidance of the term "race" in reference to themselves, and through choosing for themselves the group names by which they prefer to be addressed. Indians and Blacks do not consciously and explicitly accept the notion that they are inferior to Whites in the ways Whites have claimed. A few people in both races apparently experience feelings of inferiority as a result of having internalized White standards, but such individuals appear to be the exceptions rather than the rule. Whites rank themselves superior to both Indians and Blacks, and rank Indians above Blacks. Indians and Blacks are well aware of White ranking and frequently accept this ranking *as a statement of social facts,* but *not* as an evaluation of inherent worth. Some Indians have adopted White notions about the biological inferiority of Blacks, but have rejected such notions about themselves. Other Indians reject biological notions of superiority and inferiority altogether and see themselves as sharing the same economic and social problems that Blacks have. Blacks rank themselves below Whites and occasionally below Indians according to socio-economic criteria, but reject notions of superiority and inferiority about any race. Many Blacks remarked that Indians and Blacks are really in the same social and economic position, but that Whites try to make Indians think that they are better (and better off) than Blacks.

Although Blacks and Indians must accept or at least work within the three racial categories, they frequently avoid using the term "race" to apply to themselves. As one Black minister said at a political meeting of Indians and Blacks, "There's lots of talk about the Indian race and the Negro race and the White race. But God didn't make but one race – the human race." Blacks and Indians usually substitute the term "people" or, less often, "nationality" for "race." The use of "people" recognizes the fact of different categories of human beings, but stresses the underlying common humanity of all of them. The constructions "our people," "my people," "the people" (meaning "my or our people"), and "your people," "his people," "their people" are often used by Indians and Blacks to refer to their own and other "races."

When Whites use the term "people," however, it frequently comes to be interpreted as insulting when coupled with the modifiers "those," "these," and "you," as in the phrases "these/those people" and "you people." I was explicitly instructed by an Indian man not to use these phrases because they create distance and hostility in Indian and Black listeners. When a White uses these phrases, he offends non-Whites who hear them. The following story was told by the Indians who had been present at a political gathering attended by Indians, Blacks, and Whites:

> A White politician said to another White, in the presence of several Indians who were presumably part of the conversation, "John [a prominent White politician] is the one that can bring them. He's the only one that has the respect of these people." The Indians were offended and angry. As one Indian man explained afterward, "When a White man uses 'these people' or 'those people' or 'you people,' he's letting you know how he feels. He's saying, 'You're not one of us.' He's saying he's better."

In 1967–68, Blacks and Indians categorized Robeson County inhabitants this way:

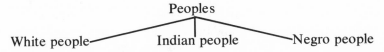

A slightly different organization of these categories could sometimes be detected, usually in political contexts:

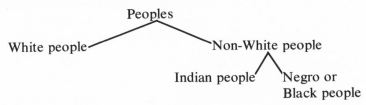

Most Blacks preferred to be called "Negro," although Black Power rhetoric was just beginning to make the term "Black" acceptable, and even preferable, particularly among Black youth. Since then, the term Black has become increasingly acceptable to those it designates. "Colored" had been an earlier term preferred by Blacks, but by 1967–68, it was considered by them to be rather offensive when used by non-Blacks, and the term "nigger" (as well as the White Southern blending of "Negro" and "nigger," "Nigra") to be very offensive. Indians seeking to be polite and courteous to Blacks rather frequently offended out of ignorance, thinking that "colored" was the most acceptable term. After a political meeting of Indians and Blacks in a rural area, a middle-aged Indian man complained misguidedly to me about the terminology that had been used by the Indian leader of the meeting, who referred to Blacks as Negroes:

> "He shouldn't have called them Negroes. He should have called them colored folks, because they don't like to be called Negroes. You know the first Indian in history was called a Croatan. A lot of people come down here and call us Croatans – they don't know any better. It's like calling a colored person a Negro."

"Croatan" was the first name under which those now called Lumbees were recognized as Indians in 1885. The complaining Indian had completely confused the "most polite" term for Blacks, but was intensely concerned about being as polite as possible.

As "Negro" began to fall out of fashion in the late 1960s and early 1970s, Indians who wanted to be courteous to Blacks and who now began to have more contact with them in schools and in political situations worried about the proper and most desirable term to apply to Blacks. For example, an Indian teacher asked me, in 1972, what I thought the most acceptable term would be for her to use in her now racially mixed classroom – "Black" or "Afro-American" or "Negro" or what? When I replied that it was a difficult problem she decided, after some deliberation, that "Afro-American" was probably the best term because it was neutral and more technical and, as such, least controversial. To her, "Black" suggested a radical political stance, and "Negro" suggested a conservative one, whereas "Afro-American" seemed not conservative but not radical either. Her goal was to avoid offending children and parents of any political persuasion as well as to avoid taking a political stance herself, saying that as an Indian it was inappropriate for her to take a public position on the politics of the Black community.

In 1967–68, most Indians preferred being called, simply, "Indians." "Lumbee" was still not a term acceptable to everyone, and "Indians" did not offend anyone. The term "Croatan" is highly insulting when used by outsiders. "Native Americans" has still not made great inroads into Indian usage except occasionally in contexts where Lumbees are primarily concerned to relate themselves to the federal government or to other Indian groups. Any term that suggests mixed-bloodedness, such as "mulatto" or "half-breed" or "mestizo," a term that Brewton Berry (1963) hoped would be a "neutral" term of reference, is viewed by Indians as unacceptable and insulting. It is one thing for Indians to discuss among themselves their varied ancestry, but they resent any outsider's doing so. This is partly because, in the South, the terms "mixed-blood" and "mulatto" have usually meant a combination of Black and non-Black ancestry. Because one cannot be a little bit Black any more than a woman can be a little bit pregnant, Robeson County Indians could not be Indians by Southern standards if they were a little bit Black. Indians have had a long and difficult struggle to be differentiated clearly from Blacks, and they become angry at any implication that they have not succeeded. As one Indian remarked, "When the Whites classified us with the Negroes in 1835, it set back our relations with the Negroes a hundred and fifty years" because Indians had to fight so hard not to be classified with Blacks.

The term everyone uses for Whites is "Whites." This term is acceptable to Whites and does not appear to be a particularly recent usage or to be in the process of being replaced. There are, for Whites, such subcategories as "Anglo-Saxons" (or "Scots"), "Jews," and "Greeks."[19] Of these, Anglo-Saxons, who are in the majority in Robeson, rank themselves highest and the others lower, but in no widely accepted order. Indians and Blacks recognize this differentiation among Whites by saying, "Jews and Greeks are White, but not really White." This was further explained by an Indian who said that because Jews and Greeks have suffered discrimination from Whites (Anglo-Saxons), too, they therefore are more understanding toward non-Whites.

In this environment of high sensitivity to racial nuances, what options do the Indians have, and how do they talk about them? One choice Indians can make is to stay "home" in Robeson County or to go away, usually to an urban place where there are employment opportunities. Gregory Peck, in his study of migration between Robeson County and Baltimore, where the largest number of urban Lumbees live (about 3,000), notes that most of the Indians who have spent some time in the city return to Robeson County (Peck 1972:108).[20] A very large number of people, both young and old, from town and from countryside in Robeson County have had some migration experience. Yet they returned. When asked why, one of the reasons almost invariably given is that they feel "more comfortable" in Robeson County. When asked why this might be so, the reply is usually that in Robeson "everyone knows who we are." "We," here, means "we Indians."

In Robeson County, an Indian no longer has to "prove himself Indian," or to go through the arduous and anxiety-producing process of negotiating a special position for himself in a social environment where there are few others like him. There may be tension in encounters between the races in Robeson County, but it is generally less than that found in encounters between Robeson County Indians and people not from Robeson. The connotations of "comfortable" are broader. It suggests a sense of well-being, of knowing the ropes, of settledness, of being, as the popular phrase has it, close to one's roots. Lumbees know that wherever they go in the United States, they will encounter people who use racial categories, and they also know that they do not fit very neatly into those categories, so that some discomfort, some difficulty is likely to ensue.

Away from home, however, where people "don't know who we are," and do not immediately recognize Lumbees as Indians, clear and insistent emblems unambiguously declaring Indian identity are sometimes needed. In an interview with a Northern newspaper reporter, a Lumbee woman living in Baltimore explained the situation this way:

"This is the first time the Lumbees have ever put any emphasis on things like costumes and dancing," Mrs. Hunt says. "In the city, it's about the only way to keep the children mindful that they're Indians and that they have something to be proud of and identify with."

In the city, Mrs. Hunt agrees, there is probably more emphasis on "Indianness" than there is at home in North Carolina.

Down there maintaining a sense of identity and a feeling for the Indian heritage is easy. In the city, it's more difficult and the children growing up in Baltimore, she believes, need the headdresses and beads and dances to remind them of what they have to be proud of.

"It's hard for us to find people in the city who will accept us as Indians with our own way of life," Mrs. Hunt says, "but we won't stop being Indians because of that, and we don't want our children to forget they're Indians" [*Akwesasne Notes* 1971:34].

If Indians return or stay "home," then what are their options? Indians tend to see themselves as able to choose between essentially two modes of behavior – "mean" or "'umble." The contrast between the two modes was brought out one evening at a gathering in our house. It consisted of a middle-aged Indian couple, an Indian woman who was their cousin, a young Indian man, a young Southern White man who worked in the Indian community but who was not a native Robesonian, my husband, and myself:

> The conversation turned to a recent court case that my husband and the White Southerner had witnessed. They described the trial, joking about the fact that one of the local White police officers had testified on behalf of an Indian who was accused of bootlegging. The officer told the White judge that the bootlegger ran a quiet place – he had no "piccolo" [jukebox], and there was no drinking on the premises. The bootlegger had come to court without a lawyer, which my husband remarked was probably a clever move. The older Indian man agreed that it was probably his best move because, he said, "They like us 'umble." The two men present at the trial then described an interchange between the judge and the bootlegger. The judge asked the bootlegger whether he had any land. The bootlegger said yes, he had a small farm. The judge asked why he didn't get his living from that. The bootlegger replied that he couldn't, that the last two years had been bad ones because of the drought. Whereupon, the judge said that he had a farm, too, and he'd had crop problems, but he didn't go selling liquor. At that point, the White Southerner was convinced he heard the bootlegger mutter under his breath, "Yes, you did." But the older Indian man said he didn't believe he'd said that, that the White Southerner must have heard wrong and that the bootlegger had probably said, "Yes, sir," because it wouldn't be smart to risk the judge hearing a remark like that. The younger Indian man agreed heartily. The older Indian man then told a story about an Indian who "wasn't too 'umble." He wouldn't act humble and even kicked the doors of the courtroom in his anger. "They threw the book at him." Everyone laughed in admiration at his "meanness."

In a situation of vulnerability, then, an Indian can respond by playing the role preferred by Whites – that of being humble – which may be "smart" because it brings less trouble, but is also painful to one's dignity. Or, he can refuse to play the role preferred by Whites, which for Indians often means a violent rejection of it (kicking the doors), or "acting mean." Rejecting the role preferred by Whites may bring penalties – having the book thrown at him– but it allows an Indian to "hold his head up" and to gain respect from fellow Indians.

Indians tend to see their options as dual – be ready to fight or be walked over. As one might expect, this often produces tension in encounters between Indians and others, particularly in situations where Indians feel at a disadvantage, such as the courtroom, because judges, juries, and lawyers tend to be White. The Indians have frequently been able to use that tension to their advantage, and the tension has existed at least since the days of the Henry Berry Lowry band, who provide to Indians today a potent image of men ready to fight. The importance of the band in fixing the tone of Indian–White relations will be discussed in the next chapter, along with what is known about earlier relations between Whites and Indians in Robeson.

2. Where did they come from and what were they like before?

The origins of the Lumbee are probably the most discussed aspect of the group, but despite an enormous volume of writings, most of it remains speculative.[1] However uncertain and poorly documented they are, the origins of the Lumbee are vital to the Indians as validation of their Indianness and important to such government agencies as the Bureau of Indian Affairs (BIA) and the Office of Economic Opportunity (OEO) because benefits may have to be conferred on the basis of their aboriginal status. Knowing where they came from is also essential to many Indians' peace of mind because such knowledge ties them to a distant past in a satisfyingly specific way rather than an unsettlingly vague one.

The first part of this chapter discusses what is known or posited about where the Lumbee came from and offers still more speculation about how they came to be as they were when the first White settlers encountered them in Robeson County in the 1700s. The remainder of the chapter is concerned with a period for which there is relatively more documentation and from which a picture is formulated of who the Lumbee's ancestors claimed to be, who their neighbors said they were, and how each behaved toward the other. During the period from about 1850 to 1885, some of the most dramatic changes in Lumbee history occurred as they protested violently their classification and treatment as "free Negroes" and maneuvered successfully for legal recognition as Indians.

Where did they come from?

In discussing the origins of the Lumbee, several threads must be kept separate: (1) the theory of their origins from Raleigh's lost colony at Roanoke proposed by Hamilton McMillan in 1885, which is now the nearly universal oral tradition of the Indians, (2) various other theories linking the Lumbee to historically documented Indian groups, such as the Cherokee and Cheraw, (3) documentary evidence that probably or

36

certainly links Lumbee ancestors to their present home in Robeson County, and (4) my own speculations about the origins of the group.

Let us look first at the documentary evidence available.[2] White Robesonian Mary Norment noted in 1875:

When the Scotch first commenced settling in Robeson County in 1747, after the disastrous battle of Culloden, (Robeson being then a part of Bladen County) the ancestors of the Locklears, Revels, Cumbas and Chavis' of to-day were living where their descendants now live [Norment 1875:26].[3]

The descendants of the families she names became Lumbee Indians. A little later, Hamilton McMillan (1888) also noted that when the first Whites settled Robeson County, they found the ancestors of the Indians already living there, but he elaborates more on their condition:

Subsequent to that date [1703] white emigrants penetrated the wilderness and in 1729 there was a settlement made on Heart's Creek, a tributary of the Cape Fear, and near the site of the present town of Fayetteville. Scotchmen arrived in what is now Richmond County in North Carolina as early as 1730. French Huguenots, in large numbers, emigrated to South Carolina after the revocation of the Edict of Nantes, and some of them had penetrated as far North as the present Northern boundary of that State, in the early part of the eighteenth century.

At the coming of white settlers there was found located on the waters of the Lumber River, a large tribe of Indians, *speaking English*, tilling the soil, owning slaves and practicing many of the arts of civilized life. They occupied the country as far West as the Pee Dee, but their principal seat was on the Lumber, extending along that river for twenty miles. They held their lands in common and land titles only became known on the approach of white men. The first grant of land to any of this tribe, of which there is written evidence in existence, was made by King George the Second in 1732, to *Henry Berry* and *James Lowrie*, two leading men of the tribe, and was located on the Lowrie Swamp, East of Lumber River in present county of Robeson in North Carolina. A subsequent grant was made to James Lowrie in 1738 [emphasis in original; McMillan 1888:13–14].[4]

White tradition thus places the ancestors of the Lumbee in Robeson County by 1750, and presumably even then they were not living in a particularly "Indian" manner.

At this point, it might well be asked who these early White settlers were. The greatest number of them were Scottish Highlanders fleeing an increasingly difficult political and economic situation at home (Meyer 1961:30–53). They began receiving land grants in the early 1730s along the upper Cape Fear River, which runs through the modern city of Fayetteville, north of Robeson County. Groups of them emigrated sporadically in 1733, 1735, 1740, 1753, and probably 1760. Emigration increased steadily from 1768 to 1774 (Meyer 1961:94). Their settlement center was located where Fayetteville now is, and their plantations and farms spread substantially north and south of there along the tributaries to the Cape Fear River and those of what is now the Lumber River in Robeson County. The Highlanders constituted the largest national group in the area, but probably never composed more than half the total population (Meyer 1961:117).

These settlers arrived speaking Gaelic, although the "gentry" among them would have spoken English and most would have had some contact with the English speakers who were their neighbors. However, Gaelic persisted at least in the homes and churches of these settlers. Some slaves were reported to have learned the language, and the last Gaelic sermon in North Carolina was not preached until 1860 (Meyer 1961:118– 19). Their churches were Presbyterian exclusively (a contrast to the Indian community, which came to worship primarily in Methodist and Baptist churches). The great majority of the newly arrived Scottish Highlanders engaged in agriculture as landlords, small freeholders, or tenants. Many arrived indented for a three- to five-year period to the gentry, and only afterward sought land of their own.

What evidence of early contacts between settlers and Indian ancestors might there be? A 1754 report from Bladen County (part of which later became Robeson) to the colonial governor of North Carolina may have reference to Lumbee ancestors as "a mixt Crew, a lawless People." The report, recorded in the *Colonial Records*, was to inform the governor of conditions in the counties so that preparations for a possible war with the French and Indians could be made.

Bladen – Col: Rutherfords Regim^t of Foot in Bladen County 441. a Troop of horse 36. A new company necessary to be made at Waggamaw James Kerr recommended for Captn

Drowning Creek on the head of Little Pedee, 50 families a mixt Crew, a lawless People, possess the Lands without patent or paying quit rents; shot a Surveyor for coming to view vacant lands being inclosed in great swamps

Quakers to attend musters or pay as in the Northern Counties; fines not high enough to oblige the Militia to attend musters No arms stores or Indians in the county

Bladen Troop Willm Davys Captn with officers 33 men The Troop wants Holsters with Blew Caps & Housings fringed, pistols, Carbines, Broad Swords or hangers with which they want to be furnished. No Indians [North Carolina 1887:161].[5]

If the report of "a mixt Crew" refers to the ancestors of the Lumbee, they appear to have displayed a spirit similar to that unequivocally found among them in the next two centuries – that is, a willingness to be defensively violent, in this case toward a surveyor viewing lands that were anything but "vacant." But the question arises, if these are Lumbee ancestors, why were there no reports of Indians in the county? There are several possible reasons for their not being referred to as Indians. First, the reporter may not have been inclined to investigate further the people who presumably shot the surveyor. Second, the White settlers may have been reluctant to report the presence of Indians in their area for fear that the governor might grant them land as had been done for the Tuscarora and Catawba in order to win their support in the coming French and Indian wars.[6] And third, eighteenth-century Whites may not have used the term "Indian" to refer to "mixed blooded" people no longer living in what Whites conceived to be a "tribal" manner.[7]

Another probable mention in the *Colonial Records* appears in 1773, when the last royal governor addressed the House of Assembly:

Mr. Speaker and Gentlemen of the House of Assembly,
    I send herewith for your consideration a representation of Mr Archibald McKissak a magistrate of the County of Bladen relative to a number of free negroes and mulattoes who infest that county and annoy its Inhabitants
                                JO. MARTIN.
New Bern, December 18th 1773   [North Carolina 1890:768].

As has been noted, initially, Lumbee ancestors were classified as "free persons of color," "free negroes," and "mulattoes." The fact that they were annoying the (presumably White) inhabitants of Bladen suggests again the kind of spirit to be so vividly expressed during the days of the Henry Berry Lowry band from 1864 to 1874.

Absolutely unequivocal references to Lumbee ancestors appear in the 1790 U.S. census, which classifies most of the Indian heads of families as "free persons of color," and a few as "free white." Very few families were listed as owning slaves, and none owned many. This census undoubtedly underenumerates Lumbee ancestors for a number of reasons. Underreporting was a general problem in that census and several reasons are recounted in its Introduction. Poor or nonexistent roads, the difficulties of navigating through swamps, and the reluctance of White enumerators to endanger their lives for the census would all have contributed to underreporting. Further, enumerators were White, would likely have been viewed with suspicion, and some would probably have been reluctant to make direct enquiries about the sensitive subject of race (cf. Beale 1958:537).

From 1790 on, there is definitive documentation showing that ancestors of the Lumbee were continuously in Robeson County and that their number was augmented by immigration. Between the middle 1700s and 1790, evidence of their presence as individuals is contained in deeds and land grants, but evidence concerning the nature of their community or their relations with their neighbors is elusive. Before that time, all we can do is speculate.

There have been many theories about where the Lumbee came from. In the middle 1800s, there were suggestions from Whites that they originated from a mixture of Indians with Portuguese and Spaniards, or from Indians and runaway slaves. A few accounts mention the marriage into the Lowry family of Tuscarora women. Norment (1875) points to separate origins for different families. But nothing in the way of a systematic theory that claimed to document the origins of the group appeared until Hamilton McMillan, a state legislator and local historian from Robeson County, proposed that the group, which had been referred to as "mulattoes," was properly designated "Indian" because they were the descendants of Sir Walter Raleigh's 1587 lost colony at Roanoke Island, Virginia (now North Carolina), and their friendly Indian neighbors. As evidence, he cited Governor John White's account of what White found when he returned to the colony after having been in England collecting supplies. White arrived back at Roanoke Island to find the colonists gone and an inscription carved in a tree suggesting that they had gone of their own volition to Croatoan, an island belonging to the friendly Indian Manteo's people. From the name of the island, McMillan derived a name for the Robeson Indians – Croatan (pronounced "crow-ah-tan," with emphasis on the last sylla-ble, as in Powha*tan*).

McMillan went on to try to trace what had happened to this amalga-mated people between 1590, when White returned to Roanoke (and shortly after departed again without having seen the colonists), and the contact of early settlers with the Robeson County descendants of the colonists and Indians in the 1700s. In this, he mentions Lawson's (1714) account of a few Hatteras Indians living on Roanoke Island who claimed that some of their ancestors were Whites and could "talk in a book" (McMillan 1888:8). In addition to travelers' accounts, McMillan cites other kinds of evidence in support of this theory – namely, that his theory corresponds with what the Indians said about where they had come from, that many of the names found among Robeson County In-dians were the same as or derived from lost colonists' names, and that the language used by the Indians in his day was "almost pure Anglo Saxon" (McMillan 1888:20). Many others have taken up this theory and have added to the broken bits of evidence, or simply repeated its assertions (e.g., Weeks, 1891, Melton 1895, Baxter 1895, Ford 1907, Fitch 1913, McPherson 1915).

But there have also been other theories developed about where and from whom the Lumbee originated. In 1913, Senator Angus W. Mc-Lean of Robeson, who was later to become governor of North Carolina, put forth the theory that the Indians were really descendants of Cherokees who refused, like those in the mountains, to remove westward. McLean maintained:

> Long before historians began to study the origin of these people they claimed to be of Cherokee descent. In fact they have always claimed that they were originally a part of the Cherokee Tribe and that they gave up their tribal relation

after they had participated with the white man in the war against the
Tuscaroras [U.S. House of Representatives 1913:20].

Many Indians supported this theory, and probably some of them initiated it. It is still sometimes advanced by Indians today. A middle-
aged Indian man who was told that we were doing a study on the Lumbee Indians pondered a bit and then said, musingly,

> "That's a new name I've had to get used to. When I was coming up
> [growing up], we went by another name – Cherokee – but that wasn't
> good enough for some, so they changed it. They took the name of the
> old winding, treacherous, dangerous, devious river [Lumbee] and
> named the people after that."[8]

Another theory has its roots in anthropologist James Mooney's
Siouan Tribes of the East (1894), which was apparently a basis on
which J. R. Swanton, another anthropologist, constructed his argument concerning the "Probable Identity of the 'Croatan' Indians"
(U.S. Senate Reports 1934:3–6). Swanton maintained that the Indian
ancestors of the "Croatans" probably came from a number of Siouan-
speaking groups in North and South Carolina, such as the Cheraw,
Keyauwee, Eno, Shakori, Waccamaw, and Cape Fear. He further
notes the possibility that "a few families or small groups of Algonquian
or Iroguian [Iroquoian] connection may have cast their lot with this
body of people, but contributions from such sources must have been
relatively insignificant" (U.S. Senate Reports 1934:6). It appears that
Swanton looked at early documentary sources to see which Indian
groups were in the general area and formulated his theory on an assumption that those groups closest to the present site of the "Croatans" would be the most probable ancestors. This may be entirely correct, but it is certainly speculative, and firm links among the groups he
mentions and the ancestors of the Lumbee remain to be established. In
1967–68, I encountered a few Indians who were either referred to as
"Cheraws" or claimed a "Cheraw" ancestor. Such people were usually said to have originated to the west of Robeson County, either in
Scotland County next door, or farther west.

There have also been other, less well articulated and argued theories
about the Indian ancestry of the Lumbee connecting them to the Mattamuskeet, the Hatteras, and the Tuscarora. What is needed is an intensive search in counties known to have contained Indians, such as
that carried out by Patrick H. Garrow (1975), who traced the presence
of the Mattamuskeet in Hyde County, North Carolina, through, for
example, land deeds and birth and marriage registers. It is possible that
by tracing family records, connections between Lumbee ancestors and
known Indian groups elsewhere can be established, but the research
would be extremely time consuming and in the end might not establish

the links, although it would surely contribute to a better understanding of local history. Such detailed research on the Lumbee has yet to be completed, but a project directed by anthropologist Robert Thomas has apparently found evidence from deeds, land grants, and wills suggesting that at least some Robeson Indian ancestors came south to Robeson County from communities along the Roanoke and Neuse rivers in North Carolina and east from Cheraw country (Robert Thomas, personal communication).

Such a formulation is supported by the slender threads of oral tradition preserved by Norment (1875) and McMillan (1888), both Robeson Whites, each with a separate bias. Norment sought to cast most of the Indians' ancestors in as poor a light as possible, and McMillan to show them in as beneficial a light as possible. Norment notes the arrival of various families from different North Carolina counties, in addition to the families who were in residence when the Whites arrived. The Lowrys, she asserts, originated in Bute County (now Franklin and Warren counties), as did the Cummingses, the Goinses, and the Brayboys; the Ransoms came from Halifax, and the Woodses from Sampson counties. She also remarks upon a Murphey married to a Cumba woman who left Robeson County about 1792 together with a Hunt and settled near Hunt's Bluff, on the Great Pee Dee River in South Carolina (Norment 1875:4, 26–7).

McMillan maintains that the Indians claimed to have come from Roanoke, in Virginia, and that they applied this name to the area around Pamlico Sound, including Tyrell, Dare, Carteret, Craven, and Jones counties (1888:19,20). Carteret, Jones, and Craven counties are at the mouth of the Neuse River. He further remarks, "Tradition in regard to their ancient dwelling places on the tributaries of Black river in the present county of Sampson are [*sic*] more definite" (McMillan 1888:25). McMillan paints a broad picture of the movements of people related to the Robeson County group:

Occasional bands of immigrants arrived on the Lumber River from ancient settlements towards the East, while others moved West towards the Pee Dee, Catawba and French Broad rivers. . . . Subsequent to the coming of white settlers a portion of the tribe went North towards the Great Lakes and some of their descendants can be found at this time in Canada, West of Lake Ontario. Another emigration occurred at a later date and the emigrants became incorporated with a tribe then located near Lake Michigan. Many families, described as white people, emigrated towards the Alleghany [*sic*] mountains and there are many families in Western North Carolina at this time, who are claimed by the tribe in Robeson County as descendants of the lost English colonists . . . [McMillan 1888:14].

Regarding the people who are said to be in Canada, west of Lake Ontario, it is intriguing that there was a group of Southern Siouan-speaking Indians, the Tutelo, who once lived along the Roanoke River and then moved progressively northward beginning about 1732. Eventually, they were taken under the protection of the League of the Iroquois (in 1753), and many ultimately followed Joseph Brant to Canada, settling on the Six Nations Reserve on Grand River. During the 1830s, about 200 Tutelos reportedly lived near Brantford, Ontario. The people known as the Tutelo by that time had absorbed elements of other Southern Siouan-speaking peoples, such as the Saponi, the Occaneechi, the Keyauwee, and the Schoccoree (DeMallie, in press).

As to the people McMillan says moved toward the Alleghenies, it is likely that some are among the ancestors of the people in scattered communities in Tennessee known derogatorily as the "Melungeons." Certainly Price (1950) has demonstrated that many of the names found among the early ancestors of at least some "Melungeon" communities are similar to those of Lumbee ancestors, and many of them are reported to have come from North Carolina originally.

In the absence of more specific information about family movements and origins, however, I would offer still more speculation concerning Lumbee ancestry that avoids naming the specific groups from which ancestors came but concentrates on the dynamics of the situation in Robeson that fostered the settlement of people of Indian ancestry from other areas. It seems a reasonable assumption that Lumbee ancestors had many different "tribal" affiliations, originally spoke several different Indian languages, and had one common goal – to find refuge from White-introduced diseases, wars, and the settlers who were sweeping through North and South Carolina. The swamps of what was to be Robeson County combined with the county's uncertain colonial status attracted people of Indian descent with a promise of protection.

There were massive dislocations of Indian populations in areas to the north and south of Robeson County. In 1711, the Tuscarora War to the north could have driven some Indians to seek refuge in the southern swamps on the border between the Carolinas. Later, in the 1730s, a smallpox epidemic raged through South Carolina and may have sent those fleeing it northward into the swamps. That Robeson provided a refuge for people – Indian, White, or Black – who sought to avoid highly organized government is also likely.

The county is located in a section of North Carolina that was, between 1712 and 1776, involved in a border dispute between the colonies of North and South Carolina. Because both colonies claimed the area, but neither could hold it, Lefler and Newsome remark, "confusion and disorder reigned throughout the region" (1963:150). Many White colonists would have hesitated to settle there because of the confusion about which colony would be legally responsible for the region, and therefore the area would provide an ideal refuge for those seeking to avoid large all-White settlements. The remnant groups who found safety in Robeson County intermarried, amalgamating into a single people that included some non-Indian neighbors who chose to live like the Indians. That the inclusion of non-Indians occurred very early is likely.

When Whites first began to settle in the county in the 1700s, the Indians already spoke English. If many were bilingual in an Indian language and English (as they might well be if they had intermarried with Whites and/or formerly been in contact with them and subsequently fled), then English would have been a good *lingua franca,* equally acceptable or unacceptable to everyone. If there were Saponi ancestors among this Robeson County group, they could have been taught English at the school run for them from 1716–18 at Christanna, a settlement designated for them on the south side of the Meherrin River in Virginia. They left Christanna around 1729 to join the Catawba to the south (DeMallie, in press).

This picture does not exclude the possibility that some of the ancestors of the Lumbee were lost colonists and their friendly Indian neighbors, nor does it necessarily exclude possible Cherokee, Siouan, or Tuscarora ancestry. Perhaps all these contributed to the population, as Dean Chavers, a Lumbee, has suggested (1971–72).

What were they like before?

The first substantive material to provide information about who the ancestors of the Lumbee said they were and what their relations with their neighbors were comes from a time of crisis for the entire South as well as for North Carolina and Robeson County. The end of the Civil War and the beginning of Reconstruction was a difficult time for Southerners of all races, but difficult in different ways. Whites suffered a humiliating and devastating military defeat and a wrenching change in their social world as slaves were emancipated and permitted to vote, while many Whites who had served prominently in the Confederate army were denied the vote until they could be declared pardoned by Congress. Blacks experienced the elation of emancipation and the fear of reprisals from Whites when they attempted to use their new freedom. And Indians found themselves locked in a desperate struggle to maintain the integrity of their community.

Even before the end of the Civil War, some Whites were treating Indians in much the way they treated Blacks. With the cessation of the fighting and the declaration of emancipation, both Indians and Blacks were free peoples and potential voters. Many Whites apparently considered this a threat to their continued dominance and became even more concerned to establish control over a recalcitrant Indian community. The Indians resisted, a few very actively and others by aiding and abetting them.

The relevant documents surviving from this difficult transition period are related primarily to the activities of an outlawed band of men led by a young man from a prosperous Indian family whose name was Henry Berry Lowry. There are hearings and depositions by Indians and Whites taken by an agent of the Freedmen's Bureau regarding the murders of Henry Berry Lowry's father and brother and an Indian named Hector Oxendine. There are accounts of the band's activities by a local White woman whose husband was reportedly killed by the band (Norment 1875, 1909) and by two reporters for the *New York Herald* who actually visited Robeson County (Townsend 1872). There is testimony given by local Whites before a joint Congressional committee investigating the Ku Klux Klan (U.S. Senate Reports 1872). And finally, there is a diary left by one of the White men who hunted the Lowry band (Wishart 1864– 72).[9] These accounts supplement the drier bones of the U.S. census. Useful secondary material for this period is available in the books of a historian, W. McKee Evans (1966, 1971), who is himself a White native of Robeson and whose family were Republicans during Reconstruction (Evans, personal communication). His volume on the Lowry band (Evans 1971) is highly regarded by many Indians.[10]

What can be learned from these and other documents about the quality of Indian life during these times? It is clear that the White community was deeply divided in its opinions about the Indians, or "mulattoes" as most referred to them, and uncoordinated in its actions toward them. They could not agree either about who the mulattoes really were or about what should be done regarding them. At the same time, enough pressure was being brought to bear on the mulatto community by some Whites to cause the formation of the Lowry band, who avenged the murders of Indians and who lived by robbing Whites. The pressure appears to have been economic as well as personal oppression. Indians had experienced land losses and were beginning to be forced to work along with Black slaves on Confederate fortifications in fever-ridden Wilmington on the coast. This they interpreted as a further move by Whites to treat them as Negroes.

Tensions over the classification of the people later recognized as Indians rose rapidly after the North Carolina constitutional revisions in 1835, which canceled many of the rights of free persons of color. Before 1835, Lumbee ancestors had been able to vote and a few had served in the War of 1812 (U.S. House of Representatives 1913:14– 15).

Classification as "free persons of color"

As a result of a series of restrictive laws termed the "Free Negro Code" by John Hope Franklin (1943), which began in 1826 and continued to be modified into the 1850s, the Indians, who had been classified as "free persons of color" at least since the 1790 census, lost their right to vote, legally bear arms without a license, or serve in the militia (Franklin 1943:63–81). They had lost their right to testify against Whites in court in 1777, when the General Assembly of North Carolina forbade "Negroes, Indians, Mulattoes, and all Persons of Mixed Blood" to be witnesses except against each other (Franklin 1943:82).

Some evidence of tensions arising from such laws may be seen in court cases involving Robeson County Indian ancestors. In 1837, Charles Oxendine was indicted in Robeson County for assault and battery. He submitted to the court and was thereupon not tried, but fined fifteen dollars. When he was unable to pay this sum, and because Oxendine was a "free negro," the sheriff was ordered to hire him out to whomever would pay his fine in the shortest time. Oxendine appealed the judgment on the grounds that the law unconstitutionally discriminated against free persons of color (*State* v. *Charles Oxendine,* 19 N.C. 417). Significantly, his case was taken on appeal by two eminent Fayetteville lawyers, Robert Strange, a U.S. Senator at the time, and George E. Badger, later Secretary of the Navy and a Whig Senator (Franklin 1943:86). The supreme court of North Carolina reversed the judgment on the grounds that Oxendine had *submitted* to the court, whereas the rule on payment of fines specified that *conviction* was necessary. It avoided ruling on the constitutionality of the law.

Lawyer Robert Strange also defended William Manuel in 1838 in a similar case. Manuel, from Sampson County, was *convicted* of assault and battery and was sentenced to pay a fine of twenty dollars. When he was unable to pay, as a free person of color, he was also bound to the sheriff, who was to hire him out until the fine was paid. Manuel appealed to the North Carolina supreme court on the grounds that imprisonment for debt is unconstitutional. The state's attorney argued that Manuel was not entitled to such protection under the constitution because, as a free person of color, he was not a citizen of the state. The judge ruled that free persons of color *are* citizens of the state if born there, but that the law can legitimately distinguish between penalties for free colored persons and those for Whites. His decision was that the defendant could discharge his fine by remaining in prison for twenty days and had to pay the costs of appeal (*State* v. *William Manuel,* 20 N.C. 144).[11]

After the General Assembly passed a law in 1840 forbidding "any Free Negro, Mulatto or Free Person of Color" to bear arms without a license, Elijah Newsom was convicted in Cumberland County, which abuts Robeson, of illegally carrying about with him a shotgun. Although he was found guilty, the judgment was arrested by the lower court on the grounds that the law prohibiting free persons of color from bearing arms was unconstitutional. When the solicitor for the state appealed, the supreme court ruled the law constitutional, simply "police regulation," as it did not prohibit free Negroes from bearing arms but merely required licenses (*State* v. *Elijah Newsom,* 27 N.C. 203). Although the 1840 law required licenses for all manner of arms – not just guns and sabers, but also daggers and bowie knives – this apparently was not stringent enough for some White Robesonians. In 1856, a group of them petitioned the General Assembly to prohibit any free Negro from possessing a gun " 'unless he is a free holder and give bond with good security and then not be allowed to carry it off the land'" (MS in Legislative Papers for 1856, as quoted in Franklin 1943:78). They also requested that only one dog be allowed to a free Negro (Franklin 1943:78, n94). "Free person of color" had become synonymous with "free Negro." Although the Robesonians' petition was denied, the legislature did pass a law in 1861 making the possession of arms by any "Negro" a misdemeanor to be punished by a fine of at least fifty dollars (Franklin 1943:78).

Robesonians had been concerned about their "free colored" population for several decades. In 1840, thirty-six of them requested that the Assembly regulate the sale of "spirits" to this troublesome population:

> "The County of Robeson is cursed with a free-coloured population that
> migrated originally from the districts round about the Roanoke and Neuse
> Rivers. They are generally indolent, roguish, improvident, and dissipated.
> Having no regard for character, they are under no restraint but what the law
> imposes. They are great topers, and so long as they can procure the
> exhilarating draught seem to forget entirely the comfort of their families. All
> that has been written against the use of ardent spirits will apply with all its force
> to them. . . . All the evils accompanying an excessive use of it afflict that
> population" [MS in Legislative Papers for 1840–41, as quoted in Franklin
> 1943:79].

This petition was not endorsed by the relevant Assembly committee, but by 1859, the Assembly had passed a law forbidding the sale or procurement of "spirituous liquors" to free persons of color, except for medicinal purposes, for which written justification from a physician or magistrate was required (Franklin 1943:81).

Meanwhile, Indian ancestors continued to appear in court, sometimes as Whites. In 1846, John Mainor and Lilly Wilkes were indicted for fornication in Robeson County, but the jury found only Mainor guilty. Mainor moved to have the judgment arrested, and the solicitor for the state appealed. Mainor was not represented by counsel in the North Carolina supreme court, but the court acquitted him on the grounds that if one defendant is acquitted, the other must be also (*State* v. *John Mainor and Lilly Wilkes,* 28 N.C. 274). Louis Hunt was acquitted in the lower Robeson County Superior Court in 1851 of murdering a slave who was the property of a prominent White family (Franklin 1943:100).

In 1853, two Indian ancestors took their cases to the North Carolina supreme court. Raiford Revels was first indicted in Robeson County for stealing a sheep said to be the property of Peter Prevatt. When it was found that the sheep was not Prevatt's, Revels was acquitted. However, he was reindicted for stealing a sheep said to be the property of someone unknown and was found guilty. This judgment was reversed in the supreme court (*State* v. *Raiford Revels,* 44 N.C. 200). The judgment against Noah Locklear was affirmed by the high court. He had been indicted in Robeson for illegally carrying about with him a rifle, a musket, and a shotgun. He was convicted upon proof that he had been carrying a shotgun. His defense was that he could not be properly indicted unless he had carried all three weapons. He was found guilty (*State* v. *Noah Locklear,* 44 N.C. 205).

Most of these cases have been cited by Franklin (1943) and others as illustrative of the situation of "free Negroes," although all of them involve people who were not considered in their locale to be the same as free people whose ancestors were Black slaves. There are no records to indicate that Lumbee ancestors were ever anything but free. Further, they formed a distinct "population," as the petition from White Robesonians suggests. Many of the surnames in other prominent "free Negro" legal cases in North Carolina are associated with Lumbee ancestors, or with groups very like them in other parts of North Carolina (e.g., the surnames Freeman, Jacobs, Chavers, Martin, Ransome, and Bell). It may be that the litigiousness of true "free Negroes" (those descended from Africans imported as slaves) in the pre–Civil War era has been overestimated.

What do such cases show about the ancestors of the Lumbee? First and foremost, they suggest a strikingly sophisticated knowledge about "how the system works" and how they might go about manipulating it. They knew how to find good counsel, and one of them, John Mainor, successfully appealed his own case to the North Carolina supreme court without counsel. Such knowledge is impossible to imagine in a genuinely "isolated" people. Further, the defendants in a number of these cases were wrestling with the legal system in an attempt to alter the law in such a way as to benefit a whole class of individuals, not just themselves (e.g., *State* v. *Oxendine, State* v. *Manuel, State* v. *Newsom*).

If the Civil War marks a crisis period for the ancestors of the Lumbee, it must be asked what we know of them on the eve of that event. From the 1850 U.S. census, it can be seen that most men designated as mulattoes were engaged in farming and laboring, whereas a few were skilled craftsmen or businessmen (carpenters, blacksmiths, shoemakers, coopers, bricklayers, furners or bakers, a merchant, and a miller). Of about 200 independent mullato households, about half are listed as owning real estate. The value given for real estate varies from $10 to $3,000, with the average value $182 and the median $100 (U.S. Census Enumerators' Reports 1850). The young men who were to become members of the Lowry band in the next decade all came from families whose real estate was valued above the median:

> Alleń Lowry, father of band members Henry Berry, Steve, and Tom, is listed as a carpenter holding real estate valued at $334.
>
> John Oxendine, father of band members Calvin and Henderson, is recorded as a farmer with real estate valued at $135.
>
> George Dial, father of band member John, is enumerated as a farmer whose real estate is valued at $400 [U.S. Census Enumerators' Reports 1850].

In addition, Hector Oxendine, who was murdered by local Whites in 1865, presumably for showing Sherman's Yankee troops where to find livestock on White farms, came from a family related to the John Oxendine family mentioned above. Hector's father was listed as a farmer with real estate valued at $75.[12]

It should be clear from this evidence that the Lowry band members and leader came from some of the more prosperous Indian families, not from among the poorest. As young men from leading families, their actions had greater impact on the Indian community than they might otherwise have had. Their activities can easily be seen as falling into what Hobsbawm has called "social banditry":

> The point about social bandits is that they are peasant outlaws whom the lord and state regard as criminals, but who remain within peasant society, and are considered by their people as heroes, as champions, avengers, fighters for justice, perhaps even leaders of liberation, and in any case as men to be admired, helped and supported [Hobsbawm 1969:13].

That there was some confusion about the racial classification of Indian ancestors from the outset is suggested by the fact that a number of families are listed as "free White" in one census and "free colored" in the next. For example, Burwell Revil is classified under "all other free persons of color'' in 1790 and the same way in 1800, but Burl Revel's family is counted as "free White" in 1810. In 1820, Burrell Revells and his family are listed as "colored free persons," as is the Burwell Revels family of the 1840 census. It is possible to follow this family through so many decades because its head was exceptionally long-lived. Emanual Carter's family is recorded in 1790 under "all other free persons of color," and in 1800 and 1810 as "free White." This suggests that some enumerators probably guessed at racial classifications on the basis of physical appearance. That in turn implies that members of the Indian community even then varied widely in appearance.

The 1850 Census Enumerators' Reports begin to provide more detailed information. Individuals within families are listed under the head of household separately by name, age, sex, and race. In this census, there are several apparently "mixed marriages" recorded. For example, Benjamin Hardin, a fifty-one-year-old mullato, heads a household with Holly Hardin, a forty-one-year-old white woman, and four Hardin children, all designated mullatoes. Jeremiah Woodell, a twenty-four-year-old White, is the head of a household containing Rhoda Woodell, a twenty-eight-year-old mulatto, and one mulatto Woodell child. There are other instances as well. The fact that White enumerators were recording racially mixed households of both types – White male with mulatto female and mulatto male with White female – suggests that such families were not unduly interfered with by Whites and perhaps that they were acceptable to Whites as part of the mulatto community. There were no instances recorded of Black and White households except where the Blacks were slaves. Thus, the present toleration of interracial couples who live in the Indian community is probably of long standing.

Henry Berry Lowry and his band. As the Civil War (or, as White Southerners call it, the War Between the States or, sometimes, the War of Northern Aggression) progressed, Indians had increasing difficulties with Whites. The economic position of the so-called mulattoes worsened. Giles Leitch, a prominent White Robeson County lawyer, testified in 1871 before a joint Congressional committee investigating "the condition of affairs in the late insurrectionary states." His testimony outlines a decline in fortune through "intemperance" and litigation:

During that war [Revolutionary War] they accumulated and amassed a large fortune and at the close of the war they were rich, their riches consisting mostly in slaves. They were colored themselves, and they owned slaves; I suppose there were a dozen heads of families, perhaps, to whom I allude particularly. Soon after the close of the revolutionary war, when law and order were reëstablished, and they could not carry on their robberies longer, they got into litigation. As a characteristic of these dozen heads of families, so it was said of them, they were intemperate. They had lawsuits, and gradually and eventually, before my recollection, before I can recollect anything much about it, they had wasted their substance in that county in litigation. They had lawsuits among themselves and with their neighbors; they were indicted for violations of the law, and were known as lawless men; just about thirty years ago [ca. 1840], I think, the last of their slaves were sold from them; I do not think they have owned any slaves within about thirty years [U.S. Senate Reports 1872:284].

With all this, the added insult of enforced labor with Black slaves, interpreted by Indians as tantamount to classifying them as Blacks, was too much to bear. Young Indian men refused to go to the fortifications and chose instead to "lie out" in the swamps where Whites often could not find them (Evans 1971:36; Norment 1875:34, 41–2). Then, in midwinter 1864–65, a White man named Harris, a man not known for his upstanding character among Whites, took two of Henry Berry Lowry's cousins by force while they were on leave from fortification work with the stated intent of returning them to work. The two young men's bodies were found shortly after that, and White and Indian opinion alike blamed Harris. Harris was in turn murdered, presumably by Indians, in January, 1865 (Evans 1971:40–1; Norment 1875:41–2). Relations between Indians and Whites were deteriorating rapidly. Furthermore, the Confederate Army was faring badly.

In March, 1865, a few days before General Sherman's troops marched through Robeson County taking draft animals as they went and foraging in field and farm, members of the White Home Guard appeared at the farm of Calvin Lowry, one of Henry Berry Lowry's brothers. Calvin, in his testimony of September 1867, regarding the murders of his father and brother, explained what had happened that day:

There was a company of men came to my place on 3rd March 1865 I was out in the field at work I saw them coming and went to meet them Part of them part of them [*sic*] was in my house & yard before I got there Searching the house When I got there they had taken a Shotgun out and gourd of powder and wanted to know who I was I said I was a Lowery and they said I was bad stock and wanted to know if I knew anything about the robbing that was going on through the country I told I heard it was going on but did not know who it was They wanted to know if I knew anything about the union prisoners and if I was harboring them I dont recollect whether I told them I had seen them but had not been harboring them They searched the Smokehouse and wanted to know if I fattened all that meat I told them I did They acknowledged there they reconed [*sic*] I did Said they wanted me to go with them . . . [NA 1868, Letter R-17].

After confiscating his guns and ammunition, Calvin maintained, the Home Guard ("the company") took him to his father's house, where they took three trunks, clothes, and a rifle as well as a demijohn of brandy, which they offered to pay for but drank anyway when Allen Lowry refused their offer. The whole Lowry family was then taken to

Robert McKenzie's. According to Calvin Lowry, in a deposition taken on October 14, 1867,

Robert McKenzie then asked, where them Union prisoners were, who was about there, and if they had not been harboring them, and if they were not with them robbing, and if he had not told them if he did not get up his boys to go to the Government fortifications, they would have to suffer for it. Allen Lowry replied that his boys were free from him & he could not rule them [NA 1868, Letter R-17].

Shortly thereafter, Allen and his son William Lowry were shot by the Home Guard. According to Calvin Lowry's deposition, the Guard afterward questioned him further concerning the whereabouts of escaped Yankee prisoners, but he claimed to know nothing. When one of the White men came at him with a bayonet, another White man stopped the first. After a warning not to help escaped prisoners, the rest of the Lowry family was released.

The White Home Guard version of this killing is, as might be expected, quite different regarding the reasons for the killing. It must be borne in mind that Indians and Whites alike were giving sworn testimony to the Lumberton agent of the Freedmen's Bureau and that it had recently become a crime to persecute someone for aiding the Union cause. Robert McKenzie, to whose home the Lowry family was taken, deposed on May 29, 1867, that he had been robbed in February 1865 by, among others, Henry Berry Lowry and Andrew Strong (Henry Berry's brother-in-law). He stated further:

The Cartload of plunder was found in Allan Lowry's house, his son William living in the same house with him, that all of the Lowrys arrested were locked up in a house and guarded, among the plunder found at Allan Lowry's house, many articles of Clothing Guns &c &c were identified by the neighbors whose houses had been robbed. That a gold head of a walking cane, was found in William Lowry's pocket, with O. G. Parsleys name on it, the cane having been reported stolen from O. G. Parsley who is now in Wilmington NC. That a jury of twelve men was chosen, and Allan William, Sinclair & Calvin Lowry were all tryed for highway robbery & found guilty, the Company which consisted of aboùt Eighty men were then consulted as to what should be done with them. And the Company voted that Allan & William Lowry should be shot forthwith [NA 1868, Letter R-10].

A few days after the Lowry killings, Sherman marched through Robeson County. Some Whites accused Indians of acting as guides for the federal troops, and one Indian, Hector Oxendine, was killed in May 1865. Elias Carlile, a White man to whose home Hector Oxendine was brought by other White men, when asked on August 23, 1867, why Oxendine had been killed, replied, "They accused him of stealing horses, and going with, and leading the 'Yankees' when they passed through'' (NA 1868, Letter R-17). Jack Carlile, a ''colored'' man, testifying on the same day:

States that he was at Elias Carliles and William Humphrey came up and asked him to go to Andrew Carliles and ask him to come up, as he wanted him to bring his gun and help to shoot a Buck. And I understood he meant the Buck to be Hector Oxendine [NA 1868, Letter R-17].

For his older sons, the killings of Allen and William Lowry must have been the final straw. One of Allen's sons, Henry Berry Lowry, thereafter led a small band of his kinsmen and friends in exacting violent revenge for the murder of his father and brother. According to all accounts, White and Indian alike, he succeeded in killing or driving out of the county everyone directly responsible for the murders. Later, in 1867, Henry Berry Lowry's mother and some of his brothers who were not in his band sought legal remedy for their wrongs by petitioning the Freedmen's Bureau. At the instigation of the bureau, the men accused by the Indians were brought before the Grand Jury in Robeson County, but the jury failed to find a true bill. The bureau then tried to have the case transferred to military court, but the headquarters of the Second Military District refused to take up the case. Radical Reconstruction had not yet begun in Congress. Obtaining legal redress under the new regime was apparently as difficult as it had been under the old. The Lowry band went on exacting its own extralegal reprisals, killing those Whites who tried to stop them and robbing others in order to live. Indian oral traditions maintain that the band redistributed at least some of their booty among their less successful fellows.

Attitudes toward the Lowry band varied among members of his own community and among Whites and Blacks, as might be expected. Henry Berry Lowry himself was quoted by Townsend, a Northern newspaper reporter, stating his position:

''My band is big enough,'' he said last week. ''They are all true men and I could not be as safe with more. We mean to live as long as we can, to kill anybody who hunts us, from the Sheriff down, and at last, if we must die, to die game.''

To another person he said. ''We are not allowed to get our living peaceably and we must take it from others. We don't kill anybody but the Ku Klux'' [Townsend 1872:26].[13]

Support for the band must have been widespread in their community because the band continued its activities for nearly ten years and its leader was never captured or killed by Whites. Giles Leitch, a Conservative lawyer from Robeson, talked about the community's support for the band in his testimony before a joint Congressional committee:

Question. Do all the men of that class [mulattoes] coöperate with Lowry in his outrages?

Answer [Leitch]. Well, sir; I think not; I do not think you can put it exactly in that light. But I think that most of them sympathize with him. I think that if a band of men were to go there for the purpose of arresting him, they would advise him of that fact in time for him to escape. I do not think they really approve of his conduct.

Question. Still they aid in sheltering him?

Answer. Yes, sir; they shelter him [U.S. Senate Reports 1872:286].

Answer [Leitch]. . . . it seems to me that, besides the terror that Lowry and his gang inspire, there is a little of sympathy, too. I think that among his class and color there is a little pride that we have been unable to take them; that he and his men can conquer and whip all who go after them [U.S. Senate Reports 1872:298].

Indians understandably seemed to be reluctant to express open support of the band to Whites. But the fearfulness of the times is communicated adequately by Jack Oxendine, father of two of the band members, who told the reporter Henderson:

" 'Fore God, dis is powerful bad country to live in; ebery now and den de Ku Kluck come in yer, and with their shootin' an' whippin' an' hangin', an' de men out by deyselves totin' dere guns, I's scart to deff'' [Townsend 1872:71].

On the other hand, not all in his community and family approved of Henry Berry Lowry's methods, even if they agreed he had been justifiably provoked. Patrick Lowry, one of Henry Berry's brothers, was interviewed by *Herald* reporter Townsend:

"My brother Harry had provocation – the same all of us had – when they killed my old father. But he has got to be a bad man, and I pray the Lord to remove him from this world, if he only repent first'' [Townsend 1872:27].

Of course, Patrick was speaking to a White outsider of whom he must have known little, and how much of what he said was for White consumption is difficult to estimate.

Whites, predictably, took a somewhat harsher view of the band. The Reverend J. H. Coble and the Reverend L. McKinnon, both accused of having been part of the company that killed Allen and William Lowry, wrote a letter of justification to Freedmen's Bureau Agent William Birney on June 8, 1867:

[of the killings of Allen and William Lowry] They were killed for house-breaking & robbery, & for nothing else. The fact is, their depredations could be borne no longer. To such an extremety [*sic*] of lawlessness did they go that some of their neighbors were compelled to abandon their homes & remove their families & goods out of the community, as was the case with Mr Robt McKenzie & others. In one word, Sir, there was no security for life or property [NA 1868, Letter R-10].

Mary Norment, whose husband had been killed, expressed even stronger sentiments about the band:

. . . they [the outlaws] seemed to fear nothing, whilst they showed a ferocity, premeditation and insolence frightful to behold; spreading terror and dismay wherever they saw fit to go; no one, not an inhabitant of the county at the time, can realize the situation; nearly all of our citizens, with here and there an honorable exception, seemed *terror-stricken* and were dumb with dismay, for they did not know at what hour the Lowrie bandits would pounce down on them like an eagle on his prey, and murder some male member of the family for some imaginary wrong, or take away from them their hard earnings [emphasis in original; Norment 1875:110].

The Yankee Townsend observed of the relationship between the band and the non-Whites of the county:

Frequent exhibitions of magnanimity distinguish his bloody course and he learned to arrogate to himself a protectorate over the interests of the mulattoes, which they return by a sort of hero-worship. There is not, probably, a negro in Scuffletown [the area of densest "mulatto" settlement] who would betray him, and his prowess is a household word in every black family in sea-board Carolina [Townsend 1872:26–7].

Blacks also seem to have been generally supportive of the outlaws. The Yankee reporter Townsend noted:

The negro waiter in the hotel at Lumberton said to me in the presence of several white men of the town: –
"They say they go up to Scuffletown to hunt Lowery; but I never knew them to go there without killing some innocent person" [Townsend 1872:34].

And from an old Black woman, he received an explanation of the band's activities and an expression of enthusiastic support:

. . . "Henry Berry Lowery aint gwying to kill nobody but them that wants to kill him. He's just a paying these white people back for killing his old father, brothers and cousins." . . . "Massta," resumed Aunt Phoebe, "this used to be a dreful hard country for poor niggers. Do you see my teeth up yer, Massta?" . . . "My massta– his name's MacQueen (or MacQuade)– knocked 'em all out wid an oak stick. . . . Oh, dis was a hard country, and Henry Berry Lowery's jess a payin' 'em back. He's only a payin' 'em back! It's better days for de brack people now. Massta, he's jess de king o' dis country" [Townsend 1872:27].

Blacks were having their own share of trouble with Whites. In 1871, a Black Republican political leader was killed by a group of Whites. Norment claimed that he was killed because he was a "co-worker" of the Lowrys (1875:102), but Townsend called him "a violent radical republican" (1872:33).

It is in this setting of violence between Indian and White, and between White and Black, at a time when White Radicals and Conservatives were vying among themselves for control of the county, that documents were produced that now allow us to formulate a picture of how Indians presented themselves, and how Whites perceived them.

Who were the people designated "mulattoes"?

The most difficult problem presented by the documentation from the 1860–75 period is that very little of it records directly what Indians said about themselves, and the small portions that do (such as the testimony given to the Grand Jury investigating the deaths of Allen and William Lowry) are directed specifically toward a White audience and concern a specific problem. Identity conceptions rarely make themselves explicit in such contexts. However, there are accounts from *New York Herald* reporters that make clear that at least some of those classified by Whites as "mulattoes" had claimed an identity different from that of Blacks for some time and were upset about the loss of lands they considered theirs.

One evening at Lumberton I sat in the office of Judge Leech [probably Giles Leitch], half a dozen [White] gentlemen present, and they described old Allan Lowery . . .

"The Lowerys," said one of the persons present, "were always savage and predatory. By conducting a sort of swamp or guerilla war during the Revolution they accumulated considerable property, and at the close of that war were landholders, slaveholders and people of the soil. Then they grew dissipated during the time of peace, and their land was levied upon to pay debts. Being Indians, with an idea that their ancestors held all this land in fee simple, they could not understand how it could be taken from them, and for years they looked upon society as having robbed them of their patrimony."

"Yes," said one present, "Allen Lowery brought me a case against a man who wished to sell a piece of property he had formely [*sic*] owned, and he couldn't be made to understand that the man had a good title for it. When they were holding the examination, just before they shot him in 1865 the old man pleaded in extenuation of the plunder found in his house that he had never been given fair play but had been cheated out of his land. He said that his grandfather had been cut across the hand in the Revolution, fighting for the State, and that the State had cheated all his family. He had the Indian sentiment deep in him, of having suffered wrong, and imparted it to all his sons. Here is Sink (Sinclair) Lowery with the same kind of notions to this day. He said a little while ago, 'We used to own all the country round here, but it was taken from use somehow' " [Townsend 1872:47–8].

Another of those sitting and talking with the reporter remarked of Allen Lowry, "He had a heap of mixed white and Indian pride. . ." (Townsend 1872:48). The two ministers who had reportedly been present at the killings of the Lowry father and son state outright in a letter dated June 8, 1967, to the Freedmen's Bureau that the Lowrys claimed to be Indians, and they do not dispute the claim:

We would premise, in the first place, that the Lowrys are believed to be free from all taint of Negro blood. They are said to be descended from the Tuscarora Indians. They have always claimed to be Indian, & disdained the idea that they are in any way connected with the African race [NA 1868, Letter R-10].

Some mulattoes were asserting their Indian identity, and some Whites had accepted their claims.[14] But there was no agreement among Whites as to this identity. Many readily acknowledged an Indian component, but disagreed about what had been added to it. Giles Leitch tried to explain just who the mulattoes were to the joint Senate and House committee in 1871:

Answer [Leitch]. The county of Robeson had about one thousand five hundred white voting population before the close of the war. Since then, since the colored population has been enfranchised, there are about three thousand voters in the county; of that one thousand five hundred additional voting population, about half were formerly slaves, and the other half are composed of a population that existed there and were never slaves, and are not white, but who since 1835 have had no right of suffrage. I am speaking now from conjecture, but I think that about one-half of that additional one thousand five hundred voters were this old free and not white population; I cannot tell with absolute certainty.

Question. Half of the colored population?

Answer. Yes, sir; half of the colored population of Robeson county were never slaves at all. In 1835 there was a State convention which disfranchised them; up to that time they had exercised the elective franchise. . . .

Question. What are they; are they negroes?

Answer. Well, sir, I desire to tell you the truth as near as I can; but really I do not know what they are; I think they are a mixture of Spanish, Portuguese and Indian. About half of them have straight black hair, and many of the characteristics of the Cherokee Indians in our State; then, as they amalgamate and mix, the hair becomes curly and kinky, and from that down to real woolen hair.

Question. You think they are mixed negroes and Indians?

Answer. I think they are mixed Portuguese, Spaniards and Indians; I mean to class the Spaniards and Portuguese as one class, and the Indians as another class. I do not think that in that class of population there is much negro blood at all; of that half of the colored population that I have attempted to describe all have been always free: I was born among them, and I reckon that I know them perfectly well. They are a thriftless, lazy, thievish and indolent population. They are called "mulattoes;" that is the name they are known by, as contradistinguished from negroes. There is a family of them by the name of Lowry, that seems to have more Indian characteristics than perhaps any of the rest of that population. I have not been able to learn the origin of that family, though for several years I have been endeavoring to do so. I think they are of Indian origin [U.S. Senate Reports 1872:283–4].

Question. I understood you to say that these seven or eight hundred persons that you designate as mulattoes are not negroes, but are a mixture of Portuguese and Spanish, white blood and Indian blood: you think they are not generally negroes?

Answer. I do not think that the negro blood predominates.

Question. The word "mulatto" means a cross between the white and negro?

Answer. Yes, sir.

Question. You do not mean the word to be understood in that sense when applied to those people?

Answer. I really do not know exactly how to describe those people. The most of them have bushy, kinky hair, and they are about the color of a cross between the white and the negro; but they do not exactly partake of the characteristics of such a cross [U.S. Senate Reports 1872:293].

And finally,

> *Question.* Who lives in Scuffletown besides them ["this Lowry set of people"]?
> *Answer* [Leitch]. The Lowry family is Indian; then there are Locklaers, Oxendines, Hunts, Joneses, and Grayboys [Brayboys]; I do not recollect how many other negro names there are. There are a dozen different families there. Some of the Lowry and Oxendine families are related by marriage. But Lowry is Indian; the balance of them are not understood to be Indian– they are mulatto; I mean colored people [U.S. Senate Reports 1872:294].[15]

Norment, however, attributes a mixture of Black blood to all the residents of "Scuffletown." In Henry Berry Lowry himself, she remarks, the various "bloods" account for his propensities. From negro blood comes his "love for rude music," from Indian blood comes his habit of "using . . . women as an auxiliary to war and plunder," and from White "cavalier" blood come his virtues – always keeping his word, never committing arson, and never insulting White females (Norment 1875:11–12). She also mentions the order in which families arrived in Robeson County and notes which ones were "probably runaway slaves" (Norment 1875:27). Norment's view of the character and habits of the mulattoes was equally unflattering:

> Pilfering chickens, stealing pigs and killing sheep for mutton were of frequent occurrence among the denizens of Scuffletown [the area in the center of Robeson County where most Indians lived] from time immemorial. A love for spirituous liquors characterized the whole population with some few exceptions. The entire mulatto race are intemperate whenever they have the means of gratifying their taste for spirituous liquors, and when under the influence of liquor they are remarkably quarrelsome and fussy, often fighting and cutting and stabbing each other with knives, or shooting each other with guns or pistols [Norment 1875:25].

Differences among Whites. Whites, then, were not in agreement with one another about exactly who the population was that had become the center of so much violence and disturbance. Even Norment could not describe Henry Berry Lowry in entirely despicable terms. He had his virtues as well as his, to her, manifest wickedness.

Some of these differences in White opinion apparently resulted from differences in political philosophy (Radical Republican vs. Conservative Democrat)[16] and the varying proximity of Whites' houses to "Scuffletown," called "the Settlement" by Indians. But then again Leitch and Norment were both Conservatives, and they disagreed about the racial composition of those they called mulattoes.

Others differed in their interpretation of, for example, the motivations of the Lowry band. A Yankee reporter found Whites generally reluctant to credit vengeance as a strong motive for the band's activities:

The disposition generally manifested by the white people of Robeson county is to put little stress upon the murder of this old man [Allen Lowery], but to ascribe the crimes of Henry Berry Lowery's band to lighter cause and to separate the motive of revenge altogether from his offenses [Townsend 1872:47].

Yet C. M. Pepper, a Robesonian whose statements about the Lowry band's deeds Norment saw fit to include in her treatise, sees vengeance as a powerful motive, one he associates with Indianness:

The event of the Lowries death which I have just mentioned, it is thought, kindled afresh in the bosom of Henry Berry the fires of revenge which are always so difficult to extinguish in the breasts of Indians. Nothing would quench that fire but blood [Norment 1875:39].

Still other Whites differed about the mulattoes' character or on what to do about them. A "Parson" Sinclair, designated by Townsend as "the fighting parson of Lumberton," is probably Colonel James Sinclair, a Presbyterian clergyman born in Scotland, who began his ministry in Robeson County before the outbreak of the Civil War. He had married a Robeson County woman and had served in the Confederate Army. He had also served, temporarily, as the Lumberton agent of the Freedmen's Bureau and later founded a Black school at Lumberton. Despite his service with the Confederate Army, he had Radical (Republican) sympathies and perhaps could be considered to be more favorably disposed toward the people he calls "free negroes" than many other Whites in Robeson (see Evans 1971:78). Sinclair spoke with the reporter Townsend in 1872 about Henry Berry Lowry:

"Lowery," answered Sinclair, "is really one of those remarkable executive spirits that arises now and then in a raw community, without advantages other than nature gave him. He has passions, but no weaknesses, and his eye is on every point at once. He has impressed that whole negro society with his power and influence. They fear and admire him. He asserts his superiority over all these whites just as well. No man who stands face to face with him can resist his quiet will, and assurance and his searching eye [*sic*]. Without fear, without hope, defying society, he is the only man we have any knowledge of down here who can play his part. Upon my word, I believe if he had lived ages ago he would have been a William the Conqueror. He reminds me of nobody but Rob Roy" (Townsend 1872:14–15].

This open admiration contrasts with the reluctant respect for Lowry's abilities expressed by Leitch and Norment.

Hardly admiring but somewhat milder in tone than Leitch and Norment is the sentiment expressed by a White man named McLeod, who lived in the Indian part of the county and who had been robbed repeatedly, losing more than $3,000 to the band. His remarks probably reflect the wariness (and perhaps the weariness) of intimacy with them:

"They took my watch," resumed McLeod, "and stopped me the other day, and seized my pocket-book. Lowery looked over its contents and said, 'Sixteen dollars, is that your whole pile? Well, I won't take that.'"

"I have no desire to see any vengeance done to them," concluded McLeod, "if they only leave the country and never return. I say let them go, for really this band looks like as if it never would be caught and never give us any peace" [Townsend 1872:60].

Norment had little sympathy for such sentiments, having lost her husband because of the band. She condemned those who expressed them as "prompted by selfish motives to refuse to aid and abet the noble men who would have risked life and all to secure a peace and quiet for those in the more immediate vicinity of the gang" (Norment 1875:31). She attributes the failure of Whites to stop the Lowry band to those Whites who would not fight them, and to intimidation and interference from Radicals, who presumably befriended the Lowrys:

Surrounded on the one hand by the robber gang and their friends, through the thick pine woods, and to a white man, the almost impenetrable swamps; on the other, Radical officials dispensing their so-called justice to the noble fellows who would have captured them [the Lowrys], and you have the situation [Norment 1875:32].

Conservative Giles Leitch was more circumspect regarding the Robeson Republican officials in his 1871 testimony:

Question. Do you think there has been any *laches* or dereliction of duty on the part of your county officers to arrest Lowry and his gang of seven men? Have your county officers done their duty in the premises, or have they not?

Answer [Leitch]. (After a pause.) I think that the sheriff, with the right to call a posse of the county, where there are three thousand voters, ought to be able to arrest seven men. I believe that there is a terror of those men on account of the certainty with which they aim; they seldom ever fail to kill whenever they shoot. I believe that that mainly is the reason why they are not captured or killed.

Question. You mean that the people generally are afraid of them?

Answer. The people generally are afraid of them. That is about the truth of it. I do not like to give it a harsher name than that [U.S. Senate Reports 1872:298].

Radical Republican–Conservative Democrat distinctions did not entirely predict the actions White Robesonians took regarding the Lowry band either. Republican Francis M. Wishart led efforts to subdue the band in 1871 until his death at their hands in 1872. But he was, apparently, an exception. Republicans did not, for the most part, participate in the hunts for the Lowry band (Evans 1971).

Divided opinion and uncoordinated action among Whites undoubtedly aided the Lowry band, as did support and cooperation from many fellow Indians and probably from some Blacks and a few Whites as well. The band struck a dramatic pose, backed by successful escapes, robberies, and killings, which told Whites that they would not tolerate their family members being killed, robbed, or abused. If the band's concern was originally for their own families, it quickly extended to demonstrating that their people were not to be intimidated lightly. The fact that the band operated for nearly ten years, despite the efforts of the White Home Guard, federal troops, and the offers of huge rewards for bounty hunters, was a source of pride for Indians and embarrassment for those Whites who felt their honor impugned by an inability to control "our mulattoes."[17] Certainly the success of the band established defensive violence as one tactic in the Indian political repertoire and reinforced the distinction between themselves and Blacks that Whites already recognized.

The end of the band came in 1874 with the death of Steve Lowry, the last active member. Several others had been killed, one had escaped altogether, one had been hung, and the leader had disappeared. Whether he was dead or out of the county has never been established. The mysterious disappearance of Henry Berry Lowry added fuel to his already legendary attributes and he became a full-fledged culture hero among his own people. A little more than a decade later, in 1885, his people had successfully maneuvered for legal recognition as Indians and obtained the right to have their own schools.

Throughout the years of the band's activities and in those that followed, the Indians were affected by larger political events in the state and nation. It was under Presidential Reconstruction that the Lowrys in 1867 futilely sought legal redress for the killings of Allen and William. The Radicals assumed control in Robeson County in 1868, at which time the Ku Klux Klan also appeared. By 1870, the Conservatives were back in power in Robeson and were in the majority in the North Carolina General Assembly, just as the Fifteenth Amendment took effect. In 1870, Robeson County had a new sheriff, a man who had been one of those accused in the killings of the Lowry father and son (Evans 1971:136), another blow to the outlawed band and to the Indian community. It was after the ascendancy of the Conservatives in 1870 that some Whites took a few of the outlaws' wives, including Rhoda Strong Lowry, Henry Berry's wife, into custody in an attempt to force the outlaws to surrender. When the outlaws replied, through an intermediary White man, they threatened bloody reprisals unless the wives were allowed to return to their homes (Norment 1875:108). It was also after the Conservatives resumed power that the Black politician, Benjamin Bethea, was murdered.

From mulattoes to Indians

After the band ceased its operations because of the deaths of most members, violence apparently lessened as Conservatives consolidated their control, but legal conditions worsened for non-Whites. The Black Codes enacted by the Conservatives in 1866 had been overthrown by the Radicals with a new constitution in 1868. But in 1875, another constitutional convention was called in which the Conservative representatives elected from Robeson played a crucial role (Lawrence 1939: 94–6). Thirty amendments were added to the state constitution; they provided, among other things, for separate schools for each race, forbade miscegenation between Whites and non-Whites, and ended local control over county governments (Lefler and Newsome 1963:471). In this climate of increasing racial restrictions, the Indians began seeking separate legal recognition and their own schools. When schools became legally segregated, most Indians refused to send their children to Black schools and were not allowed to send them to White schools.[18] In this way, for the Indians education came to be entwined with their struggle for recognition as Indians at the very beginning and was to remain closely associated with continuing efforts to establish a nationally recognized identity. Further, improvement in educational opportunities and Indian control over their own schools has long been associated for Indians and for outsiders as well with the "progress" of the people as a whole.

In 1877, the first Black teacher-training school in North Carolina was established at Fayetteville, just thirty miles north of Pembroke (Lefler and Newsome 1963:501). This may have given the Indians added impetus to establish their own schools, including a normal school, which finally came into being ten years later in 1887. By establishing themselves as Indians, and thereby as a third race, the people formerly designated "mulattoes" gained formal recognition of their position as "not Black." As we have seen, Whites already considered them as different from other "colored" people, despite the efforts of some Whites to force mulattoes to behave like Blacks, particularly during the Civil War. The 1885 legislation made the distinction a legal one and raised the status of the group to "Indian," a status that had apparently been claimed for many years by at least some of the so-called mulattoes.

But the question remains, how was this change accomplished? Indians clearly wanted it, but could not have managed it by themselves. They needed "White friends" who would support them, who would advocate raising the status of the entire group, and who could get the necessary legislation through the General Assembly. In Hamilton McMillan, they found an important White friend. McMillan was a Democratic state legislator and a local historian who was interested in the people who, he argued, were Indians. He both developed the theory that the people mistakenly called mulattoes were really descendants of Sir Walter Raleigh's lost colony and their friendly Indian neighbors, and introduced a bill for their legal recognition as "Croatan Indians" who, as such, should have separate schools. In 1885, the Indians received a legal name and the right to their own schools from the state legislature.

McMillan states that he based his theory on the remarks of many older Indians, who said they came from what he interpreted as "Roanoke," and on documents pertaining to the lost colony and to early travels in North Carolina. Unfortunately, if he took notes on Indian oral traditions concerning their origins, no one has yet uncovered them, and in his published work (McMillan 1888), there is no way to disentangle what Indians actually told him from his own arguments about their origins.

Why McMillan should have wanted to help the Indians is less easy to answer than how he did it. He seems to have maintained an interest in the improved well-being of the people, writing letters to urge their recognition by the federal government in 1890 and in 1914 (McPherson 1915:39–40, 242–3). As a Democrat whose party was still being actively challenged by Republicans in 1885, he may also have thought that if Democrats supported the recognition of the Indians, grateful Indians might cease voting for Republicans and vote in larger numbers for Democrats. He outlined the political situation among the Indians in an 1890 letter to historian Stephen B. Weeks: "In politics they are divided between the two parties of the day – perhaps 300 of them vote the Democratic ticket. The ignorant class generally vote for Republican candidates" (McMillan 1890). Indians today maintain that the bill did persuade a number of Indians to vote for Democratic candidates.[19]

Robeson County Republicans continued to be threats to Democratic rule until about 1900, when extralegal violence from the "Red Shirts" combined with Jim Crow laws to make further Republican victories impossible. The 1900 Jim Crow laws limited suffrage by means of a poll tax and a literacy test, which many non-Whites could not pass. Illiterate Whites and Indians were exempted from the literacy test under the "grandfather clause." But as late as 1897, a Republican–Populist Fusion government was elected in the state. And in 1885, Robeson County Democrats and Republicans were still locked in a struggle for dominance. Blacks were still voting, probably for Republicans. This gave the Indians leverage to pressure one or the other party to give them something in return for votes.

It also seems very likely that the Indians at least implicitly raised the specter of a repetition of Henry Berry Lowry-like behavior if their cause were completely frustrated. J. J. Blanks, an Indian minister and teacher, wrote an "Afterword" that was published in 1898 with a reprinted version of McMillan's 1888 work. The last paragraph of the essay suggests that if Whites want to see less violent behavior in Indians, they should support education for them:

> There is no race of people but have some among them who are not along an intelligent line. We have some among us who are vicious; who will drink – as the Indians used to call it – the "wonderful fire-water." And when under its influence they become crazy, the Indian passion is aroused and they very often fight each other, and will often fight for their white friends. But as the Croatans beome more and more educated this vicious nature leaves them. Therefore let us try to effect through union and co-operation among the Croatan Indians, and try to educate them, so that their progress for the next ten years may double that of the ten years just passed [Blanks in McMillan 1898:35].

In only a decade or two, the Lowry band could not have been forgotten by anyone who had lived through those times. It is likely that the Whites who praised the Indians for their "progress" after 1885 had the Lowry band in the back of their minds. McMillan makes no mention of Henry Berry Lowry, but alludes to the tensions between White and Indian communities:

> After the year 1835, these Indians who murmured greatly at the injustice done them in being classed as "Mulattoes" or "free persons of color," became suspicious of white men and at first we found difficulty in eliciting any facts relating to their past history [McMillan 1888:17].

He also recounts a speech by an old Indian that had been made in 1864 at an inquest on the killings of the young Lowrys who had been to work on fortifications. In this speech, the old Indian cited the friendship Indians had always offered Whites, contrasting it with the way Whites had treated the Indians:

> "There is the white man's blood in these veins as well as that of the Indian. In order to be great like the English, we took the white man's language and religion, for our people were told they would prosper if they would take white men's laws. In the wars between white men and Indians we always fought on the side of white men. We moved to this land and fought for liberty for white men, yet white men have treated us as negroes. Here are our young men shot down by a white man and we get no justice, and that in a land where our people were always free" [McMillan 1888:17].

McMillan appeared to consider it an injustice to classify this people as "negroes" if they had Indian and White "blood."

That his legislation had a desirable effect on the people it was designed to help seemed evident to McMillan by 1890, when he wrote to Stephen B. Weeks:

> Since the Act of Assembly recognizing them as a separate tribe (recently sustained by N.C. Supreme Court) they have become better citizens and

immediately after the passage of the Act they came near filling Lumberton Jail with violators of law. The prosecutors in all instances nearly were Croatans |McMillan 1890|.

One of the effects of the recognition of the mulattoes as Indians, whether planned or unplanned, was to split the Indian and Black communities further apart. That they were already split is evident in the refusal of most Indians to attend Black schools and, assuming McMillan was correct, in the fact that "the direst insult to a Croatan is to call him a 'nigger' " (McMillan 1890). Before formal recognition, some Indians and Blacks apparently had worshipped together and a few had gone to school together (Blanks in McMillan 1898:28–9). And before 1835, when free persons of color were disfranchised, Whites and Indians are said to have attended the same churches and sometimes the same schools:

Between 1783 and 1835 they |the Indians| attended the schools along with White people – attended the churches with whites, owned slaves and mustered and voted as white men did. Prior to 1835 they were divided as now between the parties of the day . . . |McMillan 1890|.

Those who had been considered mulattoes had managed, with the help of friendly Whites, to become legally recognized as Indians and to obtain separate schools. The change from 1870 at the height of the Lowry band's activities to 1885 was great. The Indian families who had produced and aided the outlawed men were now emphasizing their respectability and their progress to outsiders while keeping alive the traditions of the band among themselves. The Indians had successfully set and reached a goal that was to affect vitally the survival of their group as a separate people and the quality of their lives. But this success marked the beginning, not the end, of the Indian struggle for an improved life and an accepted identity.

3. What changed and how?

Not being content with changing their status from "mulatto" to "Indian" and with establishing separate schools, the Indians of Robeson County have gone on incessantly, stubbornly, and apparently tirelessly seeking to better their lot. Through persistent legal and, occasionally, extralegal political activities, they have brought about many changes. How they have managed that, often despite strong opposition, is the concern of this chapter. Factionalism and diversity have played important roles in Indian politics, but not the ones usually ascribed to them. Neither factionalism nor diversity, both difficult and usually divisive problems for reservation Indians, has inhibited the growth and development of the Lumbee, yet they have each in abundance. The fact that there have long been many factions has meant that at any one time, there is always at least one engaged in a project that would benefit the whole people. Because group improvement is a highly valued goal, along with self-improvement, often several factions are working simultaneously toward the same goal or toward several different, but equally group-benefiting, goals. Factionalism is abetted by the diversity of experience and skills brought to bear on problems by many different leaders. Such diversity of leadership and abilities has come about through differences in migration experience, education, and wealth, supplemented by the incorporation into the Indian community of people from other, similar groups. The diversity of origin and experience does not necessarily help Indians to cooperate with one another, but it does provide people who can handle many different kinds of situations and problems.

Lumbees do not have a history of effective cooperative effort except in the face of, to Indians, clear-cut, widely recognized threats from outsiders. And those outsiders who are potentially the most threatening have so far always been Whites. What organizes the Indians in cases of perceived threats is a shared point of view, a common self-image, not a formal organization. As soon as the threat disappears, so does Indian cooperation. A chronic lack of cooperation among mem-

66

bers has usually been considered a problem potentially threatening any group's survival, but the Lumbee have done quite well in just this situation. The amount of cooperation among factions, which spring up, die down, and exchange members at the drop of a hat, is little and happens seldom. But the passionate pride with which instances of cooperation are recounted and the sometimes fervent urging of their replication indicate that they are far more important factors in Lumbee motivation and imagination than might be thought from the small number of instances.

Underlying conditions

Underlying and enabling much of Lumbee success at achieving their own goals are two conditions. The first is population growth and the second is a nonreservation land base for the Indian community. These conditions do not explain Lumbee success, but they do facilitate it. Starting from diverse origins, the Indians of Robeson County have been augmented by in-migration as well as by natural increase. People from groups similar to the Lumbee in North and South Carolina have moved to Robeson County and have married there from at least the early 1800s, and probably before. This pattern continues today and has helped to swell the Indian population of Robeson County from roughly one-twentieth of the total population in 1790 to one-third in 1960. In-migration helps to explain what to some has seemed a prodigious feat of fertility (see, for example, Harper 1937, 1938; Beale 1957). Continuous in-migration has provided the Indians of Robeson County with new individuals possessed of varied backgrounds, skills, experience, and education, any of which can be brought to bear on achieving Indian goals in Robeson. Indeed, some important leaders have been born and reared outside Robeson. The relatively easy acceptance of new members into the community and the resultant diversity or heterogeneity of population is one thing that sets the Lumbee apart from many reservation Indian groups that often have great difficulty handling such differences because they can exacerbate destructive factionalism. Yet for the Lumbee, this diversity has been a source of renewal and strength.

The second important condition enabling the continued growth and viability of the Indians of Robeson County is the existence of a substantial land base. Lumbee ancestors found the extensive swampland in the interior of Robeson County a refuge, a place to eke out a living by hunting, fishing, and where possible, farming or gardening; their land was a barrier isolating them, to a degree, from Whites, who deemed the swamps inhospitable and "almost impenetrable" (Norment 1875:32). Because Whites thought the land worthless, Indians were able to obtain titles to sizable tracts of it. As one Indian man reported sardonically to me, "They thought they was takin' the old Indian." Around 1900, the land began to be drained by Whites, who began to desire it, and Indians began to be integrated into the local economy in a way that they had not previously been. Before 1900 (and indeed, for a few years thereafter), most Indians had done subsistence farming and had relied on the turpentine and lumber industry for cash income. Some had skills that brought in cash (carpentering, coopering, blacksmithing), and a few ran businesses, such as mills and ferries.

Although Robeson County land early provided some degree of economic independence and social isolation from what Indians say were the daily humiliations of non-White life in a racial system, today there are few Indians who cannot be adversely affected by concerted White efforts. Nevertheless, most have hung onto land in Robeson and many are still buying land. An enlarging population and land on which to live gave Indians a measure of bargaining power and independence in their dealings with Whites, but they did not determine the direction of Indian efforts to effect change.

Leaders and tactics

The primary mechanism through which the Indians have effected change has been politics. Almost continual political activity on the part of many different leaders using a variety of tactics has enabled the Indians to gain their ends. At any given time, there are several Indian leaders actively seeking change at the local, state, or federal levels of government. These leaders reflect the diversity of the population, as they come from various backgrounds of class, education, and place of birth, and they have different orientations, skills, and goals. In Robeson County, Indian leaders have usually been men, but women are becoming increasingly involved in politics and a few take leadership roles today. Because there is no formal Indian organization, there are no leaders elected only by Indians, so anyone can venture to lead. If a person is interested in doing something, he just does it, gathering whatever support he can muster, and using whatever strategies he thinks will work. He does not need organizational approval or election to office to be a leader.

Because there is a multiplicity of leaders and no hierarchy of leadership, there is almost constant factional strife among Lumbees. Factionalism has generally been considered a structural "problem" because it is said to contribute to disunity and, in extreme form, to the disintegration of a society. Certainly factionalism has been a great problem on some Indian reservations, such as Pine Ridge, where Dakota factions have often used violence against one another and at times almost paralyze the reservation. But I would argue that factionalism in itself is not necessarily destructive and disintegrative; its effects depend upon the context in which it occurs. As a Dakota Indian once remarked, "Why is it that when Indians disagree it's called factionalism and when Whites disagree it's called democracy?" What is crucial in distinguishing Robeson County from reservation politics is the nature of the arenas in which factional conflicts are played out. On Indian reservations there are formal political organizations, most with elective offices, which can be focal points of factional activity.[1]

Because the Lumbee have never had a formal political structure encompassing all and only Indians in Robeson County, whatever hostilities and conflicts are generated by differences among leaders and their followers cannot be focused on a single arena – such as the office of tribal chairman or tribal councilman. There is no one person or body that legally represents the entire Lumbee community. The elected offices that are present are county, state, and federal positions open to all three races (at least theoretically), and for these the competition is as much between Indians and Blacks or Whites as between Indian and Indian. Further, a person who holds such an office represents a multiracial constituency whose disparate demands he must consider if he is to be reelected. In any event, between the disfranchising Jim Crow laws (ca. 1900) and the implementation of the federal Voting Rights Act (1965), it was practically impossible for a non-White to hold elected office. The one or two Indians and Blacks who held county offices usually needed some White support and were obliged to recognize this in order to be reelected.

No Lumbee leader dominates the political scene for very long, and a leader is soon forgotten or his role minimized, even if his successes are remembered. There may be several reasons for this. There is little continuity of leadership from one period in time to another, and from one major effort to another. This is not because leaders have grown older or have died, but because a person generally does not remain in the forefront of political activities for very long. One of the reasons for this is that Indians tend to mistrust politicians, and when someone becomes particularly successful, people begin to say that he is doing well at the expense of others. Politicians are often said to suffer from the "big I, little you" syndrome.

Agitation for change is almost constant. The Lumbee attitude toward working for change was summed up by a middle-aged Indian businessman who was politically active from time to time:

He said that he and another Indian man, a prominent professional, had tried to talk to their people about the school system awhile back. They both felt strongly about it, about the fact that the quality of education could be much better. People seemed to feel he and his friend were being tough. He said that could happen when people believed in something strongly. "Nothing much happened at the time, but now it seems like a little is happening, so maybe it did some good after all. We're willing to just keep on chipping away at it. Even if it takes twenty years."

Many Lumbee attempts to change their social situation are unsuccessful, but because the Indians make so many persistent attempts, they have had a number of important successes (see Appendix). They are living proof of the efficacy of the adage, "Try, try again."

The Lumbee have developed several basic tactics in the course of their struggle for group betterment. New tactics emerge from time to time and are added to the repertoire of older ones. Although these tactics can be used by individuals, they are most effectively employed for political ends by factions. The tactics are: defensive violence, "White friends," incorporation, voting, litigation, and demonstrations.

Defensive violence. This tactic was heavily used, as we have seen, during the 1864–74 period by Henry Berry Lowry and his band. They used the tactic extremely effectively in defending themselves and in enlisting the support of the Indian community. Indians have continued to use this tactic to their advantage, such as when they routed the Ku Klux Klan in 1958 with a barrage of gunshots. Indians today regard their readiness to be defensively violent as central to their concept of who they are as a people. One middle-aged Indian, a large, powerful man, told a story about his younger days "when I used to be wild and fighting." He had since "got religion" and given up physical fighting, but not political struggle.

"This happened at [a place just over the border in South Carolina]. I was getting ready to leave when a car full of Whites started to back up into another car. I waggled my arms and called 'Whoa!' They stopped and asked me what was wrong, and I told them. They just pulled up and started back again. I yelled 'Whoa!' again. Then they stopped and asked me what was wrong again, and I told them. They got out of the car and one of the big ones grabbed me by the shirt. That's when I decided I'd take on all three of them at once. I did that, and I was on the bottom getting the worst of it when a fellow – he was an Indian boy from back home – came up with a gun and threw it on two of them, made them step on back, so it was just one to one. He told me, 'Come out from under there, Indian.' Well, I was pretty beaten down and didn't move for a minute or two, and he said, 'OK Indian, show your stuff.' That brought me out, and I took on and beat down every one of them, one at a time. That boy kept saying, 'Don't let us Indians down.'"

"White friends" as machinators and advocates. This tactic, too, is an old one, dating back at least to the Henry Berry Lowry period. There is evidence that relatives of Henry Berry Lowry enlisted the aid of a Republican sheriff during Radical Reconstruction (U.S. Senate Reports 1872:286; Townsend 1872:25–6; cf. Norment 1875:13, 74). It was arranged that Henry Berry surrender and be tried. He gave himself up to the sheriff, but apparently decided that he could not get the kind of trial he desired and subsequently escaped from jail (Evans 1971:103). In 1885, another "White friend," Hamilton McMillan, was instrumental in getting the "mulattoes" of Robeson County legally recognized as "Croatan Indians." "White friends" were extremely important in establishing early rights for the Indians, particularly because Whites dominated the political process. Today they are less important because the Indians are in a position to do more for themselves. But even now, "White friends" can play large roles. The White lawyer from the University of North Carolina who directed the case that broke "double-voting" in 1976 is an example. In a tribute to this lawyer, the Indian editor of the Lumbee newspaper, the *Carolina Indian Voice,* stated:

[The editor had just named his infant daughter and wrote this editorial as a letter to her.] We named you also in honor of Barry Nakell, a lawyer, a friend of the Lumbee Indians. Barry Nakell is a professor of law at UNC–Chapel Hill. He was our attorney when we (Indian parents) went to court and fought the evil double voting system. We won the case and double voting is no more . . . [B. Barton 1976:2].

Incorporation. Perhaps the earliest example of incorporation as a political tactic was the incorporation of the Board of Trustees in 1887 for the purpose of obtaining land and financing for the construction of the Indian Normal School. The state legislature appropriated $500 for an Indian Normal School with the stipulation that the money would be lost if Indians did not provide a building within two years (Oxendine 1934:50). The Reverend W. L. Moore, who later became the head of the Normal School, was one of the Indians most instrumental in having this bill introduced. He also wrote to the Office of Indian Affairs in 1890 in support of an Indian petition for federal aid to Croatan schools (McPherson 1915:38–9). Moore's obituary in 1931 states:

. . . Rev. W. L. Moore worked when there seemed to be no help, with the exception of 4 men. The general sentiment of the people was against, his educational program.

He called a meeting and 4 men, responded, from which the charter members of the board of trustees were chosen. At the request of Rev. W. L. Moore, the campaign was launched to secure money to erect the building. Rev. W. L. Moore gave of his funds $200 which was more than 10 fold the amount of an other donar [*sic*]. He vacated the school room, as a teacher, for one year in order to devote all his time to this school project.[2]

Formal recognition of this group of four men (who included Moore himself) is contained in the 1887 law providing for the Normal School. It designates Moore, James Oxendine, James Dial, and Preston Locklear as a "body politic and corporate, for educational purposes, in the county of Robeson, under the name and style of the trustees of the Croatan Normal School" (McPherson 1915:226). Moore is generally credited with being the "Father of the Normal School" by Indians today. He was born and reared in nearby Columbus County, not in Robeson, and he received his education, it is said, in a subscription school in Lumberton that was run by "a well-educated Negro from the North" (see also Blanks in McMillan 1898:32). Significantly, the first school was built with funds collected from both Indians and Whites and with labor donated by Indians. Oxendine states that the building was worth about $1,000 (1934:50).

Another legally incorporated group that was very active politically emerged in the 1930s. "The Siouan Lodge of the National Council of American Indians, Inc." sought unsuccessfully to have the U.S. Congress legally designate the Robeson Indians as "Siouan Indians of Lumber River" (U.S. Senate Reports 1934). They also were unsuccessful in seeking school aid from the federal government, but they did attain two important goals. One was the enrollment of twenty-two individuals as Indians under the provisions of the Indian Reorganization Act (IRA), and the second was helping to establish the Red Banks Mutual Association, a federally supported New Deal enterprise that became the longest-running cooperative from that era. It was disbanded in 1968. Although the cooperative did not live up to the expectations of many Indians, it did provide evidence of their political success and economic opportunities for a few Indian families.

The leaders of the Siouan movement were for the most part men who resided in the countryside around Pembroke, and they tended to be from less prosperous families than the leaders of the older "Cherokee" faction, several of whom lived in Pembroke and were among the best-educated Indians of their day.

A more recent example of incorporation in order to tap federal funds is the nonprofit Lumbee Regional Development Association (LRDA), begun as the Regional Development Association in 1968 by three Indians and Gerald Sider, who were the original incorporators. The Indians were all relatively young, well-educated, middle-class men. When the organization expanded upon becoming LRDA, older Indians from a greater variety of backgrounds were included and Sider was dropped. LRDA received a small starting grant through the National Congress of American Indians (NCAI) from the Ford Foundation in 1969 and began to obtain large amounts of federal money in 1971 (more than 1.5 million dollars that year).[3] In addition to channeling federal funds into the Indian community, LRDA provides a number of Indians with white collar, middle-income positions. These jobs have enabled a number of better-educated Indians to stay in the county and at the same time have employment that allowed them to use their skills. Before federal and state programs to alleviate unemployment and poverty increased these kinds of employment opportunities, many of the ambitious, well-educated Indians were forced to leave home to seek jobs suitable for their training, or to take positions in Robeson for which they were overqualified. Those who left tended to move their families to cities, usually in the North, and they return "home" to visit regularly.

Voting. Before they were disfranchised in 1835, Indians had voted (as "free persons of color"), but little is known of that period, except that they apparently voted for both Whigs and Democrats (McMillan 1890). Immediately following the Civil War, most apparently voted for Republicans, but many are said to have switched to the Democratic Party after their recognition as Indians in 1885. At that time, they were still an important force in the electorate – important enough for Democrats to try to win them away from the Republican Party with special legislation. The Indian vote was significant in 1885 largely because Blacks were also voting, and the total non-White vote could be very influential. Once Blacks were effectively disfranchised by North Carolina's Jim Crow laws and the "Red Shirt" campaigns terrorizing Black voters in 1898 and 1900, the Indian vote was less important to Whites, and voting perforce played a diminished role in Indian strategies. Before Indian voters lost their effectiveness, they managed to elect a county commissioner. Of one elected official, a very old Indian man told me with a twinkle in his eye:

> "When we were establishing schools in Raleigh, we elected an Indian representative, a Mr. [Indian surname]. He was kinda dark complected. He was asked, where do you want us to put your people – in the White schools or in the Black schools? And he was shy and said, well, put them with the Blacks. The Indians rebelled. They said, we won't go to the Black schools. Some would and some wouldn't."

After 1900, Indian voting power diminished. There were only a few elected Indian officials outside Pembroke town until the 1970s.

In 1954, an Indian, Early Bullard, was elected a judge. In a 1973 interview, he told me:

> "I served four years in the Maxton Recorder's Court. I was the first Indian elected judge, elected to two terms. I was the first that we know about – the first Indian elected by public vote to office . . . Lacy

Maynor was next after me [Lacy Maynor was judge from 1958–66]. Then we couldn't elect him anymore, it went from district to countywide. Jack Doe [a prominent local White man who was thought to control the Maxton area] didn't have any idea I'd get elected because our people had always split.''

In the 1960s, Herman Dial was elected county commissioner from Maxton District and Lacy Maynor lost the Maxton judgeship when voting for judges by district was abolished.

But voting strength remained limited to old, heavily Indian districts until after 1965. By 1965, when the federal Voting Rights Act was passed, less than half the Indians and Blacks of voting age were actually registered. Because of this, the county fell under the provisions of that act, which suspended the literacy test that had prevented many non-Whites from registering. After the act was passed, a period of intense Indian and Black activity aimed at registering voters in their communities ensued. Grants for voter registration projects and the work of several American Friends Service Committee volunteers who lived in the county from fall 1967 until fall 1969 helped to produce a great rise in non-White registration. By 1968, nearly as many non-Whites as Whites were registered, and by 1970 more non-Whites than Whites were registered.

Indians and Blacks quickly began to flex their new political muscle. In 1967–68, some Indian and Black leaders, mostly middle-aged men, put together a coalition group whose organization they left deliberately unspecific. The Indian leaders came from many different areas of the county, although much of the coordination was arranged by leaders in Pembroke. Some of the men were comfortably middle class, others among the most prosperous Indians, and still others were hard-working but much less prosperous. They varied widely in educational background and occupation. This coalition sought to use the electoral process to increase the influence of non-Whites in the county. Their organization and activities will be examined in detail in the next chapter. What is important to note here is that Indians have placed renewed emphasis on voting as a tactic for gaining their ends.

Litigation. The Lumbee have also come increasingly to use the courts to gain their objectives, although the tactic itself has been in use since before the Henry Berry Lowry days. Even the Lowrys attempted (unsuccessfully) to use the courts to bring the killers of Allen and William to justice. By 1967–68, Indians seemed to regard litigation as a tactic used effectively by Blacks in the civil rights movement, but one that did not usually work very well for Robeson Indians. Some Indians were reluctant to use the courts simply because that was what Blacks did. More avoided litigation because they felt they had little chance of winning when they had to depend on White lawyers, White judges, and mostly White juries. And indeed, many Indians who did turn to litigation against Whites lost.

However, when the Tuscarora faction (of whom more will be said shortly) began to be active in 1970, they unabashedly began using the full range of tactics developed and deployed by Blacks during the 1950s and 1960s – marches, sit-ins, and lawsuits. They instituted the "Prospect Suit" in 1970, which they hoped would secure the right of the Indians to separate schools despite the Nixon desegregation guidelines, which had brought massive desegregation to county schools in 1970. That suit was dismissed for failure to prosecute in 1978. Another suit, the "Double-Voting Suit," was initiated by some of the younger Pembroke political activists in order to end the dominance of White voters in the county school district, where students were predominantly Indian and Black. Whites were voting in their own town school districts and in the county district as well. After several appeals, the Indians finally won the "Double-Voting Suit" in 1976. That success enabled the election of a county school board composed of six Indians, one Black, and two Whites in the same year.

Demonstrations. The most recent tactic added to the Indian repertoire is demonstrations – marches, sit-ins, and nonviolent protests.

In 1970, a faction calling themselves "Tuscaroras," to distinguish themselves from other Robeson Indians, especially "Lumbees," formed to fight school integration. Theoretically, schools had been integrated under the "freedom of choice" plan for several years. But in 1967–68, schools were still basically segregated because few students "chose" to attend schools with those not of their own race. With true integration, many Indians in country areas argued that their communal integrity was being threatened by an influx of Blacks and Whites, in teaching staff as well as in student body. Fewer country Indians than town (Pembroke and Lumberton) Indians were accustomed to dealing with non-Indians on a regular and cooperative basis, and they resented the "do-nothing" attitude of town Indians, feeling that their schools were slated to become more fully integrated than the town schools.

The Indians most heavily involved in the Tuscarora movement were less well-to-do and, in general, less educated than middle-class town leaders, particularly those from Pembroke. They were also willing to be considerably more adventurous in the kinds of tactics they used. There were sit-ins in local schools, followed by arrests (sometimes even the arrests of children). Ultimately, there was a long march from Pembroke to Raleigh to dramatize their cause. At first, the group confined itself to the school issue, but then it began, as it became more sophisticated and broadly concerned in outlook, to tackle other problems, such as the welfare department, where a rally and demonstration were held. Some middle-class town Indians disliked the new "radical" tactics and felt the Tuscaroras were giving the Indians a bad name by injuring the image of respectability so carefully built up through the years. But a surprising number felt that the Tuscaroras were willing to expose themselves, to take chances that most middle-class town Indians were afraid to take. In 1973, one middle-class Indian woman from Pembroke exclaimed, "Those people have gotten out there and done things that people like me weren't willing to do because we're scared. I think they've accomplished a lot."

In short, Lumbee leaders from different areas of the county, with different interests, skills, occupations, and varying degrees of wealth and education, have used old tactics and developed new ones to use in their overall strategy of improving the opportunities of Robeson Indians in general and, at the same time, bettering the lot of their faction in particular. In the long run, the gains of any one faction have tended to benefit the Indians as a whole. Despite the free-for-all of Lumbee factional activity, there has been a surprisingly uniform direction to their aims.

I have argued that, for the Lumbee, politics has provided the primary mechanism for obtaining the changes they (or some of them) have desired. It must then be asked: What stimulates this political activity on the part of the Lumbee? Under what kinds of circumstances does it occur? Most often, it grows out of clashes between Indians and Whites, clashes that occur when Indians' ideas about themselves and their well-being conflict with Whites' ideas about them. Because Whites have been able to bring great pressure to bear in implementing their ideas, Indians have had to choose between giving in to the pressure, or fighting it. Often they have chosen to fight, and when they do, they talk about this struggle in terms of who they are, what kind of people they are, and how they should behave. These issues are at the heart of Indians' resistance to White pressures and of Whites' resistance to Indian demands.

This kind of clash simply does not occur between Blacks and Indians for at least two reasons. One is that Blacks lack the ability to impose their will on Indians, whereas Whites have considerably more ability to do this. A second is that Blacks are generally willing for other people to define themselves in whatever way they choose, as long as it does not interfere with Blacks. Indians do not threaten Blacks, and do not want to oppress them any more than they want to oppress Whites. Unless allied with Whites, neither Indians nor Blacks could enforce their will upon the other, even if they wanted to. It is important, however, that neither appears to want to. So far, improvements within each non-White community generally have not been perceived as having been made at the expense of the other.

One source of tension between Whites and Indians that has caused clashes at least since the Civil War is the Whites' classification or treatment of Indians as though they were Black. These are acts that Indians bitterly resent and angrily resist, seeing their identity and their interests jeopardized. An Indian man in his 70s explained the relation among the races this way:

> "When the Whites classified the Indians with the Negroes in 1835, that set back our relations with Negroes today. Because we had to fight so hard not to be classed with them." He elaborated this theme in a later conversation, saying, "In 1835, they crammed the Negro down our throats, and it took us fifty years to get on our feet again. Seventy-five years later we were just getting started after getting him off our backs. For 125 years, we've been trying to get him off our backs and now they're trying to put everyone together." He then told what happened at a meeting attended by Indians, Negroes, and Whites: "An Indian stood up, right in front of Negroes, and said [to the Whites], 'You've forced the Negro down our throats and now they're forcing him down yours. Don't you go pushing them off on us. If you take him, we'll take him.' And not before will we take them."

Identity conflict and change

Although most Indians were no doubt pleased with their new legal status in 1885, by 1911 they had discovered two things. One was that "Croatan" was not a tribal name recognized by historians, ethnologists, or bureaucrats in the federal government. It had no historical precedent and was based on the name of a place, not a name for a people. Anthropologist James Mooney's description of "Croatan Indians" in the *Handbook of American Indians North of Mexico,* which became a major reference work for government officials after its publication in 1907 and 1910, illustrates some of the problems the Indians encountered with their new name:

Croatan Indians. The legal designation in North Carolina for a people evidently of mixed Indian and white blood, found in various E. sections of the state, but chiefly in Robeson co., and numbering approximately 5,000. For many years they were classed with the free negroes, but steadily refused to accept such classification or to attend the negro schools or churches, claiming to be the descendants of the early native tribes and of white settlers who had intermarried with them. About 20 years ago their claim was officially recognized and they were given a separate legal existence under the title of "Croatan Indians," on the theory of descent from Raleigh's lost colony of

Croatan (q.v.). Under this name they now have separate school provision and are admitted to some privileges not accorded to the negroes. The theory of descent from the lost colony may be regarded as baseless, but the name itself serves as a convenient label for a people who combine in themselves the blood of the wasted native tribes, the early colonists or forest rovers, the runaway slaves or other negroes, and probably also of stray seamen of the Latin races from coasting vessels in the West Indian or Brazilian trade [Mooney in Hodge 1907:365].

A "convenient label" that officially suggested Negro ancestry and dismissed their lost colony origin was hardly helpful, either in consolidating local recognition as Indians or in persuading federal officials to grant them benefits. Problems with federal officials began when an 1888 petition signed by fifty-four Croatan Indians seeking federal aid for their new schools was rebuffed in 1890 (McPherson 1915:36–40). In an August 1890 letter, the Commissioner of Indian Affairs explained why to W. L. Moore, who had lobbied so effectively for the Indian Normal School:

> While I regret exceedingly that the provisions made by the State of North Carolina seem to be entirely inadequate, I find it quite impracticable to render any assistance at this time. The Government is responsible for the education of something like 36,000 Indian children and has provisions for less than half this number. So long as the immediate wards of the Government are so insufficiently provided for, I do not see how I can consistently render any assistance to the Croatans or any other civilized tribes [McPherson 1915:40].

Undaunted, in 1900 the Indians induced Representative John Bellamy of North Carolina to introduce a bill in the House to provide funds for the Croatan schools. This bill failed to become law.

Added to their failures to obtain money for schools from the federal government was the insult in the way local Whites had begun to use the name Croatan. Guy B. Johnson reported in 1939 how Whites talked about Croatans:

> For the first time, the whites and Negroes had a term which they could apply to these hitherto nameless people. They pronounced it with a sort of sneer or they shortened it to "Cro" – with the all too obvious implication. It soon became a fighting term, and for many years it has been virtually taboo in the presence of Indians [1939:520. See also Berry 1963:33].

"Cro(w)" is, of course, a White term for Blacks (as in "Jim Crow"). When I asked one of my Indian friends what kind of a bird a crow is, he replied, "a nasty black thieving bird." Another explained that Whites used the term "Croatan" to mean "half-breed, mixed-blood, someone with Negro blood." Not all Whites, apparently, accepted the Indianness of those they had formerly classified "mulattoes."

These difficulties led the Indians to request a change of name from the state legislature, and in 1911 the North Carolina General Assembly altered their name to, simply, Indians of Robeson County, "a change," Dial and Eliades point out, "that pleased nobody and settled nothing" (1975:94). The federal government does not recognize "Indians," it recognizes particular Indians with historically documented "tribal" names and affiliations (see Blu 1979b on Lumbee problems with documentation). But if their name was getting vaguer, the Indians' separateness was being reinforced as the 1911 legislature provided for separate Indian accommodation at the State Hospital for the Insane at Raleigh, and the Robeson County jail and Home for the Aged and Infirm (McPherson 1915:230). At the same time, the State Board of Education was empowered to appoint an all-Indian Board of Trustees for the Indian Normal School, and the trustees were given the right to employ and discharge teachers and "to prevent negroes from attending said school" (McPherson 1915:229).

In 1912, the Indians were at it again, seeking federal funds for a site, buildings, and maintenance for an Indian school (U.S. Senate 1912). Although a bill passed the Senate, it failed in the House, where it met resistance from a Mr. Burke, a member of the Committee on Indian Affairs, who stated:

> It is my belief that these Indians have no right to enter any Indian school
> because they are not full-blood Indians. [to Mr. McLean, a prominent White
> Robesonian later to become governor of the state] I will also say that I have
> great sympathy with people in the South in dealing with the negro. You refuse
> to recognize them. I presume it is due to the prejudice that exists in the mind of
> the people on account of color.
> MR. McLEAN: The Indians themselves recognize this feeling and respect it
> [U.S. House of Representatives 1913:19].

Mr. McLean tried to defend Indian interests, establishing their separateness from Blacks by stating that Indians, like Whites, are prejudiced against Blacks. His friendly support of the Indians was apparently thoroughgoing, as he explained why the federal government should provide a nonreservation school for the Indians and why North Carolina had not provided Indians with the same educational advantages as Whites and Blacks:

> In fact, there has always been the impression that the United States
> Government has discriminated against these Indians in favor of other Indians.
> One reason why this demand [for equal educational opportunities] has not been
> prosecuted thoroughly is on account of the fact that before the Civil War a
> breach occurred between the Indians and the whites on account of service in
> the war. After the war there arose a band of outlaws, and the feeling between
> the outlaws and the white race became so intense that it reacted and affected all
> the Indians, although probably not more than one-tenth of 1 per cent of the
> Indians had anything to do with it at all. For a long time that prejudice in the
> minds of the old people prevented us from prosecuting these demands in their
> interests. Of late years, after we saw that the little education that the State has

been able to give them has resulted in the most marked difference, they are considered among our best citizens. Of course there were always some well-behaved people among them [U.S. House of Representatives 1913:17].

Only about a month after these House hearings, the North Carolina General Assembly ratified an act changing the Indians' name to "Cherokee Indians of Robeson County," carefully delineating them from the Eastern Cherokee in western North Carolina. No benefits available to the Eastern Cherokee were to be shared with those in Robeson County. The mountain Cherokee protested vigorously, but their name was extended to Robeson County Indians anyway. Under their new name, the Indians again began seeking benefits from the federal government. In response, the Senate ordered an investigation into "the condition and tribal rights" of the people in order to determine whether the government should make "suitable provision for their support and education" (McPherson 1915:5). The result was the "McPherson Report" of 1915. O. M. McPherson visited Robeson County, interviewed Indians and Whites, and collected documents relevant to their claims. When all the evidence was in he reported:

. . . I have no hesitancy in expressing the belief that the Indians originally settled in Robeson and adjoining counties in North Carolina were an amalgamation of the Hatteras Indians with Gov. White's lost colony; the present Indians are their descendants with a further amalgamation with the early Scotch and Scotch-Irish settlers, such amalgamation continuing down to the present time, together with a small degree of amalgamation with other races [McPherson 1915:17].

The Indians had convinced someone in the federal government of their origin from the lost colony, but that was their undoing. They could not receive benefits from the federal government because the Hatteras Indians had never had a treaty with the United States (McPherson 1915:17).

What was driving the Indians in all these pleas to the federal government? McPherson provides a clue in a discussion of his interviews with Indians:

In a personal canvas of a very large number of the heads of families I found that they differed widely as to what would be the best method of extending assistance to individual families, but there was entire unanimity of opinion as to the way in which the entire body of people could best be helped, namely, in providing them with some higher institution of learning where the more ambitious of their young people could obtain a better education than is now possible and better training for useful occupations in life. . . .

In addition to the common or district schools and the normal schools for both white and colored children, the State of North Carolina has provided the youth of both these races with institutions of learning imparting instruction in agriculture and the mechanic trades, and to some extent in domestic science;

but there are no such schools of higher instruction open to these Indians. As I understand the matter, they are prohibited by law from attending these higher institutions of learning established for the education of white and colored youth [McPherson 1915:30–1].

McPherson found disagreement on methods, but agreement on the ultimate goal – a "higher institution of learning." An institution for training teachers was no longer enough.[4] The Indians saw that Whites and Blacks both had "higher institutions of learning" and that they had none – to them, a clear case of discrimination. It hurt their pride as Indians that Blacks and Whites had something that they did not, and it hurt their youths' economic opportunities.

That Indians still felt insecure about their Indian status in 1921 is suggested by the fact that in that year they persuaded the General Assembly to pass "An Act for the Protection of the Indian Public Schools of Robeson County" (Dial and Eliades 1975:99). This act provided for a committee of Indians to screen the applicants to elementary and secondary schools (the committee was expanded to include the Normal School in 1929) in order to assure themselves that only Indians would attend their schools. Adolph Dial (a Lumbee) and David Eliades suggest that the Lumbee were responding to the arrival of the "Smilings" (see Chapter 1) from Sumter County, South Carolina, who sought to enroll their children in Robeson County Indian schools:

> Although the origin of the "Smilings" is uncertain, they appear to have been the product of miscegenation and to have migrated to Robeson County from the area of Sumter, South Carolina, after World War I. While the Lumbees sympathized with the plight and problems of this group, they were unwilling to allow them into the schools they had fought so hard and suffered so grievously to get [Dial and Eliades 1975:98–9].[5]

Had the Robeson Indians been more secure in their status as Indians, presumably they would not have seen themselves as threatened by the presence, in their schools, of people whose ancestry, as one Lumbee put it to me, was "questionable." This committee formally ceased to exist after the 1954 Supreme Court *Brown* v. *Board of Education* decision.

After World War I, problems arose over the classification of individual Indians who tried to attend Indian schools outside of Robeson, such as Carlisle, and who dealt with the military. An Indian man who later became a leader in the Siouan movement explained the experiences that had caused him to become politically active. There were two especially important events, he said. The first was connected with his military service in World War I. During the war, he had been classified with Whites, although he is dark skinned. There were only two categories then – White and Negro. When, in 1922 or so, the veterans were recalled for physical examinations, he went, was given a lunch ticket to eat with Whites, but was billeted with Negroes for the night. He was angry and tried to have his night classification changed. The bureaucrat with whom he dealt was, in the Indian's words, "all set to help me until he found out that the Indians here weren't listed with the Indian Bureau in Washington. Then he told me he couldn't do anything to help me."

The second experience concerned his application to attend Carlisle Institute, an Indian training school in Pennsylvania. He applied to the school, he said, together with three or four others from Robeson. There were already some Robeson Indians at Carlisle. In 1913, they received a letter from the institute saying that they could not be admitted be- cause, according to the records in Washington, they were not Indians. The lack of national status as an Indian was brought home to him. After the war, he said, "I didn't want to go nowhere, I just wanted to stay here because here I knew what I was." Of course, "here" is also where others "knew what he was."

During the 1930s, this man joined others, formed the "Siouan Lodge of the National Council of American Indians, Inc.," attempted to gain federal recognition for Robeson Indians as "Siouan Indians of Robeson County" under the Indian Reorganization Act (IRA – also known as the Wheeler-Howard Act), and worked on obtaining a resettlement project for Indians. The organization of the Siouan movement departed from earlier organizations in that it explicitly sought participation from people throughout the countryside. The "General Council of the Siouan Indians" wrote to request that it be recognized by the Depart- ment of the Interior "as the appropriate representative of the Siouan Indians of North Carolina in all future activities of the Department that may affect our people." In this letter, the organization is explained. It states that, in 1933, each of sixteen communities in Robeson and two adjoining counties held an election and elected a representative to the General Council. Each community also elected a chairman, a secre- tary, and a treasurer. The representatives of the communities, who formed the General Council, met and elected a secretary, chairman, chief councilman, and a delegate. The term of office was to expire November 1, 1937, "unless reelected." No one received any pay for their services and all those elected could be recalled by a majority of votes in the community (MS, Robeson County Collection 1935–42).

In 1933, a bill introduced into the U.S. Senate provided for the en- rollment of the Robeson Indians as Cheraw Indians and permitted their children to attend government Indian schools (U.S. Senate Reports 1934:1). However, the Secretary of the Interior objected to the bill, stating that it would be too costly to provide school facilities, that in any event the federal government had no treaty relations with these particular Indians and should not "assume the burden of the education of their children," but that he favored legislation to "clarify the status of these Indians." He suggested that they be designated "Siouan Indians of the Lumber River" rather than "Cheraw Indians," on the basis of a report by anthropologist John R. Swanton of the Smithsonian Institution (U.S. Senate Reports 1934:1–6).

One of the men active in trying to have these bills passed explained that they had first had a bill for the name "Cheraw," but there were too many other names, so they took the name "Siouan" because it was the family name for all the groups. He said that his own grandmother was a Pee Dee and his father's father was a Cheraw. "There are many Cheraw here," he added. His feeling was that it would not be fair to take the name of any one of the remnants and apply it to the whole group, because the identity of the others would be lost. He claimed that the 1933–34 bill got to the second reading in the House, when the local Representative, a White man, killed it in 1934.[6]

Other activities undertaken by the Siouan General Council were more successful. They were able to enroll twenty-two individuals as one-half or more Indian under the IRA.[7] These individuals thereby could request a reservation from the Secretary of the Interior. Not until the 1970s was any further action taken. Then, several descendants of these twenty-two and a few of those enrolled petitioned the Bureau of Indian Affairs (BIA) and the Secretary of the Interior for a reservation. When the Department of the Interior argued that the Indians lacked standing to do this, the Indians took the issue to court, where it was decided that the Indians did have standing. They are now (1979) waiting to hear more about whether they will be awarded a reservation.

A White nonlocal lawyer working with the group seeking a reservation told me in 1972 that land had been surveyed for a reservation in the 1930s, but that the proposal had never been enacted. The "Tuscarora" faction has been particularly active in the current maneuvering for a reservation. Although the BIA has been supportive of Lumbee-Tuscarora attempts to get Indian benefits from other agencies, and of the bill that removes language in the 1956 Lumbee law prohibiting benefits, it has not been particularly encouraging about reservation status for "Tuscaroras," the "Eastern Carolina Indian Organization" (ECIO), or Lumbees.[8] When a delegation of Tuscaroras visited the BIA in 1972, they were reportedly told by the Commissioner of Indian Affairs that many people do not look favorably on new tribes being developed or on new reservations being formed.

One of the leaders active in the 1930s stated in 1967 that the "Siouans" had deliberately halted their efforts to get a reservation. He said that he had worked to have individuals from different families enrolled as Indians under the BIA because:

> "It was important to establish a floor. We wanted land from the government, too. We carried it all the way up to getting a reservation, but we stopped just short of that because we found out what it would mean to have a reservation just like the wild Indians. Why it would set us back a hundred years! We've already gone beyond that stage, and we don't want to go back."

At hearings in Washington, which this man and several other Indians had attended, the assistant "director" of the BIA reportedly asked, "Why enroll twenty-two and leave 18,000 out?" The answer was "to establish a base," which would help to combat problems, such as being turned away from Carlisle, and "to represent families" – to have people enrolled from different families.

The General Council of Siouan Indians was also instrumental in obtaining a federally assisted cooperative project at Red Banks, an area just west of Pembroke. This project was begun in 1938 and was terminated in 1968, making it the longest-running New Deal cooperative of its kind. Initially, enthusiasm for the project was high, but problems emerged rather quickly. In May, 1941, several letters to federal officials were written by tenants on the cooperative and by members of the General Council as well as the chairman of the Pembroke Farmers' Association.[9] A letter of May 3, 1941, from several Indians to government officials, registers complaints, both general and specific:

One thing as was stressed in the reports was "work relief for Indians," which was not carried out. The appropriation that was made for the project, we believe, has not been used properly as we should have had more results. The buildings have been thrown loosely together and not according to contracts, let by the Farm Security Administration.

The land let to home steaders was not all cleared as stated in the contracts, the land was not drained and ready for cultivation when it was taken over by the homesteaders, the allotments of cotton and tobacco that was originally on the land has been transferred and cut until there are very few homesteaders who have enough money crop to live on much less enough to pay the Government for the land and money that has been borrowed. . . .

. . . If the project can be placed with the Indian Office let us know how it can be done, if not we want a man who will not be prejudice against the Indians to be sent here instead of [Joe Doakes], for we disgusted with him and his set up here and at Raleigh. We have completely lost confidence in the local office and Raleigh. Most all of their promises have never been kept that they have made to the people, even the Home Demonstration Department has never done anything except stay in the office. As for the farm supervisor we do not want him on the farms for he insulted and tried to discourage the farmers and told them to leave the farms [MS, typewritten draft of letter, Robeson County Collection 1935–42].

A draft of another letter, of April 2, 1942, indicates that the first letter received no response. It states, in part, "It seems that so long as we have local white people in charge it will continue to go backward instead of being a success." At least some Indians were defining Whites as part of their problem.

By the time the Red Banks Mutual Association disbanded in 1968, membership had dropped from fifteen families to five, with ten other families living on the farm and working as day laborers. The federal government had apparently attempted to dissolve the cooperative in the late 1940s, but the Indians insisted on the terms of their ninety-nine-year lease. In the end, this stubbornness paid off, for the fifteen families were given opportunities to buy farms with reasonable government loans at the dissolution of the mutual association. Earl Deese, the manager of the association, said, "If a man got sick or too old to work he lost his membership" (*News and Observer* 1968:8). The five voting members of the association were given the opportunity to buy farms from 130 to 300 acres. Three other families were given thirty-three-year rural housing loans to provide them with new or remodeled homes and one acre of land. Each of the remaining seven families was granted an economic opportunity loan for a house and four acres (*News and Observer* 1968:8).

Ella Deloria, a Dakota Indian and anthropologist, reported in 1940 that there were two factions among the Indians of Robeson County – those who supported a Cherokee identity and those who tried to have the bill for a Siouan identity passed (E. Deloria 1940). Deloria had gone to Pembroke for the Farm Security Administration to devise a pageant for the Robeson Indians. She and the pageant, "The Life Story of a People," were both still recalled with enthusiasm in 1967–68. One old Indian man who had met her spoke well of her and then added, "She knew her people," meaning that she had recognized the Robesonians as Indians. A few of the young men, some of whom had not been born when the pageant took place in 1940 and 1941, talked eagerly of reproducing it or producing something like it. Eventually, the idea of having another pageant was transformed into plans for an outdoor drama similar to "Unto These Hills" given at Cherokee and "The Lost Colony" done at Manteo. The Lumbee drama, "Strike at the Wind," is about Henry Berry Lowry and began public presentations in the summer of 1976.

That there was a large amount of activity centering around maintaining an Indian identity in the 1930s until the start of World War II, when many Lumbee men went off to war, is evident. In addition to the Siouan Lodge and Cherokee factions, the Indian pageant, and the cooperative farm, there was a "Longhouse Movement." Ella Deloria reported that a Mohawk from Saint Regis had come to Robeson County in 1938 and had organized a group of Indians, taught them dances and songs, and left. The Indians built a large log house (the "Long House") and were holding three-hour meetings in it once a week in 1940 when Deloria was there (E. Deloria 1940).

After World War II, many Indian veterans chafed upon their return to Robeson County when they found the old three-way segregation system unchanged. Dial and Eliades provide an account given by a veteran shortly after his return home (1975:156). He went to a dance with Indian and White friends, but was told by a policeman that he could not go in because he was Indian. He found the incident disturbing. Another veteran told me his experience:

> "In 1945 or '46, I applied to UNC [University of North Carolina, Chapel Hill]. I had six battle stars. They said they didn't accept Indians from Robeson County. Occasionally they'd slip in the back door at the University of South Carolina. They said we'll let you in if you'll get Chancellor "Smith" [a White man] to modify his statement. He wouldn't. At Western North Carolina, they said, we'll let you know, we have to meet with the Board of Trustees. I went to [a Western college] that summer. When I went there, I had a telegram from Western Carolina accepting me. But the next year I transferred to [a Northern urban college]. Indians from the West could come here and go to school, but here we are living here right in the state, taxpayers and all, and we can't go."

Experiences like these encouraged political activism.

At the end of the war, when Pembroke State College (formerly the Normal School) opened its doors to other Indians who were federally recognized, Indians from other areas of the United States began to attend, helping to create a greater consciousness, among some Robeson Indians, of larger Indian problems. In 1951, Pembroke State College for Indians was finally fully accredited by the Southern Association of Colleges and Secondary Schools and, in 1953, it began admitting Whites.[10] Because of the Supreme Court desegregation ruling in 1954, the college was thereafter technically open to Blacks. Few Blacks attended, however, and even in 1968–69, they were less than 1 percent of the student body. It is said that when the White president of the college was interviewed by reporters about "desegregation" in 1954, he caustically remarked, "You weren't here last year when we integrated with Whites, why are you here this year?"

The early 1950s were also a time of increased political activity centering around a new name for the Indians. In 1951, a delegation of Indians appeared before the North Carolina General Assembly in support of a bill introduced by the state senator from Robeson County that would change their name to Lumbee Indians, the old name of the river that cuts across the center of Robeson County and along which the Indian population is concentrated. The legislative committee decided that the Indians should "think over the matter for a couple of years," and if they continued to desire the change, it could be made (*The State* 1951:3). In justification of the new name, D. F. Lowry, one of the Indian leaders seeking the change, wrote to *The State* in 1952:

> The first white settlers found a large tribe of Indians living on the Lumbee River in what is now Robeson County – a mixture of colonial blood with Indian blood, not only of White's colony; but, with other colonies following and with many tribes of Indians; hence, we haven't any right to be called any one of the various tribal names; but, should take the geographical name, which is Lumbee Indians, because we were discovered on the Lumbee River [Lowry 1952:24].

Reverend D. F. Lowry, a nephew (brother's son) of Henry Berry, was a man of many talents and varied experience and was highly respected by Indians and Whites alike. He was an early graduate of the Normal School before it was standardized, which meant, he said, "you can study anything you want to." After he was graduated, he was principal of the college (the Normal School, called "the college" by the Indians) for a while, and then he went to Piedmont Business College in Virginia. For a time, he was business manager of Pembroke Supply Company, a large local firm owned by Whites, but then took a Civil Service exam. Of it, he said:

> When I went down to tell them I wanted to take the exam, they said, "You can't be a rural letter carrier, that's a White man's job." And I just laughed because I'd graduated from a White college [the business college in Virginia]. The exam lasted for four hours. There were twenty-four White men and one Indian. I worked it out in an hour and a half. I drove a buggy down there – that was before cars. As I was walking down the street to get my horse, I hear somebody running down the street after me. He was panting hard, time he got to me. And he was a feller who had finished the exam sometime after me. And he asked me what was my name. I told him, and he wanted to know where did I come from. I said Elrod. And he said he was a big landowner over in [another part of the county], and he just went around taking every test that came up, and he said he never had been beat before. He wanted to know where I went to school. And I told him the college, and I had been to Duke University for training one summer, and to Greensboro College and to Nashville."

When I asked him how long he had carried the mail, he replied that he took the mail route for thirty years, he taught for twenty years, and he preached for forty years.

The General Assembly did pass legislation designating the Indians as Lumbees in 1953, after the Indians voted in 1952 on whether they wanted a new name. Dial and Eliades suggest that there was some opposition to the idea of one more name (1975:157). Whatever the opposition, it was not effective at the polls and those who voted overwhelmingly favored the new name (Dial and Eliades 1975:157, 159). The Indians then took their case to Congress, and in 1956, at long last, they were legally recognized as Indians by the federal government under the name Lumbee. The only difficulty in the federal law was a clause at the end, which stated:

Nothing in this Act shall make such Indians eligible for any services performed by the United States for Indians because of their status as Indians, and none of the statutes of the United States which affect Indians because of their status as Indians shall be applicable to the Lumbee Indians [Public Law 570, as quoted in Dial and Eliades 1975:187].

The Indians, who had gotten a collective foot in the federal door with the enrollment of twenty-two people in the 1930s, were stuck halfway through with this 1956 act. But halfway was better than one foot, and since 1971, both Lumbees and the Tuscarora faction have been actively campaigning to have the restrictive clause removed through further Congressional legislation. In 1971, Senator B. Everett Jordan of North Carolina introduced a bill (S.2763) to that effect:

Since 1960 a number of Federal agencies have opened their programs and services to all American Indians. This bill would assure that Lumbee Indians be treated as other Indian groups and would enable them to have full access to all Federal programs and services except those administered for reservation Indians by the Bureau of Indian Affairs [B. E. Jordan 1971].

This particular bill failed to pass, and similar legislation has been proposed several times since then, so far unsuccessfully.

In 1958, the Lumbee found themselves catapulted into national headlines for the first time since the Henry Berry Lowry days, and the relations between Indians and Whites in Robeson County were being discussed across the country. One January night "hundreds" of whooping, angry, gun-shooting Indians broke up a Ku Klux Klan rally that had been called to intimidate them, and the rest of the country's imagination was captured for a brief moment. What is more, the Indians routed the Klan so thoroughly that they have not been able to hold another rally in Robeson County since 1958.

The Klan had started agitating in Robeson County before the night of the now famous rally. They burned crosses and sent threats to Indians. One of those threatened reportedly was a White woman who had been dating an Indian man;[11] another threat went to a family who moved into what some considered a "White" neighborhood. These incidents served to anger and arouse the Indians, as did a series of inflammatory letters by Klansmen to a local newspaper. Klan threat was answered by Indian counterthreat. The Klan scheduled a rally for a field near

Maxton, a town at the western edge of the county, and some Indians immediately proclaimed that they would not allow it. One of the primary instigators of this Klan activity was the Reverend James W. Cole (known to Indians as "Catfish Cole") of South Carolina. He was scheduled to be a speaker at the rally. During the period of increasing tension before the rally, Lumbees received telegrams from Indians of various tribes in many parts of the United States offering moral support. A few offered to "send braves," as Lumbees put it. The rally received national news attention and some reporters were present at the event. Afterward, Malvina Reynolds, a folksinger, wrote and recorded a song about it entitled "The Ballad of Maxton Field."

Thus, the confrontation was set, and on the night of the rally, Indians from across the county (and, as Indians tell it, from all the cities to which Lumbees have migrated as well as from nearby military installations) took up guns and other weapons and drove off to the rally. The Indians surrounded the field where the rally was to take place, and, as it began, they doused a single lightbulb over the speaker's platform with a shot, and in the ensuing dark, gunfire and shouting predominated. When it was over, the Klansmen had fled and no one had been seriously injured. Afterward, a photographer took a picture of two Indians, Charlie Warriax and Simeon Oxendine, draped in a Ku Klux Klan flag. This photograph appeared in *Life* magazine, and the first Lumbee I ever met was carrying it in her wallet in 1966. Of the effects of these events, Simeon Oxendine stated to Dial and Eliades, "We killed the Klan once and for all. We did the right thing for all people" (1975:162).

And indeed, the Klan has not returned publicly to Robeson County. In 1966, it sought to hold another rally there in order to regain the prestige it had lost in 1958. Many Indians threatened that they would never allow a Klan rally to take place in Robeson. And because some Indians feared that it would be impossible to prevent serious bloodshed a second time, they persuaded authorities in the state capital to issue an injunction against the Klan, preventing them from holding the rally. Although the legality of the injunction was questionable (the American Civil Liberties Union later took the case for the Klan), it was effective. No rally was held.

Many of the Indian participants in these events were veterans of World War II, and no one today is given credit for leading the Indians. Once again Indians had resorted flamboyantly to defensive violence as a political tactic, but this time there was no one heroic leader, and "the Indian people" have become the hero in the retelling of the story.

With the return to defensive violence, the Lumbee story seems to have come full circle back to the Henry Berry Lowry days. But new possibilities emerged in the 1960s and new tactics began to be used. The net result of the brief and relatively unbloody return to defensive violence was, apparently, increased wariness and respect on the part of many Whites, and amplified pride on the part of Indians. This new situation helped Indians to take advantage of the possibilities opening before them and helped Whites to accept such Indian behavior, however reluctantly. What the new possibilities were and how Indians, Whites, and Blacks reacted to them is dealt with in the next chapter.

4. What are they trying to do now?

Since their disfranchisement in 1835, one aspect of Indian political strategy had been to distinguish themselves from Blacks by having as little to do with them as possible in order to avoid accusations of Black ancestry and to bolster claims to an Indian identity. Then, in a striking reversal of strategy, some Indians began to advocate working with Blacks in order to further Indian aims. In 1967–68, a Black–Indian coalition was formed with the notion that the two groups shared common interests and that these interests were best served by cooperation.

There were several conditions that now made such cooperation an attractive possibility for Indians. First, they had been fully accepted as Indians by local Whites and increasingly by the federal government and other Indian groups. Therefore, they felt relatively more secure in their Indian status than they had before. Second, the 1965 federal Voting Rights Act made an Indian–Black voting majority attainable for the first time in this century. And third, Indian respect for Blacks had increased during the 1950s and early 1960s as the civil rights movement made great changes throughout the South. Many Indians uneasily admitted that they had been outdone by Blacks and were being accorded certain rights and privileges because Blacks had won them, not because Indians had done so. For Indians, who were accustomed to thinking of themselves as being in the forefront of obtaining concessions from Whites, this was not a particularly comfortable feeling.

Some Indians threw themselves into coalition activities with Blacks – because it seemed in their interests to do so, because they could once more be at the forefront of gaining benefits for their people, and because they could cease to feel themselves outdone if they became part of the doing. There was also a growing sense among some Indians that they had shared with Blacks the experience of discrimination, a bond that in some evoked deep empathy.

The Indians and Blacks who participated in the coalition risked incurring the displeasure of Whites, some of whom were powerful. Most appeared to be motivated by a genuine concern for the welfare of their

91

own people and stood to lose more than they could gain as individuals, though a few may have increased their individual fortune. All were breaking new ground by attempting to cooperate with each other, and no one in the coalition could be considered especially "typical" because of that. The attitudes and values of these men and women increasingly have become those expressed by others in their communities in the 1970s. Although the coalition was largely unsuccessful in achieving its immediate goals in 1968, it set the tenor of relations among the races and the character of political action for the next decade. It also laid the foundation for the impressive non-White electoral victories to come.

It is within the larger context of county politics that the coalition movement must be understood; therefore, this chapter will discuss the structure of county political offices and of the local Democratic Party, which has controlled the county since the turn of the century. By concentrating on the aims and activities of the 1967–68 coalition, relations between Blacks, Whites, and Indians become clearer, and some of the differences between Black and Indian approaches to politics that produce tensions as well as grounds for cooperation are thrown into high relief. One coalition meeting is described and analyzed in detail in order to illustrate differences in Black and Indian styles and attitudes, and to provide evidence for my claim that political events and meetings are shaped by identity concepts and in turn can be a force in altering them.

County politics

V. O. Key, in his study of Southern politics, characterized the North Carolina of the 1940s as a "progressive plutocracy," more moderate on racial issues, possessing a more liberal press and a higher level of industrialization than most other Southern states. Industrialization had given rise to a financial and business elite who in turn heavily influenced politics. "For half a century an economic oligarchy has held sway," Key asserted (1949:211). He found North Carolinians proud but not complacent (1949:206). The picture had changed by the mid-1970s. According to Jack Bass and Walter DeVries,

The progressive image the state projected in the late 1940s has evolved into a progressive myth that remains accepted as fact by much of the state's native leadership, despite ample evidence to the contrary [1977:219].

North Carolina's reputation for being moderate on racial issues persists in the face of evidence that belies it. Key had no more than finished his study before race became an issue in the 1950 Senate campaign between progressive Frank Graham, president of the University of North Carolina, and conservative Willis Smith, a former president of the American Bar Association. During the campaign, Graham was accused of favoring "Mingling of the Races," of supporting school desegregation, and of being a Communist sympathizer (Bass and DeVries 1977:220).[1] Graham, who had been expected to win, lost. Race had suddenly become *the* issue in a particularly ugly way, and it has remained an issue in one form or another in nearly every election since 1950 (Bass and DeVries 1977:221). The economic situation of North Carolina's industries has already been discussed. The state has fallen behind in average hourly wages and is attracting industries that pay even lower average wages. This is obviously related to the fact that North Carolina has lagged behind all other Southern states in union activity (Bass and DeVries 1977:239):

> But compared with states like Arkansas, Louisiana, Tennessee, and Texas, union membership in North Carolina is low and organized labor remains relatively weak. The legacy of bitter and bloody textile strikes in the 1920s and 1930s and repressive measures (often sanctioned by government) against union organizers in the 1950s have all contributed to labor weakness. And government policy still reflects the unspoken concern of business to discourage union growth [Bass and DeVries 1977:241].

If Key's assessment of North Carolina's politics in the 1940s does not hold for the 1970s, some of the underlying features he has pointed out do. One feature of Southern politics, a feature that distinguishes it from much of the rest of the country, was made vividly clear by Key. The county is the crucial political unit throughout the South (in Louisiana "counties" are called "parishes"). North Carolina is no exception. The county political organizations still form the basis for state politics, and, since 1900, state politics have been dominated by the Democratic Party. Not until 1972 did North Carolina have a Republican governor, and even then local offices in most areas went to Democrats. If Indians were to have political power at the local level, rather than just influence, they needed to affect the county Democratic Party organization as well as the formal county political structure.

The ability to wield political power became a possibility for non-Whites in Robeson County with the passage by Congress of the Voting Rights Act of 1965. This act allowed for massive non-White voter registration by eliminating the use of "tests or devices" as qualifications for registration in counties where less than 50 percent of the people of voting age were registered on November 1, 1964, or where less than 50 percent of these same people voted in the presidential election of November 1964 (see section 4, Public Law 89-110). By 1964, a poll tax had been eliminated but a literacy test was required of voters in Robeson County (Fleer 1968:17–19). The literacy test called for prospective voters to be able to read and write, and to interpret parts of the North Carolina constitution. This test had effectively barred many non-Whites from registering to vote, and Indians and Blacks frequently mentioned it as a deterrent, arguing that it was applied arbitrarily. At one of the coalition political meetings, an Indian spoke to the gathered Indians and Blacks. He told the following joke dramatizing the difficulties of registration:

> "A Negro was going to register to vote. He goes in and the Whites in charge of registration hand him a Chinese newspaper and tell him he's got to read it and tell them what it says in order to be eligible to vote. He says, 'It says, Ain't no Negro going to register here today.'"

In 1966, only 9,401 Blacks and Indians were registered of a potential 21,424 (according to statistics compiled by the State Board of Elections). Ten years later, in September, 1976, 26,944 Blacks and Indians were registered – roughly 6,000 more non-White registered voters than White (*Carolina Indian Voice* 1976b:12).

Public office

Although there had been some attempts by Indians and Blacks to gain county political offices before 1968, such efforts were necessarily limited to the few districts or precincts where substantial numbers of non-White voters were registered.

In 1967–68, Robeson County was governed by a County Commission composed of six commissioners elected from six districts within the county. In 1968, a seventh commissioner was added when the old Lumberton District was split in two. In 1967, five commissioners were White and one was Indian. By 1977, three commissioners were Indian and four were White. These commissioners appointed a county manager, who administered the everyday affairs of the county and acted as advisor to the commissioners. In 1966, the county manager explained to me that he acted as liaison between the commissioners and the various county departments, such as Registrar of Deeds, Welfare, Board of Education, and Sheriff's Office. He said he had "no real authority" because he could not hire and fire people without the approval of the commissioners.

Although members of the County Board of Education and certain department heads within the county are elected – for example, county sheriff, registrar of deeds, treasurer – the county commissioners can powerfully affect these departments because they allocate funds for them. One White county official told me that although some department heads are elected and can theoretically hire and fire whom they please, in fact they do not, because the money for their departments comes from the commission. Therefore, he said, before hiring someone, a department head checks with the commissioner from whose area the prospective employee comes. Then, "If the commissioner likes him [the prospective employee], he stays; if not, it wouldn't be too smart to keep him."

The commissioners also control appointments to the County Welfare Department, an important agency to non-Whites. For Indians, the most highly charged and potentially explosive issues centered around the Welfare Department, the County Board of Education, and the Sheriff's Office. These agencies had important and controversial impact on non-Whites, and in 1967–68, all were controlled by Whites whose behavior sometimes enraged Indians. The head of the Welfare Department has since changed, following a demonstration by "Tuscaroras," and the county school board is now (1979) dominated by Indians and Blacks. With the increased registration of non-White voters after 1968, an Indian has run for sheriff and lost.

Commissioners make policy decisions that can profoundly affect the quality of life in the county. They can induce factories to locate in the county by offering reduced tax rates, they can require or abate antipollution devices in these factories, they decide which ambulances are to serve the county at large, and which federal aid programs to adopt. For example, while I was living in Robeson County, the commissioners decided to switch from the surplus food assistance program to food stamps, a decision of considerable importance to those with low incomes.

In addition to the popularly elected county offices, there are state offices for which Robesonians regularly run. North Carolina's governing body is a bicameral General Assembly, which sits biennially.[2] In 1968, Robeson County voters elected one state senator and, with Hoke and Scotland counties, four state representatives, all White men. The senator and two representatives were Robesonians in 1967. These positions are vitally important to the county, because such representatives can introduce or kill legislation affecting their own areas, and because they can channel state funds into their locality. For example, when a Black Robesonian was elected in 1970 to the state house of representatives, he soon introduced equal opportunity legislation, which became law.

The incorporated towns in Robeson County are administered through their own elected officials, usually a mayor and councilmen, sometimes with the assistance of a town manager. The only town in the county controlled by non-Whites is Pembroke, the "Indian town." Although Pembroke has been heavily Indian from its inception, its governing officials were White for many years. From 1895, when the town was incorporated, until 1917, these officials were elected and were White. Thereafter until 1946, they were appointed by the governor who, "apparently as the result of a gentleman's agreement," appointed one or two Indian commissioners out of four. The mayor was White, under this arrangement (Dial and Eliades 1975:143). Dial and Eliades report what happened in 1945:

In 1945, a group of Lumbees went to the governor and asked that the citizens be allowed to elect their officials in a democratic manner. According to local sources, the governor consulted the three most influential whites in Pembroke as to how they felt on the matter and when they replied favorably, he granted the Indians' request for democracy. The fact that the governor was mainly concerned with the white reaction, not with the will of the majority, says a great deal about prevailing attitudes and policies [1975:143].

Since the offices have again become elective, the mayor has always been an Indian man. In 1967, two councilmen were Indians and two were Whites, but by 1974, all of the town's elected offices were held by Indians. The town councilmen and mayor appoint a chief of police, hire a town clerk, and are responsible for running the town generally. In the early 1970s, the town erected public housing with federal assistance.

The largest town (some would say the only city) in Robeson is Lumberton, the county seat (see Table 1). In 1967, the mayor and all the members of the city council were White. As the county seat of a White-dominated county, Lumberton was referred to by Indians and Blacks as the center of the county's "power structure." Often the term "the boys in Lumberton" was used to refer to all politically powerful Whites in Robeson County (even though they did not all come from or reside in Lumberton) as well as to politically powerful Whites living in that town. Lumberton was seen as a place whose White inhabitants were especially resistant to changes desired by Blacks and Indians.

Several other towns, smaller than Lumberton but larger than Pembroke, figured importantly in the life of the county: Fairmont and Rowland to the south of Pembroke, Maxton (near which the Klan rally was forcibly dissolved) to the west, and Red Springs and Saint Pauls to the north (see Map 2 and Table 1 for locations and population). Among these smaller towns, Red Springs was singled out by Indians as being the "worst" in terms of racial prejudice against Indians. For many years Indians had not been allowed to own land within the town limits of Red Springs. On the other hand, Maxton, Lumberton, and Fairmont had particularly active and successfully organized Black communities.

Each of the "White" towns (except Saint Pauls) had a separate school district with its own board of education elected from within the district. In addition, there was a County Board of Education that administered all schools not in one of the special districts. Most of the students outside the special districts were Indian and Black children. Although voters in the special districts could vote for members of the County Board of Education as well as for members of their own town board of education, voters not in the special districts could vote only for the county board. This situation came to be characterized by Indians as "double voting" because the people in the special, heavily White districts voted for two boards of education, and in so doing controlled the county board, which supervised mostly non-White children. Most Indians felt strongly that this was unfair, and in 1973, several Indians filed suit against the Robeson County Board of Education, seeking to outlaw this voting procedure. In 1976, the Indians won their case in the U.S. Court of Appeals. In the first county school board election (1976) after the elimination of "double voting," two Whites, one Black, and six Indians won positions.

County Democratic Party organization

The Democratic Party's county organization is based on precincts. The registered Democrats of a precinct who attend a publicly announced meeting vote for delegates to the county convention and for a precinct committee, which in turn elects its own officers. The precinct elections are held biennially, in the same years as elections. Of course, not all registered Democratic voters participate in these elections, but those who do tend to be the most politically concerned and active members of the party. As Jack D. Fleer puts it, "The precinct meeting is generally sparsely attended but attracts persons who have a greater commitment to party affairs" (Fleer 1968:42). In 1968, the rules for the composition of the precinct committee specified that there be five men and five women, all registered Democrats present at their election. Immediately after their election, the committee had to choose from its number a chairman and a vice-chairman, one a man and the other a woman not from the same immediate family. The committee also named a secretary-treasurer.

Although the responsibilities of the Democratic precinct committee are vague, in general these are the people who work hardest campaigning and getting out the vote. In studies in three urban areas of North Carolina, it was revealed that precinct officials considered personal contact and communication with voters to be the most frequent kind of campaigning. "The personal touch remains an important ingredient in the vitality of political parties and is achieved through casual and/or more systematic canvassing'' (Fleer 1968:44). In Robeson County, the "personal touch" is of vital importance, and casual canvassing is more common than a systematic effort.

The chairman and vice-chairman of each precinct, along with the presidents of the Democratic Women's Club and the Young Democratic Club, form the County Executive Committee, which elects a county chairman, from one to three vice-chairmen, a secretary, and a treasurer. Either the chairman or the first vice-chairman must be a woman, and the other a man. As Fleer remarks, "The county executive committee and its chairman have developed as a significant focal point in the organization of state and national political parties" (1968:47). These county Democratic leaders participate heavily in dispensing patronage, recruiting candidates, fund raising, and running the local organization. Fleer cities a survey that reported that 80 percent of North Carolina Democratic county chairmen dispensed patronage positions, while 90 percent of North Carolina Republican chairmen had no patronage to dispense (1968:48).

The Democratic County Executive Committee also recommends party members for positions on the County Board of Elections. The Robeson County Board of Elections has long had three members— two Democrats and one Republican, selected by the State Board of Elections from lists submitted by the state Democratic and Republican chairmen. Until 1972, the board in Robeson was entirely White, but at that time, a White and a Black Democrat were appointed along with an Indian Republican. All were new members. When the members of this new board met to elect officers, a controversy erupted. The Black Democrat moved that the Indian Republican be chairman, not knowing, he later said, that the Indian was a Republican. The motion was passed unanimously. When later queried about his vote by a reporter for a Lumberton newspaper, the White Democrat stated, "I knew he was a Republican but I was out-voted two to one and I went along for the sake of harmony. I feel this board has go[t] to work together" (Goodyear 1972:1). Before the meeting was over, leading county Democrats had heard about the unprecedented election of a Republican chairman in a predominantly Democratic county, and had persuaded the Black Democrat to withdraw his motion. He then moved that the White Democrat be chairman over the protests of the Indian Republican. The White Democrat became acting chairman until the whole affair could be adjudicated by the State Board of Elections, which finally declared, just before the 1972 elections, that the Indian was the official chairman (*The Robesonian* 1972:1). In the interim, there were many editorials, the resignation of a key member of the board's staff, and letters to the editor from individuals of various races.

One of the interesting things about this incident is what it shows about

race relations and party affiliations. Initially, in a spirit of cooperation between non-Whites, the Black nominated the Indian, apparently assuming that he was a Democrat. The White went along to preserve a harmonious working relationship and probably to avoid the
appearance of racial bias. What upset all these good intentions was party
politics. The Black may be seen as a mediator, making nominations –
first the Indian and then the White. Indians, both Democrats and Republicans, became angry over the controversy, because, many said, an
Indian was being discriminated against. They also recognized the importance of having non-Whites in control of election procedures because of
prior difficulties in registration and voting procedures.

The Democratic Executive Committee also has influence in the matter
of appointing people to fill vacated positions formerly held by Democrats. In 1973, an Indian man explained how an Indian had come to be
chosen to replace a White for the office of state representative:

> He asserted that until recently, the Executive Committee of the County
> Democratic Party chose replacements when elected officers were va-
> cated. But they reorganized within the last two or three years and
> changed the rules. Instead, two special committees were set up for just
> such contingencies – one to fill vacancies for the state house of rep-
> resentatives and one to fill state senate vacancies. For the house com-
> mittee, they selected Indians and Blacks – as he put it, "to give them
> positions but without expecting that there would be power attached to
> it." When a house vacancy materialized upon the death of a White
> incumbent, the house committee supported an Indian replacement and
> was able to maneuver this appointment successfully through the meet-
> ing of delegates from other counties in the district.

Before Indian and Black voting increased, they were not selected for
such committees.

The County Democratic Convention, composed of the County Executive Committee and delegates elected by the precincts, elects delegates
to the State Democratic Convention. These delegates in turn elect members to various district committees. The state Democratic organization
is responsible for fund raising, campaigning, and planning the state convention. Because the Democratic Party in North Carolina is very much
the majority party, nomination in a primary election is tantamount, for
most offices, to election. In Robeson County the real struggle takes
place over the primary election.

The coalition

Because so many fewer Indians and Blacks than Whites had been registered to vote before 1968, non-White efforts to participate in the formal

structures of elected office and the Democratic Party were largely doomed to failure. By 1968, however, participation was brought within reach if a few more non-White voters could be registered and persuaded to vote, and if Blacks and Indians would support one another's candidates. This possibility stimulated the growth of an organization of Blacks and Indians, which they sometimes called "the Movement" (see also Sider 1971). This coalition organization grew out of Indian and Black ongoing voter registeration projects. One such Indian project was under way in 1967 when I arrived in Robeson County for a seventeen-month stay, and efforts continued throughout that time and well into the 1970s.

How were they organized?

Some Black and Indian leaders, particularly those who were involved in early voter registration efforts, began to try to coordinate their activities and to promote local organization. Ultimately, a hierarchical structure resembling that of the County Democratic Party emerged. "Shadow" precinct organizations were set up, complete with officers, in as many precincts as possible. Of course, those precincts with the most potential non-White voters were organized first, and some precincts were never organized at all because, as one of the Indian leaders commented in a coalition meeting:

> "I've been over to [two predominantly White precincts], but we haven't been able to get anyone in there. No one felt they could be in control of their own interests. And it wouldn't be to our interest to register people who can't control their own interests. They'd go and vote against us."

The precinct organizations met with increasing frequency as the primary election approached, and the chairman and vice-chairman of each precinct met periodically with one another, with other locally important Black and Indian leaders, and with the coalition candidates at "countywide" meetings. In the countywide meetings, these Indian and Black leaders, nearly all men, could coordinate activities throughout the county, reaffirm commitments to their common program, and air difficulties among themselves. Much of the actual planning, however, took place in small groups of leaders, which coalesced as the occasion demanded and as the ties of friendship and ambition dictated. When they had decided something or thoroughly discussed a problem, the men in the small planning groups (for they were invariably men) would then "spread the word" by approaching others who were prominent in the coalition and who in turn either informed others casually or else brought the matter up in the next countywide meeting.

The only "outsiders" present in any of the coalition political meetings were a few nonlocal Whites – my husband, myself, and sometimes people from voter registration projects. Indians and Blacks appeared to contribute their opinions about equally frequently in the large countywide meetings, but unevenly in the smaller precinct meetings where the relative numbers of Blacks and Indians varied greatly.

What did they want and how did they try to get it?

The explicit goals of the coalition were (1) the registration of non-White voters, (2) the election of non-Whites to county offices, and (3) the active participation of non-Whites in the county Democratic Party organization. One of the difficulties in accomplishing the goals was logistic. In rural areas, where most Indians and many Blacks live, houses are dispersed and people busy with their work. Many families do not have their own transportation, and public transportation is almost nonexistent. If people are to be registered or to vote, then transportation must be made available to them. In addition, the vital primary election is held in early May, a time when those who follow agricultural pursuits are heavily engaged in working their fields. In 1968, a runoff election for one county commissioner was held in June, also a time of intense agricultural activity. The precinct elections are usually held not long after the primary and present the same difficulty.

Registration. The coalition sought to register enough non-White voters to outnumber registered Whites. In this they were somewhat successful, in part because there were several voter registration drives mounted by other groups in the county as well. By the 1968 primary election, there were about as many Indians and Blacks registered as Whites. In 1966, there had been 9,401 non-Whites registered to vote; in 1968, there were 14,471 (Robeson County Board of Elections). Although non-White voter registration increased markedly, more Whites were also registered. White registration gained sharply in Lumberton when, a few weeks before the primary elections, a special liquor election was held. Lumberton residents were to decide whether or not they would allow the sale of liquor within the town limits by authorizing a state-regulated retail store to be located there. Antiliquor forces were galvanized, ministers preached against alcohol, and many new White voters were registered in this highly emotional campaign. In the event,

Lumberton voters rejected the sale of liquor in their town, to the delight of many in Pembroke, who gleefully remarked that Lumberton people would have to come to Pembroke to buy their liquor, thereby augmenting the revenues of the Indian town. Pembroke had voted *for* a state liquor store. But perhaps the most important outcome of Lumberton's liquor vote was that by the time the primary election was held, about 200 more Whites than non-Whites were registered voters.

In order to increase registration, the coalition precinct organizations were supposed to make surveys of registered and nonregistered voters that would pinpoint areas where efforts should be concentrated. These surveys also gave coalition workers an opportunity to campaign for their candidates and an idea where to put their efforts to get out the vote. As the primaries neared, it became obvious that greater numbers of non-Whites could be registered in those precincts where many of them remained unregistered. For the effort expended there, more new voters could be registered in a shorter time than in precincts where nearly all the eligible non-White voters were already registered.

In general, registration efforts encountered various problems. At first, there were too few registrars in the county, and they were nearly all White, available for too few hours, or available when non-Whites found it difficult to meet them. After much delay, assistants (commissioners) were appointed, some of whom were non-White. These assistants could register people to vote if the registrar signed the application afterward. Reports of specific difficulties flourished. One White registrar, it was said, kept a large vicious dog unchained in his yard, and many people were afraid to approach his house, where they had to register. Indians and Blacks reported incidents of insults from White registrars, harassment from White landlords, and sometimes threats, as a result of their registration activities.

Non-White candidates. The coalition wanted to run non-White candidates who were not dependent upon White support for various state and local offices. It was hoped that such candidates, if elected, would recognize their debt to "the people." There were several elective offices that Blacks and Indians considered to be of prime importance. They wanted more representation on the county school board, which was then composed of seven members – five Whites, one Indian, and one Black. The positions of county commissioner, county sheriff, state representative, and state senator were also considered important, although in this election the coalition did not produce candidates for all these offices. For statewide elective offices, the coalition officially endorsed no one, because, many argued, they should concentrate on local issues and should not risk splitting their constituency by supporting one or another state or national candidate. There was some friction over this issue between Black and Indian leaders. Most Black leaders wanted the coalition to endorse the Black candidate for governor, Reginald Hawkins, and most Indian leaders felt that they would harm support for local candidates, especially among Indian voters, by such a move. In the primary, the Black vote went heavily for Hawkins, and, because a few Indians campaigned strongly for him also, he received part of the Indian vote as well.

The local candidates did not run openly as fellow coalition candidates. Rather, they declared for office as individuals and depended on a campaign of speaking at the coalition political meetings to make their commitments clear. Because there were four positions open for the county school board and because, in the last election, voters had been required to vote for as many candidates as there were positions in order to have their votes counted, the coalition supported four candidates – two Blacks and two Indians.

In the past this "vote for all" rule had hampered non-White efforts to elect their own candidates since they had always had to vote for one or more Whites as well as their Indian and/or Black candidates. If someone voted for only one candidate, his or her ballot was discounted. Unfortunately, at just the time when plans were being made by the coalition to run four candidates for four positions, the rule was changed and voters could vote for "one to four" candidates. Had the coalition known that "single shot" voting would be permitted, their plan would no doubt have been different. As it was, they found themselves with four candidates of decidedly uneven strength to support. The nominations for school board candidates were made in two separate meetings – one with all Blacks in which the two Black candidates were nominated, and one with all Indians in which the two Indian candidates were chosen.

One of the strategies of the coalition was to have their candidates wait until the very end of the filing period before announcing their candidacies in order to forestall what Indians and Blacks feared would be White attempts to run "their own" Indians and Blacks. As one Indian candidate put it while addressing a coalition meeting:

> "We un-Whites are not too well liked. The [White power] structure is waiting for us to name our own candidates so they can get some more non-Whites to run. They want to get a little white Indian, a little white Negro. That would shell off enough of our own little boys and little girls who have to go along with the power structure because of their jobs. But when they get in to vote, they can vote however they want."

Indians, when they use the terms "white Indian" and "white Negro" refer, of course, not to the color of a person's skin but to the "color" of

his political stance. A "white" Indian or Negro is one who accommo-
dates himself to the Whites in positions of power, espouses White values, and desires to "live like Whites."

In their campaigns, the candidates relied on the precinct organizations to persuade voters in their areas to vote for them. Most coalition
candidates appeared at nearly every coalition-organized precinct to
speak at a meeting at least once. In addition, they were introduced at a
rally for the Black candidate for governor, Reginald Hawkins, in Lumberton. Candidates also relied on their own personal networks of kin
and friends to campaign for them, and they sometimes spoke at other
gatherings than coalition-sponsored ones. As the election approached,
most took advertisements in the local newspapers.

The coalition selected and endorsed candidates, supported their
campaigns, and then faced the task of producing votes for them on
primary election day. Both Indians and Blacks worried about what
Whites might do to non-White voters and how they might best counteract White efforts to manipulate the vote. At one of the precinct
meetings, a Black leader told of an incident that, he said, had occurred
in the last election:

> "Some voters went down to the polls last time, and the [White] poll
> watchers helped them to vote, thinking that they didn't know how to
> read and write. But they did, so they knew what was happening.
> Those poll watchers said, 'Well here, if you don't want this man, you
> just X him out over here on the side.'" [The "X" on the side would,
> of course, be a vote "for," not "against," a candidate.]

At another meeting, an Indian warned, "Let them [Whites] help you
register. But don't let them help you on election day."

To help them get voters to the polls, the precinct organizations were
to use the registration surveys they had made. Elaborate plans were
drawn up for election day procedures. There was to be a central coordinating office equipped with several telephones and staffed by telephone answerers and troubleshooters who could be dispatched to precincts that reported difficulties. It was hoped that cars and drivers
could be provided to areas that needed them, for some Indians and
several college students from a nearby private college had volunteered
to drive people to the polls. Indeed, these volunteers were very helpful,
but, as it turned out, there simply were not enough drivers produced
anywhere in the county to effect a heavy turnout of non-White voters.
There were plans to have people in each organized precinct keep a
rough tally of how many and what kind of voters entered each polling
place in order to determine where later efforts to take people to the
polls should be directed. Several precincts actually participated in this
tallying, and the central office was able to assign drivers to areas that

most needed them. In addition, the central office received complaints about difficulties with voting officials in the precincts.

Indians and Blacks reported trouble from several precincts, but the most complaints were received from precincts in the county commission district where the incumbent White was being challenged by another White and a Black. In one of those precincts, it was reported that voting officials would not allow friends or relatives to help voters who could not read, even though the voters desired them to help. In addition, some White precinct voting officials were said to be watching people mark their ballots. In Robeson County at this time, there were no voting machines (which, one Indian remarked, was a good thing because machines are "something we don't know nothing about"). Instead, voters received paper ballots, which they marked with pencils and deposited in locked boxes. In some precincts, separate "booths" allowed the voter privacy; in others, several voters might stand beside one another in front of a long table to mark their ballots. In the latter case, maintaining the secrecy of one's ballot was considerably more difficult than in the former.

Other complaints charged that people who were properly registered and who had not voted found that they were unable to vote because, they were told, they had already voted. Some non-Whites with registration cards were told they could not vote because their names had not been recorded in the local books (even when they had been recorded at the Board of Elections in Lumberton). In one precinct, an American Friends volunteer, a young White man from the North, reported that while he was canvassing for voters, he was elbowed sharply by two or three local White men, one of whom declared, "White people who help niggers ought to be shot!" In another instance, a precinct refused to allow non-Whites to watch the votes being counted, despite the fact that it was their legal right to do so. Upon hearing of this, an Indian went to the precinct in question, watched the counting for about an hour, and was then ordered to leave by law enforcement officers, who apparently ignored his protests that he had a legal right to be there.

In response to the problems arising at the polls during the primary election, a few concerned Indians and nonlocal Whites telephoned the White chairman of the Board of Elections in Lumberton. Reportedly, in the first few conversations, he agreed to remedy the difficulties, but as the number of problems (and calls) increased, he became less responsive and ultimately told a caller not to bother him with any more informal complaints. After that, an employee of the federal Department of Justice was contacted, who suggested that affidavits concerning violations be drawn up and sent to him, and that for the remainder of election day, voters could be taken to vote at the County Board of

Elections if they were turned away in the precincts. The second suggestion was logistically impossible to implement, but the first was followed, and affidavits were sworn to and sent to Washington. When there was no response to these from the Department of Justice, the same employee was again contacted. There was some urgency because one primary contest for a county commission seat entered a runoff election scheduled for June. The employee reportedly told his caller that three things could be done in Robeson. First, an attempt could be made to work through the State Board of Elections; second, people could be instructed to "stand up and complain" immediately when they believed violations had occurred; and third, a rumor could be spread that the Federal Bureau of Investigation (FBI) was in the county watching the runoff election. He said he could be of no further help.

Because the Black candidate for a county commission seat had received more votes than the two White candidates, but had failed to get a majority, the White incumbent runner-up called for a runoff. Non-Whites had feared that this might happen and had talked about it in political meetings. But voter turnout in the primary election was extremely light everywhere, particularly among non-White voters. After the primary, many Indians and Blacks claimed what had happened was that the people who ordinarily drove non-Whites to the polls had been "paid to stay home" by Whites. And the coalition simply was not strong enough to make up for many of the regular drivers not driving. It also lacked the funds to pay people for their services, which White candidates often provided.

In the runoff election, the Black candidate lost, but allegedly one of the effects of his running was to drive the price of votes up from one dollar to five dollars a vote. Further, an incident occurred on runoff election day that resulted in the first case brought under a provision of the 1968 Civil Rights Act protecting civil rights workers. One young American Friends volunteer, another White Northerner, claimed that he had been threatened by an uncle of the White incumbent candidate for county commissioner. The young man had been driving people, mostly non-Whites, to the polls. While he was at the polling place, the uncle, as he sat in his car, reportedly brandished a gun and told the volunteer that he had "better get the hell back where you come from." An Indian claimed that the uncle had also pointed a gun at a group of Indians and shouted, "I know you voted for that damn nigger. I'll kill every goddamn one of you nigger-loving Indians." The man was charged with threatening and intimidating an Indian woman and the young Northern Quaker who had been encouraging Indians and Blacks to vote, but when the case finally came to court, he was acquitted.

The results of the 1968 primary and runoff elections were disappointing to those active in the coalition. Only one man supported by the coalition was elected, a man who had also been strongly supported by Whites and who had not taken an active role in the coalition movement.

Increased participation in the Democratic Party organization. The third coalition goal was to create precinct organizations that could, in the aftermath of the primary elections, take over regular Democratic Party precinct organizations. The rules of party organization were explained in the coalition-organized "shadow" precincts just before the party precinct elections were to take place. In these preparation meetings, people were cautioned about the ploys Whites had reportedly used in the past to keep Blacks and Indians from substantial participation. The few precincts that already had non-White leadership explained how they had accomplished it.

Non-Whites were urged to arrive before the time specified for the start of precinct meetings because, it was said, Whites sometimes locked the doors at that time. A few coalition precincts concentrated on disseminating knowledge of *Robert's Rules of Order,* so that Whites could not use esoteric regulations of procedure to hamper their efforts. In some precincts a lack of familiarity with these rules did prevent non-Whites from attaining their goal.

On the whole, the coalition's attempts at precinct takeovers were more successful than their efforts to get their candidates elected. Non-Whites did gain control of several new precincts. In this, they were aided by the element of surprise. Whites were not expecting these moves and were unprepared for them. In the next Democratic precinct elections (after the 1970 primary election), Whites regained control of one or two precincts, but non-Whites took over several more. Even in 1968, the effects of non-White precinct activity in the Democratic Party could begin to be seen at the County Executive Committee meeting, at which an Indian and a Black were elected and a White woman reelected as vice-chairmen of the County Democratic Party. By 1976, the chairman of the County Democratic Party was a prominent Black minister.

Although the 1968 coalition efforts seemed at the time to be disappointingly unsuccessful, they nevertheless paved the way for important gains in 1970, when more precincts came under non-White control, and one or two local offices went to non-Whites. That year, one of the state representatives elected from Robeson's district was a Black man, the second Black man to be elected to the state legislature since Reconstruction. In 1966, this man, the Reverend J. J. Johnson, had been the first Black man elected as a town commissioner in Fairmont. Sub-

sequent elections have produced more non-White victories and have
made it virtually impossible for a White to be elected without substantial non-White support, support that is to some extent recognized and
rewarded by Whites when they accede to office. In 1968, three non-
Whites held elective county offices. By 1976, there were twelve non-
Whites in such positions. The structure of coalition has apparently
changed since 1968. In 1970, instead of trying to have a single coalition
organization, Blacks and Indians organized separately and consulted
with one another more informally, through a few leaders. That this was
effective is manifest from the election and Democratic precinct victories that year. Such flexibility in coordination between Blacks and
Indians has so far not hindered gains for both groups and may well have
contributed to their success.

What was going on in the coalition?

Coalition political gatherings, particularly formal ones, set the tone of
coalition efforts, provided an arena for the expression of Indian identity, demanded dialogue between Blacks and Indians, and even, for
those Indians involved, helped to create a new sense of Indianness. In
order to talk about these matters substantively, I have included here a
lengthy description of one particular coalition meeting. It was perhaps
the third or fourth countywide meeting and was preceded by many precinct meetings all over the county. It took place about a month and a
half before the primary election in a medium-sized town. The coalition
candidates had been nominated and all but two had indicated that they
would run. I have eliminated the names of those involved and have
occasionally disguised their sex, but I have not altered their "race."

A countywide coalition meeting (1968).

An Indian leader, a man with wide knowledge of the county as a
whole and with speaking experience in most precincts, chaired the
meeting. He brought the meeting to order and gave an opening
speech: "I've been watching the political scene. Revolution is in the
news – the political structure is being torn asunder. We have a new
candidate for President – one of the Kennedy boys [Robert] – then
you come on down to the state and to the county and to the local.
People are through with political agreements people made a hundred
years ago. The way change comes about is by meeting as you are
doing. Someone said, 'A riot is the unheard voices taking action.'
Here in Robeson County, we can upset the structure with a powerful
weapon, the pencil [ballots are marked by pencils]. The boys in
Chicago may have to do other things [there had been riots in Northern

cities recently]. Let's take our citizenship to the polls and cast our ballots. In any organization you've got to stay ahead. We're going to have three telephones for the central office – we need to know how many cars, how many miles, how much gas you need. We're attempting to see the ballots at 2:30 at night when they get through counting. It will take a lot of people to carry out this program. Two people at each poll – to mark down every person who goes in the box. From each hour we need to know how many from what groups that went in that place [the polling place]. We need at least two runners – to telephone to the central office. And we're going to need heaven knows how many to watch each other that day to keep us straight. This is going to follow through on the surveys you made. The precinct chairman won't be able to do anything except run in and vote. He's going to stay on top of his people. Now we don't want a boss, no. He's just going to look after his people. Let's have no drinking – get drunk the day after if you have to get drunk.''

Under the call for old business, a prominent Black leader who had been nominated to be a candidate at the last meeting explained why he would not run this time – because he wants to wait until there are more Indians and Blacks registered, so that he can run and win. The chairman praised this decision saying, ''He has let us out from under another power structure. Despite what you'd call a draft. Anybody can run, too few can run and win.''

As new business, an Indian precinct chairman raised the question of how the campaigns of the candidates should be run. He asked, ''Should there be a central campaign manager or should each take care of his own?'' The chairman replied, ''We can give suggestions, but we shouldn't come out and try to map a plan for the candidates. This is my idea. Let's have discussion.''

A Black minister-leader responded strongly with ''Let the candidate assume his own responsibility,'' and an Indian candidate backed him up: ''That's the way I see it.''

Another Indian, reacting to the Indian chairman's comment that anyone could run but few could win, raised the issue of his own prospective candidacy: ''Maybe [the Black man who has just declined to be a candidate] is a big man after all, and maybe some of the rest of us should do the same. I came to the meeting to find out from you as to whether I should finally file. If I'm not supposed to be in there, then I don't want to be there. If you want to see the picture of the county changed – then it's our decision together. . . . If I do run at your request, I would like to partially do my own choosing, but I would like for everyone in the county to feel that they are my campaign managers. . . . We're all going to have to be campaigners if we're going to win. . . . Beat the floaters to the punch on this brain-washing deal. Either ignore it, laugh, or tell your neighbor, 'Here we go again.' If you still say you want me to go, and you'll all go with me, I'll run.'' There followed a chorus of encouraging comments.

A Black candidate for another office outlined his position: ''As a candidate for [an office], I'll choose someone to work with me. But I need help. We've been turned to and fro by our fellow brothers. Now it's time to get ourselves together as a people. We have to keep the other fellow from tearing down the structure we have built, keep him from brain-washing us. Even though I am defeated, I would like to know the people were behind me. It's time to move some obstacles out of the way. Each of you can be a campaign manager."

The Indian chairman then reminded everyone that filing time was near, and that White-supported candidates had already begun filing. He reiterated that Whites, once the coalition candidates filed, would try to have other – "their own" – Blacks and Indians file in order to split the non-White vote. He cautioned, "They'll split you off and have a run-off. We want to make it home the first time."

Then an Indian candidate was recognized: "We have to put a bell on the cat. To some people it seems to be better to criticize than to praise. The Indian gives praise to someone who's dead. Who gives it while a man's living? But you hear for weeks afterward what a good man he was. We have to start running toward something instead of away from it. A man [a White man] came to see me, and he tried to tell me not to run – he said they [Whites] didn't think they could support two non-White candidates this time. I said if they couldn't support two of us, how could they support the thirty or forty thousand of us in the county? The situation in Robeson County can only be known, by and large, by a non-White. Only one of us can know what it's actually like – others might know about it, but they don't actually know." He went on to urge that people "do their homework" by registering voters and disseminating information and then "pass the exam" by getting out the vote. "It's a popular thing for us here in Robeson County to go away from home – to Detroit, Baltimore – to get away from that bad old place. Many have gained status by this horizontal move. We don't want our children to have to leave here."

A third Indian candidate spoke up: "You go away from home and run into the same thing again. Three brothers were plowing cotton one day, and they were talking about running for something. A White man came and gave two brothers cigarettes. He split them. We've got to equalize and be as one." He talked further about "the Whites and how they put the Indians down, and the Negroes." "I got called to jury duty one time. I was the only Indian on the jury. They called all the others 'Mr.' and they called me 'Joe'. They asked me if I knew 'Mr. Smith' [a White man]. I said, 'No, I don't know David.' But I wish I had the words back in my mouth. I wish I'd said, 'No, Tom, I don't know David.'" This was received with laughter and remarks of approval.

Then the chairman recognized a Black candidate: "I'm glad we've come together to discuss our purpose and intentions. I'm with you one hundred percent. The Bible says, 'Behold how good it is for brothers to dwell together in unity.'" After developing that theme, he complained, briefly, that one of the Indian candidates had already filed for candidacy and that the filing had been reported in another county's newspaper. He said he understood the candidates had agreed to wait until later.

Reverting to the campaign theme, the chairman urged, "Make them [the candidates] rich with what we've got – our votes. We should do this. For the love of our county and for the love of our people. Listen

to everything that's being said and don't say anything. Don't talk."
He then called for reports from several people on registration progress
in the precincts.

After the reports had been given, the Indian man who had started
the discussion about candidates and the organization of their campaigns returned to the issue, saying, "We don't want to be their
mouthpiece, but they can use our help in different parts of the county.
If we're going to be loose as jelly, we're not going to get this stuff
out." Unsuccessfully, the chairman tried to discourage this line of
discussion, but a Black leader pursued it, maintaining, "The candidates are running for us, they're not running for themselves. I'm not
talking about programs, now, I'm talking about money." To which an
Indian precinct chairman added, "We're going to have to help him
[the candidate]. He can't foot the bill. When we can put someone in,
then we can ask him to do things." He urged people to attend a benefit
dinner at which boxes of food would be auctioned off. Then he ended
"Don't give up, you've got the chance. You've got to get them to the
polls. Daddy should have done this and it would be a better place for
us today."

There followed discussion from several Blacks. In response to one
Black minister's suggestion that the group should have a name and
officers in order to make it clearer to people who the group is and
what it wants to do, another Black countered, "Maybe we shouldn't
organize *now* – I stress *now*. Every other organization with a name
we've ever had has flunked out. A group doesn't mean anything more
with a name. There ought to be an organization, but not now. If we
have a president and treasurer and so on, they'll be able to pick us off.
Now they don't know who's who. Let's not change it yet. Not before
the election. Let's try this out one time." In the general discussion
about this, most people expressed an aversion to creating a formal
organization. An Indian precinct chairman concluded, "It's better to
have a group where nobody's at the top."

Finally, the Indian who brought up the issue of what to do for candidates reminded people again that this point had still not been resolved. One of the Indian candidates rose and tried to pull the discussion together: "I agree we need organization. I also agree with some
other things that were said about timing. Let's wait until after the election. Right now the candidates should meet and discuss things. Then
they can bring what they decide back to the group – to say what we
want to do. Some things that Mr. Timmy might want to do might hurt
me and some things that I do might hurt Mr. Timmy – so we can't run
together."

The Black leader who opposed formal organization suggested, "We
do need some coordination. There should be a coordinating commitee
of Indians and Negroes to get some understanding. Misunderstanding
has kept us apart. A committee of three or five – let's have them plan
things and we can all be a part of it."

A Black precinct chairman moved that the candidates get together,
and the move was seconded by an Indian. One of the Indian precinct
chairmen offered his precinct's help. Another spoke of the need for
the "non-White race" to work for all three races. He proposed an

amendment to the previous motion – that the precinct chairmen meet with the candidates. The amendment passed.

One of the Indian precinct chairmen complained that he thought all along it was only precinct chairmen who would attend these countywide meetings and have a voice. But the meeting chairman explained, "That was only a planning stage." He cited the lack of county organization, of formal rules for the group. Then he called for a motion to adjourn.

Issues explicitly raised. A number of issues were raised in the meeting just described, and most of them were dominant and recurring in other meetings as well. Some were raised and dropped; others ran thematically throughout the meeting. Behind these issues, the ways they were articulated, and by whom, lay other, implicit issues concerning differences between Blacks and Indians in style, conceptions of leadership, and the organization of their communities.

One concern common to both Indians and Blacks, raised in this meeting by an Indian candidate, was the distressing flow of young people out of Robeson County. It was generally assumed that young people left the county to seek better employment opportunities and, particularly among Blacks, a less oppressive social environment. Older Blacks and Indians lamented the out-migration of their youth – as the Indian said, "We don't want our children to have to leave here." It was assumed by everyone that if social and economic conditions could be improved in Robeson, fewer young people would feel compelled to leave. Numbers of Indian and Black young people do leave the county each year, but their migration patterns differ considerably. Whereas many Indian migrants eventually return to Robeson County to live, many Black migrants do not, although Blacks tend to return to visit.

This difference in migration patterns has to do with, among other things, differences in the groups with which Blacks and Indians identify. Blacks from Robeson identify with American Blacks generally, and particularly with other Southern Blacks. The reference group for them is a large one, scattered across the United States, rooted less to a particular place than to a particular people. Recently the notion of ultimate rootedness in Africa, from which ancestors were taken as slaves, has emerged (e.g., Haley 1976), but there has been no development of a localized common source of identity defined by any one place in the United States. In contrast, the reference group for Lumbees is "Indians in Robeson County," and this group can be extended to related Indians in the surrounding counties. Their group identity is geographically rooted to one relatively small area of the United States, as is the identity of so many other Indian groups. Their orientation is revealed, for example, by the continued use of "home" to mean Robeson

County, even in the second generation of Northern urban Lumbee families. Some Lumbee families never return to Robeson to live, but a surprising number of their children, who have been reared in the urban North, choose to attend college at Pembroke State University and sometimes stay to live in the county.

There was one comment made by an Indian candidate that stands out, for it was the only statement of its kind that I heard at any political gathering. The assertion that "the situation in Robeson County can only be known, by and large, by a non-White [i.e., "one of us"]" cut in two directions. On the one hand, it affirmed solidarity between Indians and Blacks in an only-we-insiders-can-know-what-it's-like way. On the other hand, it excluded Whites from this knowledge. Whether it excluded or included those nonlocal Whites present at the meeting – two anthropologists and two or three voter registration project workers – is not clear. We could have been exempted by the "by and large" clause or included because we were beginning to presume that we knew something about the situation. It may, in short, have reflected some ambivalence toward "we outsiders" on the part of the speaker, but not outright hostility because this same man had been instrumental in supporting both anthropologists and project workers in their separate endeavors.

Other subjects were strongly reiterated throughout the meeting and appeared in one form or another in all the meetings. One such topic was Indian–Black solidarity. Black and Indian solidarity was, as everyone explicitly recognized, vitally important for making the coalition work. Both Indians and Blacks espoused unity, but each in slightly different ways. Blacks tended to stress brotherhood, biblically enjoined or otherwise, and unity as a moral good. The appeal was to "get ourselves together as a people." Indians, however, tended to emphasize the other side of the coin – unity *against* the Whites who threaten to split "us." For Indians, the unity lay perhaps more in the necessity and challenge of common opposition than in a moral idea of the brotherhood of mankind. Indians repeatedly used the phrase "we non-Whites," a new concept for them. Both Blacks and Indians warned of possible White maneuvers to defeat them and told stories about how Whites would try to divide them. Throughout the political meeting (and in others), the significant but absent others were local Whites. Strategy and tactics were planned in relation to what they might be expected to do and sentiment was appealed to on the basis of what they had already done. But Indians more often than Blacks recounted specific tales of White insults or oppression, such as the jury incident mentioned by one Indian candidate and the Whites' warning that they would not support another's candidacy.

For Indians, particularly, these incidents served to whip up enthusiasm and commitment for the coalition enterprise. As many said
themselves, one sure way to unite Indians in Robeson is for Whites to
threaten or insult them. Indians also seemed to assume that the recounting of incidents in which Whites wronged Indians or Blacks
would have the same effect on Blacks that it did on Indians, which was
not entirely the case. If Blacks were not particularly instilled with a
proud, fighting spirit by the telling of such incidents, they were not
offended by them and were usually engaged by them. But Blacks'
source of commitment lay elsewhere, in religion and the greater moral
good – positive, not negative, forces. Indians and Blacks in this respect
were complementary – the positive and the negative, each able to be
sympathetic if not entirely moved in the same way by the other's
grounds.

Because of their approach to cooperation and encouraging commitment, Indians sprinkled meetings with accounts like these:

> "You're driving along the highway and the highway patrol comes
> over. You're doing 40 in a 35 mile zone. He's your servant. When
> you want to know what you're being charged with, then he gets mad.
> You've made him your boss man. You go to court. On the left and the
> right, except in the front, are non-White. Except the black robe
> [judge] and solicitor [prosecutor]. You try to convince that White
> judge that his White friend who's driving *your* car down *your* road
> told a lie. He gives you a sentence. You get mad, so you want to
> appeal. Two hundred dollars. Doing you like a cow, milking you dry.
> You're going to have a jury. Then you got to have a lawyer. They're
> still milking the bag. Then to pay the lawyer, you got to go to the
> lender. Back to the power structure. People who are your servants,
> you have made your bosses."

> In the all-Indian nominations meeting, someone remarked that he
> had been at a Black businessman's store in a nearby town when a
> White man came in saying that the Indians are setting up to rule the
> county. Another Indian remarked, "He's trying to split the Indians
> from the colored folks."

> In a countywide meeting, an Indian told a story of a Negro and an
> Indian who were walking down the street: "The Negro had a ham on
> his shoulder. He bumped into the Indian and they fell to fighting. A
> White man came along and picked up that ham and kept on going. He
> just walked off with the ham."

> An Indian told a political gathering of Indians and Blacks, who nod-
> ded and commented in vigorous assent, "Whites say to Indians, 'If
> you go with them [Blacks], you're nothing but nigger-lovers,' and
> they say to the Negroes, 'Don't join those damn Croatans, they'll cut
> your throat!'"[3]

Blacks mentioned such incidents much less often during the political
meetings. A few years later a Black leader, who was elected to the

North Carolina House of Representatives in 1970 from Robeson and two other counties, told a White reporter:

"The strategy in Robeson County," says Rep. Johnson, "has been to keep black people and Indians separate to avoid the political impact they would have together. If the two groups ever built a coalition, they would control everything in the county, and that's well known" [Gaillard 1971a:35].

William Willis (1963) has termed this kind of White strategy "divide and rule" in his discussion of the colonial period. Although both Indians and Blacks recognized White efforts to split them, it was difficult to counteract those efforts. One reason is that there are differences between Indians and Blacks concerning goals and reasons for cooperation. Many Indians and Blacks agreed that together the two had the potential to gain electoral control. But Indians often talked as if Indians and Blacks do not share the same problems, a viewpoint encouraged by Whites. Even Whites who were generally sympathetic toward Indian problems did not think an Indian–Black coalition was a good idea. As one such man said, "Indians would be foolish to throw in their lot with the Negroes and take on all the Negro problems as well as their own." But Blacks talked as though Indians and Blacks *do* have the same problems, while recognizing that Indians frequently do not see this. When Indians seemed to act as though Indian and Black problems were different, Blacks became uneasy and suspicious.

Both Indians and Blacks also realize that an obstacle to overcoming their differences is that so many members of each group are vulnerable to White pressures. This vulnerability was widely recognized but hard to protect against. There was an attempt made in the all-Indian nominations meeting for the school board to select candidates who were tougher and less vulnerable than others. Several Indians who were not present were suggested and discussed. For almost every nominee, someone mentioned that his income was fairly secure ("He owns his own land," or "He rents his shop from a [Indian] neighbor"). Of one nominee, it was said,

"He's a independent liver – he's a [occupation]. He had a contract for [a prominent White man], was cursed, and walked off the job, with his men. He'll weigh out his own decision, not like some on there now. And they'll [those on the current board] go against their people every time. We need someone to go in there and fight for the people."

Three stories that circulated during and just after the primary campaigns exemplify how Indians and Blacks say they can be "got to." First, there was a politically active Indian bootlegger who suddenly "was turned around" (switched sides) just before an election.[4] People explained this switch, saying that the "ATCU [Alcohol Tax Control Unit] men" or "the revenuers" caught him with too much non-tax-paid liquor in his possession. He was already on probation, so that he could have been sent to jail. It was said that the "sheriff" or one of his men arrived at the bootlegger's place after he had been caught, and told the ATCU men that they could leave because he would take care of everything himself. The next day the bootlegger "changed his mind" about his political commitments. Several Indians said that the sheriff (or his men) had made a deal with the bootlegger – the bootlegger would not be prosecuted if he changed his political ways. Indians seemed to make this assertion resignedly, expressing an attitude that the bootlegger, or any reasonable person in a similar predicament, could not be expected to do anything else. There were no bitter recriminations.

The second story concerned a politically active Indian man with a small business, who suddenly was deluged by tax inspectors as he began to be effective in his political work. It was said that when a local tax man found nothing wrong, a state inspector appeared. When he found nothing wrong, a federal inspector arrived and claimed to find that several thousand dollars were owed the government. The arrival of the inspectors was attributed to the machinations of the "White power structure," who wanted to stop this man's political activities by pressuring him economically.

A third story, circulated during the campaign activity preceding the primary election, maintained that one of the Blacks who was active in the coalition had begun to be harassed. He was a veteran, a man who refused to play a "humble" role, but who was not flamboyant or particularly obvious in his refusal. It was said that White law enforcement officers began watching his house, stopping his car to question him and to check for violations, and even threatening him.

Whether these stories are true or not does not especially matter here, because people treated them as if they were and cited them as situations representative of general conditions in the county. They were repeated as examples of "how they [the Whites] keep us down." Indians used the recounting of incidents like these to arouse their anger and resentment toward Whites, thereby motivating themselves to try to change the situation. Furthermore, by focusing on White attempts to split Blacks and Indians, Indians avoided confronting their own role in maintaining the split. Implicit in some Indian statements was a threat of ultimate recourse to violence, as in the oblique reference to Northern urban riots which, it was hinted, result from minorities being unable to work effectively within the system. Blacks never, even indirectly, suggested violence as a possible but undesirable alternative. Rather, in these meetings they were given to making broader analytical statements about political affairs and tended to be more concerned to map out the goals of the coalition and how they might be accomplished. Part of this pragmatic concern may have been related to some Blacks' fears that Indians might, given the opportunity, cut them out of the decision-making process.

Both Indians and Blacks were concerned about the organization of activities, but each in slightly different ways. Indeed, in this particular meeting, how various activities ought to be organized was the most difficult problem addressed. The organization for election day had been worked out in advance and was simply presented by the Indian chairman of the meeting. There was no discussion of it, and everyone agreed to it. But the twin organizational problems of how to get the candidates moving and how the coalition itself should be run required considerably more discussion. It was an Indian who raised the problem of the candidates and a Black who raised the issue of the coalition itself. In general, everyone agreed that a high degree of individualism ought to be allowed the candidates, but Blacks were concerned to fix upon some kind of formal meeting among them. An Indian quickly added that the precinct chairmen ought to attend as well, further democratizing the meeting.

In the discussion about the structure of the coalition, everyone agreed, in principle, about the need for circumspection in order to avoid retribution from Whites. Blacks were more divided over the issue of organization than Indians, although most did not desire a formal structure at the top, largely for pragmatic reasons – "They'll be able to pick us off." The division between two Black leaders in the meeting could be traced to rivalries between these men, each a leader in a different county town. Indians rejected formal organization rather unanimously, but for a different reason. As one Indian said, "It's better to have a group where nobody's at the top." These differences in attitude and approach reflect more thoroughgoing differences in Indian and Black ideas about leadership and politics and in the structures of the two communities, all implicit issues in the discussion at the meeting.

Issues implicitly raised. In saying that it is *better* not to have anyone at the top, the Indian precinct chairman reiterated a common moral motif in Indian discussions about leadership, as did the meeting chairman when he specified, "We don't want a boss, no." Political leaders, many Indians told me, often become "big I, little you," meaning they "get above themselves" and "forget their people." A leader who displays this syndrome is said to have lost his "commonness." Here "common" refers to oneness with others rather than to something vulgar or second-rate, and to say of someone, "He's common," is a compliment. An Indian man said in praise of a prominent middle-class Indian, "He's common. He'll go down with the boys and chew tobacco with them and talk with them. He hasn't got above himself."

Individual Indians have praise for their favorite leaders, but on the whole, leaders are said to be in politics for personal prestige and material gain, although they should only be concerned to obtain beneficial changes for their people. Indians continually asked, concerning one leader or another, "What's in it for him?" And they tended to evaluate Black leaders in the same light. Comments such as these were frequently heard:

> An Indian evaluated two Indian leaders with: "I can't believe they'd be working so hard unless there's something in it for them."

> Another Indian remarked of a different Indian leader: "He's out for himself. He used to talk a lot about the Indian people, but you don't hear it anymore – he'd take the side he thinks has the most advantage for him."

> An Indian maintained that two Black leaders "are both out for money."

> Of an Indian officeholder, another Indian observed, "He's been [in the office] so long he thinks he owns it. He doesn't do a thing."

> Of an Indian precinct chairman in the coalition movement, it was claimed, "He's been bought off to work for [a White candidate]."

> In response to a question about what he meant by "top echelon Indians," an Indian explained the problems of leadership: "We haven't had any top echelon Indians. The Indian race hasn't had anyone to look up to the way the Negroes have Martin Luther King. [This statement was made before King was assassinated.] The closest person we have to it down here is [a prominent Indian leader]. The Indian race doesn't like to see anyone get ahead, and when a man gets ahead, they cut him down. We need twenty or thirty top echelon Indians like [the same prominent Indian leader]. But when he started getting ahead, he made more enemies than friends."

Such remarks help make clear why the Indian meeting chairman specified that a precinct chairman should not be a boss, but should "look after his people." The Indian ideal is that leaders should be selflessly concerned for their own people, but most assert that in reality leaders "are in it for themselves." Thus, individual Indians may favor or believe in the virtues of a particular leader, but followers tend to be fickle and to regard their leaders with a certain amount of suspicion, watching for indications of the "big I, little you." There is a strong reluctance among most Indians to praise or honor leaders until they are either dead or very old and no longer active. Many expressed the opinion that political leaders were no better than anyone else, but thought they were.

Blacks, on the other hand, had more confidence in their leaders and supported them more consistently. Many Black leaders were ministers, a position that gave them experience in organization and community leadership. Other leaders were businessmen whose clients were primarily other Blacks. Still others were simply men highly respected in their own localities. There has been great controversy about the role played by Black ministers and churches in political activism, with some analysts arguing that they have been in the forefront of creating change and others maintaining that they have obstructed or delayed change (see, e.g., Marx 1967:94– 105). The role of ministers and churches probably has varied widely from one area to another and over time. No political activity in Robeson could be considered strongly or flamboyantly militant, unless any seeking after change is to be defined as militancy. Yet, Blacks and Indians were (and are still) determinedly active. In 1967–68, Black church organizations and ministers were playing important leadership roles in political activity. Whether they would have done so if more militant groups had not been active in other, particularly urban, areas and if militancy had not been widespread at that time cannot be known. But because there had been more militant activities elsewhere (such as sit-ins, marches, and even the violent urban eruptions in Watts, Newark, and Detroit), the organizing work of Blacks and Indians in Robeson County did not appear as "radical" or as threatening to local Whites as it undoubtedly would have several years earlier.[5]

Black leaders, both ministers and nonministers, appear to wear the mantle of leadership comfortably and proudly, with assurance in the loyalty of their fellows. Their relationship with followers is based on mutual trust (after testing) and shared responsibilities. Blacks do not follow their leaders blindly or uncritically, but once having evaluated and tested a leader, they allow him authority.

Indian followers, on the other hand, only reluctantly and exceedingly warily "follow" their leaders. Indians do not readily delegate authority or decision-making powers to their leaders, and leadership is constantly contested. An Indian leader can never be entirely sure of his constituency from one day to the next, and must attempt to maintain a precarious balance between an aura of authority ("big I, little you") and an image of working for his own people ("commonness"), for Indians expect their leaders to have both these qualities, even if one of them is considered undesirable. A person must manifest both if he is to be a leader. If he is too "common," he will not set himself apart from his fellows and therefore will not be able to lead; if he is too self-aggrandizing and assertive, he will alienate his followers.

Another significant contrast between Indian and Black leaders today is that almost no prominent Indian leaders are ministers, and no Indian minister-leader has a middle-class congregation, whereas several important Black leaders are the heads of large middle-class churches, and many Black leaders are ministers. Why this should be is not entirely clear, because there have been several important Indian minister-leaders in the past, such as W. L. Moore, who was instrumental in obtaining and running the Indian Normal School in the late 1880s, and Doctor Fuller Lowry, who was prominently active in having the group recognized as the Lumbee by both the state and federal governments in the 1950s.

Black–Indian differences in leadership can be traced, at least in part, to the changing nature of political involvement – lately, the increase in emphasis on mobilizing voters – and to organizational, stylistic, and moral-orientation dissimilarities. Blacks develop leaders through organizational experience, often in the church, an old organization that has been recurrently important politically. Indian leaders usually do not have such organizational experience either in churches or in voluntary organizations, although many have business experience as farmers, professionals, or store owners and managers. Leadership styles are correspondingly different. Black leaders deal with issues more frequently than do Indians, and they have a strong organizational sense with a cooperative style. Indian leadership style is more personality oriented, highly individualistic, and entrepreneurial. When an issue arises, Indian leaders relate themselves to it or ignore it, but even when they involve themselves with an issue, they do not present themselves in terms of it. Instead, they rely on their persona, with the attitude, "People know who I am." At the moment, few issues are compelling ones for most Indian ministers. An important exception (the only one during 1967–68) occurred when Indian ministers became active over the issue of liquor elections in 1968. In this case, ministers preached sermons encouraging their congregations to vote against allowing state liquor stores to be established in the county. They were, for the most part, unsuccessful, and Pembroke, the Indian town, voted to have a state liquor store.

Leadership styles are in turn related to different ideas about how people ought to behave. Indians place heavy emphasis on each individual's ability to choose whether or not "to live right." This moral individualism makes possible the judging (often harsh) of each person. Ministers are expected by Indians to behave with particularly high principles in every area of their lives. Blacks, although agreeing that it is, to a degree, the choice of the individual to behave as he does, place their emphasis on cooperation within the group, on "treating people right" even more than on "doing right." A Black minister is expected to be a good organizer (able to persuade people to cooperate) and, as a corollary, a good orator, but he is not necessarily expected to be much better than ordinary men in other areas of his life. Hence, perhaps, so much Black joking about the sexual peccadilloes of ministers. Black and Indian values about individuality, moral right, and how individuals ought to behave in the best of all possible worlds are not *very* different and not contradictory. But the emphasis placed on one aspect or another of moral right or on a particular value in any given context does vary and, in this case, can result in different conceptions of leadership and different behavior on the part of leaders and followers. Such variation in values and ideas feeds into the historical role of the church in both communities and into their different community structures.

Black and Indian leadership differences were recognized by Whites, who commented on the cooperation they saw among Black leaders and between Black leaders and their followers, in contrast to the apparent testiness between Indian leaders and their followers, which so often led to fragmentation. One White politician claimed that whereas he could be assured of a bloc vote from certain Black leaders, he could never depend on such a vote from Indians. He said there were no Indian leaders who could produce enough votes to make bargaining with them worthwhile. "Indians," he asserted, "will split their votes no matter what."

The separate styles of Black and Indian leadership are embedded in very differently organized communities. Blacks in Robeson County had several highly organized centers of activity, one in each of the larger towns. The ministers of the most important churches in each of the towns were political leaders, men who were accustomed to organizing their people. A Black leader, whether a minister or not, had a respected place in his locality and usually an income not directly dependent on local Whites. The Black population in each town could, through the leaders there, be mobilized for activity, sometimes integrating nearby country Blacks into its network. By 1967, Black organizations in one or two towns had demonstrated effective action in attaining goals set within their own locality. In one case, a successful Black boycott of businesses persuaded White businessmen to hire Blacks. In another, a Black town councilman had been elected. The Black leaders from one town know those from another and have demonstrated their ability to cooperate, despite the rivalries for paramount influence among them. They are aided in their efforts by followers who, when they share a similar perception of a situation, can act in concert.

The multicentered Black community with its several organized foci may be contrasted with the Indian community, which has a single but unorganized center. Pembroke, the Indian town, is located in the center of the county, and is also often used as a symbol for the Indian community as a whole (to outsiders), a showcase for Indian achievements in the arts, education, and business. Although Pembroke does have a high concentration of Indian-owned and -managed businesses, Indian schools, and the formerly Indian college, it is in some ways less highly organized politically than many rural areas. In Pembroke, many leaders are vying for followers, thereby creating rich soil for factionalism. Indeed, intense factional activity is characteristic of Pembroke even more than of other Indian areas.

Indians live mostly in the rural areas of the county, unlike Blacks, most of whom live in towns. There are several named rural localities that are singled out by Indians as containing particularly heavy concentrations of Indians. Each of these localities – such as Saddletree, Magnolia, Prospect, and Alfordsville – has several leaders, who also compete with one another and with the leaders of other localities. Rivalry has grown up between Pembroke and the other Indian areas, a rivalry that is expressed most vividly and sometimes violently (in fist fights, for example) in encounters between young Indian men from different areas. The older men who have become political leaders usually content themselves with verbal disputes. Unlike the Black community, nowhere is the Indian community highly organized, unified, or cooperative. Many people attend churches regularly and even fervently, but Indian churches do not operate today as other than religious institutions. Indian ministers cooperate with one another, but for planning such events as revival meetings, not political gatherings. What holds the Indian community together is not interlocking formal organizations.

One result of emphasis on entrepreneurial political leadership, moral individualism, and a lack of formal organization linking the Indian localities together is rampant factionalism, except when some clear-cut threat to the Indian community is perceived. Then, there is a coalescence of Indian public opinion and, often, concerted action. There have been dramatic examples of this kind of behavior widely approved by Indian opinion, as we have seen in the Henry Berry Lowry band's activities and in the 1958 Indian reaction to the Ku Klux Klan. But two minor incidents occurred while I was in Robeson County that, on a smaller scale, elicited the same response. Both were interpreted by many Indians as threatening the status and well-being of their people, generally provoked anger, and produced considerable moral and some material support for the central figures. In each incident, however, only a few Indians were very active in their support.

One incident culminated in court, where an Indian man was accused of being drunk and disorderly and resisting arrest and a White woman of drunken driving, and "resisting the discharge of an officer's duty." The couple had filed a countersuit against several White officers. Both were middle-aged and had been riding in a car together with a couple of young Indian men when they were stopped by a White state trooper, who took them to the jail in Lumberton. The case was complicated, but essentially the Indians who became active supporters of the Indian man and the White woman said that they felt the two had been arrested because they were an interracial couple. Some even added that they thought the woman had previously dated a relative of the White trooper, and that the trooper "just couldn't stand to see her with an Indian."

The couple claimed that they had been beaten by the arresting trooper and some fellow officers, and had fought back. The beatings were interpreted by many Indians as further evidence of police harassment. In court, the officers did not deny that they had beaten the two, but claimed that the couple had started the fighting. Throughout the couple's trial, most Whites referred to the White woman defendant as "Mrs. ———" and to the Indian man by his first name. In discussing the case, Indians did not seem concerned about the nature of the charges, but focused on the treatment of the couple by the troopers. Indians from various economic backgrounds and political persuasions actively supported the two defendants and many others voiced their sympathy and encouragement for the couple. Although no one mentioned it explicitly, it could be argued that, by their actions, the White troopers were seen as attempting to erode an unofficial but locally accepted Indian "right" to date and marry Whites unmolestedly, a "right" denied Blacks.

The second incident involved a crippled Indian youth who stopped at a gasoline station owned by a White man who was also a city councilman in a "White" town. According to an account in the Indian-owned newspaper, which derived from an interview with the Indian youth, he had asked to use the restroom, and the White owner became angry when the Indian did not immediately reappear. As the Indian left the restroom, he allegedly was stopped by the owner, who then kicked him and shouted imprecations and insults.[6] Two actions followed the incident. First, a group of young Indian men went to the service station and reportedly "messed it up," letting the owner know that they were retaliating for the kicking incident and threatening him with physical violence if he ever abused an Indian again ("We told him we'd cut his head off"). And second, the Indian brought suit against the owner. Again, a few Indians participated actively in support of the young Indian man, and Indian public opinion was stoutly against the White for having attacked the Indian. Neither of the suits filed by Indians in these two incidents was successful.

This concerted, angry, and sometimes violent defensive Indian response is triggered by what Indians see as attacks on Indians as a people, on their Indianness. Denials of Indian identity (as Indians see it) or threats to Indian status tend to unite Indian opinion and to some degree Indian action. Since Indians claim that they are a "mean" people, a people who stand up for themselves to Whites, it would not be in keeping with that conception to ignore overt threats and insults. Notably, only Whites appear to evoke this united, hostile response, either because Blacks do not insult and threaten or because they are not perceived by Indians as directly threatening. Blacks are, however, perceived by many Indians to be an indirect threat, insofar as Whites try to lump Indians and Blacks together and to treat them both in the same insulting way. This is why, for many years, Indians have refused to marry Blacks (those who do are ostracized from the Indian community) or to attend Black schools. It is important that as Blacks have successfully demanded and obtained better treatment from Whites, relations between Blacks and Indians have improved. Indians have increased respect for Blacks as they stand up for themselves, and have less to fear from being lumped with them under the neutral term "non-White" as Blacks are treated less badly by Whites.

Blacks' reactions to insult and even attacks from Whites are very different from Indians'. In Robeson County, Blacks simply do not retaliate either directly or violently. In nearby Monroe, North Carolina, when Blacks did take up guns defensively, it did not, in the end, go well for them. In the summer of 1957, not long before the Indians broke up the Ku Klux Klan rally in Robeson, a group of Blacks from Monroe led by Robert Williams "shot up an armed motorcade of the Ku Klux Klan, *including two police cars,* which had come to attack the home of Dr. Albert E. Perry, vice-president of the Monroe chapter of the National Association for the Advancement of Colored People [NAACP]" (Robert Williams 1962:39). Williams maintains:

The lawful authorites of Monroe and North Carolina acted to enforce order *only after, and as a direct result of, our being armed.* Previously they had connived with the Ku Klux Klan in the racist violence against our people. Self-defense prevented bloodshed and forced the law to establish order [1962:41].

Monroe is in southern North Carolina, about midway between Charlotte and Pembroke. In 1957, this county seat reportedly had a population of 11,000, of which about one-quarter were Blacks (Robert Williams 1962:50; see p. 4 "errata"). Williams and other veterans returned from Korea began to revitalize the dwindling membership of the local chapter of the NAACP, and had successfully pressed for integrating the public library. When they began demanding access to the local swimming pool, having been told that a separate swimming pool could not be promised the Black community, the Ku Klux Klan swung into action. Although the NAACP asked only that Blacks be allowed to swim on one or two separate days each week, they were denied their request, and so began a campaign of brief stand-ins as Blacks repeatedly asked for admission (Robert Williams 1962:52–3). When the Klan began intimidating individual Blacks and Black appeals for protection failed to bring aid, Williams wrote to the National Rifle Association requesting a charter, which was granted. Finally, when a Klan motorcade reportedly attacked another Black leader's house, the armed Blacks repelled the Klan with gunfire (Robert Williams 1962:57). The immediate outcome, Williams states, was that the Klan "stopped raiding our community" and some laws began being enforced (1962:57).

However, in the long run, the policy of violent self-defense for the Blacks of Monroe was crushed. One of the Black leaders, a local doctor, was convicted of performing illegal abortions and thereby lost his license to practice medicine. Williams says that the doctor was Catholic, and that testimony in his favor was given by a man who had been the head of the county medical department, who said that the Black doctor had refused to file sterilization permits on the grounds that it was against his religious beliefs (1962:58). Williams himself, as is widely known, was accused of kidnapping and, fearing that he could not get a fair trial and that he might be killed before being brought to trial, fled the country in 1961. He maintains that he had taken a White couple into his home for their own protection after they had driven into an angry Black community during a period of severe racial tensions. Some Blacks claimed that they had seen this couple earlier in a Klan caravan driving through the Negro neighborhood (Robert Williams 1962:84–90). When local police closed in, they failed to find Williams, who eventually made his way to Cuba. He finally returned to the United States in 1969 Robert Cohen 1972:357). Here, Black armed self-defense ultimately failed to protect Black leaders and brought to the Black community increased harassment from Whites. In the Indian case, armed self-defense increased White respect for the Indians and did not result in retaliation against Indians.

Williams points out one possible reason for the difference in White reactions, as he seeks to explain why the White press virtually ignored the Blacks' attack against the Klan, while the Indians' encounter with them was splashed in headlines across the country:

The national press played up the Indian–Klan fight because they didn't consider this a great threat – the Indians are a tiny minority and people could laugh at the incident as a sentimental joke – but no one wanted Negroes to get the impression that this was an accepted way to deal with the Klan. So the white press maintained a complete blackout about the Monroe fight [Robert Williams 1962:57–8].

Certainly in Robeson County itself, Blacks have traditionally been more vulnerable than Indians to direct White retaliation. At first, they lived interspersed among Whites and did not have swamps into which they could retreat and lie low. Later, they were economically more dependent on Whites than Indians were. Instead of direct, violent confrontation, Blacks in Robeson have used legal methods and nonviolent tactics to gain their ends. As Blacks have succeeded with these, Indians have also come to adopt them or to use them more often.

An example may make the contrast in Robeson County clear. Shortly after I settled in Pembroke, some Blacks had gone to a restaurant run by Whites that did not serve Blacks. Reportedly, when the Blacks asked for food, Whites threw ammonia in their faces. Rather than retaliate with further violence, which Indians probably would have done, the Blacks contacted a lawyer and filed suit while Black leaders helped to cool tempers. In the kicking incident, several Indian men had retaliated by "messing up" the White's service station while Indian leaders tried to keep them from physically harming the White. Only then did the Indian file a lawsuit against the White.

In the past, there have been several reasons for Indians' reluctance to go to court. One is that judges and juries are predominantly White. Another is that until 1972 there were no Lumbee lawyers licensed to practice in Robeson County. Blacks have had access to Black lawyers for a much longer time and can more easily obtain good experienced lawyers, often through the NAACP. Indians have been reluctant to use Black lawyers because they felt that so doing might prejudice White judges and juries against them even more than the usual amount. In this they may have been correct, for if Indians had Black lawyers, it might suggest to Whites that an alliance many fear is becoming a reality. Indians could, and sometimes did, hire White lawyers, but often felt that White lawyers could not be fully trusted because, it was said, they might just decide to "make a deal" with those White judges and the other White lawyers. Finally, many Indians simply cannot afford legal assistance. In the 1970s, the legal situation has changed dramatically. Whereas in 1967 there were no Indian lawyers practicing in Robeson County, in 1977, ten years later, there are seven. Also in the 1970s, Indians have turned increasingly to the kinds of lawsuits brought so successfully by Blacks (e.g., the "Double-Voting Suit," and the "Prospect Suit").

During the 1967–68 coalition movement, some Indians were explicitly beginning to define themselves as sharing some of the same problems Blacks have. They began, in political contexts, to refer to themselves as "non-Whites" and even "un-Whites." They had long explicitly defined themselves (in part) as "not Black" and are now explicitly stressing the "not White" aspect of their identity. Until recently, Indians had no need to stress the "not White," because Whites stressed it so strongly. But now, the disappearance of many institutionalized forms of segregation and increased intermarriage with Whites, combined with a realization of shared problems with Blacks, have led Indians to emphasize what Blacks and Indians have in common – the fact that they have been and still are being discriminated against by Whites because of their respective "races."

Both "not White" and "not Black" have, during at least the more than 100 years for which there are substantive records, been components of Indian identity. But the emphasis is in the process of changing from "not Black" to "non-White." This represents a significant alteration from the period when Indians were terribly concerned to define themselves as having nothing in common with Blacks – not "blood," behavior, or political aims. Before the Civil War, "not Black" meant "free" and "never slaves" to Indians. Afterward, it came to mean "having our own name and our own schools" and "not marrying Blacks." With the coming of the Jim Crow laws, about 1900, "not Black" came progressively to mean being assigned separate facilities and accorded separate treatment in racial etiquette. As the social context has changed with the civil rights movements in the 1950s and 1960s, the distinction between Black and Indian imposed from the outside has lessened, and Indians have focused more on behavioral differences between the groups as distinguishing features, such as different responses to White intimidation. "Not Black" is now less a part of Indians' public presentation of themselves and "not White" more a part. They have already established themselves as "not Black" in the eyes of Blacks and Whites, and now want to emphasize to others that they are "not White" either.

In 1967–68, Indians were still divided among themselves in their attitudes toward Blacks. Some Indians spoke about Blacks in denigrating ways, much as many Whites did. These Indians did not, by and large, participate in coalition activities. But the spectrum of opinion was wide, and there were many who did not wish to associate socially with Blacks but who maintained that Blacks were being badly treated by Whites and had a right to better conditions and treatment. Still others (among them, most of those in the coalition) sought to forge a new relationship with Blacks, and fought, more or less successfully, the old prejudice against Blacks.[7] In all, there must have been hundreds of

Indians active to some degree in the coalition. It remains to be seen how much and in what ways Indian concepts of their identity will be altered by their political involvements, but some changes are already under way.

One of the stylistic differences between Blacks and Indians is that Blacks much more frequently than Indians invoke biblical examples and language in their discussions and exhortations. Brotherhood was, for Blacks, a powerful and often-appealed-to image, representing their sense of community, which they now were attempting to extend to Indians, their strong ethic of looking after one another, and the biblical sanction for this.[8] Indians rarely used such imagery, emphasizing instead the common political plight of Blacks and Indians – powerlessness – perhaps because "brotherhood" suggested a more intimate connection between the two communities, with overtones of a "blood" bond they have been forced to deny. Although Indians were apparently not offended by the appeals to brotherhood and did not reject them, they did not frame their own arguments and pleas in terms of it.

A religiously based appeal cannot be rejected out of hand by either Indians or Blacks, because members of both communities, whether active church members or not, take religion seriously. Both communities have many churches and "preachers," most of which are fundamentalist and Protestant. One of the differences between them lies in how they relate religion to political action. Indians tended to separate religious and political activities, and a few Indian ministers even told their congregations that they should not participate in any way, even to vote. These men had not been "bought off" by Whites, and I never heard anyone say that they had been. Rather, they simply seemed to believe in the "rightness" of their stand. The rationale behind this position was a variation on the "If God had intended such-and-such to happen, it would happen" theme.

A middle-aged, middle-class Indian provided an example of this rationale in a discussion about religion with two Northern White men:

> "The Bible tells us what is true and what isn't true," he said. "Everything is foreordained. The Bible is absolute, not relative. The Devil is what makes things bad: God makes things good. Because everything is foreordained, there's no point in trying to change things. If God wants things changed, He'll change them."
> In the ensuing interchange, one of the White men pursued the problem of activism further, asking, "If, on a Sunday, you could either help someone or go to church, what would you do?"
> The Indian queried, "You mean I couldn't do both?" to which the reply was, "No." After giving the matter some thought, the Indian decided, "I'd go to church because the Lord requires that you honor him above all."

This discussion reflects an especially extreme form of fundamentalist conservatism that, although it was not common, occurred frequently enough to create problems for activist organizers. If taken literally and seriously, this rationale makes politics 'both unnecessary and even wrong, because it would be presumptuous of mere men to try to accomplish things that God has not ordained.

Indians often consider politics and politicians to be dishonest, immoral, and serving the petty interests of man, not the higher ones of God. People who actively associate themselves with politics can become tainted by baseness. Good religious people will try to resist sin and will not abet the inevitable sins of politicians by participating in politics. Attitudes such as these create another barrier to increased political participation among Indians.

For Blacks, there is neither a rigid separation between religion and politics nor an idea that politics is sinful as such. Although Gary Marx found that the more time Blacks spent in church, the less time they spent on politics (Marx 1967:100), in Robeson County, most politically active Blacks were also church activists and were certainly, in their own eyes, believing religious people. Unlike Indians, most Blacks were of the "God helps them who helps themselves" persuasion rather than the "If God had intended . . ." view.

Both Indians and Blacks who were involved in coalition politics applied moral, religiously sanctioned standards to their political behavior. For example, they were concerned to act uprightly themselves and to be "fair" to Whites. As one Indian put it at an Indian and Black coalition meeting:

> "They're [the Whites] afraid that we'll do them like they've done us. All Black's as bad as all White – we just want a share. We don't want it all, just a little piece of it. They think we want to take over the county."

Indeed, in one or two instances where non-Whites were successful in gaining control of Democratic Party precinct committees, they elected a couple of Whites to the committees, and in one case chose a White as one of the two most important offices. They did this explicitly to show that they would not behave toward Whites as they saw Whites behave toward them. This attitude has clear roots in the biblical injunction to "do unto others as you would have them do unto you."

Another frequent concern was honesty. Because politics so often appeared to require lying, both Blacks and Indians expressed concern that individuals maintain high standards of personal honesty. Indians urged one another not to commit themselves to any particular candidate, in order to avoid pressure from Whites. One could listen to arguments for a candidate, but should not give one's word to vote for a candidate and then not do it. A few more pragmatic Indians advocated taking a White politician's money and then voting according to the heart (for a non-White candidate), but these suggestions were not well received, as many Indians and Blacks interpreted such behavior as lying, an immoral or sinful act.

> In a precinct meeting, an Indian leader maintained, "We have to get out and talk to people in the community, because people are scared. If you have to take a man's money, you can take it and still vote how you want." The most prominent Black leader in the precinct responded disapprovingly with, "That would be a lie." To which the Indian replied, "I don't mean people *should* take money, I never would. But if they *have* to, then they can do what they want anyway."

Political cynicism is not an approved mode of thought and behavior for most Indians and Blacks.

Indian–Black tensions

Finally, the meeting described here reveals some of the tensions between Indians and Blacks that make creating a coalition difficult. One Indian candidate became slightly nettled at the Indian chairman's hint that a proposed Black candidate had done well by the group in withdrawing his candidacy because his chances of winning were slim. The Indian candidate did not like either the Indian chairman's implicit criticism or the implied invidious distinction between himself and the Black candidate. The same Indian candidate was the target of a Black candidate's criticism. The Black was annoyed because the Indian had announced his candidacy sooner than the date the candidates had agreed upon.

In instances like this where some specific act or incident provoked Black mistrust and anger, Blacks usually confronted Indians directly. In a precinct meeting, a Black leader confronted the Indians present with an example of Indian prejudice against Blacks:

> In response to discussion among the Indians about how divided they were, the Black leader said, "Now, the Negroes are split too." He then explained that he and some other Negroes had applied to join the Lumbee Recreation Center, an Indian-owned and -managed park with boating, bathing, and golfing facilities, but their money was sent back. "I've looked very carefully at the board of directors, and there isn't a single Negro name on it, but there are some Whites. Now some Negroes think all Indians are like that. Now, I don't think that, but some do." Several Indians immediately expressed disapproval of what had happened at the Recreation Center, and one commented, "If they

used federal funds, it should be public, it shouldn't be segregated."
Other Indians protested that while some Indians are like that, not all
are.

At another precinct meeting, two Blacks had arrived in an openly angry
mood, furious that they had been left out of the school board nomination meeting and blaming one or two Indian leaders for failing to communicate the time and place of the meeting, which they characterized
as a deliberate omission. The Indian leaders were not present at the
meeting, and the Indians who were present hastened to disavow the
behavior of the leaders and to express their own solidarity with Blacks.

Indians expressed their distrust of Blacks much more obliquely.
Rather than bringing up the subject of their immediate concern, they
would, for example, mention an incident unrelated to any of the Blacks
in the coalition in which Blacks betrayed Indians by siding with
Whites. In one meeting, an Indian remarked upon the case of a Black
leader in a nearby town, a man not active in the coalition, "who is a
traitor and who is in with the Lumberton gang. He's a disgrace to his
race and to the county." Here, Lumberton, the county seat, is used to
stand for "the White power structure." Such indirect references usually served to heighten tensions between the two groups, whereas the
more direct challenges by Blacks tended to release them, at least temporarily. I did not witness or hear about any instances in the coalition
meetings where Indians thought that they had been insulted or
threatened by Blacks.

However, such an instance did occur just after a rally in Lumberton
for the 1968 Black candidate for governor. As I returned from the rally
in a carload of Indians, one Indian fumed about an encounter he had
had with a Black minister as everyone walked away from the rally.

> The Indian had encountered a Black minister. He said the minister
> claimed that the minister's father was a Cherokee Indian, his grand-
> mother on his mother's side was a Negro, and his mother's father was
> a White man. The Indian then understood the minister to assert that
> his father used to say, "Where the Lumbees come from, there were
> Negroes they started up from." The Indian was furious, called the
> minister a liar and said, "If I wasn't feeling so good tonight, I would
> have popped him one. I get mad when anyone talks that way. I'm an
> Indian and proud of it – but I don't think I'm better'n anybody else. I
> just can't stand for someone to grind it into me." He went on to say
> that he knew the Lumbee had come from the lost colony. "Some got
> lost, some intermarried, but the names were the same – Lowry and
> Oxendine. And Locklear – that's Scotch."
>
> Another Indian spoke up, expressing surprise at the incident be-
> cause he had heard the minister too, but had heard him differently. "I
> thought he said his father said that the Lumbee got started from 'his
> people' and they must have just drifted down there." Since the minis-

ter's father was a Cherokee, "his people" would then be Indians, not
Negroes. The first Indian remained unconvinced of the other's interpretation.

Here the first Indian considered himself insulted by what he took to be
an imputation that Lumbees have Negro ancestry. And his response
was verbal – to call the man a liar to his face. Such a direct insult as
calling someone a liar would probably have resulted in a fight if directed toward another Indian, but the Black shrugged it off. This kind
of interchange was relatively rare, especially among those working for
the movement. Notably, the Indian who responded so angrily was one
of the few Indian members of the NAACP and one of the few actively
to support the Black candidate for governor. He was firmly committed
to the success of the coalition and worked very hard to attain it. He was
a hot-tempered person, which accounts more for his reaction than anything else.

Both Indian and Black leaders worried about maintaining smooth
working relations with one another. At a countywide meeting, an Indian candidate reminded those gathered that they should focus on their
common goals, and not be distracted from those goals by too much
concentration on their relations with each other, by telling the following story:

> "A Negro came into town one day to catch a bus for Selma, Alabama,
> to go to a big demonstration. While he's waiting for that bus, he steps
> on a scale to weigh himself. The scale gives out a little card, and on it
> it says, 'You're a Negro, you weigh 130 pounds, and you're waiting
> for a bus to take to Selma, Alabama, for the demonstration.' He was
> mighty surprised, so when he sees an Indian coming down the street
> with his blanket on, he calls him over and tells him about it. So the
> Indian gets on the scale, and the scale prints out a card which says,
> 'You're an Indian, you weigh 160 pounds, and you were minding your
> own business before that Negro called you over here.' They were
> both puzzled, so finally the Negro borrows the Indian's blanket and
> steps on the scale. The card this time says, 'You're still a Negro, you
> still weigh 130 pounds, and you were on your way to Selma, Alabama,
> to demonstrate, and you've fooled around with that Indian so long
> you've missed your bus.' Let's don't miss the bus."

In attempting to promote good working relations between them,
most Indians and Blacks in the coalition behaved toward one another in
what each considered a very polite manner. The problem was that what
Indians thought polite, Blacks sometimes did not, but because it was
clear that good will and not slight was intended, Blacks bore the gaffes
relatively well. By the same token, Blacks sometimes inadvertently, in
an attempt to be polite, offended Indians, who also chose not to make
issues of these mistakes. Such errors of understanding, however, had

the effect of erecting yet another barrier (or reinforcing those already present) to the development of relaxed and trusting closeness between Blacks and Indians. Neither group relaxed its watchfulness and wariness in dealing with the other.

In this chapter, I have examined the goals, strategy, and accomplishments of the 1967–68 coalition movement against a background of values, concepts, and beliefs that mold political behavior and of social organizational features in terms of which political activity occurs. The coalition between Blacks and Indians marked the beginning of a new period of electoral gains for both groups and of a changing emphasis in the concept of Indianness for Indians. More and more Indians are beginning to fit their concept of who they are into the general category "non-White," which they share with Blacks. This contrasts strongly with their earlier insistence on their "not Black" identity, which they shared with Whites. Both have always been present, but the emphasis has shifted. "Not Black" and "non-White" do not exhaust the content of Indian identity. They are both different expressions of it that continually appear publicly when they are in contact with people of other races. There is also a positive "we Indian" element to Indian identity, which will be discussed at length in the next chapter.

5. Who do they say they are?

Indians' ideas about who they are and what kind of people they are have been an important driving force behind their political behavior. When their view of themselves has been challenged or threatened, Indians have responded with one or another mode of political action, whether defending themselves violently, lobbying for favorable laws, instituting lawsuits, or registering voters. They have also tended to interpret threats to their social and economic well-being as threats to their identity. In order to understand more about why they react as they do and how matters come to be conceived as threats to Indian identity, one must know what their identity constructs are and (insofar as there is evidence) what they have been.

But the question "Wherein does Lumbee Indian identity lie?" does not have an obvious answer in a situation where everyone, Lumbees and most neighbors alike, speaks English, is Christian, works at similar occupations, and lives in a house that resembles those inhabited by others. Lumbees have no "exotic" rituals, dances, songs, or crafts, nor do they dress distinctively. To make matters worse, Indians articulate coherently only one aspect of their group identity, which means that part of it is not obvious (in any organized way) to Lumbees themselves. It is the burden of this chapter to uncover and make explicit the Indians' sometimes obscure notions about who they are as a people and how they express these notions.

How do Indians talk about themselves?

There are two major aspects of Indian identity. One is an articulate, well-formulated aspect, which is essentially an explanation, an intellectual account of the origins of the group couched in terms that are meaningful to relevant outsiders, such as local Whites and people in the federal bureaucracy. The second aspect is inarticulately expressed and

134

only loosely or ill-formulated, an often unselfconscious moral and emotional blueprint of "who we are."

An intellectual account

The well-formulated account of "who we are" is always quite self-consciously presented, to outsiders and to other Indians. Today, most Indians recite McMillan's theory of the Roanoke lost colony origins as fact. They have apparently been doing this since McMillan's theory was advanced in the middle 1880s. Whether they simply adopted this convenient story because it was helpful to their cause or whether it was widely adopted because it fit many features of their own oral tradition, as McMillan claims, or for both reasons, is difficult to say on the basis of evidence now available. There is no known record of an Indian version of their origins before McMillan's (1888).

The lost colony account of the origins of the group is more than a colorful story. It makes important claims in ways that are especially potent to a White Southern audience. For example, the autochthonous "we were here first" declaration of Indian ancestry is augmented by a claim of ancestry from the first White settlers as well, which argues for doubly original status.

McMillan posited that the Roanoke colonists, who had presumably departed to Croatoan with their friendly Indian neighbors, were eventually forced to move inland and southward by hostile Indians, finally settling along the Lumber River, where early Scottish settlers found them. When the Scots encountered them, the Indians were said to be living in houses similar to those of Whites, speaking an obsolete dialect of English, cultivating the soil, and owning slaves. The dual origin from Whites and Indians thus also "explains" the lack of distinctively "Indian" social and cultural features reported by the White settlers. Presumably, the Indians gave up their indigenous habits to emulate the Europeans, a view flattering to Whites. That this is what happened is also suggested by McMillan's version of a speech given by "an old Indian, named George Lowrie," in 1864 and recounted by McMillan in 1888: "In order to be great like the English, we took the white man's language and religion, for our people were told they would prosper if they would take white men's laws" (1888:17). Today, Indians say, "We never had tribal ways," meaning that there are no preserved traditions that are usually thought to be associated with "tribes." The lost colony story also in effect accounts for the physical appearance of the Indians – their great variety of physical type – by pointing to an early mixture of Indian with White "blood."

Finally, sometimes a claim to nobility on one or both sides is made. It is said that one of the children who came to America with the soon-to-be-lost colonists was the offspring of Sir Walter Raleigh and Elizabeth Throgmorton, one of Queen Elizabeth I's ladies-in-waiting. This child's name is supposed to have been Henry Berry (Lucas and Groome 1940:vii–ix; Lowrey 1960:9, 29). On the Indian side, the nobility comes from Manteo, an Indian who had been taken from Roanoke to England by the earlier Amidas and Barlowe (1584) expedition and who was returned to Roanoke with Raleigh's colony. Manteo was created Lord of Roanoke. It is with Manteo's people that the lost colonists are said to have amalgamated (McMillan 1888:2–9; L. Barton 1967:20–1).

This "history" speaks with great appeal to Southern Whites, who are past-conscious and genealogy-constructing. The story is a compelling blend of Romanticism, light and dark nobility, and pre-Mayflower settlement. And it has perhaps special resonance in Robeson County, where so many White settlers are of Scottish ancestry, for the Indian claims are to English ancestry – in England, at least, of higher status than Scottish ancestry.

Although the lost colony origin story was attractive and even convincing to local Whites, federal bureaucrats have generally found it less plausible (McPherson 1915 is a notable exception). They prefer written documentation, and the lost colony story is sketchy and full of holes at best, particularly for the period between the disappearance of the colony at Roanoke Island in the 1500s and the appearance of Lumbee ancestors in what is now Robeson County in the 1700s. That is partly why the Robeson Indians have made additional formal claims of infusions from other Indian populations – in the hopes that this ancestry will be more acceptable to bureaucrats and more demonstrable to historians. And, partly, these claims represent various Indians' attempts to satisfy themselves about where they came from.

As we have seen, both Indians and historians disagree about what name most accurately reflects the ancestry of the group. Indians have devoted a great amount of political energy to the question of what name best represents their people. The "Tuscaroras" are evidence that such controversy and its attendant political activity continues in the Indian community. But documentation for all the proposed Indian antecedents remains problematic, and such reasoned voices as Dean Chavers's, a Lumbee Indian, are fundamentally unsatisfying to anyone who desires a single, straightforward, and uncomplex "answer." Chavers states:

The truth of the Lumbee origins (which will probably never be settled satisfactorily because of the paucity of written documents) is probably that *all*

the theoretical population sources contributed to the present population
[emphasis in original; 1971–72:12].

Linked to the origin stories, which serve both as a "charter" in
Malinowski's sense, and as an explanation for some of the obviously
problematic aspects of the group, is the Lumbee presentation of themselves as a progressive people. There is pride in recounting that "we
have come from there to here," improving life along the way. Both
origin stories and the image of progress are, I think, designed to speak
to outsiders in terms of White middle-class values. They also speak to
those Indians who share the values of independence, upward mobility,
and "respectability." Indians know that Whites often respond favorably to evidence of Indian "improvement" in wealth, education, and
gentility.

For many years, Indians have proudly announced their "progressiveness." In 1898, the Reverend J. J. Blanks, an Indian minister,
called attention to the progress his people had made because of their access to education (Blanks in McMillan 1898:35). Clifton Oxendine, for
many years a teacher at Pembroke State College, pointed in 1934 to
progress in the improved economic status of many Indians, the steady
upgrading of scholastic standards at the Indian Normal School, an increase in the number of Indians to receive advanced degrees, and the
acquisition of more land by Indians (1934:56–61). Clarence Lowrey, a
Lumbee, remarks, "The Lumbees have made remarkable progress in
the social and economic world particularly in the past fifty years"
(1960:59). Lew Barton, also a Lumbee writer, points to improvements
in education (1967:136–7), and historians Adolph Dial (a Lumbee) and
David Eliades report gains on all fronts from business to politics to
education (1975:141–72).

A virtue of "progress" is that it can be counted both a moral and an
economic good. Lumbee "progressiveness" at once sets them apart (in
their own eyes) from reservation Indians, accounts for the differences
between them, and gives Lumbees moral merit if not a traditional kind
of "Indianness." In a recent flurry of statements in the *Carolina Indian
Voice,* the theme of "progress" was reiterated.

[Detroit Michigan, is a city where many Lumbees live. One of the newspapers
there carried an article which portrayed the Lumbee in terms offensive to
them, characterizing them as a backward people and as a racial mixture of
Negro, Indian, and White. Mr. and Mrs. Gerald D. Locklear, Lumbees living
in Michigan, reacted with a letter to the offending Detroit newspaper, which
was also printed in the Lumbee newspaper. The letter stated, in part:]
"I happen to be a Lumbee Indian and feel your article is a slap in the face about
my people. We are not a small number of people in the South, and a racial
mixture of Negro, White and Indian as you imply. We are a proud people of
Indian ancestry.

"Do you have to be a government ward or tribe to be identified as an Indian? It seems to me you are ignorant of the facts of Indians and have everyone stereo-typed as reservation Indians. If you would check the records you would find the Lumbee Indians to be the most progressive Indians any place in the U.S.A."

[In the same issue of the Lumbee newspaper, Adolph Dial told an interviewer:] "All of our blood runs red. Purity of race, and that includes whites, simply does not exist. She [the Detroit reporter] misses the whole point that Lumbee Indians are proud and progressive folk and that they have clung to their heritage against insurmountable odds."

[The editor of the Indian newspaper further asserted,] "We are free and progressive and proud of our heritage and accomplishments" [*Carolina Indian Voice,* 1977:6].

Of all the accomplishments pointed to with pride, educational improvements are perhaps the most frequently cited and the most actively sought after. Indeed, educational goals have produced a great amount of Indian political activity from 1885 until the present. Improved education has come to symbolize high status, prestige, "progressiveness," opportunity for improvement, upward mobility, and community pride. Better educational opportunities have enabled a segment of the Lumbee to become solidly middle class. By obtaining a separate school system, the Indians established themselves visibly and firmly as separate people and at the same time were able to institute some local controls. Although Indians could not govern how much money was allocated to their educational system (they could only lobby), they could, through local school committees, Normal School and college trustees, and Indian teachers and principals, control much of what went on at individual schools. For the most part, teachers were hired and fired by school committees, unless a particular teacher had aroused the animosity of Whites in positions of influence or power. In such cases, the County Board of Education, until the 1970s dominated by Whites, might veto the hiring or promotion of a troublesome individual.

The Lumbee today see themselves as a people who have made great educational progress, and who have struggled hard to provide opportunities for their children. When the 1970 Nixon desegregation guidelines required more than token integration in Robeson County schools, many Indians were disturbed by the prospect of losing even their small measure of control over local schools. It was around this issue that the breakaway "Tuscarora" group of Robeson County Indians organized themselves to protest the loss of Indian control. Helen Schierbeck, a Lumbee Indian working for the U.S. Office of Education in Washington, D.C., outlined Indian concern for education and their progress toward better educational opportunities.

"The Lumbee Indians feel the desegregation plan [for total desegregation throughout the South, to be accomplished by busing] is discriminatory against them, will destroy the Indian public schools which they built themselves and to which their identity and heritage is inextricably bound, and will unnecessarily bus their children long distances across the county to schools not close to their homes. . . .

"(3) They began their own school systems in 1887. Land was given by local Indian people, the school building was constructed by local people, and teachers were hired from the outside by local people and brought into the community to teach.

"(4) Today there are 10,000 Indian children in the county public schools attending 4 Indian high schools and 6 Indian elementary schools. Some 400 Indians are the teachers and administrators in these schools.

"(5) The Indian school facilities are worth in excess of 10 million dollars today. These schools have been brought up to this level by the hard work of the Lumbee people themselves. They raised through box suppers and other fund-raising activities over a million dollars in this last quarter of a century to bring their schools up to standard.

"(6) A national survey of Indian education funded by U.S.O.E. [U.S. Office of Education] has stated that Lumbee Indian students stay in school longer and achieve on a more equal part with non-Indian students because of the Indian teachers and administrators.[1]

"American Indian community development, in terms of the creation of their own institutions, like schools, businesses, and churches, must be permitted the freedom to organize and maintain their identity, until they feel free to move in other directions. To do otherwise will thwart the true meaning of democracy" [*The Robesonian* 1970b:1,2].

Indian teachers and parents are still contributing to their schools in a number of ways. Teachers frequently have to clean their own schoolrooms, because funds are not provided for adequate custodial services. The allocation for school supplies is usually low (in one case, a primary school teacher told me that she has been allowed only $1.25 per pupil per year), so teachers often buy additional supplies with their own funds. Parents and teachers contribute time and money to fund-raising enterprises because many schools lack such basic facilities as playground equipment, which must then be purchased privately. Indians pay for their schools both through county taxes and by private subsidies. The struggle for recognition as Indians has been paralleled by a struggle for improved educational facilities and opportunities, and the two struggles have become so intertwined that, for Lumbees today, educational achievements are part of their identity as Indians.

In addition to the constantly improving schools, perhaps symbolized best for Indians in the changing status of the original "Croatan Normal School" to Pembroke Indian College, Pembroke State College, and finally, to Pembroke State University, other achievements are cited as indicators of Lumbee progress: an increase in the number of professionals, the publication of an Indian newspaper, the increasing number of Indian businesses and Indians holding elected office, and, more recently, the founding of a Lumbee bank (1971) and the opening of a heavily Indian cooperative tobacco warehouse (1977). In earlier years, such accomplishments were viewed by Indians as setting them apart from Blacks; more recently, they have come to be seen as setting them apart from reservation Indians (about whose life most Lumbees know little).

An emotional and moral blueprint

The first aspect of Lumbee identity, then, is composed of a presentation of "where we came from and how far we've gotten from there," of origins and progress, both explicitly couched in terms meaningful to Whites as well as to Indians. By contrast, the second aspect is not explicitly formulated in any coherent whole, but is expressed bit by bit in a variety of contexts.

That Lumbees themselves have difficulty articulating anything but the first aspect of their identity is illustrated in a discussion that took place at the First Convocation of American Indian Scholars between Adolph Dial, an historian and a Lumbee, and several other Indians present:[2]

EMERSON ECKIWARDI [Commanche]: I am Commanche, southwestern Oklahoma. I understand that Lumbees, in addition to a few other tribes, are not recognized as an Indian tribe as we understand it. I am wondering what criteria, if any, were used by the government in not recognizing you people as Indian tribes.

ADOLPH DIAL [Lumbee]: If you're saying: Do you have the Bureau of Indian Affairs there; do [you] have a reservation; do you have the United States Government looking after you, then the answer is no. We do not have them. In 1954, by congressional action, we were recognized as Lumbee Indians.

EMERSON ECKIWARDI: I guess, what I mean specifically, is – for instance – do you have a language of your own? Do you have a special culture?

ADOLPH DIAL: Well, you could get into a definition of a culture. But I know what you are asking. You are saying are Lumbees like Commanche. Right?

EMERSON ECKIWARDI: Yes.

ADOLPH DIAL: And Navajo or some other groups. And I would say that we are quite different. On the other hand, I would like to point out that with all the obstacles, we have been one of the most progressive groups in the United States, and I am not trying to take anything away from anyone. We have in our public schools, out of eight or ten thousand students, about three hundred and fifty Lumbees in Robinson [Robeson] County with college degrees. They are teaching in public schools, and have received their degrees from all over the country. . . .

JEANNETTE HENRY [Eastern Cherokee]: I think the question is being asked: how do you determine that any individual is a Lumbee Indian?

ADOLPH DIAL: Okay, alright. The question is, how do you determine whether an individual is a Lumbee. One writer said once that a Lumbee is what he says he is.[3] How do you like that one?

JEANNETTE HENRY: The question in the minds of the participants is this: If you do not have treaty rights with the United States government; if you do not have a tribal form of society or any vestiges of it; if you do not have a language; if you do not have any parts of your culture remaining . . . if, in other words, you could pass right out of here and become a white man, then what are you? I think this is the crucial point, because the Lumbee may be what everybody else is going to become in twenty or fifty years.

ADOLPH DIAL: We have thirty school systems today. I was a principal of Prospect Union School, grades one through twelve, about seven hundred students. Forty per cent of them were Lockleer [Locklear] and I will give anyone a thousand dollars to show me a Lockleer [Locklear] that doesn't trace back to Robinson [Robeson] County. And those Lockleers [Locklears] are Lumbees, as long ago as ten thousand years. What you are saying, though is that because of our origin, because of our Lost Colony origin, when we lost many things that other tribes have, we may not be considered Indian?

A SPEAKER [probably Lumbee]: We lost, yes, including favor with our own people.

ADOLPH DIAL: I think the important thing is that we share your problems. And I say further, that until all Indians are ready to work together and fight for a common cause, nothing good will come of it. I am sure there is no one in the country today doing any more than the Lumbees for Indian people.

A SPEAKER: Mr. Kaniatobe [Choctaw], I don't think anybody is quite satisfied with the answers being given so far to the question, which is: How do we know we're Indians, and particularly how do the Lumbees know?

ADOLPH DIAL: All right. If you come right down to it, I know you look at me, and you say, you look a little bit Indian. But I can tell you, that you show a little white. Yes! So let's get right down to it. How many, actually how many pure people are left in this country today? Pure Indians? Just like any other group of people, what happens to the Indian when he moves to Chicago or any other urban area. They often intermarry. But the point is *today* – how much significance are you going to put on this thing? The significance is that the American Indian is being mistreated. We need to work together for a common cause. We need to be somebody.

RAY CROSS [Mandan-Hidatsa]: You speak of discrimination, common causes. I think you miss one small point with the problem we are facing in the American Indian in our history. The program in the Historical Society [American Indian Historical Society] is to preserve culture, language, Indian identity, tribal identity. Sure, we can preserve what is left of the Lumbee culture, if you can find it.

ADOLPH DIAL: Yes, you can preserve what is left of it, which is the people who are left.

LEW BARTON [Lumbee]: That is what we are trying to do, and we are fighting for all we are worth. . . .

DON WANATEE [Mesquakie]: The name itself does not make the tribe, because back home we are known as the Tami Indians and we are not Tami Indians. We are not even properly named "Indians," . . . we are the People.

We are Mesquakie People . . . People of the Red Earth. But they continue to call us second class folks – Tami Indians, because we live geographically near Tami. . . . I don't think it's the name, I think it's the person. Like the good man over there said if he's a Lumbee, he's a Lumbee. I believe him.

JEANNETTE HENRY: Well said. There's no doubt that he's a Lumbee, and there is no doubt about the existence of this group of people, that they are Indian people. The tragedy of it is that there is no other way to describe the predicament in which native people find themselves. The Lumbee people are now where they have been for hundreds of years. They have recognized themselves always as Indians. They are mixed. There is so much difference between the Lumbee and Commanche situations that here there is room for other and broader work. But the situation is alike in this sense: the Lumbees are ignored in the literature, just as the Commanches are. I can show you areas in California where the Indians there don't know who they are, yet they know they are Indians. They have been wiped out as tribes during the Gold Rush [*Indian Voices* 1970:120–3].

Here, a Lumbee seeks to explain to other Indians, in terms that they will understand, in what ways the Lumbees are Indians. Many Indians taking part in the discussion sound sympathetic and appear to be trying to understand the perplexing case of Indians who lack identifiably "Indian" culture traits. Dial cites Lumbee origins, their progressiveness, and their Indian "blood." Yet he does not articulate the kinds of things Lumbees say to one another about who they are. In formal situations where they must defend their identity as Indians, Lumbees simply do not argue on the basis of the behavioral characteristics that they identify as "Indian" to one another. For Lumbees, it is essentially a constellation of behavioral characteristics that gives potent meaning to the term "Indian" when they apply it to themselves. The constellation provides a moral and emotional blueprint of "who we are."

These behavioral characteristics are all qualities that imply action – to be visible, to be most meaningful, they must be acted out. They come up, time and time again, in many different situations. They arise sometimes in the context of an Indian describing to outsiders "what Indians are like." At other times, the same characteristics crop up in stories told by one Indian to another, or in gatherings where little attention is paid to a White anthropologist. No one puts them all together, or at least I never heard anyone do it. But a number of Indians who have read earlier attempts to work this argument out have pronounced it valid. One Indian read a paper I wrote on this subject, and when he had finished, he said, "Well, I never thought about it that way before, but it seems all right." We then walked a few blocks to the home of another anthropologist, and when we entered, the Indian was asked what he thought about the paper. He replied, "Oh, it's all right, but there's nothing in it we didn't already know." I took that to be confirmation that I was on the right track.

Just what are these behavioral characteristics that Indians so often apply to themselves? The central ones, so far as I can see, are: pride, "meanness," and cohesiveness (what Indians call "sticking together"). But there are additional characteristics that are also important and help to define a "real Indian": "talking Indian" (speaking a variant of English often described as a "dialect"), keeping one's word, and owning land in Robeson County. All these "behavioral characteristics" function as symbols of Indian identity, as models for ideal behavior, as expressive of the Indian self. Lumbees see themselves as an integral part of a larger society, and their notions about themselves have developed within the context of that larger society. This is not to say that their identity has been "caused" or created by the larger society. Rather, identity is created and maintained through the complex interaction of Indian ideas and activities with those of their neighbors over a period of time.

Pride. At the center of the constellation of behavioral attributes is a quality to which all others are linked and without which none of the others can be said to be "Indian." This quality is pride, claimed by Indians today and ascribed to their behavior by Whites since the earliest substantive reports. A White Robesonian, it will be recalled, told the reporter Townsend in 1872 that Allen Lowry "had a heap of mixed white and Indian pride . . ." (Townsend 1872:48). Of Henry Berry Lowry himself, Townsend states that there were "reports of his proud and unintimidated bearing" while he was in jail under a Republican sheriff (1872:26). McMillan later maintained: "They are a proud race, boasting alike of their English and Indian blood, hospitable to strangers and ever ready to do friendly offices for white people" (1888:21). Indian pride may not have changed, but White interpretation of their "friendliness" had. What is difficult to ascertain from these early reports is whether Indians considered pride an identifying characteristic of their Indianness.

In his 1939 article, Guy B. Johnson records White remarks about Indians:

The white farmers, for their part, recognize this independence of the Indian when they say, "If you want a tenant to take care of your land and make money, get an Indian. *But don't try to boss him.* He wears his pride like a sore thumb" [emphasis in original; G. Johnson 1939:522].

Indians today say of themselves, "We're a proud people," or "I'm an Indian and proud of it." For Indians, being proud is having and expressing a feeling of self-respect and self-worth in their Indianness, in having an Indian identity and proclaiming it. "Acting proud" (instead of "being proud") is less desirable, although sometimes a concomitant of having pride, because it means "being egotistical" or arrogant.

Explaining what people were like in Robeson County to two anthropologists, an Indian man stated, "There's one thing Indians and the Chinese have in common – pride." But pride also emerged in formal contexts where the main audience was Indian, not White. On Veteran's Day in 1967, a Lumbee military man returned to Pembroke to give a speech after the usual parade. He said:

> "I have a prescription for you. Not one your local doctor can fill. Pride is the prescription. . . . I'm proud of my people because they have days like this. They're not sitting in at the Pentagon or rioting in Detroit or New Jersey."

There were some who argued that pride in Indianness was increasing. In 1972, an Indian elementary school teacher remarked that she thought Indian schoolchildren were much prouder of being Indian now than they had been several years ago, because when she asked them "Do you know any Indians?" they used to say "No," but now they say "Yes." And an Indian man noted in 1973 that "until a few years ago, many Indians from Robeson County in most urban areas tried to hide their Indian identity and place of origin."

It may be that with recent Lumbee successes on the local level, increasing involvement in national Indian affairs (in the Coalition of Eastern Native Americans, the BIA, the Indian Claims Commission, the Indian Policy Review Board, and even in the American Indian Movement), and the communication of these activities in national newspapers as well as in the local Indian newspaper, Indian children have come to identify earlier and more strongly as Indians, and those away from home are more willing to be recognized for what they are.

Meanness. The behavioral characteristic Indians today appear to take most pride in is what they call their "meanness," as in the proudly proclaimed statement "We Indians, we're a mean people." "Mean" is a term suggesting not miserliness or pettiness, but a sensitivity to insult coupled with a tendency to react to insults quickly, violently, and implacably. It does not signify, for Indians, "small" or "base" but rather "touchiness" and a willingness to "stand up for oneself" against others.

When meanness is turned outward, against Whites, it is considered a particularly good quality. For example, Henry Berry Lowry is characterized with pride as having been a "mean" man. When acted upon, meanness enables Indians to retaliate against threats and insults from Whites, and suggests that they will not be afraid to be violent and unyielding in their own defense, if need be.

Meanness turned inward, against other Indians, is considered a problem because it can and does result in the troubling of one Indian by another, fistfights, cuttings, shootings, or just verbal threats.

> Two Indian men were discussing the possibility of having a Lumbee Indian Day which would bring Lumbees together for a celebration and possibly a pageant similar to one organized by the anthropologist Ella Deloria, a Dakota, in 1940. An anthropologist asked whether it would also be an opportunity to politicize people, or to organize them for action. Both Indians immediately agreed that there couldn't be political agitation because there would be fighting. One said, "There might be fighting anyway when you put all those Indians together." The other responded, "That's Indians for you – you put them together at something like this and there'll be some fighting and cutting."

An Indian woman also complained about Indian "meanness" toward Indians and explained that it was one reason she wanted to move from the heavily Indian area where she was living.

> The woman and her husband ran a typical crossroads country store with groceries, candy, and cold soft drinks inside, and gasoline pumps outside. She said that there had been a number of fatal accidents near the store, one of which she had witnessed. It was a particularly bloody accident involving children. She also mentioned that they had been robbed several times. In the worst robbery, they lost $800, and they knew who had done it because they saw him. He was someone who came into the store often and knew the place well. When he had finished in the store, he entered the bedroom at the back, at which point, she said, they could have shot him or could have called "the law." But they didn't. Instead, they chased him out by waving a gun at him. When I asked why they hadn't had him arrested, she said, "His family lives right around here. There are mean people in this area." She feared that the family would have torn up the store "and maybe us" if she and her husband had told who it was. It was because of the mean people and because of the accidents that she said she wanted to move away from there.

On the whole, however, meanness is highly valued as the quality that, along with pride, enables Indians to "stand up for themselves" against Whites and differentiates Indians (in their own minds) from Blacks.

Whites, needless to say, are less enamored of the quality of meanness in Indians. They know that direct insults and frontal attacks on Indians bring retaliation, and most Whites try to avoid angering them. A White who "messes with" an Indian and reaps a violent retaliation is not supported by others in the White community, who say he should have known better because "everyone knows how Indians are." If a Black were to respond violently to a similar provocation, he would be classified as "uppity" and would be punished. Privately, Whites say that only some Indians are mean, and they express physical fear of such Indians. Several Whites, upon finding out that my husband and I lived in Pembroke, asked, "Aren't you *afraid* to live out there with those Indians?" Interestingly enough, when Indians were told of this White question, many were surprised to hear that Whites feared them, despite these same Indians' repeated stress on their meanness. By contrast, Whites do not admit openly to being afraid of Blacks.

Publicly, Whites now stress the changes that have occurred in the Indian community, contrasting the current achievements and respectability of the Indians with their disreputability during the Henry Berry Lowry period. In 1967, when I stopped at a Lumberton printery looking for a copy of Norment's (1875) book on the Lowry band, I was told that they had had many copies of the reprinted (1909) version, but that they had sold them all for fifty cents a copy to a New York dealer some time before. When I asked whether they had plans to reprint the book again, the woman said, "No, the Indians wouldn't like it." When asked why, she continued, "That's the way they were a long time ago, and they wouldn't like to be reminded because they're not that way any more."

A retaliatory spirit among Indians has long been noticed by Whites. Townsend reported that Henry Berry Lowry had witnessed the killings of his father and brother, and, "There he swore eternal vengeance against the perpetrators of the act" (1872:52). Although he did not use the term "mean," Townsend says that both leader and band "have shown a ferocity, a premeditation and an insolence frightful to understand . . ." (1872:65). Norment also mentions Henry Berry Lowry's vengefulness (1875). McMillan states publicly, "They are peaceable in disposition, but when aroused by repeated injury, they will fight desperately" (1888:21) and privately, in a letter to Weeks, "They are revengeful and never forget an injury" (McMillan 1890). He further reports that "an old citizen" said of the Indians, "'They never forget a kindness, an injury, nor a debt'" (McMillan 1888:27).

But most Whites since the 1880s seem to have preferred to emphasize the "progress" Indians have made rather than their uncertain temper. Representative John Bellamy of North Carolina, in remarks to the U.S. House supporting federal aid for Robeson County Indian education, stated in 1900:

The leader, Henry Berry Lowery, was finally killed, peace and quiet was again restored, and under the benign influence and rule of our people, inaugurated in the year 1887, they are becoming good citizens [Bellamy 1900:7].

In an appendix to the reprinted Norment volume (1909), Colonel F. A. Olds, who visited Robeson County from Raleigh, North Carolina, reported:

Assurances were given that these people had made as much relative improvement in the past 25 years as any others in their section of the State or in any other part of it, yet they started at zero. Of course there is plenty of room for further improvement. They are domestic in their life and need only two things, these being abstention from liquor and the cultivation of a higher standard of morals in home life. They have been the prey of designing white men, who have gone in their section for evil purposes . . . [Olds in Norment 1909:165].

The State has provided a separate normal school for these people; the Governor has addressed them; they are being aroused to fresh pride in their ancestry and in learning and their development is becoming rapid [Olds in Norment 1909:187].

U.S. Senator Angus W. McLean from Robeson County also testified on behalf of the Indians to obtain school funds from the federal government in 1913: "Of late years, after we saw that the little education that the State has been able to give them has resulted in the most marked difference, they are considered among our best citizens" (U.S. House of Representatives 1913:17). Senator Simmons, also of North Carolina, stated at the same hearings:

I want to say that these Indians have manifested in the last 15 or 20 years a very remarkable interest in agriculture especially. They have disclosed an ambition which we hardly thought that race possessed for their children. They are trying to send their children to the higher schools, and they are poor people. . . . I do not think there is any class of our people in recent years that have shown more interest in trying to educate their children than they have [U.S. House of Representatives 1913:11].

Robert C. Lawrence, a prominent White lawyer in Robeson, wrote of the Indians in 1939: "These people have made and are still making much progress, due largely to the excellent normal school provided for them by the state and located at Pembroke" (Lawrence 1939:113–14).

White praise for Indian "progressiveness" can be seen to match Indian pride expressed in it. The Indians chose their imagery well in relation to a White audience.

Cohesiveness. Closely related to both "meanness" and "pride" is a third self-ascribed Indian quality – what Indians call "sticking together." This quality is highly valued, if problematic, and Indians often enjoin one another to exhibit this behavior, particularly in political contexts. Such statements as "I'm for my people first – the Lumbee have to stick together" and "If you don't go out of your way to help another Lumbee, you ain't worth nothing" were common. Once, in a gathering of young Indian men, one of them explained to an anthropologist, "If an Indian sees another Indian, they're drawn together like – to a magnet. Indians won't stay by themselves; it's in their blood not to."

On the other hand, in discussions of "who our real enemies are," Indians often say "ourselves." One Indian maintained, "Our neighbors are sticking us.'' These comments reflect the tendency of Indians to mobilize mutual support in some circumstances and to fragment into factions in others. The situations in which Indians "stick together" best are the same ones that elicit Indian meanness – those in which Whites are seen as threatening Indian identity.

In a *Carolina Indian Voice* editorial, outrage at perceived discrimination, the specter of Henry Berry Lowry, and an appeal to stick together are combined:

Many Indians made a concerted effort to see that the county school board was tri-racial. From the lips of several Indian figures came the soothing message: "They have changed; let us not do unto them what they have done unto us." *WE WERE BETRAYED!* Indian candidates were *massacred* in the white precincts. . . . The 1976 Democratic Primary clearly shows that there is as much white racism here in Robeson as there was in the days of Henry Berry Lowrie. The question we pose today: Is there still as much Indian courage and determination?

Unless we act forcefully all will be lost; we cannot allow such a challenge to go unanswered if we are to survive. We must re-group before the 1978 elections. Is it not time that we think of our own people [*Carolina Indian Voice*, 1976a:2]?

White Robesonians complained during the reign of the Lowry band that the "mulattoes" were protecting the band and giving them information that allowed them to elude their White pursuers (Norment 1875, Townsend 1872). But thereafter, Whites characterized Indians either as avoiding other races or as fragmented into factions. McMillan stated, "The great mass shun notoriety and carefully avoid places where crowds of other races assemble" (1888:21). Later, G. Johnson found, "In his work, the Indian's aim is to have as little to do with white people as possible" (1939:521), and he points to a "lack of strong group solidarity, the presence of factions, and the timidity of leaders" (1939:523). Yet, he says, he does not desire to convey the impression that Indians are disorganized and unstable (G. Johnson 1939:523). Here is more evidence for the presence of factions that do not disorganize, the other side of the sticking-together-in-the-face-of-White-intimidation coin. Cohesiveness is activated when direct threats or insults from Whites are perceived, but there can be a passive kind of cohesiveness in a common avoidance by Indians of other races. And when Indians are not being actively cohesive, they tend to fragment into factions.

Traditions expressive of Indianness

The three most important and most general behavioral characteristics – meanness, pride, and cohesiveness – are all embedded in two traditions considered by Indians to be vital events in their history. Significantly, these events are rarely mentioned by local Whites today as the most important ones in Indian history. Their role in Lumbee history is thus minimized by Whites, who prefer to picture Indians in their "progressive" mode rather than their "aggressive" one. The two traditions are, not surprisingly, tales of the Henry Berry Lowry band, and of the Ku Klux Klan rally. Indians who recount these stories do so with passion and intensity, often laced with ironic humor. These qualities are not present in the telling of origin stories.

Henry Berry Lowry

The story of Henry Berry Lowry is the most complex and elaborately embroidered tradition found among the Lumbee. It is the oral tradition, not the written documentation, that concerns me here. One version of the story was told to me by an elderly Indian man in a formal intervjew at his home. He was once politically very active and was an educated, religious man. He, a young Indian man, and I sat talking in the dignified old man's backyard one summer evening in 1973:

> "Now I'll tell you something everybody doesn't know. When they wanted the Indians to go to work [on the Confederate fortifications in Wilmington], Henry Berry Lowry says, 'We won't go.' James [Lowry] III had a son named William who married a Cherokee Indian girl. Down the line somewhere, one of 'em married a Tuscarora Indian girl. William was a soldier in the Revolutionary War, and drew a pension for life. He had a son named Allen Lowry. Allen Lowry had a son named Calvin Lowry. . . . And another son named Henry Berry Lowry. . . .
>
> "A Scotchman named Bob McKenzie owned 250 acres of land. His land adjoined Allen Lowry's 250 acres. These foreigners had a habit of taking some of their own food or stock or goods and slipping them over on their Indian neighbor's land. Then they would accuse their neighbor of stealing and get their land. The Home Guards was the law. One day McKenzie told Allen, 'The Home Guards told me to tell you to move off'n this land.' And Allen had some friends among the Home Guards, so he knew it wasn't true. He said, 'The Home Guard told me to stay on this land' [with a chuckle]. So McKenzie sent his slaves to put harnesses in Allen's shelter, and they hid meat in the shockets of corn in the field. McKenzie comes to him the next morning and accuses him of having stolen harnesses and meat. Allen says, 'I've got all the harnesses and meat I need without stealing.' McKenzie says, 'Well, let's just look around.' So they find the stolen harnesses and meat. Allen says, 'You put it there, I didn't.' McKenzie goes off and comes back with the Home Guard. They arrested Allen and his wife and William, Sinclair, Calvin, and Aunt Pursh [sons and a daughter of Allen Lowry]. They carried them over to McKenzie's.

"Aunt Pursh told me she was locked up in the smokehouse. She heard the Home Guard say, 'What'll we do with 'em?' Another one said 'Let's set the smokehouse afire and burn all of them up.' Another says, 'No, there's women and children in there. Those women and children didn't go out there stealing. The first one strikes a fire, I'll kill him.' Then they took them out of the house and put Allen and William [his son] in a cart with some shovels. And they went toward Allen Lowry's home. They got out there and made them dig a grave.

"And about that time there was much commotion about. Henry Berry was about seventeen years old, and he had crawled through the bushes near to where they were. When they got the grave dug, they blindfolded Allen and William and made them stand with their backs to the grave. Then the leader lined up the Home Guard and told them to get their rifles out. Then he said, 'When I count three, shoot – and your conscience won't bother you because you won't know which bullet killed them' [ironically]. They shot them and covered them up so fast they didn't even get to die good. An after they had left, Henry Berry stood up and swore by the God Who made him he wouldn't stop 'til he killed the last one of those Home Guards.

"And he had a White friend. And his White friend said, 'I don't blame you, I'd do the same thing.' He [the White friend] ordered him a gun. It cost $100 – you know you could get a gun in those days for two, three dollars. Its fittings were all brass, and it could shoot two miles. Henry Berry said he would stay out in the woods until he killed every one of those Home Guards. And he did [triumphantly]!

"They would send soldiers, send men after him. They would send a crew of men inside after him. They would fool the people – they were his friends. They would tell him to go off this way [pointing right], and then they would shoot up in the trees and start shouting, 'Get him! That way! Look out, he's getting away!' And when the others come up and said, 'Which way'd he go?' they'd say, 'This way' [pointing left]. And they never could get him.

"Then 500 soldiers come to Moss Neck [a railroad stop somewhere near the center of a broad Indian area derisively named "Scuffletown" by Whites and called "the Settlement" by Indians]. And the general came to Henry's mother and told her to send for him to meet them, that they wouldn't hurt him. Said they weren't after him, that they would have done the same as him. So they met him and talked with him, and they put a uniform on him like the other soldiers. And he was with them the whole time they were hunting him. I know because his brothers used to help hive bees for Calvin. He was a beekeeper. Down in Devil's Den [said to be the principal hideout of the Lowry band] – the new road going to Hopewell church goes by Devil's Den – they met him several times while they were down there looking after the hogs. He hunted with the soldiers the whole time. The brothers looked up one day and saw some soldiers, and he was right among them. They didn't give any sign, but they recognized him. Marcus Dial, Noah's daddy, said the day before the soldiers were to leave, he saw Henry Berry. He had a black spot on his face – a lot of Lowry's have a black spot on their face [pointing to his cheek and laughing]. Henry Berry called him over and said, 'The general says he wants me to go back with him. He'll bandage several of our faces.' Dial said, 'I'd go with 'em.' Said he went to Moss Neck the next day, and they had several soldiers bandaged. He went off with them soldiers.

"Allen Lowry was prosperous, and all his sons were carpenters. He had a deed to his land, but times got bad, and the sheriff got the deed [for auction]. But William had been off making money, and he heard about it and came home and got that sheriff's deed. So William had the deed. And McKenzie killed the two fellows who had the deeds. But today the Indians own McKenzie's land.''

In this account, as in most other Indian versions explaining why Henry Berry Lowry became violent, it is the murder of Allen and William, for which Henry Berry swears vengeance, that starts the band on the road to killings and robbery. The relations between the Lowrys and their White neighbors are also said to be "typical" of Indian–White relations at that time. The initial difficulty between Allen Lowry and his White neighbor is described in terms of White covetousness of Indian wealth and land. In a classic case of White "greediness," the White neighbor dishonestly arranges to take Indian land and goods. This kind of difficulty is one reported and passed down in the oral traditions of many families as having been encountered by their ancestors. A neighboring White ties his mule or leaves some of his goods on an Indian's property, and later "finds" the "stolen goods," and demands land or goods or money in restitution.[4] The Lowry family's experiences with the deceit of White neighbors are said by Indians today to have been like those of other Indian families, but the punishment meted out to the Lowrys was more extreme, beyond what could be tolerated without retribution.

There is also mention of a "White friend" who agreed that the killings were a real provocation for retaliation, and who supplied Henry Berry with a special gun. At least here, not all Whites are portrayed as wanting to injure Indians.

Throughout the story runs a theme of outwitting and outdoing Whites who were chasing the band, either by other Indians misdirecting the pursuing Whites, or by the outlaws disguising themselves, in this case as soldiers. These are the parts of the Lowry saga that give Indians special pleasure and they are usually told in an ironic manner.

Finally, the disappearance of the leader himself allows for an upbeat ending. What caused his disappearance and how it was managed, despite a huge reward for him dead or alive, is still the subject of much speculation. Some Indians say that he tired of running and fighting and so managed to escape the county (in the version just recounted, by railroad, disguised as a bandaged federal soldier). Thereafter, some say, he went to Mexico, or, simply, "West." A variant escape story similar to one described in Lucas and Groome's (1941) novel about Henry Berry Lowry was told to me by a young Indian boy about fourteen or fifteen years old. He described the band's leader as "a kind of Robin Hood."

> "Henry Berry Lowry got started because they wanted his land. They shot his father – his family. After a trial for stealing hogs or hams or something. Afterward Henry Berry Lowry hunted down and killed everyone on the jury, one at a time.
>
> "He married [pause] – I don't remember her name, but whenever they'd put him in jail, she'd go to visit and when the sheriff had turned his back, she'd pull out a pipe and clonk him on the head and they'd escape [with enthusiasm].
>
> "One time he told everybody he'd rob a bank in Lumberton – no one believed him. But he went on in and dragged the safe out of the bank into the street. He shot it open and got away before anyone could catch him, and he left the safe in the middle of the road.
>
> "After awhile he was getting old – they never caught him – and he went out hunting with a rifle. And he shot himself in the head. And they found him and buried him quick. But what really happened was that he shot a deer, and took its insides out and put them on his head, so everybody thought he was shot. But he really wasn't. And he let them bury him. But then he got away."

Some Indians have said that Henry Berry Lowry returned as an old man to visit his family before he died of old age. Others deny that he ever came home again. Whatever may actually have happened, it is certain that Henry Berry Lowry lived a colorful and, for a time, violent life and then simply disappeared from view.

This, of course, is the very stuff of which good legends are made, and, indeed, even the Whites of his own time attributed to him heroic, larger-than-life qualities, at the same time that they excoriated him. Norment reports that Henry Berry Lowry could run and never tire, was always alert, drank but never became intoxicated, and that he always carried eighty pounds of arms with him and was able to run, swim, and tramp through the swamps with this remarkable burden. She describes Henry Berry as handsome, attractive to women, and musical (Norment 1875:10–12).

There are probably as many Lowry band anecdotes as there are storytellers, but some incidents have found their way into many people's repertoires. The robbery of the safe from the county seat and its subsequent discovery in the middle of the road never failed to be a source of amusement for both teller and listeners. The sly fun poked at Whites – the White sheriff, unable to prevent robbery even in his stronghold, is taunted along with the whole "White" town of Lumberton by the placing of the empty safe where everyone could see what had happened – is obvious, and suggests that Henry Berry and his band had a sense of humor. There is a trickster quality about the band in some of these versions.

Three other commonly told anecdotes further illustrate Indian attitudes about earlier times, their assumptions about Whites, and the behavioral models they hold up to themselves for emulation. The first story concerns the tactics used by the sheriff and his men to capture the Indian band. Frustrated in their plans to hunt the Indians through the swamps, the sheriff took some of the outlawed men's wives into custody, including Henry Berry's beautiful wife, Rhoda. Her beauty is as remarked upon today as it was in the accounts written then (see Townsend 1872, Norment 1875). The sheriff sent word to the outlaws that he would hold the wives until members of the band gave themselves up. Henry Berry's response to this threat was to send a note by way of a White neighbor saying that if the women, who were not responsible for their husbands, were not released, the band would wreak vengeance on the entire county. The women were released promptly, at the insistence of other Whites, and this tactic was not repeated. For Indians, the story serves as a reminder that Whites will cease to "play by the rules" when it suits them. In this case, the treatment of the women strikes Indians as particularly unjust, as Henry Berry and his band were acknowledged by their White enemies never to have molested a White woman, although they had many opportunities to have done so. And the unspoken moral of the story is, of course, that prompt and forceful resistance to White demands is effective.

A second anecdote recounts the adventures of a White Northerner who was hired secretly by local Whites to be a spy. He ingratiated himself with the band by making friends with the Indians, being useful to the Indian community, and, some say, by teaching Indian children. Eventually a plan evolved for the spy to lead the band and their families out of Robeson County and into the West or Mexico. Indians say that the band members were tired of fighting but were afraid to stop, lest they be killed or jailed, so they decided that the only way to find peace was to leave the county. Somehow the band discovered that the spy had betrayed them to local Whites, who were planning an ambush along their route. The band quickly changed its arrangements, captured the spy, took him into the swamp, and killed him, first permitting him to write a letter to his wife, which they then posted. In this story, a very treacherous White is repaid by his own death. Nevertheless, even if he does not behave honorably, the Indians do allow him the courtesy of a last letter to his wife, thereby refusing to treat Whites as badly as they are treated by them. The ultimate powerlessness of the band to break out of the cycle of violence in which they had been caught, could not end, and for which they were not entirely responsible, is clear.

A third anecdote relates the cleverness of Henry Berry Lowry. As usual, the Home Guard was searching for Henry Berry Lowry. This time,

> ". . . they caught up with him along the river and started shooting at him. He jumped into the river, grabbed a boat, flipped it over, and swam away underneath it, with all those men shooting and trying to get him."

The elderly Indian man who told me this story prefaced it with the remark that Henry Berry Lowry "was smart." There are several other clever escape tales about Henry Berry Lowry, in some of which he is aided by his beautiful wife.

The series of stories about Henry Berry Lowry are vividly told and avidly heard. His name and exploits are frequently invoked by Indians today either in exhortations to other Indians to stand up for themselves or in implicit warnings to Whites about what happens when they push Indians too far.[5] Henry Berry Lowry has become, for Robeson County Indians, a culture hero, a man representative of highly regarded Indian qualities. He always kept his word, was dignified and proud, came from a well-to-do landowning family, married an Indian woman of legendary beauty and cleverness, was "mean" enough to stand up for his family and his people, and "stuck together" with his band members and with fellow Indians generally. In addition, he possessed a sense of humor and was handsome, intelligent, strong, and quick-witted. The fact that he was never captured or killed for almost a ten-year period demonstrates his ingenuity and leadership and the strong support of the Indian community for the band.

Throughout the Henry Berry Lowry stories runs a theme of betrayal by Whites, of disappointment in their behavior, with a counterpoint still hinting at the possibility of Indian–White rapprochement. Betrayal can be seen in the spy's behavior, the actions of the Lowry's neighbor in depositing what he would claim to be stolen goods on Lowry land, the shooting without proper trial of two members of a prominent Indian family, and before that, the treatment of Indians as though they were Blacks. Indeed, this treatment is usually cited as the background for Indian dissatisfaction and anger at that period. To classify Indians in the same category as Blacks – and slaves at that – was too great an indignity, too great an insult, and too great a threat to their identity. One of the elderly men who told me stories of Henry Berry Lowry began by speaking about difficulties current in the county in 1971 – troubles over Whites enforcing integration in schools. Many Indians were convinced that Indians and Blacks were being integrated while Whites "integrated" less often and then only with Indians. The old Indian man leaned toward me and explained,

"Confidentially, our problems today come from the fact that Whites have tried to make Indians and Negroes merge. In the old days, at the end of the Civil War, Indians were conscripted to work alongside Blacks on the batteries down at Wilmington. The Indians wouldn't go. Some of those who wouldn't go were the Lowry band."

As counterpoint to the themes of White tyranny, there are suggestions that all Whites are not bad, and that Indians and Whites might yet work together. Henry Berry Lowry went to a White man to ask him to carry a message to the sheriff, and is said to have once surrendered voluntarily to the sheriff in the hope of a fair and speedy trial. A "White friend" ordered a gun for him. Thus, the strong theme of betrayal and treachery by Whites is moderated slightly by a muted role for "White friends." This stands in contrast to the image presented by Indians in their telling of the origin story – "we have always been the White man's friend."

It is only relatively recently – perhaps with the lessening of political dependence on "White friends" – that Henry Berry Lowry has been publicly esteemed before Whites. Earlier, although the Indians repeated these stories to Henry Berry Lowry's glory among themselves, they did not generally acknowledge to Whites that they thought him worthy of emulation. But now, Indian approbation of Henry Berry Lowry has become so acceptable in the public forum that an award is named for him. A 1975 article in the *Carolina Indian Voice* discusses the Henry Berry Lowry Memorial Award to be given at the annual Lumbee Homecoming Day and describes what Henry Berry stands for, at least to many Indians:

For the fifth time in history, the Lumbee community is paying homage to this "Robinhood of the Lumbee Indians." . . .

Henry Berry Lowery symbolizes the hopes and aspirations of all Lumbee Indians. All nominations are to recognize an outstanding Lumbee Indian who has demonstrated pride in his Indian heritage and background; who has worked diligently against racial injustices; who has been an advocate voice for Indian people under a dominant society; and has contributed in a worthwhile manner to the Lumbee Indians and Lumbee Community [*Carolina Indian Voice*, 1975:3].

Henry Berry Lowry and his band have become figures whose goals and actions should, at least in some respects, be emulated. In a 1972 speech at a political rally exhorting Indians to action, a young Indian declaimed:

We must learn to unite and stand together against people like [a prominent and influential White landowner]. Only about a hundred years ago, another group of Indians under the leadership of Henry Berry made a stand. I do not subscribe to the theory that Henry Berry acted solely out of revenge, and with only a few followers. Those were terrible days; the very existence of the Indian people was at stake. How much of the fighting was done by just plain Indians such as you and I? By their stand, these people showed that the Indian will not tolerate physical intimidation, but will meet violence with violence. We did not have to repeat this response again until 1958 at the Battle of Maxton [the routing of the Ku Klux Klan]. Here a number of just plain Indians vowed to risk all for the right of the Indian people to exist unmolested.

Let me make myself perfectly clear: I am not advocating violence. These are merely illustrations of what our people can do when they are willing to fight for what is right and just [Brooks 1972:5].

Here a linkage in spirit between Henry Berry Lowry's band and the routing of the Ku Klux Klan is made. The stories that surround the 1958 Klan incident form the last tradition of prime importance to Indians in recounting who they are among themselves. The first tradition, which illustrates concern with who outsiders say they are, deals with the origins of the group and is wound about with the themes of "White man's friend" and "progressiveness." The second tradition tells of Henry Berry Lowry and his band, illustrating what Indians can do when they defend themselves stoutly and stick together against Whites, not all of whom make trouble for Indians. The third tradition recounts the Indian encounter with the Ku Klux Klan in 1958 and represents, for most Lumbees, one of the rare instances of unified Indian opinion backed by unified action. It is the quintessential instance of Indians "getting together" to meet White threats. I never heard any dissenting Indian voice concerning the Klan rally, whereas even now, although Indians are proud of Henry Berry's exploits, a few will say that he ought not to have killed so many men or robbed so many houses, that he carried things too far. At the Klan rally, things were carried precisely far enough.

The Ku Klux Klan rally

On the night of the rally, angry Indians arrived from all over the county and beyond. Many were drawn by the publicity that preceded the rally, and nearly everyone brought a weapon, most a gun. The Indians began to cluster along three sides of the field where the rally was to take place, leaving only the swampy side unmanned. As the rally opened, there were "war cries," a shot shattered the lightbulb over the speaker's platform, and the air rang with gunshots. Indians say that the Klansmen ran off into the swamp, and, according to some, "They didn't come out for three days" because they were so frightened. Surprisingly, despite all the gunfire, no one was seriously hurt. When I enquired whether there had been any policemen or troopers or deputies at the rally, one Indian replied that yes, there had been several cars full of them. When I asked what they were doing while all the shooting took place, he answered jocularly, "They stayed right in their cars."

All of the Indians I talked with about the Klan incident stressed that there were many Indian participants – "hundreds."[6] Whatever the precise number of Indians may have been, I do not remember having talked with an adult male Lumbee old enough to have participated who did not claim to have been present at the rally.

The basic story of the Klan rout is amplified in various ways. A few Indians recounted the number and variety of weapons that had been assembled for the confrontation – rifles, shotguns, pistols, and even hand grenades ("bushelbaskets full of them"). An Indian woman whose husband had been at the rally explained the Klan incident this way:

> She said it all started when an Indian woman moved into an ordinary neighborhood in Lumberton, which was not an especially unusual event. "But 'Catfish Cole' from South Carolina got wind of it and started saying how he was a Klansman and they don't allow that." A cross was burned on the woman's lawn. She moved out and lived with a neighbor until the trouble was over. Cole wrote letters to *The Robesonian* [a White-owned Lumberton paper] which became increasingly vituperative – "nasty." "He threatened to do all kinds of things to the woman if she didn't leave that neighborhood. He said in South Carolina they don't have such things, and they shouldn't here either." Some Indians wrote answering letters to the newspaper, and anger began to build in the Indian community. Then Cole announced a meeting in a field in Maxton with a swamp on one side. About twenty-five Klansmen and their wives and children attended. "Cole was supposed to speak, but he'd been warned if he took one step on that platform he'd be killed. The police were out in droves. The Klansmen were armed, and there was a lightbulb over the platform. The Lumbees were milling around. While the sheriff was still arguing with Cole and trying to get him not to speak off to one side, someone shot out the light bulb. Then suddenly there were shots zinging all over the field everywhich way. It was a miracle no one was killed or hurt." I asked, "What happened to the police?" She responded, "They disappeared into squad cars." When asked if there had been any Indian spokesmen, she said no, that there had been a group of Indians who had met with the sheriff before the rally to ask him to tell Cole that if Cole spoke, they would kill him. "That was the only time I've ever seen the Indians get together on anything. Everyone I know (all the men) and everyone I know of was there."
>
> Later, she heard reports that when the shooting started, Cole ran for the swamp and wasn't seen for two days, leaving his wife and children behind. After a while, some Indians pushed her stuck car out of the sand and helped her on her way.
>
> The Klan has not returned. "I don't think there are any members in the county – it was outsiders." She said the Klan did try to hold another meeting, but that "they wouldn't dare show up for that."

In a later discussion, when asked about a local man who I had been told was a Klansman, this same woman replied, "They burned a cross in his yard after the Klan trouble in 1958. He left town for awhile, and then he came back. He wouldn't dare be [a Klansman]. We watch him too closely." She seemed to evaluate this man in terms of what he actually does rather than what he might think. She expressed no particular dislike or condemnation of him.

An Indian man who was present at the rally had a slightly different version of what happened. The major difference in the two accounts is in the degree of organization attributed to the Indians.

> He claimed that he and seven or more carloads of Indian men, all armed, had planned their activities. They had decided to "get" the Klan if they shot any Indians. "And after we got the Klan we were going to go into Lumberton and clean it out." If it came to "getting" the Klan, two groups of men had been prepared – one patrolling the field to ensure that no Klansmen escaped, and one patrolling to keep an eye on photographers to make sure there were no records of what they were doing. It was arranged that the Indians would "drift in" in two cars at a time so that the police would not realize what was afoot. After the rally, this man went with the seven carloads of men, still armed, into Lumberton to see whether the sheriff had any Indians locked up. They got the sheriff to come out to talk, and when the sheriff saw all the man and guns, he tried to placate them. The Indians held by the sheriff were speedily released.

Despite the differences in emphasis and the disagreement about how organized the Indian activities were, both these accounts express the basic Ku Klux Klan rally theme – that of unified and armed Indians violently resisting attempts to intimidate them. But these armed and violent men, unlike the Lowry band, do not have any one generally recognized leader. By 1967–68, at least, all the Indians to whom I talked about the Klan incident failed to mention the names of leaders – no one was being given credit for having organized resistance to the Klan. Perhaps just as indicative was the fact that one man, who had been credited as being a leader by national news media, was frequently criticized for apparently claiming that role. In contrast to the Lowry band, whose exploits are often couched in terms of their leader, the Indians at the Klan rally are talked about as united by common interest and feelings of anger and outrage, not by a powerful leader.

When the Klan proposed to hold another rally in Robeson County in 1966, the Indians again threatened that they would not allow the rally to take place. An Indian professional was overheard to exclaim that he would fight the Klan if they came, adding "I know I'm supposed to be a [professional] but I'm still a Lumbee!" Because some Indians felt that it would be impossible to avoid serious bloodshed a second time, a few of them went to Raleigh and persuaded authorities to issue an injunction preventing the Klan from holding its meeting. The rally was not held, nor have there been any public displays of Klan activity in Robeson County from 1958 to 1979.

In accounts of the Klan, as in those of the Lowry band, "violent men with guns" are the central figures, but this time they are "all adult Indian men" rather than "an Indian leader and his band." Here there are no overtones of the "White friend" or suggestions of possible rapprochement as there are in the Lowry band and origin traditions. The Klan tradition strongly emphasizes Indian identity characteristics of pride, meanness, and sticking together. And, like the Lowry band stories, Klan stories often display Indian humor – in the wry telling of the Klansmen's desertion of their wives, who were then helped by Indians, and in the reticent behavior of the sheriff's men. Whether all the events took place exactly as recounted is not as important as the fact that the events are taken to be fundamentally true (whatever the embroidery) and are displayed as an expression of Indian identity and Indian success by Indians today.

The Klan, in its most recent incarnation, has been strong in North Carolina, particularly in the eastern sections of the state. In 1967–68, a large billboard beside the interstate highway running through Fayetteville, North Carolina, betokened Klan strength. It read, "Support your United Klans – fight integration and Communism." The message was accompanied by a large robed and hooded figure on horseback. Fayetteville is only about thirty-five miles north of Pembroke. The continued undefaced existence of the billboard surprised me, particularly because Fayetteville is the home of Fort Bragg and Pope Air Force Base, one of the nation's largest (and during the Vietnam War, one of the most active) military bases. As such, it is staffed by many people who might find the billboard offensive. When I expressed my surprise to Lumbees, a typical response was, "Oh, that's Fayetteville. If it were here in Robeson County, it wouldn't last more than a day." But no one seemed to feel particularly threatened by the presence of the sign in a neighboring county.

The Klan itself is a small minority fringe of the White community, and many Robeson Whites deplore Klan activities. Because of this disagreement among themselves, the White community in Robeson County did not present a unified front or have a single strong response to the Indians' attack on the Klan, and, so far as I know, there were no unpleasant repercussions for any of the Indians involved in the incident. Indeed, *Life* magazine reported that Indians "found they had now earned new sympathy and admiration from the whites" (*Life* 1958b:36). According to the same article, a White police chief said, " 'The rally . . . has developed a bond of friendship between the whites and Indians that never developed before' " (*Life* 1958b:36).

None of the Whites I have talked with had good words for the Klan. Several Whites were of the same opinion as the Indian woman whose version of the Klan rally is presented here – it was all the work of "outside agitators from South Carolina." Certainly no White admits openly that he is a member of the Ku Klux Klan. The Klan incident is rarely raised spontaneously by Whites in conversation. It, like the exploits of Henry Berry Lowry, is something most Whites would prefer not to emphasize, and it presents an aspect of Indian behavior of which they must be wary.

Other behavioral qualities of Indianness

"Talking Indian," keeping one's word, and owning land in Robeson County are also behavioral qualities used by Indians to characterize what Indians do, ought to do, and are, but they are of secondary importance, elaborations on the tone set by pride, meanness, and cohesiveness. All the behavioral characteristics are conceived by Indians as particularly "Indian" attributes that are or can be acted out in varying degrees by Indian individuals. Most of the characteristics have been identified as "Indian behavior" for many years by White observers.

"Talking Indian"

"Dialect" is an important identifying feature of Indianness.[7] But whether or not any particular Indian speaks the "Indian dialect" is often a matter of choice. Many Indians, particularly middle-class people, can switch into and out of the "Indian dialect" depending upon the circumstances. When speaking to audiences of Whites, such Indians tend consciously to approximate the "good grammar" that they have been taught in school because they are aware that Whites sometimes stigmatize them for their "dialect." "Talking Indian" can be a mark of solidarity among Indians, but it can also be a source of self-consciousness and embarrassment for Indians when they speak with Whites. The distress over Indian speech patterns expressed by a middle-class Indian woman was perhaps unusually great, but conveys an attitude that was not uncommon among Indians of her class:

> At a formal public hearing attended by members of all three races, testimony was taken from individuals of each race. A few days later, a middle-class Indian expressed her concern about the image presented by "the Indian people" to Whites and Blacks at the gathering. She said she thought the best person she saw testifying was a Negro, and that

"our people" had not spoken as well. When I said I thought some had done quite well, she said, "Yes, but none of them can talk – they all use the wrong verbs and don't know their plurals. That's the trouble with most of us."

Unfortunately, the distinction between prescriptive grammar and descriptive grammar is not made in Robeson County schools, and children are taught that the only "good" English is the standard form taught in their classes.

Whites have long recognized a distinctiveness in Indian speech. McMillan described it as "almost pure Anglo Saxon" and listed the pronunciation of several words as evidence (1888:20, 26). In 1919, anthropologist Elsie Clews Parsons visited Robeson County. She was told about Indians by a white farmer of Scottish ancestry:

. . . how much they kept to themselves, mixing with neither whites nor colored; how they had a different "tone" in speaking, "sounds French" (I [E.C.P.] failed to notice it in any instance) and how they were "a very kind people until they got mad," – testimony to their "fierce temper," when aroused, that I got later from whites and Negroes [E. Parsons 1919:385].

From Indians, she heard that the last speaker of the Cherokee language (the Indians were officially Cherokees at this time) had died eight years before her visit. She found that "Mr. Lowrie [the "town historian"] himself knew a few words, – *waka* ("cow," Spanish *vaca* I), *sola* ("good-morning"). I met nobody else who knew any Indian words at all" (E. Parsons 1919:385). It is quite possible that Parsons was being "put on" by the Indians she spoke with. During my stay in Robeson, I heard several stories told by Indians about how they had fooled Whites by playing on White notions about "Indian ways." The Indians reported these incidents as amusing examples of White gullibility, White stereotyping, and at the same time poked fun at themselves for their lack of "Indian" characteristics.

One man told a story about "some tourist who came down from Ohio or Indiana or Kentucky" and stopped at a local gas station in Pembroke. The White tourist asked the Indian gas station attendant where he could see some Croatans, not realizing that the attendant was an Indian or that the term Croatan was highly insulting. So the attendant said he would show the tourist a Croatan and then introduced him to a prominent White landowner who lived in Pembroke. The White landowner went along with the joke, pretending to be an Indian. Another Indian explained that he used "to Indian talk the Whites" in a Northern city where he worked for a short period. He said they really thought he could speak an Indian language, an idea that appeared to amuse him very much, as he had simply rattled off a string of nonsense syllables.

Today Whites and Blacks say that Indians speak a distinctive "dialect," but in practice they often have difficulty recognizing it. Indians do usually recognize other speakers of their own "dialect." Although speaking the "Indian dialect" marks one as Indian, not all Indians speak it. Some Indians have been reared away from Robeson County and have speech patterns from other areas. When an Indian cannot or does not "talk like an Indian" to other Indians he may be open to a charge of snobbery if he does not explain himself. One Indian woman was surprised to find another who was apparently not snobbish and yet did not speak the Indian "dialect":

> Two women met for the first time in an Indian-owned restaurant. Both were well within the Indian range of physical appearance, on the light skinned end of the range. One woman, speaking with the "Indian dialect," asked the other what her name was. The first woman chose to speak in the "Indian dialect" rather than in a way approximating White norms of speech, which I had also heard her use at times. The other woman replied with a surname that was not distinctively Indian, so the first asked her where she lived. The answer was the name of a heavily Indian area, so the first woman asked in a surprised voice, "Are you an Indian?" When the reply was affirmative, the first woman exclaimed, "Why, you don't talk like an Indian!" The explanation the second woman gave for this circumstance was that she had spent many years away from Robeson County and had either lost her accent or never developed it.

This interchange also illustrates quite well how Indians identify one another – through a combination of geographic, surname, physical appearance, and contextual and behavioral cues. Physical appearance is the least reliable indicator, place of residence is slightly better, surnames are sometimes decisive, but behavioral features and context are the best of all. Of course a few Indians exhibit none of the expected features and so must be asked outright about their identity, though that is considered slightly impolite and avoided if possible.

But because it is almost impossible and even potentially dangerous for Indians or anyone else in Robeson County to deal with a person whose race is unknown, a small rudeness is preferred to ambiguity. For example, when a dark-skinned friend from the North visited my husband and me in Pembroke, he met an Indian neighbor. In the course of conversation, the Indian burst out, "I'm about to pop. What nationality are you?" When our friend replied, "American," the Indian persisted, asking "What else?" to which the response was "Filipino." The Indian shook his head and commented, "You could be one of us." Our Northern friend fell within the very wide range of possible Indian physical appearance, but exhibited none of the other expected "Indian" characteristics except presence in Robeson County.

"Keeping your word"

Another behavioral characteristic, of which Indians are proud, is their reputation for keeping their word. This is an important point of honor for Whites and of honesty for Indians. For Indians, to break one's word after having given it "would be a lie," and therefore a sin. The moral commitment of giving one's word is considered by most Indians to be binding. Most politically active Indians encouraged others to refrain from "giving your word" to opposition candidates rather than give it and break it. For this reason, many politicians have difficulty extracting promises from Indian constituents.

Whites have pointed out this behavioral quality since the Henry Berry Lowry days. Even Norment, whose husband the band had presumably killed, stated of Henry Berry Lowry:

His cavalier scrupulousness may also be observed in the matter of a promise or a treaty. Those most robbed and outraged by this bandit give him credit for complying strictly to his word. Like the rattlesnake, he generally warned before he struck [Norment 1875:12].

Of course, Norment attributed this fine quality to the influence of Henry Berry Lowry's White ancestry – his "cavalier blood." A Northern reporter for a New York newspaper provides evidence of similar sentiments among other local Whites. When he asked a merchant in one of the towns near the Indian settlement whether Henry Berry would be likely to grant him an interview, the merchant replied:

"Yes, if he could be made to understand that your intentions were pacific. The large reward now out for him, amounting, for himself and party, to about forty-five thousand dollars, taken dead or alive, makes him apprehensive of assassination. But if he were to promise not to injure you, you could go anywhere to see him with perfect impunity." This was general testimony [Townsend 1872:17].

McMillan, in his 1888 pamphlet, extended this honest virtue to the rest of Henry Berry Lowry's people:

"They never forget a kindness, an injury, nor a debt," said an old citizen. "They may not pay you when a debt is due, but they seldom forget an obligation and are sure to pay you after a time" [1888:27].

Owning land in Robeson County

For Lumbees, an important aspect of their Indianness lies in their relationship to the land of Robeson County, which is, they feel, properly and best expressed through their ownership of that land. Robeson

County land is not merely an economic investment, a commodity to be bought cheaply and sold dearly, but a homeland, the geographic focus for the Indian community, the place "where we people have our roots and where we belong." The refrain, "This land belonged to our fathers," emerges repeatedly in conversations about either land or Whites. Even Indians who have lived away from Robeson for years, or who have been reared in other parts of the country, regard Robeson County as home (see, e.g., Peck 1972). A Baltimore Lumbee, the head of the Indian Center in that city, told a reporter in 1970:

"I've never heard one of our people refer to Baltimore as home," says Herbert Locklear, director of the Indian Center and an official with the city Department of Social Services.

"People who have been here 20 years will ask me when was the last time I was home, and they mean North Carolina, not my house in Baltimore" [Akwesasne Notes 1971:34].

More than a means of livelihood, for Indians, landowning is an end in itself. Ownership is more important in many cases than the amount of money to be made from land. As one Indian commented wryly, "Indians would rather have land than money." And indeed, the demand for land in Indian areas is so great that land values are now much higher than the productivity of the land alone warrants. Today Indians could do much better in rational economic terms by acquiring other assets than land. And they know they could.

Because of the high value placed on land ownership, even of small plots, the allocation of wealth for land in most Indian families is relatively high. Even Indians who leave the county for long periods of time often buy land to which they plan one day to return, either when they have made enough money elsewhere to finance themselves in Robeson or when they retire. There is also a strong feeling among Indians that land now belonging to Indians should be kept in Indian hands. One older Indian man told me that a group of Indians had banded together to pay $19,000 for sixteen acres of land in an "Indian section" in order to prevent a White corporation from purchasing it. This amount was considerably above the normal market value of the land at that time. Most Indians say that they prefer to own land near other Indians. As one rather conservative middle-class Indian put it, "Most people prefer friends among their own. Most of my friends are from my own people, and people seem happier among their own." Many Indians expressed the sentiment that they felt "more comfortable among our own people."

For Lumbees, then, Robeson County land has great symbolic as well as economic significance. It has an association with ancestors ("We were here first") and validates continuing Indian existence. It has in the past stood for a style of life common to most Indians and still common to many – a rural and agriculturally based style that is rapidly changing with the increased industrialization of the area. In this vein, a seventy-three-year-old Indian man told a reporter:

"I think white people got a feelin' against the Indian," says Mr. Locklear. "Reckon they want our land, but I held on to mine. . . . It's in m' blood, this lan* is. Never done nothin' but farmin' all my life." And has he ever thought about moving away from Robeson County? "No sir! No sir, I have not. . . . There's no other place like it. No sir, I wouldn' move if I lived to be 140" [ellipses in original; Gaillard 1971b:5].

Although land no longer provides the economic mainstay for many Indian families, and despite changes in livelihood, Indians continue to value land highly. To own land is to express one's Indianness, to be truly Indian.

Indian attachment to land is long-standing. In 1872, Townsend reported a conversation among White Robesonians, who noted that Allen Lowry said he "had been cheated out of his land." Another said that the Indians had the idea that their ancestors had held "all this land in fee simple." That the feeling of having been wronged over the loss of their land was being passed on to the next generation was suggested by one White man's account of Allen's son, Sinclair, who said, " 'We used to own all the country round here, but it was taken from us somehow' " (Townsend 1872:48). McMillan claimed, "They held their lands in common and land titles only became known on the approach of white men. . . . Many of these people at a later period purchased their lands from persons who obtained large patents from the King" (1888:14). He also stated that they were "almost universally land holders" (1888:24).

Later, Indians testified before Congressional committees about their landholding. During the 1912 Senate Committee on Indian Affairs hearings, an Indian, R. N. S. Locklear, was asked, "Are your people nearly all landowners?" To which he replied, "No sir, they are not all," which he later amended to "Nearly all, yes sir" (U.S. Senate 1912:6). In 1913, at House hearings on the same bill, there were further questions about property ownership. One of the Senators from North Carolina, testifying in support of federal aid to Robeson County Indian education, was asked whether the Indians held their property in severalty, to which the answer was affirmative. When further questioned as to whether they received it from the federal government, the Senator replied:

No, sir. We do not know exactly how they did acquire it. The title is now based upon possession so long that the State presumes a grant. The bulk of these Indians, the 6,000 in Robeson County, live in one township, or rather one settlement around this little town of Pembroke [U.S. House of Representatives 1913:10].

At the same proceedings, Mr. Locklear, an Indian, was asked about Indian landholdings:

> MR. BURKE: To what extent do you people own your land there?
> MR. LOCKLEAR: I do not get the question. How much per head?
> MR. BURKE: What portion of you have farms?
> MR. LOCKLEAR: Well, about 25 per cent of them own small farms, anywhere from 1 acre to 25 or 50 acres [U.S. House of Representatives 1913:26].

Clifton Oxendine, also an Indian, noted in his 1934 M.A. thesis, "In the main, the Indians are law-abiding, great believers in owning land, and are industrious workers" (Oxendine 1934:60).

By 1935, assertions that nearly every Indian owned land were no longer being made. In a report to the U.S. Commissioner of Indian Affairs, Fred A. Baker, the superintendent of the Sisseton Sioux Indian Agency on temporary assignment in Robeson County, described the situation as he found it during an investigation into the possibility of obtaining federally funded land for the Indians:

> They hailed with joy the offer of the government; many of the old people could not restrain their feelings, – tears filled many eyes and flowed down furrowed cheeks. We must confess to the fact that our own feelings were deeply touched as the old people expressed so deep a longing to have a piece of land on which they could live in peace without fear of ejectment by a landlord. Inquiry revealed that only about fifteen families out of every hundred owned any land; that eighty-five percent of the Indians were tenants or "share-croppers" and farm laborers. A small number of the Indians have attained a considerable degree of financial independence; own their own homes and farm considerable land. A number are landlords and rent lands to other members of the group [Robeson County Collection 1935–42].

Lumbee Lew Barton writes:

> It is obvious that the Indians could have known nothing about land grants, deeds, and the like, until the approach of the white man. When the settlers did approach, they began promptly to complain about the lands held by the Indians, lands which they coveted for themselves. . . . Since the Indians were there first, and especially since they got legal title to their lands later on, they feel that they are the ones who have a problem. . . . The theory seems to be that, if the Indians are kept poor enough, they will eventually be compelled to sell – and at sacrifice prices. But land in Robeson County today is seldom for sale at any price; and when it is, it usually brings a price probably in excess of its real worth [1967:43–4].

When I asked a prosperous elderly Indian man in 1973 how he had accumulated so much land, he said,

> "By hard work and denied of everything you could get along without. You had to clear it, ditch it, get the stumps out. But we didn't deny ourselves of something to eat. I always had whatever I wanted to eat. . . . In our country here a man could live if he wanted to and save

some. . . . I've always spent all we had on land. Our land's paid for
and we don't owe nobody nothing.''

For this man, land and his own hard work had enabled him to prosper –
but more than that, owning land gave him dignity, place, a sense of
independence and continuity. He told where his father had been born,
what land his family had held, who had owned it before, and who
would inherit it.

But the genuine economic independence that land ownership can
confer on Indians today is much less than it conferred on their ancestors. The reasons for lessened independence are manifold – the change
from subsistence gardening and farming to agricultural integration into
a national market; the increasing costs of farming (seed, fertilizer,
machinery), which frequently require credit that must be obtained from
White institutions (banks, stores); and the escalating demands for con-
sumer goods such as large cars, color televisions, and household
appliances. Although land ownership initially enabled Indians to
choose a pattern of life that allowed most of them to avoid daily direct
and intimate contact with Whites, it did not enable them to escape the
political and economic consequences of life within a racially divided
society. Indians were often able to mute or elude daily humiliations
from the racial code of conduct, but even the most withdrawn have had
increasingly to deal with both Whites and Blacks.

What the Lumbee have done is to develop a notion of themselves
that is expressed in two quite different modes – one formal and the
other informal. One mode of expression is used primarily for presenting themselves to outsiders, especially Whites, and entails the recita-
tion of their origins in the lost colony and miscellaneous Indian groups
as well as the demonstration of their progressiveness in terms appeal-
ing both to middle-class White standards and to themselves.

The second mode of expression is largely implicit; it sets a general
tone and describes qualities to be valued and acted upon as the individual chooses. This mode is not coherently and articulately presented
either to insiders or outsiders – it is not a logically ordered statement of
Indianness, as the recounting of origins is. Rather, it appears in bits and
pieces in many different contexts where Indians present themselves to
one another or to the inquisitive outsider. It outlines an ideal of particularly ''Indian'' behavior, a design for being and feeling Indian, in terms
of which one can choose to act. Thus, an Indian may choose to act out
these characteristics that are said to epitomize Indianness, or not, and
he may then be judged on this basis. The fact that all these behavioral
qualities have an action component – that one can demonstrate one's
Indianness by acting upon them – ties in strongly with the continuous
and many-faceted nature of Indian political activity. Indians, in being

Indian, in their concept of themselves as a people, see themselves as active, as acting upon the world. Not all Robeson Indians exhibit the behavioral qualities outlined here, although most, I think, would subscribe to them in a general way. But many do act upon one or another or several qualities enough of the time to cause outside observers to remark upon it, and enough of the time to validate their claims of who they are to themselves.

If the Indian versions of their origins have been numerous and often changing, the behavioral characteristics ascribed to the Indians have been remarkably constant. Unfortunately, there are no known early records of how Indians conceptualized themselves, so that we cannot know for certain how closely the observed (or attributed) behavior corresponded with Indians' images of themselves.

How Lumbee notions about their Indianness fit with membership in the Indian community now and how that affects their relationships with Black and Indian neighbors is observable, however, and will be explored in the next chapter.

6. What difference does who they say they are make?

If Lumbees speak, as they do and frequently, of their origins, their progress, and their behavioral characteristics, what has that to do with other people's conceptions of them and with how the Lumbee community is constituted?

First, Lumbees' ideas about their group identity draw upon different kinds of symbols than do Whites' and Blacks' notions about themselves. The Indians have resisted using the racial symbolism of physical appearance so characteristic of American, and especially Southern American tradition, and have employed instead what can be called "ethnic" symbolism emphasizing history and culture (this last point is more fully explored in Chapter 7). Lumbees themselves, of course, would not put the matter this way and have not seen their use of symbols in these terms. Whether their "resistance" to racial symbolism was a carefully calculated strategy or, more likely, an unconscious rejection of a demeaning classification system probably cannot, at this point, be determined. What is clear is that Blacks and Whites both draw upon racial imagery to characterize themselves and each other, while doing so from quite different basic assumptions and assigning quite different meanings to the same symbols.

To present its own identity, each group has employed symbols used, often for other purposes and with other meanings, in all the groups. Thus all the groups draw upon a common "pool" of symbols for constructing their identity concepts. This means that the symbols used for identity are not unique to any one group. It also means that confusion and tension can arise when a symbol has different meanings attached to it, or (what is the same thing) is used in different ways by two or more different groups.

Second, Lumbees' ideas about themselves as a group have facilitated the absorption of new members into the Indian community, thereby augmenting the community in sheer numbers as well as in diversified experience and skills.

169

Membership in the Lumbee community

In order to see how ideas about who they are might affect membership in the Indian community, it is necessary to specify who the members of the "Indian community" are. Not all members of the community are Lumbee Indians. Non-Lumbees become members of the community by identifying with it and interacting primarily with other community members. Membership is thus both optional and loosely defined. It is precisely this "vagueness," the failure to draw definite lines about membership, that has enabled outsiders to amalgamate with Lumbees and to operate as members of the community if not as Lumbees.

Most members of the Indian community in Robeson County are, of course, Lumbees.[1] A person is a Lumbee by birth if he has one socially recognized Lumbee parent and no socially recognized Black parent. There is no distinction among Lumbees based on what percentage of Lumbee "blood" an Indian might have. This is distinctly at variance with definitions of Indianness on reservations where people are enrolled and labeled as "full-bloods," "half-bloods," "quarter-bloods," etc. As Robert Daniels (writing about the Dakota) has pointed out, this distinction often appears to have more to do with life-style than with biology, but administrators and others persist in treating these categories of "blood quanta" as reflective of biological parentage and "real" Indian identity (Daniels 1970).[2]

Among themselves, the Lumbee have never made these distinctions of "degrees of Indianness" based on "blood." All Lumbees are considered equally entitled to be Lumbee, however many ancestors were not Lumbees, so long as none were socially recognized as Blacks. There is, not surprisingly, a distinction in "degrees of Indianness" based on behavior. Those Indians who act out the behavioral characteristics that exemplify Indianness to the fullest degree are said to be "real Indians." Those who "act like Whites" are said to be "not really Indian." By this, it is meant that they do not behave according to Indian values, *not that they are not Indians.* A person who is "not really Indian" is fully a Lumbee; he just is not behaving the way a Lumbee ought to, by community standards. He is not, in short, living his Indianness.

Although the phrase "real Indian" is one employed by Indians throughout the county, I never heard anyone claim to *be* a real Indian.[3] "Real old-timey Indian" is an identity ascribed to one by others, not claimed for oneself. This identity has positive and negative aspects. On the positive side, it suggests an admirably greater degree of authenticity, of linkage with the past, of disregard for White values and ways. For this reason, those pointed out as real Indians tend to be living in backcountry areas, away from daily contacts with Whites, and they tend to be among the less well off. Therefore, on the negative side, a real Indian identity suggests the negative qualities of little material wealth, a lack of sophistication and possibly formal education, and few of the physical comforts middle-class Indians have. It is a status to be admired in others but not perhaps one to which many aspire, because having it implies not having many of the physical comforts a large number of Indians would like to have.

A contrast with the concept of the "real Indian" is offered by the notion of the "brick house Indian." A brick house Indian is one who is said to be similar to Whites in materialistic "middle-class" desires and in neglect of community. To be accused of being a brick house Indian is to be reproached for being too self-interested; but to be accused of being a "White Indian" is to be condemned for having betrayed "our people" by adopting White values wholesale and by siding with Whites politically, a far more serious charge. The "White" middle-class life-style at issue here, in which physical comforts and status symbols play large roles, is embodied in the possession of a brick, rather than a frame, house. Not all Indians who live in brick houses are considered brick house Indians, of course. The phrase refers to a materially oriented style of life for which the brick house is a symbol, not a diagnostic feature. A brick house Indian may be envied for his comforts, but he is not admired. Brick house Indians cannot be real Indians because they are too oriented toward White ways, are thought to be too willing to sacrifice the good of the Indian community for their own ends, to be too concerned with accumulating assets for themselves to look after their neighbors' needs. Pembroke is often said to contain more brick house Indians than any other area of Robeson County. None of the real Indians about whom I was told lived there.

A second category of people who are members of the Lumbee community are not Lumbees, but are Whites who have married Lumbees. Both White males and White females have married into the Lumbee community, and all that I know about come from outside Robeson County, though not necessarily outside the South. Until recently, such marriages had to take place outside North Carolina, because laws prevented "interracial" marriage within the state. But once such White–Indian couples settle in Robeson County, they are not disturbed by local Whites.

The attitude of Indians toward such marriages varied greatly. In families with a proud tradition of "We marry only Indians," these matches were discouraged. In other families with an equally proud tradition of intermarriage with both Whites and Indians, the matches were contemplated happily. The in-married Whites themselves are more or less well integrated into the Indian community, depending on how they behave. In the case of one White woman whose married name was distinctively Indian, many younger Indians assumed that she was Indian because she was so actively a part of the Indian community. The older Indians, of course, remembered her origins. In the case of another whose married name was equally Indian, everyone knew that she was White, and many held this against her because they did not like her. Whether she participated less because she was disliked or was disliked because she participated less, or both, is uncertain. But in both cases, the children of the women and their Indian husbands were considered full-fledged Lumbees by birth. It may be that Whites were expected to act more like Lumbees than Lumbees were in order to be fully accepted as members of the Indian community. They may be expected to "prove" themselves by not "acting like Whites."

The third category of people who are members of the Lumbee community are non-Lumbee Indians from outside Robeson County. A few Indians from reservations or with reservation history have married Lumbees and settled in Robeson County. Their children are considered Lumbees and are no more "Indian" than anyone else. But by far the largest number of Indians originally from outside Robeson County come from nonreservation groups similar to the Lumbee located in North or South Carolina – such as the groups now known as the Haliwa (Halifax and Warren counties, North Carolina), the Coharie (Sampson County, North Carolina), the Waccamaw (Columbus County, North Carolina), the Indians of Person County (North Carolina), and related people in a few nearby counties of South Carolina (Blu n.d.). All these named groups achieved legal recognition as Indians after the Robeson County group was designated Indians by the North Carolina legislature. Several of the groups patterned their requests for recognition after the Robeson group's successful petitions (for example, the Coharie and the Haliwa). Most of the Indians from these other nearby groups who now reside in Robeson County have married Lumbees, but a few couples from outside also have moved into Robeson. Their children then have married Lumbees. Once the Robeson County Indians have accepted the group from which such individuals come as Indian, there is no barrier to further individual in-migration and marriage. However, the initial definition of these other groups as Indian has sometimes been problematic.

In a discussion about the relations between these groups and the Lumbee, a middle-aged Lumbee man explained the reluctance of Robeson County Indians to accept new groups as equals:

> He stated that groups "of questionable backgrounds" needed to "establish their identity in their own realms." When asked who these

groups were, he responded that usually a derogatory name was assigned to them and that many are now expanding and finding new difficulties in their situations. When this happens, "if they are not accepted in the normal way, they try to contact others with similar problems," such as the Lumbee. "Robeson County Indians are advanced, and they won't accept people of questionable origin."

He then gave an example of "how a breakthrough comes" in the relations between groups. An Indian preacher from Robeson County went to work among Indians in a rather distant North Carolina county as a missionary. He was sympathetic to their problems because, as a Robeson Indian, he was familiar with them. Those he encountered were "a group of nice looking people." He brought a family back to Robeson with him in order for the child in the family to be educated. The family then intermarried here. The young man of the family became a leading professional, and the daughter of a prominent Lumbee family who was very much against "outsiders" married the young man. That one intermarriage opened the door to others.

Individual marriages have been taking place over a long period of time between some groups. The relationship between Robeson County and Sampson County Indians is close and of long standing. In the 1850 U.S. census, the first census to list county of origin for each family member, a number of marriages between Robesonians and Sampsonians are already recorded. One of the men born in Sampson County, Hardy Bell, whose occupation is given as merchant and whose real estate is valued at $3,000, was the wealthiest "mulatto" listed in 1850 (U.S. Census Enumerators' Reports 1850). Both Bell and his wife, Nancy, came from Sampson County, and their children married Robeson Indians. Mary Norment, a White Robesonian, says of Bell:

One of the family, namely Hardy Bell, moved to Lumberton about 1840, and commenced merchandising. He succeeded in this line of business very well until he died. For several years he was the most prominent merchant in Lumberton, Lumberton being called in Robeson "Hardy Bell's town," as a burlesque [1875:27].

From the 1850 U.S. Census Enumerators' Reports, it appears that about one-quarter of the independent "mulatto" households (by "independent" I mean those not listed under a White head of household) contained at least one adult member who was born in another county or another state. The counties from which most outsiders originate are Cumberland, Sampson, and Anson counties in North Carolina. Cumberland adjoins Robeson, and Sampson adjoins Cumberland. This suggests that the process of concentration and migration into Robeson County has been going on for at least 120 years.

That Sampson County and Robeson County Indians continued to intermarry and to have other contacts with one another is indicated in a pamphlet printed in 1916, which argued for separate state-supported

schools for Sampson County Indians. Sampson Indians petitioned the
state of North Carolina on the basis of their kinship with Robeson
"Croatans."

Your petitioners further respectfully show that they are the same race and
blood and a part of the same people, held by the same ties of racial and social
intercourse as the Croatan Indians of Robeson County, many of whom were
former residents of Sampson County, and with whom they have married and
intermarried. That since the State of North Carolina has been so just and
generous as to provide special and separate school advantages for our brothers
and kinsmen, in Robeson County, as well as in the counties of Richmond,
Scotland, Hoke, Person and Cumberland, we now appeal to you for the same
just and generous recognition from the State of North Carolina and from your
Honorable Board, in Sampson County, that we may share equal advantages
with them as people of the same race and blood, and as loyal citizens of the
State [reprinted in Butler 1916:6].

In addition to listing several marriages that had taken.place between
Sampson County and Robeson County Indians, the pamphlet mentions
that the first teachers in two Sampson County schools, beginning in
1910 and 1911, were "Croatans from Robeson County" (Butler
1916:40–2, 44).

An Indian from Sampson County, C. D. Brewington, later (in the
1950s) published a pamphlet drawing many interconnections between
several Indian groups in North Carolina and attempting to relate them
to Indian groups of the 1600s and 1700s. Brewington, an educator and
minister who married a Robeson County woman and moved from
Sampson to Robeson, categorizes several groups, including Robeson
and Sampson Indians, as "Eastern North Carolina Indians":

I have no hesitance in expressing the belief that the Eastern North Carolina
Indians are an amalgamation of the Five Civilized Tribes with John White's
Lost Colony, and that the present Indians are their descendants, with further
amalgamation continuing down to the present time. These amalgamated
Indians were first found over two hundred and fifty years ago in Eastern North
Carolina on the banks of the Cape Fear and its tributaries, including Conarie
[Coharie]; both big and little Coharie, South River and Mingo, also the Neuse
and Lumbee Rivers. These rivers are found in Sampson and adjoining counties,
where they are living to this day [Brewington n.d.:6].

Although some groups, like the Sampson County Indians (now
known as the Coharie), have long intermarried with Robeson Indians,
other groups have not been immediately acceptable to Robeson Indians. In order to weed out people "of questionable origin," the Robeson group established a racial screening committee for Indian schools
in the 1920s. Ultimately, however, many groups have been approved
for intermarriage, and often Indian teachers or preachers from Robeson have been instrumental in defining the groups with whom they
have worked as acceptably Indian.

Individuals migrating from other groups apparently find acceptance more readily than larger numbers of people arriving within a short span of time. A case in point is the group, remarked upon earlier, whom the Lumbee call the "Smilings." This group from Sumter County, South Carolina, apparently arrived between about 1906 and 1925 to settle in Robeson County.[4] Lumbees refused to allow "Smiling" children admittance to their schools, and eventually the group sued and obtained a fourth school in the then segregated Robeson County system. That arrangement ended in the late 1950s, and although there was prejudice still evident on the part of some Lumbees toward the "Smilings" in 1967–68, it appeared to be diminishing. A Lumbee man who lived near their settlement claimed,

> "A lot of the Smilings out where I live are blond-headed and blue-eyed. The old ones used to be terrible thieves – they'd steal mules and horses and cows and paint them. But the ones now aren't like that."

Another Lumbee who knew and had worked with many Independent Indians explained Lumbee–Smiling relations this way:

> During the 1930s, what he called the "Council of Racial Purity" [the racial screening committee for the Indian schools] had denied the Smilings entry into the Robeson County Indian schools. There was a court case brought by Smilings and eventually the county had to provide separate schools for them. He said that a distant relative of his had married a Smiling, was cut off from the family, and is living in the Smiling area. In general, however, he thought that prejudice was growing less. He said, "They're a wonderful people."
> Initially he took the position that they were a very distinct group. But then he said there were hardly any of them, so how could they keep their identity? "They don't need their identity anymore. They're on their way to extinction as a group anyway."

Many Lumbees were reluctant to talk about the Smilings, apparently embarrassed by the subject.

> An Indian man offered to show us around the county not long after we arrived. My husband asked whether he knew anything about the Smilings, to which the Indian demanded, "What have you heard about them?" When my husband responded, "A group different from the Lumbee," the Indian muttered, "They [Lumbees] don't think they're [Smilings] Indian – they [Lumbees] don't think they're [Smilings] like us. It's a sensitive subject." He then changed the subject.

Still another Indian, in a discussion of groups considered by Lumbees to be "of questionable background," was confronted with the proposition that some people said the Smilings were Indian, Negro, and White. To this he quickly and rather nervously replied, "No, the Smilings are a separate group with a separate identity."

The interconnections between Robeson Indians and similar people elsewhere are based on intermarriage and the exchange of ideas and expertise. The Robeson group's early successes inspired other groups to attempt similar legal feats. For example, a Haliwa man told me at the annual Haliwa Homecoming in 1973 that he had gone to Robeson County many years ago, before the Haliwas had recognition. He said, "I'd heard about Robeson County and wanted to see for myself." He met a Robeson Indian from an active and influential family and said that since that time the Robeson man and his brothers had "helped the people here a lot, and now we have our own recognition." He also mentioned other contacts with the Robeson group, including intermarriage. One Indian maintained that the Robeson County schools, and particularly the Normal School–college, had "changed the complexion of the marginal groups" by training teachers for many of the groups (see also Butler 1916). He spoke of the need for such groups "to establish their identity in their own realms."

Skin color or physical appearance is not in itself a barrier to the acceptance of a non-Lumbee into the Lumbee community. But the darker an unknown person is, the more closely his claims to Indianness are likely to be scrutinized, and skin color is widely commented upon, light skin, on the whole, being preferred to dark. But just because a person has dark skin, he is not excluded from recognition as a Lumbee, so long, again, as one of his parents is a socially recognized Lumbee and neither a socially recognized Black.

There is a certain amount of joking about skin color, which can rapidly lead to insult if the two parties are not close or are not in a good mood. A rather dark Indian man, upon greeting his aging, lighter-skinned father, of whom he was fond, called out, "Hey, black boy," to which the father responded, "Hey, white boy." This comfortable joking was made possible by the closeness of their relationship, which allowed a presumption of good will, and perhaps by the inverted play of contrasts between epithets and actual skin color. In another instance in which an Indian man reportedly called a younger Indian "black boy," the young man reacted strongly to what he probably correctly perceived as an intended insult. He is said to have gone to his car and returned with a shotgun, with which he killed the insulting Indian. The Indian who told this story ended it by saying, "If you live by the sword, you die by the sword." Such is the power of words.

The term "black Indian," sometimes used to designate individual darker-skinned Indians, is never used in direct address unless either insult or joking is intended. It refers only to the person's skin color, not to his behavioral characteristics. In this, then, it is not the true obverse of the term "White Indian," which denotes a person's life-style, values, and behavior. "White Indian" is a term of criticism, of harsh judgment against the individual so categorized, who could choose to act otherwise – that is, to "act like an Indian" instead of "like a White." "Black Indian" carries no moral judgment. It is a reflection of aesthetic preferences, not moral ones. A dark-skinned Indian can, if he behaves appropriately, be considered a "reâl Indian," whereas an Indian who behaves like a White can never be so considered. Conceivably a person could be referred to as both a "black Indian" and a "White Indian," if a dark-skinned individual were to adopt White values and neglect Indian ones. It must also be said that I never heard anyone use both these terms to describe one individual.

Sometimes the aesthetic preference for light skin can be very strong. Not long after our arrival in Robeson County, I observed a teenaged Indian girl, whom I thought to be very beautiful, at church. Curious, after the service I asked an Indian in the congregation who she was. I described her as beautiful, explained what she had been wearing and where she had been sitting, to no avail. The person I asked simply could not imagine who I was talking about and could not recall seeing a particularly beautiful girl sitting where I described her as having sat. This encounter was repeated with two or three more Indians, as I became more and more puzzled about why I could not find anyone to identify the girl. Finally I found someone who recalled a girl sitting in the place I mentioned and wearing the appropriate clothes. But the Indian who could at last identify her looked at me incredulously and exclaimed, "But she's not beautiful! She's too dark." When I checked further, I discovered that my description of beauty had confounded people. They could not understand how I could find the girl beautiful. But when I consulted with other Whites who knew her, they all attributed great beauty to her.

Preferences for light skin can affect the choice of marriage partners or cause favoritism on the part of parents and grandparents. A dark-skinned Indian woman was heard to remark to her lighter-skinned Indian husband, "You married me even though I'm dark." And of a White man married to a relatively dark Indian woman, an Indian woman remarked, "He married her and she's dark." Another Indian woman, describing an encounter in an Indian store between a White Northerner and an Indian who had entered, said, "This man [entering] was dark, and I'm sure he [the Northern White] thought he was a Negro, but he was an Indian." Parents and grandparents were reported sometimes to favor light-skinned over dark-skinned children and grandchildren. An Indian told me that his mother came from South Carolina and had married a Robeson County man. The parents and children used to visit his mother's mother in South Carolina, who always told him that he was too dark and she did not like him. "She just told me right out I was too dark. . . . I never thought my father got his due from her, because she said he was dark too." This clear favoritism based on color preference created a very painful situation for the grandson.

Thus it may be seen that, in certain contexts, Indians consider skin color to be important. Some Indians have absorbed White values regarding skin color, and all the Indians I talked to assumed that Whites preferred light skin to dark. But however deeply the aesthetic preference for light skin may be embedded in some Indians, Robeson County Indians have apparently never split their community along color lines. Other similar Indian communities have. Reportedly both Sampson County Indians and one other group have gone through periods in which lines were drawn within the group on the basis of color and presumed Black ancestry, with a lighter-skinned group seeking to exclude a darker-skinned group from membership.

George F. Butler mentions that the Sampson County community split over the enrollment of children who, it was deemed by some Indians, "contained negro blood to the prohibitive degree" (1916:31). He adds that the exclusion of these children in 1911 or 1912 "created confusion and friction in this Indian school," which, along with the subsequent annoyance of the County Board of Education, led to the 1913 cancellation of provision for Indian schools by the state legislature (Butler 1916:32). There is also note made of the fact that between 1912 and 1916, some taxpayers listed as Indians in 1912 were forced off the Indian tax list "as they were known to contain negro blood" (Butler 1916:33). Here we have people who have at one point been considered members of the Indian community being formally excluded at another because of their presumed Negro heritage.

A similar exclusionary process was at work, at least for a time, in an Indian community in northern North Carolina. Pollitzer, Menegaz-Bock, and Herion (1966) were primarily concerned with blood factors and gene frequencies in their analysis of the community, but they mention that in 1958 and 1959 when they did their study, they found a schism in the group:

. . . criteria for membership in the Indian Association were being rigorously applied and two distinct groups had begun to come into being, the one more Negroid in appearance than the other [Pollitzer, Menegaz-Bock, and Herion 1966:35].

When the split first began, "psychological and political factors caused the withdrawal of a phenotypically less Negroid element from a more Negroid one" (Pollitzer, Menegaz-Bock, and Herion 1966:36). But they also note that the schism was not maintained, as competition between the two factions increased:

In 1957, a segment of this population, considering itself to be Indian, formed an exclusive association. They succeeded in establishing their own schools, which were soon recognized and supported by the state. The remainder of the isolate was considered to be Negro, and their children attended Negro schools. Membership in the Indian Association was by invitation; only those who appeared to be healthy and non-Negroid were invited to become members. Friction between the two groups soon developed. As tensions increased, the leaders strengthened the Indian Association with new members by lowering both the racial and health barriers. As a result, the two groups now are similar in physical appearance [Pollitzer, Menegaz-Bok, and Herion 1966:27–8].

A permanent split apparently occurred in Columbus County, North Carolina. Franklin Frazier interviewed some people in the "colored" community for his 1939 study, *The Negro Family in the United States.* From their reports, it appears that before the Civil War there was a large community that had been labeled "mulatto." Some apparently claimed to be Indian, but all set themselves apart from the slaves, taking pride in their free ancestry and referring to themselves as a "nationality" and "the tribe" (Frazier 1939:236;237,n 28). Of this group originally classified as "mulattoes," Frazier claims, some set themselves apart as Indians, others "entered the white race," and many merged into the general Negro population (1939:236–7).

After the Indians and those who claimed to be Indians set themselves apart as a distinct race, the members of the colored community in Columbus County ceased to regard their group as a peculiar race and came to think of themselves as a part of the general Negro population [Frazier 1939:236–7].

Frazier goes on to remark that many of those who chose a Black identity went on to become prominent leaders, both in the county and in the state.[5]

Whatever tensions have been encountered over skin color and/or reputed Black ancestry, the Lumbee have not resolved them by casting out members of the group. Guy B. Johnson, who did fieldwork among the Robeson Indians in the 1930s, suggests how tensions at one period were resolved:

In 1885, when the Indians were legally declared a separate race and were named Croatan, they faced the problem of deciding just who was Indian and who was not. They wanted to weed out those who were considered "undesirables," but it was difficult for them to draw the line. They evidently fell back on a sort of pragmatic definition, viz.: an Indian is a person called an Indian by other Indians. It was as if they had said, "All right, everyone who is already in can stay in, but woe unto anybody with Negro blood who tries to get in hereafter" [1939:519].

He also says that a split between light and dark Indians is "incipient but never openly admitted" (G. Johnson 1939:520).

Robeson Indians appear always to have had many factions, but none has crystallized along color or imputed-ancestry lines clearly and definitively enough to result in a community split that counts some people as members of the group and some as nonmembers. By not creating strict blood-quantum rules of membership and by emphasizing behavioral characteristics, Robeson Indians have opened the way for relatively easy admittance and acceptance of new people into the Lumbee community. In refusing to define membership in terms of presumed biological ancestry, either in degrees of Indian "blood" or in notions of "racially" determined appearance, the Indians have rejected White criteria and set up their own. Physical appearance is obviously significant to Indians because they know that Whites evaluate them on that basis, but Lumbees today refuse, and insofar as can be determined in the past refused, to characterize themselves as a group according to physical appearance. They do not refer to themselves as having "red" skin (or "copper" skin, or whatever) and straight dark hair, for example, even though early White observers described some of them in that light (Norment 1875, Leitch in U.S. Senate Reports 1872).

By casting their identity in terms of behavioral characteristics, Lumbees have enabled people who are willing to behave like Lumbees to live easily among them.

> One afternoon an Indian woman was driving me home when we passed an Indian man who disliked me and my husband. The woman suggested, teasingly, that we stop to talk to him. I responded, in the same vein, that I thought he would enjoy seeing us. She laughed and said we shouldn't take him seriously, and I said "We don't – he's just foolish." She looked over with a start and exclaimed, "You've been here so long you're even talking like us." When I asked what she meant, she replied, "That's just what we say – 'he's foolish.'" She went on to say that we had become part of the community and were into everything. Then she repeated approvingly what the wife of a White couple who have lived actively in the Indian community for many years and whose son has married a Lumbee woman had said. The White woman told the Indian woman that she doesn't know how to act around White people anymore and that White people make her uneasy.

Although non-Lumbee newcomers never "become" Lumbees, their children or grandchildren usually do through the marriage of a parent or grandparent into the Lumbee community. The White couple mentioned above are considered by Lumbees to be very actively part of the Indian community, but not to be Indians. Their son's children, however, are Indians, through their mother. In this way, outsiders are incorporated into the community relatively smoothly, and in a generation or two, their descendants become, simply, Lumbees. This process adds to the growth of the group in numbers and to its range of individual talents and perspectives.

Lumbees' concepts of their Indian identity also have repercussions in the Black and White communities. Both Blacks' and Whites' group identities and their relations with Indians are affected.

Black, White, and Indian identity concepts

It has become a truism that groups define themselves in relation to one another. Certainly each of the three major communities in Robeson County does just that. But the notion of contrast by itself does not help us very much to understand what goes on in Robeson or elsewhere. There are at least two reasons why it does not.

First, the notion that groups always define themselves in contrast to one another tends to obscure one option that may be available to some people, which is merger into one or another of the supposedly contrastive groups. And second, such a notion fails to develop what is potentially the most interesting line of enquiry, which is the content of the dimensions of contrast. In any social situation, there are many apparently possible contrasts, yet only a few are selected for emphasis, as Lévi-Strauss has demonstrated in his essay on totemism (1963). This raises the questions of why certain dimensions have been chosen and what their emotional and intellectual quality has to do with the way people think and behave.

Regarding identity options, it might well be asked whether Lumbee ancestors had the option of merging with one or the other of their neighbors. Ordinarily, "might have been" arguments seem out of place and off the point, but here a discussion of possibilities can be illuminating. Let us look initially at the logical possibilities that may have existed, *given* the social milieu and the views of Whites about the "mulattoes," and *assuming* the Lumbee to be the sheerly self-maximizing people they have sometimes been counted.

A few social scientists have assumed that the Lumbee are motivated principally by their desire not to be Black. They want not to be Black, the reasoning goes, so that they can escape the stigma and discrimination suffered by Blacks. Actually, it is said, they would like to be White, but failing that will "settle" for being Indian:

The Indian, then, is forever on the defensive. He feels that there is always a question mark hanging over him. His wish to escape the stigma of Negro kinship, and thus to be identified with the white man, is uppermost in his mind. It is this wish which dominates his behavior and determines his modes of personal adjustment to the other races [G. Johnson 1939:519].

These are all "reluctant Indians" – Nanticokes, Chickahominy, Lumbees. Most of them would doubtless prefer to be whites. But, since that goal is beyond their reach, they will settle for Indian. It is better to be red than black – even an off-shade of red [Berry 1963:161].

Such statements as Berry's and Johnson's confuse the Indian point of view with a White outsider's point of view. For an Indian, being White is hardly the *summum bonum* implied here. I have argued in the previous chapter that a Lumbee desire not to be Black is matched by a desire not to be White either, and that both these "negatives" are balanced by a positive notion of what their Indianness means to them. They have consistently sought recognition as original Americans, "Indians," as Whites call them.

Leaving my argument aside for a moment, let us assume for the sake of discussion that Lumbee ancestors really did want to be White. Could they have accomplished that? Many Lumbees are light skinned (and many have been since at least the middle of the last century, if Norment [1875] and Townsend [1872] are to be believed). By casting off darker-skinned relatives and friends, they could probably eventually have been classified as White by applying the same energy to that goal as they have to being recognized as Indians. I say "probably" because that appears to be what has happened to some of the so-called Brass Ankles, Melungeons, and Rockingham County Indians.

Brewton Berry states in a 1945 article that most of the South Carolina Brass Ankles, who are said to have Indian, Negro, and White ancestry, "have persistently fought for white status, and their efforts have met with a surprising degree of success" (1945:36). In many counties they had at that time been admitted to White schools, churches, and restaurants; in others they were still excluded. More recent research in 1976 indicates that many Brass Ankles (a bitterly resented term) have married people whose all-White ancestry has never been questioned and that a number of communities in which they formerly lived have disappeared. Even the Whites who still distinguish between themselves and Brass Ankles in conversations with a White outsider make no distinctions in face-to-face behavior between ordinary Whites and Brass Ankles (Gildemeister 1977 and personal communication).

The derogatorily named Melungeons of Tennessee and Kentucky, to whom some ancestors of the Lumbee may be related, were formerly segregated in separate schools and said by local Whites to possess Indian, Negro, and White "blood." After a struggle with Whites, they have now been largely accepted by local Whites as "White" (Price 1950, 1951).

In Rockingham County, North Carolina, a group of people who did not gain legal recognition as Indians are reported to have split in 1931 along color lines between those who attempted to gain recognition as

Whites and those who claimed an Indian identity. The latter said that they were descended from White men who fought in the Civil War for the Confederacy and from the full-blooded Indian women who married them (Nunn 1937). Recent information is scarce, but it appears that at least some of the group were recognized as White (and some as Indians and Blacks) by U.S. census enumerators in 1950 (Beale 1957).

These examples suggest that if enough Robeson County Indians had desired strongly to be White, they might well have accomplished that, despite inevitable White objections, particularly if the Indian community split along color lines.

No one has ever hinted that Indians wanted to be Black, but if they had, they might easily have merged with the Black community, as Whites wanted them to, and Blacks probably would not have objected. The situation in nearby Columbus County, North Carolina is, perhaps, illustrative. According to Frazier (1939:236–7), some members of the "free Negro" community merged with Blacks, others with Whites, and the remainder claimed to be Indians (today recognized as "Waccamaw-Siouans").

There might even have been other non-Indian identities available to Lumbee ancestors. As we have seen, some Whites at the critical juncture after the Civil War attributed to the group "Spanish" and "Portuguese" ancestry. If Indians had been motivated to emphasize this kind of ancestry, they might have been able to gain recognition as Europeans, albeit "dark" Europeans. The "Turk-Americans" of South Carolina, who are now classified as White but who nevertheless preserve a distinctive community, have claimed Turkish and White ancestry (Kaye 1963, Trillin 1969, White 1975b). As early as 1790, the ancestors of the "Turk-Americans" petitioned the South Carolina legislature to treat them according to White rather than Negro laws because they were, they argued, "subjects of the Emperor of Morocco" (*Journal of the House of Representatives*, Wed. Jan. 20, 1790, as quoted in Berry 1963:187). They were successful in being accorded this right. The group had separate schools until 1950, when they began litigation to gain admission to White schools. The litigation finally procured for them the right of admission.

So far, this discussion has been concerned with logical possibilities or "options" open to Indian ancestors *if* those ancestors had been motivated toward one or another of them. The notion of "option" or "choice" obviously implies that the actors see themselves with an array of possibilities. If the actors do not perceive themselves to have options, they cannot make a choice. Unfortunately, there is no evidence to show whether Indian ancestors thought they had a choice of group identities.

All we have are accounts of the way they behaved. Judging from these, they have single-mindedly claimed to be autochthonous and have struggled for legal status reflecting that claim.

That they should have done so for more than a hundred years from an entirely negative motivation (the desire not to be Black) is psychologically improbable (cf. Eriskson 1966, 1968), to say the least. The Indians have been concerned all the while with enabling their community to flourish, with providing for themselves the opportunity to be together in their own ways, and with keeping their "ethos" alive. Indianness has at least enough of these positive aspects to be emotionally satisfying and intellectually compelling to many of those who claim it. The fact that to be Indian is to be "not Black" may have had advantages, but these rather meager material advantages should not be mistaken for major motivations. Concern for keeping the community together and preserving its integrity is much more likely to be a major motivating force. If Indians were to become White or Black or anything else, they would have to negate and forget their Indian heritage, their sense of community and place.

In the 1970s, individual Lumbee Indians do have a choice. Many of the lighter Indians know that they can easily "pass" for Whites. One such woman, angry at the frustrations of coping with political maneuverings by Whites, proclaimed, "I could go away from this county and be White. Why should I stay here and put up with this?" The question was a rhetorical one, for the woman had no intention of leaving the county or her Indian identity behind. She was proud of her Indianness and of her people (as she later said), and she was angry that Indians should be denied benefits and rights accorded to Whites. She did not want to *be* White, but she did want to have similar opportunities and benefits. Given the possibility that many Indians now could leave Robeson County and "become" White, *and they know they could,* the fact that they do not (or that so few do) cannot be explained if they are motivated, as Berry and G. Johnson maintain, by a desire not to be Black combined with a desire to be White.

Indian ideas about identity are attached to symbols that contrast along certain dimensions with the identity symbols of Blacks and Whites. Logically, these Indian identity symbols could have come from a number of different domains. The Indians could, for example, have used symbolism related to the racial system for describing their group identity. They could have called themselves "red"- or "copper"-skinned people, terms that are no more or less descriptive of "real" skin color than "white" or "black." Or, they could have focused on "blood," with all its race and kinship connotations, particularly if they had virtually eliminated marriages with outsiders by, say, prohibiting the offspring of such unions from attending Indian schools. Rules could have been constructed along genealogical or "blood" lines and could have required a minimal percentage of Robeson Indian "blood" for admittance. But the Indians did not take up any of these possibilities. Indians do not use racial symbols in projecting their group image at all – instead they use "ethnic" imagery based on folk history and behavioral characteristics.[6] In the next chapter, I will argue that, in the United States, "ethnicity" is importantly tied to group notions of history and culture, and that this sets it apart from "race," which is based on folk notions about biology. Blacks and Whites, however, do use the physical appearance imagery of racial dogma with which to identify themselves and each other, although each group attaches different meanings to the images. Furthermore, in Robeson County, Whites and Blacks define themselves explicitly in terms of one another but not in relation to Indians. Indians define themselves implicitly in relation to the other two. Let us look at the symbolism used by each of the groups, how it fits into the symbolism employed by the others, and what some of the implications of these differences are for the relations of one group with another.

Whites

For both Whites and non-Whites, *the* symbol of Whiteness is white skin. To Whites, white skin represents their aesthetic, moral, intellectual, and biological superiority and their concomitant "natural" social supremacy over non-Whites. It is Whiteness, represented by white skin, that is "naturally" superior, not light skin in and of itself. Light skin confers superiority only upon a person who is socially recognized as White and is presumed born of two White parents. Light skin does not make a Black or an Indian White. Beyond a general agreement among Whites concerning this superiority and supremacy, there is little elaboration of the concept of Whiteness (even those Whites who do not hold this view recognize that the majority of Whites do).

This lack of elaboration is an indication of one of the fundamental differences between White identity and the two varieties of non-White identity. "White," for most Whites in Robeson County, is a category of persons into which they fit, not a "people" (sharing, as *Webster's* puts it, "common culture, tradition, or sense of kinship") to which they belong. For a Black or an Indian, however, Blackness or Indianness does identify him with a people, gives him a style of being, and a sense of belonging with others who are like him in important and fundamental ways. It would be easy, if not terribly enlightening, to argue that developing a sense of common enterprise and unity is a good adaptive strategy for people like Indians and Blacks who have needed such a mechanism to hold them together and to enable their survival in relation to the more powerful and dominant Whites. Whites, because at least theoretically they were on top (even if only some "really" were), needed no such concept of their being "a people." There is, no doubt, some truth in this, but by these standards one would expect Whites now to be busily constructing a concept of their unity as a people (or something akin to that) because their dominance is seriously challenged and, at least in the political realm, lessening rapidly. Yet there is no evidence to suggest that Robeson Whites are coalescing into "a people" either in concept or in practice.

Leaving aside a rather crude causal schema for the moment, let us try to understand what kind of a category "White" is for Whites and to see how that relates to the kinds of connections and divisions that exist among them. There is a tendency among Robesonians of all groups to categorize events, objects, behavior, and situations as either "natural" or "unnatural." Whites often exhibit this tendency when talking about race. For Whites, "White," "Black," and "Indian" are "natural" categories of people, "God-given" because God intentionally created visible differences among people. Further, Whites tend to view much of the behavior and many of the "aptitudes" they associate with each race as inherent. In 1969, a prominent White politician in Robeson County gave an interview to the editor of the Indian newspaper who was, at that time, a young Northern White man. The politician must have been well aware that tensions existed between the Indian and White communities and that there had been a rapid increase in non-White voters. Therefore, what he said and the straightforward manner in which he expressed it surprised even the most cynical Indians and a good many Whites. He told the editor, for the record:

"The reason industry has been attracted to Robeson County is because the three races get along so well. Of course, different races have different aptitudes."
". . . niggers make good brickmasons . . . they have a lot of patience."
". . . Indians make good mechanics and are good with their hands."
". . . whites make good clerical workers and things such as that" [ellipses and quotes in original; *The Lumbee* 1969:2].

The White politician retired from politics not long afterward, and many said his retirement had been precipitated by the publication of this interview.

In 1967–68, many, though by no means all, Whites talked in terms of a rather standard stereotype of Blacks – namely, that Blacks are physically unattractive, have an unpleasant body odor, are lazy, unintelligent, dissembling, musical, good at sports, and uncaring about other

Blacks. These physical, intellectual, and moral characteristics are all said to be tied to one another, to be "natural" qualities of Blacks inherited with and carried by their "Black blood." Whites, in short, view Blacks as a category of human beings, not as a people with common cultural traditions. Neither do Whites conceive of Blacks as a moral community.

Because Whites tend to view behavior as somewhat inherent, it is frequently said of an individual's actions, "It's his nature to do that." Such a phrase may be applied to a White, a Black, or an Indian. Because at least some behavior is seen as inherent, Whites do not hold Blacks or anyone else entirely accountable for all their actions. In the case of Blacks, it is said that they, like children, sometimes cannot help themselves. But this attitude does not extend to certain areas of behavior, as any Black man accused of having raped a White woman discovers. In such a case, the Black man is deemed entirely responsible for his actions. Whites can also justify punishment on the grounds that Blacks, like children, must be governed strictly in order to be taught proper behavior.

In this case, Whites define Blacks in terms similar to those with which they define themselves – namely, as a category rather than as a people. Whites have assigned Blacks particular characteristics that are seen as polar opposites of the presumed virtues of Whites. If White skin epitomizes beauty, which reaches its apogee in Southern White womanhood, Black skin is ugly, presumably particularly so in Black men. If Blacks are uncontrolled and impulsive, Whites are there to provide order and guidance, the governance of chaos. Whites and Blacks become, in this White system of thought, reciprocals of one another, a positive and a negative image of human nature.

Indians obtrude into White conversation and purview much less often and less thoroughgoingly. Whites tend to differ widely in their opinions about who and what Indians are and where, in the moral scale of things, they fit. There is no widely accepted stereotype of Indians, whereas there is of Blacks. In general, however, Whites seem to view Indians as a community or a people rather than simply as a category. Indians are conceived by most Whites to have a moral order, at least among themselves. It is "natural," a White may say, for an Indian to be proud – one cannot be surprised at his proud behavior. This quality appears to have been accepted as "Indian" behavior and to have inspired irritation alternating or tinged with respect (see also Blu 1977).

Overlaying this penchant for interpreting people, behavior, events, and things in "natural" terms is the motif of individualism. The individual case, the individual exception, concern for the individual as opposed to his class or race or occupation group – all are constant counterpoints to the generalities expressed in "natural" arguments and assumptions (see also, for example, Moreland 1958:186). Thus one may encounter a White who insists, "Nigras are all lazy and ignorant," and who in the next breath points out an exception: "Of course not all of them are like that. Take the [surname] family. They're all hardworking and they've all made something of themselves." The ability of an individual to do "anything he puts his mind to, if only he's willing to work" is taken for granted.

This constant reference to the individual both reflects and reinforces a heavy emphasis on personal knowledge, relationships, and experiences that pervades everyday life for everyone in Robeson County. People are urged by ministers of the gospel to "accept Christ as your personal Savior." A man gives his word or accepts another man's as absolutely binding when the two "know" each other. In an argument someone will cite to great effect the evidence of "my own personal experience."

But, in the end, the "individual case," the known exception, serves only to leaven the heavy dough of "natural" existence. It allows Whites in particular to absorb exceptions to their dicta about race without changing the basic concepts, without seeing a challenge to their way of thinking. Although Blacks and Indians share, to a degree, the talk of "natural" things as well as the personalism and individualism, non-Whites do not apply these ideas in the same way to race.

Among Whites, a consciousness of who they are, of their common classification as Whites, does not result in even the temporary submerging of the deep divisions between classes, political parties, and ideologies, and between Whites of different national origins. Whites have failed to develop the sense of themselves as a people that has helped Indians and Blacks to bridge (upon occasion) whatever divisions of class, political opinion, and differences in origin exist in their communities. White class divisons are pronounced, and the economic and social distance between poor and rich is great. The poverty among some Whites is similar to that of poor Blacks or Indians who live with hunger, inadequate housing, and illness sometimes caused by malnutrition. The contrast between the poor and the "working class" of regularly employed, adequately clothed, housed, and fed Whites is great enough, but the gulf between poor Whites and upper-class (or, as most designate themselves, "upper-middle-class") Whites is enormous. Upper-class Whites control the financial and social life of the county – and, until recently, the political life as well. The White middle class has been rapidly expanding and some have moved into positions of considerable influence as well. Indians and Blacks are well aware of these divisions within the White community. One old Indian man contrasted class divisions in the White community with those in the Indian:

> "Indians have classes just like you do – different classes of people. But at the same time we're one people, not like Whites. For example, if you do something to a White man who's an important man – like [a prominent local White] – there'd be some Whites not so high up who would be glad. But if you hit an Indian, even if he's an ordinary man, then everyone will have sympathy for him, same as if you hit an important Indian."

For Indians and Blacks, "racial" identity – Indianness or Blackness – often overrides the differences within the group. One Indian pointed out, regarding Indian unity: "People act together because there is no other choice. They don't really see eye to eye." Indians and Blacks have developed a sense of "the common good" as well as a clear view of who they say they must unite against – that is, Whites. But Indians and Blacks also have evolved emotional satisfaction in their self-proclaimed unity, and an expressive style that each is proud of.

Politics has always been a source of division and fundamental disagreement among Whites. After the differences during the Revolution between Tories and Whigs, there began to be differences over the abolition of slavery, and over whether or not to stay within the Union. Robeson County, as has been pointed out, had a strong Republican contingent before and after the Civil War, a split that the Indians used to their advantage in gaining recognition as Croatan Indians. Today political differences are somewhat more complicated. Whites are now mostly Democrats, but the Republicans have recently made gains (including among a few of the more prosperous Indians), and there are even a few who claimed American Party membership when George Wallace ran as its candidate for President. Of these, White Republicans tend to be rather elitist and very conservative in fiscal policy, and American Party people tend to be conservative and populist. Among Democrats, there is a split between the conservatives and the "liberals." These liberals should not be confused with Northern liberals, for their aims and ideals are often different. Southern liberals tend to be more racially conservative and more populist than their Northern counterparts and can be distinguished best from other Southerners by their more relaxed attitude about race and their concern for creating opportunities for the disadvantaged. In 1967–68, there was still, among liberal Southerners (who are mostly Democrats), little explicit talk of absolute equality. Rather, equal opportunity was emphasized.

Whites of all party affiliations and philosophical positions supported "our country" and considered themselves patriotic with a fervor not usually so uniformly found in other sections of the United States. It is, perhaps, a little surprising that the same people at one moment remind a Yankee outsider of the viciousness and vindictiveness of the Yankees during and after the War Between the States and at the next moment extoll the virtues of the United States today in contrast to the vices of Communism. An editorial in a local White newspaper discussed this patriotism in the light of Fourth of July celebrations that had just been held:

> What is gratifying about the celebration of patriotic occasions is the reaffirmation of love of country. This does not necessarily mean endorsement of all national policies, both international and domestic. It does mean a sustaining love of this land and its people, the principles upon which it was founded, and its purposes [*The Robesonian,* 1970a:8A].

It may be that this patriotic attitude, among other things, helped White Southerners in Robeson County and elsewhere to accept the massive changes brought about by the demolition of legal segregation. In Robeson County, there has been a certain amount of legal maneuvering to avoid full-scale integration, and only the normal amount of buying votes or drivers. There has been no hysteria, no racist appeals, and no organized violent resistance from Whites, as there has been in some other areas of the South. Indeed, it is an interesting question why Whites in Robeson County, who clearly perceived the non-White threat to their continued political domination of the county and who have by now (1979) experienced the loss of their absolute control, did not offer more resistance.

There are also ethnic divisions among Whites that stem from differences in national origin and religious background. The most significant of these divisons occur between Anglo-Saxon-Americans (who are, in this area, mostly of Scottish origin), Jewish-Americans, and Greek-Americans. It may be that these divisions have helped to prevent Whites from thinking of themselves as a single people with a common history and traditions. In Robeson County, Jewish-Americans make up probably less than .5 percent of the White population, and Greek-Americans are even fewer in number. But because so many Jewish- and Greek-Americans are substantial businessmen, they have an influence greater than simple numbers would suggest. Although there is no systematic discrimination against either Jews or Greeks in Robeson County (clubs and voluntary organizations accept them as members), many Anglo-Saxons have stereotypical views of both groups and a few emphasize the negative elements of the stereotypes. When I remarked about the lack of discrimination to an "expatriate" White North Carolinian living in New York, he observed wryly, "That's true for that part of North Carolina, as long as the Jews are from the right class. There's no discrimination, just denigration."

Anglo-Saxons say of Jews that they are sober, industrious, family oriented (or "clannish" to those who would slur), and shrewd businessmen (or "clever cheaters" to those who resent them). It is said that Jews are primarily motivated by desire for economic gain. Combined with economic success, these qualities can be either respected or resented, and Anglo-Saxons appear to be divided, with more expressing respect for than resentment of Jews (Blu 1977). Jews are unquestionably accorded White status, but are said to be "different than the rest of us." And most Anglo-Saxons still do not want their children to marry Jews (nor do Jews generally want their children to marry non-Jews). Indians and Blacks recognize this division among Whites, classifying Jews and Greeks as "White, but not really White." An Indian explained this by saying that Jews and Greeks have suffered discrimination from Whites, too, and that, therefore, they are more understanding toward non-Whites.

And indeed, many Jewish and Greek merchants and businessmen have been in the forefront of providing opportunities for Blacks and Indians to fill jobs formerly reserved exclusively for Whites. They do not publicize their efforts to increase opportunities for fear that their own positions in the White community (and the status of their ethnic groups) might be jeopardized. Although some efforts of Greek and Jewish businessmen, such as the hiring of non-White sales or supervisory personnel, could be viewed as being good for business so long as White customers are not lost, the privately declared motivation is usually stated in terms of easing racial discrimination or opening employment opportunities to everyone. Awareness among Greeks and Jews that either they or their ancestors have suffered discrimination, if not necessarily of the same kind, does often, they say, enable them to sympathize with non-Whites. Sometimes acts are purely philanthropic. In the early 1970s, a Jewish professional, upon his retirement, gave his professional library and office equipment to a young Indian man, who was thus enabled to establish himself independently from Whites. Had it not been for this gift, the Indian could not have afforded to be independent. But this kind of support is given quietly by Jews and Greeks, who have no desire to antagonize other Whites by appearing to favor non-Whites.

The Whites' concept of their own Whiteness, then, differs greatly from the group concepts held by Indians and Blacks. Whites consider themselves to be classifiable under a single category by virtue of their presumed inherent superiority, which is symbolized by white skin. But they do not imagine themselves to share a common history or origin, and if they were to stress origins and historical tradition, that might serve only to emphasize the divisions among the White ethnic groups.

No sense of Whiteness has developed to override the divisions of class, ethnicity, and political ideology or party affiliations present among Whites.

Blacks and Indians, however, have developed strong group concepts of themselves that emphasize shared characteristics and common traditions, and these concepts have enabled them at times to act with unity, submerging their differences. The fact that those who now constitute the Lumbee Indians probably originated from Indian groups of different linguistic stocks and were augmented by marriage with people from similar groups as well as with non-Indians has been discussed. The origins of Robeson County Blacks are more obscure because less investigated, but it is likely that the slaves who were brought by the early settlers came from diverse groups in Africa and the Caribbean and that these were later joined by other slaves with equally disparate origins. Peter Wood in *Black Majority* (1974) has painstakingly documented an original diversity among colonial Blacks in South Carolina that has subsequently been obscured by, among other things, a general sense of Blackness or Negritude among Blacks.

Blacks

Blacks do have a notion of themselves as a people, as sharing common experiences, characteristics, and "culture." They see themselves as "naturally" more expressive, more caring, and more considerate than Whites. For Blacks, these qualities are symbolized primarily by dark skin and by an inherent quality, "soul," which is latent in all Blacks but may or may not be manifest in particular individuals. "Soul" is a complicated concept that represents much of what is conceived to be good about Blackness – style, spontaneity, sincerity, "heart," and the ability to transform suffering into beauty or humor (see also Keil 1966 and Hannerz 1969 on "soul"). Blacks have, essentially, taken a characteristic that represents them in the racial schema used by Whites – namely, dark skin – and have used it to stand for themselves as a people, but have changed the meanings attached to it by Whites and at the same time elaborated the concept so that it is no longer simply categorizing. Whereas, for Whites, White skin is *the* symbol of their Whiteness, for Blacks, Black skin is only the foremost symbol of their Blackness. Other aspects of physical appearance have secondary significance and also stand for Blackness – such as tightly curled or kinky hair, thick lips, and a broad nose. These characteristics do not, literally and by themselves, indicate Blackness. Rather, they stand for Blackness in a general way. A White person with swarthy skin, kinky hair, thick lips, and a broad nose is still White.

These secondary physical characteristics said by Blacks and Whites alike to symbolize "Blackness" are valued by individual Blacks sometimes negatively and sometimes positively, depending upon the person and the context. One rather dark Negro said, referring to light-skinned Blacks, "You know what all the people like me say. If you look like one of them [a White], you are one of them." In discussing the hiring of a rural Negro deputy sheriff, another Black man said, "We don't want to get one of those 'red Negroes' hired – we want one you can tell from down the block." In both these remarks, the speakers were acknowledging and rejecting an older preference among Whites and in some Negro circles for "White" physical characteristics – light skin, wavy or straight hair, thin lips, and narrow nose. Such "White" characteristics are called "good" and the Negro ones "bad" by both Indians and Blacks. For Indians, the terms have the obvious meanings – many quite genuinely prefer the lighter, "Whiter" characteristics and make aesthetic judgments on the basis of them. But Blacks often invert the meanings, so that "good" comes to mean "ugly," "bad," or "undesirable," and "bad" comes to mean "beautiful," "good," "wonderful," or "desirable."

This kind of inversion was particularly evident in 1967–68. In Robeson County at that time, most Blacks referred to themselves as Negroes, but the urban Black Power movement was beginning to make itself felt. A Black Power leader from an urban center in North Carolina made several influential visits to Robeson County, speaking to large groups at meetings in churches and making contact with local Black political leaders. By the end of 1968, the younger people and some of the politicians were using Black Power rhetoric and referring to themselves as Blacks. For a few years after that, preferred terminology wavered between "Black" and "Negro" (pronounced "Kneegrow," not "Nig-rah"), with "Black" finally gaining the edge.

What the Black Power movement did was explicitly to invert the meanings attached to dark or "black" skin by Whites. For Whites, dark skin stands for ugliness, lack of virtue, and inferiority. Black Power asserts that "Black is beautiful." One of the images used by the Black Power leader in his talks in Robeson County was vivid and well received by Black audiences. He told of going swimming as a boy. When he came up from under water, he said, he would always throw his head back as though to get his hair out of his eyes the way White people had to do. The audience laughed heartily and sympathetically, as it was obvious to everyone that his hair would have continued to be closely curled around his head both in and out of the water and would never have been anywhere near his eyes. He then went on to point out how long it had taken him to recognize this as a virtue, and to learn to appreciate the kind of hair he had for its beauty and practical advantages. He then went on to talk more generally of how good it was to be Black.

With this explicitness and a ''Black is beautiful'' rhetoric, the Black Power leader sought to fight the ambivalence some Blacks had come to feel about themselves when they partially and perhaps even unconsciously accepted White evaluations of their worth, which conflict with the stated evaluations of Blackness or Negroness presented by their own people. Some Indians suffer from a similar ambivalence stemming from conflicting White and Indian evaluations of Indianness. However, many Blacks (and Indians) have maintained a positive image of themselves as a people and as individuals, despite White evaluations to the contrary. Black Power rhetoric enabled people for the first time in recent history to speak publicly and explicitly of themselves in terms that directly contradicted the White stereotype of Blacks. In this, then, one may see that Blacks define themselves partly and explicitly in reference to Whites, saying of themselves ''Blacks treat people better'' or are ''truer Christians'' than Whites. It is perhaps interesting to note that one older White woman from a prominent Robeson family regularly attended Negro churches because, she said, they had ''true religion,'' which she felt most White churches lacked. Other Whites regarded her as very eccentric but did not interfere with her. The symbols used by both Whites and Blacks to identify themselves and each other (though with different meanings attached to them) are those found in racial dogma. Blacks have supplemented physical-appearance imagery with the internal expressive qualities of ''soul'' and ''heart.''

A shared perception of the past is also important to Blacks' notions of themselves as people. Many families have preserved stories told by ex-slave grandparents and great-grandparents. Blacks have come to see themselves as having been forcibly taken by Whites from their African homeland and thrown into a terrible new life of slavery in which they were forbidden to preserve most of their former ways of life. Feelings of frustration, resentment, anger, and vulnerability aroused by thoughts of this past are often compounded by the present experience of powerlessness. Cut off from their distant African past, Blacks have often been looked down upon by Whites, who say that they have no culture, no traditions, are not fully civilized. In Robeson County, Blacks have increasingly incorporated recent national events into their view of themselves as a people rather than looking to newly created or imported Africanisms as some urban Blacks have done. The life and death of Dr. Martin Luther King, the success of sit-ins and demonstrations in other areas of the South, the urban disorders of the late 1960s all became part of the ongoing story of Black people in the United States, thereby emphasizing an identification with all Black people, wherever they are. This contrasts with the Indian identification with a place (Robeson County and the surrounding area) that stands for the Indians who live there. Robeson County Indians (and other Indians who have a land base) identify with Indians from other places only at a distance and in a very removed way. Their primary concern and interest remains centered upon their own localized group.

Blacks sometimes trace their sensitivity, concern, and caring for one another to the shared perception of the enslavement of Black ancestors and present discrimination. The common suffering known to have been experienced by ancestors and often experienced by the present generation helps create a bond among Blacks and reinforces the notion of themselves as a people.

The "natural" imagery used by Whites to talk about "the races" and their respective behavior patterns is repeated in Black discussions about themselves and others. If Blacks claim they "just naturally" have soul (although no one argues that all Blacks *have* soul, only the capacity for it), they maintain that Whites are "naturally" self-interested. Given this assumption about Whites, Blacks have concentrated in their political activities on making it clear to Whites that it is in their own self-interest to cooperate with Blacks. Such tactics as boycotts and litigation are preferred to physical intimidation. So far as I know, Blacks in Robeson County have never used direct physical confrontations with Whites. In a boycott, a merchant can be given graphic proof that his business will suffer if he does not hire Black personnel.

With such a view of Whites, Blacks have a few illusions about what they can expect from Whites. If they get more than they expected, well and good. If not, they are not so much disappointed as confirmed in their view of White nature. Importantly, and in distinct contrast with White views, Blacks do not believe that the social order is fixed, a "given" in the nature of things, however much they may attribute a particular individual's tendencies to his nature. Rather, for Blacks, the social order is a negotiable reality, something it is possible to change. And, of course, Blacks have changed the social reality. Everyone in Robeson County in 1967 recognized that legal segregation had been struck down because of the successful efforts of Blacks all over the country. Like Whites, Blacks do not hold individuals entirely accountable for their actions since, to a degree, what people do follows from their nature. In this, they are more forgiving of White behavior than Indians are. Indians expect more because they have a view of people as able to choose their actions and morally responsible for them. From the Indian point of view, if Whites are greedy, it is because Whites have chosen to be so, not because they are "naturally" that way.

Whites and Blacks, then, share various symbols for, and even (in a limited way) approaches to, interpreting human behavior. But this similarity is deceptive because the meanings attached to the symbols are often different (though they are also sometimes the same, which only adds to the confusion), and the approaches are used rather rigidly in the case of Whites and much more flexibly in the case of Blacks. Whites and Blacks therefore frequently *sound* as though they are communicating fully with one another, when this is in fact not the case. Whites say that they understand Blacks, but they often do not realize that Blacks are carrying on a many-leveled discourse susceptible to multiple interpretations and having several sets of meanings intertwined. The complexity of Black discourse emerged, for me, in 1966 in a courtroom full of people from all three races:

> During a session of magistrate's court in Robeson County a case involving a knifing incident between two young Black men was being tried. One of the witnesses called was the Black owner of the entertainment establishment where the incident took place. He was probably a bootlegger, since most such places of entertainment are dependent upon illegal alcohol in this legally dry county, and as such, I was told, he was quite likely paying off the county sheriff to leave him alone. He appeared to be a well-known figure – to both Blacks and Whites in the courtroom. In recounting his version of the incident, he explained that he had gone outside his establishment to try to calm things down between the two men – and found himself suddenly between two drawn knives. In response to a question about what happened next, he replied, "I ducked out fast. I don't know what happened next, because I was too busy getting out of there." His manner of presentation was rather theatrical, with shrugs, eye-rolling and a self-mocking tone – self-mocking at his implied cowardice in wanting to get out fast. He got a laugh from everyone, White, Black and Indian, and appeared pleased with his performance.

Here, he was presenting Whites with a living example of their stereotype of Blacks as he humorously emphasized witlessness, lack of knowledge, and cowardice. By validating the stereotype, he avoided trouble with Whites, and, at the same time, he avoided giving testimony favoring either of the two principals, both of whom had family and friends who patronized his establishment. But he was also playing to the Blacks in the audience, mocking, in his self-mocking, the White stereotype. Whites seemed quite unaware of this level of communication, while Blacks enjoyed precisely that unawareness.

Whatever the differences between White and Black images of themselves and each other, Whites and Blacks usually can communicate effectively with one another when they try, although Whites are sometimes unintentionally insulting. Indians, however, present a different matter.

Indians

Both Blacks and Whites are often confused by Indians and are rather wary of them. To them, Indians are a mass of contradictions – cohesive and threatening one moment, fragmented and fighting among themselves the next; angry one moment, reticent the next; touchy about insults, but often apparently nonchalant about what Blacks think are fundamental forms of discrimination, such as all-White juries or (until 1970) separate schools. Neither Whites nor Blacks have well-developed and widely shared views on what makes Indians do what they do, aside from an all-encompassing and vague "pride."

In practical terms, this has meant that both Blacks and Whites deal with Indians rather circumspectly in face-to-face situations. Neither wholly trusts Indians. Blacks know that many Indians consider themselves better than Blacks, and they fear that, given the opportunity, Indians will ally themselves with Whites. Whites are uneasy because of their inability to predict what Indians will do and because Indian leaders are not able to produce a consistent and disciplined following, so that when political deals are made with Indians, Whites are never sure whether they will come unstuck.

Indians, for their part, have difficulty dealing with both Blacks and Whites, partly because of differences in their concepts about one another, and partly because Indians tend to interpret others' behavior as they would their own. As has been pointed out, Indians use behavioral characteristics with which to symbolize to themselves their identity as a people. These characteristics express and reaffirm Indian-ness and are seen as a matter of moral choice rather than as inherent or "natural." Because Indians consider these characteristics to be matters of choice dependent upon individual decision, they tend to evaluate Indians, and others as well, in moral terms rather than "natural" ones. The decision to act like an Indian or to be "really" Indian is a moral one. If Indians may choose whether or not to act like Indians, then, from the Indian point of view, Whites and Blacks may choose whether to act like Whites or Blacks. Whites, who are said to be greedy and to lie, may choose *not* to behave that way. To Indians, the more moral action is *not* to behave like a White.

White behavior is often held up as an example of what not to do, or as the kind of behavior to be condemned whenever it is encountered. In a precinct political gathering, an Indian woman responded to accusations made by two Blacks present that certain Indian leaders had deceived the Blacks by saying angrily, "We've been lied to by Whites for three hundred years, and we're not going to be lied to by Indians now."

At the same meeting, one of the Blacks, indignant at feeling that Indian coalition leaders had made an important decision without consulting him, referred to some Indians as "yellow people," suggesting people whose social identity is dark but whose skin is light (as in the Black phrase "high-yellow"), whose orientation is correspondingly White, and at the same time who are cowardly. This insult was not picked up by any of the Indians present, either because they did not understand it or because they chose to ignore it in the interests of furthering the coalition. Instead of becoming angry at the Blacks, the Indians present expressed anger at other Indians and tried to soothe the feelings of the irate Black leaders.

One Indian way of dealing with Whites is, as has been noted, to avoid face-to-face contact with Whites insofar as that is feasible. One young Indian man, in response to my questions about what kinds of people Whites are, said a White is "someone you have as little to do with as possible, someone with White skin. You don't *know* him." Indians find Whites to be nearly as problematic as Whites find Indians. This is because although Indians mistrust Whites, they keep hoping for the best in White behavior. Indians appear to be profound believers in the perfectability of humankind. They are frequently disappointed, but apparently confirmed in their faith often enough to allow them to keep hoping.

Indians' attitudes towards Blacks are complex and in the process of changing. Some Indians appear to have adopted the White stereotype about Blacks, at least in part, and have a negative view of Blacks. Sometimes even those Indians who have worked hardest at creating new ties between the two groups retain somewhat negative images of Blacks. An Indian coalition worker once remarked, "Everybody knows the reason the White man brought the Black man over here is that he couldn't do nothing with the Indians. He couldn't make them [Indians] work and do what he wanted them to, but the Negro would." Many Indians reject some or all of the White stereotype, but have an unclear idea of who Blacks are. On the one hand, Blacks are people who have earned Indian respect for leading the struggle against racial discrimination in recent years, a discrimination in some degree shared by Indians and Blacks. A middle-aged Indian man explained the relationship between Blacks and Indians:

> "If you're a member of a minority group around here, you have to be a certain way." And then, elaborating in answer to the comment "I know what you mean, but I'd like to hear it in your own words," he went on: "You have to be liberal about race and you have to keep moving. We're a small group, and we have trouble accomplishing anything on the state level, let alone in Washington. As the Negro moves forward, it carries the Indians with them."

On the other hand, some Indians bitterly resented the fact that the only reason they could now eat in restaurants formerly closed to them was because "the Negroes opened it up for us."

Indians also mistrust Blacks, although for different reasons than they mistrust Whites. With their straightforward, yet reticent manner of presentation, Indians cannot seem to understand a Black expressive, complex style of behavior with its double entendres, put ons, and inverted meanings. To Indians it all seems so much deviousness and dishonesty. And because Blacks do not "stand up for themselves" in the way that Indians do, Indians view them as weak and liable to ally themselves with Whites at the expense of Indians.

> After the primary election and the runoff, when it was clear that the coalition movement had been badly beaten, an Indian leader began to talk about what was now happening. He said that the Whites are trying to put together a coalition with the Negroes, and he mentioned the names of some Black leaders he thought had "gone over," and others who were being courted. He said that if that White–Black coalition works, "the Indians will have to fight." He was very angry and disappointed.

Whites are known to have the power to do things that will affect Indians directly and are worrisome for that reason. Blacks have not had that power, but Indians worry that they will get it by making an alliance with Whites, cutting out the Indians altogether.

In short, it could be said that Whites are disliked for what they do, and Blacks mistrusted for what they do not do. One young Indian man summed it up this way:

> "When an Indian meets a Black, he thinks he's a doormat. He [the Black] lets the Whites walk all over him and the Indian can't understand why he doesn't stand up for himself. He [the Indian] thinks it's funny he [the Black] doesn't.
>
> "When an Indian meets a White man, he thinks, 'I know you've been doing me all my life, and you're going to keep on doing it. You think you're better than me. But don't let me know you think that or I'll bust your head.'"

7. Where does the Lumbee problem lead?

The headlines on the front page of a widely distributed, free Manhattan newspaper proclaimed " 'Ethnic' Now is Something Special. Call it a touch of class" (*Wisdoms Child*, Nov. 15, 1977, p. 1). In the late 1970s, "ethnic" has become a fashionable and even desirable quality to most Manhattanites and perhaps to most New Yorkers. People proudly announce their heritage and ancestry, searching for the "exotica" that makes them "one of us" and "different from others." It was not always so. From the 1930s through the early 1960s, the New York city colleges, then tuition free and a golden opportunity for immigrants and their children, offered courses, sometimes mandatory, in speech. At that time immigrants wanted their children to speak "good English." As late as the early 1960s, a young man born and reared in Queens was forced to take a speech class at Queens College to "correct" his thoroughly American Queens accent. By the late 1970s, this kind of requirement had become unthinkable at any of the city colleges.

What, it might be asked, does ethnicity in New York City in the late 1970s have to do with Lumbee Indians in North Carolina in the late 1960s? For me, the striking changes in attitudes toward ethnicity in New York suggested that parallel changes might be occurring in Robeson County and elsewhere. And indeed, there appears to have been a widespread alteration in the popular vocabulary expressive of social differences across the nation.

When I worked and lived in Robeson, inequalities were characterized in racial terms by Whites, Indians, and Blacks. Of course, members of the three groups referred to different aspects or kinds of inequality when they used the term "race," as I have already remarked. Nevertheless, at a political meeting of Blacks and Indians in 1968, a Black minister both recognized and rejected the usual way of talking about social differences in terms of race:

> "People talk about the 'Indian race' and the 'Negro race' and the 'White race'. But God didn't make but one race – the human race."

At that time I heard no one – neither this man nor anyone else in the county – characterize social differences in "ethnic" terms. But by 1973, another Black minister from Robeson County, in a commencement speech at a nearby Black state university, was using the term "ethnic groups" to describe Blacks and others:

Black Power means the consolidation of economics, political, social and educational resources of all black people. It embraces other ethnic groups by unifying them to bring about pressure upon the society to make favorable changes for blacks and the rest of the society. . . . Black and beautiful with brain power and production power equals soul control [J. Johnson n.d.:33–4].

Such changes are related to the career of Blacks in the 1960s and to the concomitant "resurgence" or "revitalization" of ethnicity among many ethnic groups in the United States. This revitalization was as dramatic as it was unexpected, as most previous theories had predicted ever-increasing assimilation and homogenization, referring to the United States as a "melting pot." Apparently the definition of ethnicity (and possibly race) is in the process of changing. If that is the case, what happens when basic concepts for describing social differences and inequalities change, and what effects might such changes have on ideas about dominance and hierarchy in the United States? A consideration of these questions leads to the still larger issue of how the concepts of "ethnicity" and "ethnic group" have been used in attempts to analyze other cultures and societies also undergoing a revitalization of certain kinds of social difference. Ultimately, it must be asked how useful such concepts have proved in these cross-cultural contexts. As these kinds of concerns may seem rather removed from the intensive study of the Lumbee presented here, the question of how the Lumbee can lead to these broader concerns is raised.

The "Lumbee problem" and American ethnicity

First and last, *The Lumbee Problem* in the title of this work is one of how differences among people are conceived, worked out, and changed over time. The impact of local and national ideas of "race" and "ethnicity" on Indian strategy has perforce been great. Indians have sought to present themselves as a separate people who can be fitted into the categories prevalent in the larger society, however much the meaning of those categories must be stretched or changed. Initially, they were recognized as a distinct "race," albeit one with communal aspects. Yet, by insisting all along on their "peoplehood," their cohesiveness, and their aboriginal past, the Indians of Robeson County have used what is now perceived as "ethnic" imagery.

The milieu in which the Lumbee have worked for change is pervaded by racial considerations and discrimination. Although it is possible to imagine social differentiation to which no notions of inequality or evaluations as better and worse are attached, such cases are apparently exceedingly rare (see, for example, LeVine and Campbell 1972). More often, where there are social differences, there are also material and/or ideological inequalities attached to those differences.

By entitling this volume *The Lumbee Problem,* I have meant to call attention in a multifaceted way to their identity. First, the Indians have themselves had to face the problem of formulating concepts of who they are as a group in such a way as to speak to outsiders without doing violence to their own notions of themselves. In seeking recognition as Indians, the Lumbee have long encountered resistance, also a problem. Second, the career of the Lumbee presents an interpretive problem to the social analyst by posing the question of how they have managed to change their legal status from "free persons of color" to "Lumbee Indians" in less than 100 years. There is the further difficulty of understanding wherein their distinctiveness lies and how that distinctiveness is maintained in a situation where differences are not immediately obvious, even to Robesonians. Third, there is a problem of how a study of the Lumbee can highlight certain conceptual features of the interplay between concepts of race and ethnicity.

As I have presented it, "the Lumbee problem" is how a particular "ethnic" group, the Lumbee Indians of Robeson County, has changed – and in changing maintained – its group identity. In the subtitle of this volume, *The Making of an American Indian People,* I mean to imply that the Lumbee have achieved full recognition as Indians largely through their taking an active role on their own behalf. They have been anything but passively accepting of a situation "imposed from above" and have thereby managed, enlisting the aid of outsiders when necessary, to change their life situation (cf. the interpretation of Sider 1976). I do not mean, in the subtitle, to imply that Robeson County Indians have manufactured their Indian identity spuriously, out of whole cloth, as some have suggested (e.g., Milling 1940). On the contrary, I argue that they began from their own traditional conviction that they were descended from Indians and proceeded gradually to persuade others to recognize them, legally and socially, as Indians. In the process of convincing others of their Indianness, Robeson County Indians have altered some aspects of their ideas about who they are (their origins from particular Indian groups), changed the emphasis of other aspects (from "not Black" to, increasingly, "non-White"), and apparently maintained still others (what I have called "behavioral characteristics"), though with different emphases at different periods.

In analyzing the Lumbee problem, I indicate that ideas and concepts have been driving forces for change through political activity as well as powerful influences for continuity. For this reason, symbols have been a key area for analysis. By carefully investigating the meaning of Lumbee identity, it is possible to see why some changes are sought and others resisted, and how a sense of continuity is maintained at the same time. I have tried to understand, among other things, some of the intentions and motivations of actors (see Skinner 1972). For the Lumbee, their own idea of who they are, as a people, is now and has long been an animating agent in their political activities, and these activities have in turn brought about changes in their legal status, living conditions, and, to an extent, their ideas about themselves. (For example, pride has prompted certain political actions, the success of which increases pride.) Specifying some of the powerful symbols that inspire and motivate Lumbees and identifying the circumstances in which the symbols tend to be acted upon is an important aspect of the analysis. What the triggering circumstances are is conditioned by the nature and content of the symbols. And, of course, some symbols change their meaning (and their ability to animate) with altered social circumstances.

From this symbolic and political analysis of a particular situation in which "ethnic identity" plays a vital role, my theoretical concerns have turned to the broader areas of the meaning and analytic utility of the concept "ethnicity" in wider social contexts. Of what relevance is this study of the Lumbee to the now fashionable and increasingly murky area labeled "ethnicity?" Throughout the following discussion, I intend to raise larger issues rather than to settle any of them definitively, to suggest implications rather than to "prove" points.

Ideas of "race" and "ethnic group" in America[1]

In order to see more clearly in what sense the Lumbee can be considered an "ethnic" group, it is necessary to make clear what is meant by both "race" and "ethnic group," as these terms are used in the United States. One difficulty inherent in defining each of the terms is that the way laymen (or the "folk") use the terms has sometimes been rather uncritically adopted in scientific discussions and has at other times itself been influenced by popularized social science. Yet there are important differences between folk and scientific usages that ought to be noted.

The discussion of race in Chapter 1 pointed to the differences between definitions used by biologists and physical anthropologists on the one hand and the popular or folk definition on the other. For scientists, a race is a subgroup within a species. Members of one species do not or cannot breed with members of another species, but members of different races with the same species can and often do breed with one another. Human beings, of course, all belong to the same species, *Homo sapiens*. It is because there has been so much interbreeding among members of *Homo sapiens* that the boundaries between human populations are not clear and unambiguous. Therefore, there are disagreements among scientists about which populations ought to be considered races, what the genetic differences between them are, and what such differences might mean for human beings (cf. Garn 1960, Dobzhansky 1962, Hulse 1963, Mayr 1963, Montagu 1964, Jensen 1969 and 1971, Shockley 1972, Buettner-Janusch 1973, Molnar 1975). Some physical anthropologists have urged that "race," as a biological term, not be applied to human populations. Race, they argue, is essentially a term designating social categories and ought to be used solely in that sense, if at all (e.g., Montagu 1964, Buettner-Janusch 1973). Social scientists usually treat races as social or cultural categories.

For laymen who use the term race, there is, perhaps, slightly more agreement about what it signifies. For them, it classifies individual human beings according to their presumed biological differences and, for most, ranks them as inferior or superior on this basis. An individual's biological makeup is believed to be manifest in his physical appearance, and particularly in the color of skin, texture of hair, and shape of nose. Individuals are assumed to exhibit biologically determined character, personality, and intelligence differences. Those considered members of the same race are thought to be basically similar physically, morally, and behaviorally.[2]

As I have already noted, in 1967–68, many Whites in Robeson County said that Blacks, because of their racial biology, lacked membership in a moral community and did not care for or help one another– that is, they were not cohesive as a people. The "Negro race" was not considered a *group* by Whites, but merely a *collection* of individuals, all of whom were presumed to be biologically similar.

It is along the dimension of moral community that race contrasts most vividly with the folk category "ethnic group" as it is used today. For American laymen, ethnic groups are precisely what races are not. Ethnics are at least potentially members of groups, not just aggregations of individuals. Ethnic groups are seen by the folk to have members who share common interests and are capable of acting together on the basis of those interests. In short, they are interest groups, whether actual or potential. Seeing ethnic groups as interest groups appears to be a relatively new phenomenon, which seems to be linked with the recent career of American Blacks.

Ethnic categorization, for the folk, is a classification of individuals as members of groups that are distinguished from one another on the basis of "heritage" or "background" – that is, nationality of ancestors, language, race, religion, customs, historical events, or any combination of these. The folk contrast between ethnicity and race might be characterized in Lévi-Straussian terms, in that race is conceived to be a division "in nature," whereas ethnicity is conceived as a division "in culture."[3] This apparently has not always been the case, as immigrant groups from Europe were often described initially with racial imagery by those already in residence during the 1800s and early 1900s.

For social scientists, the term "ethnic group" was initially developed to describe people who were perceived as obviously different from "ordinary" or "dominant" members of a society.[4] Max Weber elaborated the notion of "*'ethnische' Gruppen*" (ethnic groups) or "*ethnische Gemeinschaften*" (ethnic communities), using the Jews in Europe and Blacks in the United States as extreme cases, or as "pariah" groups with a caste-like structure. In his discussion of "ethnic honor" and its relation to conceptions of "chosen people," he takes the Jews as exemplars (Weber 1968:391, 933–4; 1956:239, 536–7). Significantly, Weber analytically separates two aspects – the conceptual and the social – that are fused in the folk definition of ethnic groups. That is, he distinguishes the subjective belief in ethnic group membership from the formation and activities of a group based on a belief in common ethnicity:

> The belief in group affinity, regardless of whether it has any objective foundation, can have important consequences especially for the formation of a political community. We shall call "ethnic groups" those human groups that entertain a subjective belief in their common descent because of similarities of physical type or of customs or both, or because of memories of colonization and migration; this belief must be important for the propagation of group formation [*Vergemeinschaften*]; conversely, it does not matter whether or not an objective blood relationship exists [1968:389].

Ethnic identity, then, serves to facilitate group formation but does not guarantee it. Further, Weber argues, political organization tends to inspire a belief in common ethnicity, while the belief can at the same time encourage political groupings. The belief in common ethnicity can persist even when the political community to which it was attached dissolves (Weber 1968:389).

As to the relationship between ethnicity and race, Weber notes that race depends on the inheritance of physical characteristics or "traits" acquired through actual common descent, whereas ethnicity is based on an *assumption* of common descent, not necessarily on true common descent. For Weber, "racial" distinctions are physical ones, the implications of which must be scientifically investigated rather than assumed. Such investigation, however, is made difficult by the fact that many "traits" ascribed to racial differences can be accounted for by social factors and by the fact that obvious physical differences can give rise to both "consciousness of kind" and political groupings. In this way, racial differences can be one among other factors that give rise to ethnic consciousness. Other factors that can contribute to a sense of ethnicity are common language and customs, a memory of actual migration, common religion, and political action both past and present (Weber 1968:236–8). Certainly Weber was skeptical of "racial" theories of behavior, although he did not rule out the possibility that physiological differences might have an influence on behavior (see also Manasse 1947).

Weber's treatment of ethnicity and race is part of an attempt to generalize about processes of group formation and political action and is thus not directly tied to the analysis of any specific time or place, however much he may use the situation of Jews in Europe as a model. His work contrasts with the early landmark studies of ethnicity in the United States, particularly with that of W. Lloyd Warner and his associates on the Yankee City (Newburyport, Massachusetts) project. In the series of volumes produced from fieldwork and interviews conducted in the 1930s, the place and mobility of ethnic groups in Yankee City is an important issue. Unlike Weber, however, Warner and his associates fail to distinguish between ethnic "consciousness of kind" and ethnic groups as social entities. For them, ethnic group membership is based on claimed or ascribed status *and* participation in the activities of the group. Stephan Thernstrom, in his reanalysis of Newburyport from an historical point of view, remarks, "any citizen who did not fulfill these two criteria, amazingly, Warner classified a 'Yankee'" (1964:231).

As a result of this restrictive definition of ethnicity, Warner was able to proclaim that "Yankees" were numerically dominant, constituting well over half the total population (Warner and Lunt 1941:213). However, Thernstrom argues that by 1885 immigrants and their children were nearly half the population and that most of the "Yankees" were not from old Newburyport families (1964:195–6). By the 1930s, "an overwhelming majority" of community members were immigrants and their children and grandchildren (Thernstrom 1964:231).

Whatever their actual number, Yankees were certainly symbolically dominant in Warner's Newburyport. They set the tone of life, and those who claimed to be and were recognized as "old Yankee families" were widely admired, emulated, and generally conceded to be the "upper uppers." The place of Yankees in the ethnic scheme of things appears at first to be somewhat problematic. In the first Yankee City volume, Warner and Lunt (1941) logically list all the groups said to be possessed of similar kinds of distinctive features at the opening of their discussion on ethnic groups. In the list, "Natives, or Yankees" and "Negroes" are included along with Irish, French Canadians, Jews, and other "immigrant" groups. However, they note, "We ordinarily do not speak of the natives, or Yankees, as an ethnic group. This is simply a device to avoid terminological difficulties" (Warner and Lunt 1941:211; 211, n 1). That the decision to eliminate "Yankees" from consideration as "ethnics" was more than terminological convenience is evident from their statement about the Yankees' views:

> Thus it became evident that many individuals, despite the fact of their birth in the United States or even in Yankee City, were nevertheless regarded by the native group as "foreigners" and were constrained to this role in certain areas of social relations by the pressure of Yankee opinion [Warner and Lunt 1941:212].

Here is a case where the "logic" of investigation suggests that all the groups are similar in some respects, but because the natives' categories do not fit the logic of investigation, something must be done. The "something" in Warner's case was to adopt, rather uncritically, the Yankee view of ethnic relations.[5]

In a later volume (Warner and Srole 1945), "Yankees" are characterized not just as "native" but also as "dominant" and are contrasted with ethnic groups, or "cultural minorities." Significantly too, "Negroes" are classified as a "racial group" or "color caste" rather than as an ethnic group. In other words, race and ethnicity, which were apparently merged in the earlier schema, are later separated and ranked. Yankees rank "ethnic groups" as inferior to themselves and "racial groups" as inferior to ethnic groups. An ethnic group is said to possess "a divergent set of cultural traits which are evaluated by the host society as inferior," while racial groups "are divergent biologically rather than culturally" (Warner and Srole 1945:285).

Warner and Srole then explore the symbolic significance of ethnicity as opposed to race:

> The cultural traits of the ethnic group, which have become symbols of inferior status, can be and are changed in time; but the physical traits which have become symbols of inferior status are permanent [1945:285].

Unfortunately, this is a good example of the confusion that results from failing to distinguish objective observation from the natives' symbolic linkages, a confusion that produces misleading symbolic analysis. It is true that the cultural traits of an ethnic group can be changed over time, but they symbolize what Edward Shils (1957) has called "primordial attachments," what Clifford Geertz (1963) terms "cultural 'givens,'" and what Max Weber (1968) would include in his "subjective belief in ethnicity." That is, from an ethnic's point of view, the cultural traits distinguishing his group from other groups are "given," are felt to be in the nature of the unchanging because they are firmly rooted in the past, whether or not that is actually the case. To Warner's Yankees, these "cultural traits" appeared changeable. By contrast, the physical "traits" of race are by no means permanent, as genes flow and interbreeding takes place. Rather, the physical traits represent or symbolize immutability and permanence, especially to the "dominant" members of society.

Finally, Warner and Srole note that ethnicity in the United States is not quite the same as that in Europe, because "the roots of the minorities of Europe are buried deeply in the soil of the dominant country," whereas "in the United States the ethnic group's origins are known and felt to be 'foreign'" (1945:283). Here, the problem of fitting American Indians into the American framework emerges and is buried in a footnote as an exception. The implication is that American Indians are considered to be an ethnic minority but not an immigrant one. They would, of course, be "foreign" in the sense of "alien in character" to Warner's Yankees. Whether the difference between European and American ethnicity is correctly and completely characterized or not, Warner and Srole at least see that social differences in the two areas are not identical. However, they do not pursue this point.

If Warner and Srole (1945) reflect a Yankee view of ethnicity in their separation of race from ethnic groups, other American studies, many of which can be found in sociology journals published during the 1930s and 1940s, treated "Negroes" and "Orientals" along with groups of European origin as "ethnic groups." That at least some laymen persisted in the view that race and ethnicity are separate matters is reflected in an incident that took place in the late 1960s. A colleague teaching in a major Eastern city had prepared a course on urban ethnicity focused upon readings about Blacks and Hispanics. Her predominantly White Catholic students complained about the prolonged discussion of Blacks, claiming "Blacks aren't ethnics – we're ethnics."

Now, in the late 1970s, ethnic reference has become much broader for both social scientists and laymen. It encompasses Blacks, American Indians, Hispanics, and even White Anglo-Saxon Protestants (WASPs), in addition to the traditional so-called hyphenated Americans (e.g., Irish-, Italian-, Polish-Americans). The progressive ethnicization of WASPs (see Fallers 1973, Lorinskas 1974, Allen 1975) is highly significant, for the term ethnic was originally contrasted, in American scientific consciousness, if not in linguistic category, with

WASP. What was not WASP in the United States was "foreign" or "ethnic." But if WASPs are becoming just another kind of ethnic group, their symbolic dominance should be less great today than it has been in the past.[6]

Lest the contrast between racial and ethnic categorizing be over-drawn, it should be noted that ethnicity and race are currently in-tertwined in popular as well as social scientific conceptions. On the one hand, ethnicity is sometimes seen as a factor in race when laymen add cultural factors to the defining physical features of race. On the other hand, race is frequently recognized as a background factor in ethnicity. Decidedly, it is merely one of several – along with others such as com-mon history, customs, language, and religion. Even among social sci-entists, race permeates the classification of ethnics. Thanks to Michael Novak (1971), we now have the term "white ethnics" to refer to Polish-, Italian-, Greek-, and Slavic-Americans. Formerly, these groups were simply "ethnics." Implicitly, the contrast of "White ethnics" must be with "Black ethnics" or "dark ethnics," but so far we have been spared these last terms. Perhaps because of Novak's popular writings and because it makes explicit a formerly implicit divi-sion, the term "White ethnics" is now used by many people who are not academics.

As ethnicity has become more "fashionable" in lay and social scien-tific circles and as more individuals assert what they see as a positive aspect of their personal identity, race has become a less socially ac-ceptable way of referring to people and a less desirable personal iden-tity to claim. At the same time that many Americans are shifting to an expanded ethnic classification from a racial one, the racial aspects of ethnic groups are being emphasized in a way that they formerly were not, and "cultural" aspects of race are often added or stressed. Race is not disappearing so much as being altered and subsumed under a differ-ent rubric. As this occurs, voluntaristic attitudes about ethnicity – that one can choose how much and in many cases whether to participate in an ethnic identity – are being heightened.

Ethnic identity in the United States may be optional in two respects. In American terms, in order for an individual to claim an ethnic identity legitimately, one or more of his relatively immediate ancestors must have possessed that identity. If an individual has ancestors with several different ethnic identities, he may then legitimately choose which he will "be" from among them, all things being equal. Because all things are almost never equal, a person may be swayed in his choice by the circumstances of his upbringing within one or another ethnic commun-ity, by the assumptions of others, by the relative status ranking of one group over another as expressed in his social circle, or by how he views what has happened to him. An individual may even try to insist on being recognized as having more than one ethnic identity. This position appears to be difficult to maintain, but one hears, in New York City at any rate, of increasing numbers of children who, when confronted by their friends' questions, "Are you White or are you Black?" or "Are you Irish or are you Italian?" insistently assert "Both!" Whether they can continue to maintain this position as they grow older remains to be seen. But the "right" to emphasize one side or another of one's ethnic ancestry seems well established. There is no "right" to choose one's "racial" ancestry, as race is currently conceived, but if race and ethnicity become progressively intertwined in a new way, it is possible that being Black will, in years to come, be more a matter of individual choice and less a matter of assignment by others.

In addition to having the theoretical "choice" of ethnic identities from several of one's ancestors, an individual has the option of deciding to what extent he will involve himself with other like ethnics, and to what extent he commits himself to his ethnic identity.[7] Some people choose to minimize their ethnicity, rarely interacting with others of similar ethnic identity and ignoring whatever traditional aspects might be associated with such an identity. Others choose to live within a community that strongly emphasizes its ethnicity, proudly and explicitly carrying on traditions associated with it. For example, some Jews in the South have chosen to "assimilate," to minimize their Jewishness by changing their religious affiliation, marrying gentiles, and failing to pass on to their children a sense of Jewish tradition (see Dinnerstein and Palsson 1973). Other Southern Jews have opted to stress their Jewish heritage and to practice their religion even when they are excluded from neighborhoods and clubs (or, in the past, from voting in some states), or when congregations are so small that they must share a circuit-riding rabbi, as Robeson County Jews do.

Between virtually opting out of one's ethnicity and centering one's life around it, there are many intermediate possibilities. The kinds and numbers of involvements with those of similar ethnicity, the degree to which an individual acts upon the traditions and values he is taught, and the amount of emotional satisfaction or suffering experienced over his ethnicity differs from individual to individual. In Robeson County, Indians recognize this kind of gradation, explicitly view it as a matter of individual choice (with moral overtones), and mark the ends of the spectrum with the labels "real old-timey Indian" and "White Indian" or "brick house Indian."

Thus there are at least some options for the individual who has been assigned or ascribed a legitimate claim to ethnic identity at birth. But the individual does not, according to American folk notions about ethnicity, have the option to change his ethnic identity to something entirely different. He is thought to be born with a limited set of possible ethnic identities and, at best, he is allowed to choose among them. The only way to claim an ethnic identity to which one is not entitled by birth is to "pass," to pretend to ancestry not one's own. "Passing" is also the only way to change one's racial status, about which there is conceived to be no choice.

If neither race nor ethnicity can legitimately be changed (aside from the optional aspects noted), the evaluation, or rank, of a race or ethnic group can, in either case, be changed. The Irish, who were often considered by other White Southerners to be inferior to Blacks before the Civil War, rose above Blacks in the estimation of other Whites after the war. The Mississippi Chinese worked successfully at raising their status as a group from below that of Blacks, whom they were supposed to replace as agricultural workers after the Civil War, to "almost White" by the late 1960s (Loewen 1971).

Returning to the question of how the Lumbee fit into concepts of race and ethnic group as they have been outlined here, it may be said that they have been conceived as a "race" by Whites, that they have long conceived of themselves as "a people" (that is, in "ethnic" terms), and that they are now considered an "ethnic group" in popular as well as social scientific parlance. The Lumbee have emphasized their past in their ideas about who they are and have operated effectively as an "interest group." They exhibit Weber's "consciousness of kind" and have undertaken political activity guided by that consciousness. They consider themselves and are considered by others to be members of a moral community.

Blacks as pivotal figures in recent changes

Assuming that there is a widespread shift in the United States from classifying people according to race to classifying them as ethnics, the key to understanding the changing basis of classification must be the recent career of Blacks. Blacks are the people, in a racial classification, in contrast to whom Whites define themselves. Blacks are also in the forefront of the resurgence of claims to ethnic identity that became so apparent in the 1960s. Whether located in the North or South, Blacks can no longer be seen as incapable of organizing themselves for their common good. Rather, they have come to be viewed as having organized themselves effectively, both nationally and locally, in order to compel recognition of their rights and compliance with the Constitution. Other people, witnessing the success of Blacks, have begun asserting or reasserting their ethnic identity, and thereby their right to membership in an ethnic group concerned with protecting their own interests (see, for example, V. Deloria 1969, Clancy 1971, Galush 1974, Maruyama 1974, Radzialowski 1974, G. Rosen 1974, Vecoli 1974, Glazer 1974, Glazer and Moynihan 1975). Martin Kilson has remarked that the resurgence of urban White ethnicity has an "anti-Negro orientation" (1975:260).

Vigorous Black claims to an ethnic, as opposed to a racial, identity represented a marked change. According to Kilson:

The new black ethnicity is, then, initially an effort to redress this inferior ethnic characterization [by Whites]. What is more – and what lends a special force to black neo-ethnicity – Negroes themselves share the belief that in some basic way, they do not possess a full measure of ethnic attributes [1975:237].

Unlike the ethnicity of white social groups, black ethnicity lacked until recently the quality of authenticity – that is, a true and viable heritage, unquestionable in its capacity to shape and sustain a cohesive identity or awareness [1975:243].

Further, he sees Black ethnicity as particularly dependent on politics for continued revitalization (1975:244).

Although not all ethnic groups are interest groups, the new effectiveness of ethnic groups as interest groups apparently induces more people to stress their ethnicity and join together in a common interest. As Blacks have effectively defined and defended their interests as a group, perceptions by Blacks of their own abilities and strengths as a group have changed, as have others' perceptions of Blacks. Some groups have explicitly copied Black strategies and tactics; other groups have adopted the tactics but denied that they are emulating Blacks. Whatever non-Blacks say, however, it seems clear that Blacks have provided, through their success and the widespread publicity attendant upon that success, a stimulus for other groups to organize themselves as interest groups.[8]

But people derive more from membership in an ethnic group than simple economic or political self-interest suggests. There is the attractiveness of a "we feeling," or, in Durkheimian terms, communal solidarity, derived from associating with others perceived as like oneself in important basic ways (cf. Isaacs 1974 on basic group identity). The associations with other members of an ethnic group may provide satisfaction, warmth, and comfortableness during leisure activities, religious observances, or neighborhood living. It should be clear that those who consider themselves members of an ethnic group "get something out of it," and that the something is actually many things, with possibilities ranging from economic and political advantages to psychic support and a feeling of being comfortable among one's fellows. But what are some of the broader implications of a shift from a racial to an ethnic classification?

Dominance and hierarchy

If Americans are shifting from a predominantly racial to a predominantly ethnic classification of people, there should be a concomitant change in the symbols of dominance, status, and hierarchy. By the term "hierarchy," I do not mean to suggest, as Louis Dumont does, a holistic relationship in which the larger encompasses the smaller (1970:xii). Instead, I use it to mean merely a graded or ranked series. "Dominance" here means the ascendancy of one set or group of people over another. If one group controls economic opportunities and financing and has the ability to cut off another group's access to these, it may be said to be economically dominant. So too, if one set of people hold all or a majority of the important political offices and wield the most political influence, thereby denying participation to another set of people, the first set can be said to be politically dominant over the second.[9]

A group of people may also be said to be "symbolically dominant" over another. This concept is somewhat more complicated, for it has to do with meanings given to items, circumstances, events, words. If one group is to dominate another symbolically, it must persuade the other, by whatever means – force or education or religion – to accept, to some degree, the dominant group's definition of the subordinate group and that group's inferior "place" in society. When the definitions, values, and interpretations of the dominant group have been more or less internalized and accepted by the subordinate group, the first may then be said to be symbolically dominant over the second. This concept is useful in thinking about why so many women, who are in numbers a majority in the United States, have accepted the notion that they are inferior to men in a variety of important ways and have helped to inculcate in their children the same notion. Men may thus be said to be symbolically dominant.

"Symbolic domination" is one of the ways in which one group can establish what Antonio Gramsci (1971) calls "hegemony" over another. Hegemony for him is "indirect" dominance, the intellectual and moral leadership made possible by the consent of those led, in contrast with "direct" dominance made possible by force, or command exercised through governmental structures.[10] Symbolic domination is one way of securing the "minimum [and perhaps more] of voluntary compliance" necessary for Max Weber's "genuine domination" (1968:212). "Voluntary compliance" would be facilitated if followers accept the validity or efficacy of symbols and meanings that help legitimize the authority of their leaders.

In the racial schema, not only are Whites clearly politically and economically dominant over Blacks, but physical attributes symbolizing their superiority, such as light skin and wavy or straight hair, are also dominant symbols for what is good or desirable. Thus, light skin becomes "good skin" to Blacks, whereas dark skin is characterized as "bad skin." The symbols associated with Whiteness come to have precedence even among Blacks, and hence the almost caste-within-a-caste structure at least formerly to be found in many Black communities, with lighter-skinned people regarded more highly than darker-skinned ones.[11] As Ira Berlin (1974) has shown, various historical events contributed to the dominance of light over dark as symbol and as social advantage. In the racial system of the United States, Whites are clearly on top, socially and economically, as well as symbolically, and are the people whose standards should be adhered to, whether out of necessity or admiration or both. The symbols of dominance in this system are unambiguous and clear-cut.

However, as people shift to an ethnic schema, the picture is less clear, more ambiguous. Although initially ethnic groups were clearly culturally contrasted with WASPs, that contrast is no longer sharp because WASPs have increasingly come to see themselves and to be seen by others as an ethnic group, similar in nature to other ethnic groups. Today, the idea is spreading that "everyone is an ethnic of one group or another," as one of my Italian-American students proclaimed in 1975. If we grant that WASPs are becoming ethnics, the question arises of how such groups are to be ranked when they are *all* conceived as minority groups, each struggling to protect and further its own interests (cf. Bell 1975). Instead of a simple ranking of White over Black, we now have a multiplicity of groups vying with one another for political and economic dominance, and for symbolic dominance as well. It may be that if E. Digby Baltzell (1964) is correct and the American elite is becoming more obviously and proportionally multiethnic, this change contributes to an ambiguity in symbols of dominance.

I would argue that today's system of ethnic classification, when it includes WASPs and Blacks, does not provide a simple, coherent set of symbols of domination. It should be noted, of course, that the resurgence of ethnicity comes at a time when most ethnics have, as Lloyd Fallers has pointed out (1973:25–6), achieved native facility in manipulating what are basically Anglo-Saxon institutions, such as North American forms of law and government, as well as an Anglo-Saxon language, English. If in the current generation ethnics are less different from one another than their ancestors were, they have certainly come to value at least some of their present differences and show no wish to absorb or emulate more Anglo-Saxon values and traditions. In effect, the rise of ethnicity can be seen as a rejection of the symbolic domination of WASP culture combined with an acceptance of many institutions that had their origins in WASP culture.

The implications of this change in symbolic dominance are important to the groups themselves and for understanding changing concepts of American society. One widely recognized implication is that symbols that were formerly negatively valued are becoming positively valued (e.g., continued use of a non-English language). For Blacks, physical features formerly considered undesirable, such as dark skin and kinky hair, are coming to be considered beautiful and desirable. However, the negative-to-positive process is not a simple inversion but is an additive process, because characteristics formerly highly valued, such as light skin and straight hair, do not necessarily become undesirable. Being a Black as a constituent of a race is undesirable because it means being considered innately inferior, but being a Black as part of an ethnic group is desirable because it means being a member of a cohesive group that is seen as actively and, at least to a degree, successfully combating the disadvantages of its minority status, thereby engendering self-respect as well as respect from others. As Erik Erikson (1968) and others have pointed out, a positive evaluation of one's ethnic identity is important for psychic well-being.

A second implication of the shift is that with increased emphasis on ethnicity in place of race must come an increased concern with historical matters. Not only are the members of one ethnic group concerned with their own past, as a group, but members of another ethnic group must also be concerned with it insofar as they must interact with and understand the first group. Historical traditions and experiences are considered important features linking members of an ethnic group because they are part of a common heritage. But history is logically superfluous for the classification of people into races, for race is assumed to be based on current biological differences and not on historical ones. I do not argue that a racially divided society is one in which there is no interest in history, for the Southern United States is clearly both racially divided and extremely conscious of its past. But I would argue that a concern with history is not logically necessary in a racially divided society in the way that it is in an ethnically divided society. History, as perceived by both insiders and outsiders, is at the core of ethnic identification, which makes more understandable the urgent demands from ethnic groups to rewrite and expand history.[12] As a Black woman remarked in a 1977 television interview, "We come from someplace, we're not just a color."[13] History is not a frill, it is at the heart of a symbolic structure of ethnicity in the United States.

The symbols representing racial distinctions are manifestly different from those representing ethnic ones. They are, in David M. Schneider's terms, drawn from different "domains" (1968; see also Schneider and Smith 1973). The racial symbols are those of physical appearance, drawn from the realm of folk biology. Unlike racial symbols, ethnic symbols in the United States are taken from many different domains. One is the realm of ultimate national origin, signifying the countries and cultures from which relevant ancestors came. Another is linguistic, or broadly cultural (as Hispanic). In the case of the Jews, the designation can be thought of either as primarily religious or as primarily referring to origin in the first Israel, or both. For many ethnics, food is conceived to be an important feature of their ethnicity, as is the particular role of the mother (Schneider 1968). There are, then, a wide variety of symbols taken from many domains that can represent ethnic diversity – food, music, kinship, nationality, religion, language, and culture, as well as race. Such symbolic variety provides ethnicity with richness of resonance and allows for complexity of presentation; the single focus of folk biological imagery cannot do the same for race.

All the symbols used to stand for and to express ethnic identity have in common a perceived link to an ethnic group's past. That is, if certain music or food, the special role of the mother, or a common language or religion are said to obtain in a particular group, that fact is deemed (rightly or wrongly) to be rooted in the group's past, a result of the group's historical development. The traditional or folk history of a group is at the core of its ethnic identity and is irrelevant to its racial identity except insofar as it indicates a common "point" of origin from which a race is thought to have sprung (e.g., Blacks from Africa). The quality of a history has no part in a purely racial identity (which is, perhaps, why people from so many different backgrounds, or ethnic heritages, can be lumped together in the racial schema as "White" or "Black"). But the content and the interpretation of traditional history is vital to understanding the "ethnic experience" that distinguishes an Irish-American from an Italian-American or an Hispanic-American from an Afro-American. The interpretation of a group's history is frequently different among insiders and outsiders, and attempts are now being made to bridge that gap by, for example, the teaching of various ethnic groups' histories in public schools. Although a laudable enterprise, this may be fraught with difficulties.

A major difficulty is that two kinds of history are too often confused with one another. One is the documentary history of a group of people compiled by competent historians (or those adopting their methods) and based on a variety of specified sources, each of which is documented and evaluated. The other is the folk history of a group – the traditions, written and oral, that are passed among members of the ethnic group itself and that are deemed to confer unity and meaning upon the group. (A third type may intrude – the folk history about one group created by another, but this often reduces to stereotypes.) The two are usually enmeshed in a knotty way, now at odds with one another, now in apparent agreement, again, the one feeding back into the other, creating scholarly havoc for those seeking to understand. Indeed, sometimes the tensions between the two can stimulate change, as has been the case with the Lumbee and the various accounts of their history.

If the perceived past is central to ethnic identity in the United States, then it ought to make a difference what kind of past a group sees itself (and is seen by others) as having. Thus, we might expect the following kinds of groups to have rather different views of themselves because of their pasts:

1   descendants of original Americans, or American Indians, many of whom now live in what Robert Thomas (n.d.) has called "enclaves" in rural areas of the country. Such groups are aware that they "were here first," and tend to resent the loss of their land and their independence. After the attempt to banish them to "Indian territory" (the Removals of the 1830s and 1840s), when it became clear that White settlers would move over the whole continent, Whites could not entertain fantasies of eliminating the Indians by sending them "back where they came from." The only alternatives were accommodation or genocide.

2   descendants of early European settlers, who tend to have a notion of their ancestors as "pioneers" or "founders," developers of the nation and bringers of civilization. For many years, these people have been dominant over Indians, Blacks, and later immigrants. Unlike Blacks and later immigrants, they see themselves as having had a place in "building the nation," a place they often deny to others.

3   descendants of African slaves, who see themselves as having been brought by force, against their will, to labor for others. Dominant Whites have sometimes entertained fantasies of sending Blacks back to Africa. Blacks themselves have from time to time entertained ideas of a return to Africa (and some have gone), but for most Blacks this has not been either a real possibility or an attractive fantasy. Most have long regarded themselves as Americans, but Americans separated involuntarily from their African past. This involuntary separation is a source of resentment.

4   descendents of later immigrants, some of whom were fleeing persecution and who therefore did not entertain the notion of "return" to their homelands, and some of whom "chose" to leave their homelands for "the land of opportunity." Among the latter, the possibility, however unrealistic, of a return to their ancestral

lands could be considered. The descendants of early European settlers have sometimes entertained fantasies of sending all the later immigrants back "where they came from."

How useful this kind of schema might be in analyzing the larger category of "American ethnic groups" must be investigated elsewhere. But because of the importance of notions of the past to American ethnics, it seems a promising line of enquiry.[14]

What the impact of a change in classification schema from racial to ethnic will be is difficult to say. Some have predicted that increasing competition among ethnic groups will tear the society apart. Others, like Novak, have expressed hope that those ethnic groups having common interests will learn to cooperate with each other (Novak 1974). At the conceptual or cultural level, if WASPs are no longer at what Fallers calls the cultural center and Shils the moral center of the United States, it is not clear who, if anyone, is at that symbolic center. What can be said with certainty is that if the simplistic and clearly defined model of dominant–subordinate relations among human beings offered by the racial schema in the United States is no longer adequate, then Americans must logically replace that model. Perhaps they will replace it with a more complex one composed of a variety of ethnic groups whose relations to one another are in flux and in which dominance is not (at least not yet) clearly defined or symbolized. What the ethnic system in the United States does seem to offer is a wider range of symbols from a number of domains and varieties of behavior that provide a challenge to people who would integrate them into an altered, more complex world view, whether from a scientific or a commonsense perspective.

How useful is the concept of "ethnicity"?

So far, the discussion of ethnic groups has pertained exclusively to the way they are conceived and acted upon in the United States. Because it is both a social scientific and a "native" concept (probably popularized from social science), "ethnic group" is a useful way of talking about and analyzing what goes on in the United States, so long as the changes in its impact and usage are kept in mind. It is useful because it is part of the conceptual paraphernalia of "the natives," who think and act on the basis of their perceptions. It is not merely a disguise for class relationships, as some have argued. Rather, it increasingly cuts across class lines as members of ethnic groups grow more diverse in their economic and social status. Just why class consciousness in the United States should be less widespread and, on the whole, less deeply felt than ethnic consciousness is a matter for another inquiry. It is enough, here, to state that it is.

In American society, the term "ethnic" has a familiar meaning for actors. It is no theorist's abstract idea, but a possibly motivating factor in behavior, an indubitably shaping factor in cognition, and an apparently deep-seated factor in affect. For a social scientist to ignore such an important native concept in his attempt to understand American behavior would be foolhardy.

It must next be asked how useful a concept "ethnic group" or "ethnicity" is for understanding what happens outside the United States. In what sense or senses is "ethnicity" generalizable or relevant in cross-cultural contexts? Max Weber was skeptical about the analytical use of the concept:

All in all, the notion of "ethnically" determined social action subsumes phenomena that a rigorous sociological analysis . . . would have to distinguish carefully. . . . *It is certain that in this process the collective term "ethnic" would be abandoned, for it is unsuitable for a really rigorous analysis.* However, we do not pursue sociology for its own sake and therefore limit ourselves to showing briefly *the diverse factors that are hidden behind this semingly uniform phenomenon.*

The concept of the "ethnic" group . . . dissolves if we define our terms exactly . . . [emphasis mine; Weber 1968:394–5].

After intensive study of the Lumbee problem, and a more extensive study of ethnicity in several other national contexts, I have come to a slightly more contentious conclusion than Weber – namely, that (1) most current generalizing discussions of ethnicity are based on an American folk concept of ethnicity, however much "scientific" jargon has been added, and (2) none of the generalizations yet offered about "ethnicity" stands up under cross-cultural scrutiny unless it is so general as to be analytically and even descriptively useless. "Ethnicity" is now more widely used than Weber would probably have imagined, and it has been applied to situations past and present all over the world, in "new nations" and old, in the West and in the East. But when ethnicity has come to refer to everything from tribalism to religious sects, from City men in London to the shifting identities of Shan and Kachin, from regionalism to race, it is difficult to see that it has any universal utility either as an analytic tool or as a descriptive one.

In defense of this somewhat extreme position, I will briefly consider some attempts to construct broad definitions of ethnicity and of ethnic groups and proceed to show that they will not work in particular and, I admit, carefully selected cases. The definitions considered here have been put forward by American sociologists and anthropologists as well as by anthropologists from other countries. Although they do not all agree with one another, they fall within a restricted range.

Some definitions

For Harold Isaacs (1974), an American sociologist, belonging to an ethnic group gives one "basic group identity," which is ascribed at birth, is composed of "primordial affinities and attachments" (after Shils 1957), and which potentially makes a group a "candidate for nationhood" (after Geertz 1963). It is associated with a perceived common past, is affected by the shaping circumstances of the present, and may involve many elements – a name, history and origins of the group, nationality (or tribe), physical appearance, language, religion, value system, and/or geography. This is a description, essentially, of the possibilities of the current American folk category of ethnic identity or ethnic group. Isaacs, however, explicitly seeks to take into account great cross-cultural variation. He therefore suggests that the emphasis on one element or another may vary, and that not all elements may be present in any one case. He presents an elegant synthesis of what ethnicity "is," but is not particularly concerned to specify the ways in which ethnicity (or basic group identity) can be used in various contexts.

Two more American sociologists, Nathan Glazer and Daniel Patrick Moynihan (1975), are concerned almost exclusively with the way ethnicity is used, and they assume that it is basically a means of advancing the interests of a group. They are careful to add that it is *not only* a means of advancing interests, for it is combined with an affective tie that is important in itself, but that can be overridden by "rational interest." They reject the notion that this tie is "primordial" because, to them, "primordial" is a fixed notion, dividing people into immutable, enduring categories, whereas many of the groups they want to identify as "ethnic" are of recent origins. This misconstrues the original use of primordial by Edward Shils (1957), who employs it to refer to ties and sentiments that individuals *feel* are basic and terribly important, deep-seated factors (see also Geertz 1963). He does not mean that they have to have felt such feelings for a long time, or that they cannot change. But for Glazer and Moynihan, ethnicity is of importance primarily as a mobilizing principle for potential interest groups, and just how the affective ties fit in is not clear. Further, there is no discussion of how such nonprimordial affective ties of ethnicity differ from affective ties between members of other kinds of interest groups. The notion that ethnic groups are at least potential interest groups is, of course, an aspect of the American folk conception.

It could be argued – unfairly, to be sure – that as American sociologists, these authors are insufficiently aware (which they are not) of cross-cultural differences and perhaps too deeply embedded in their own culture to notice that they are recapitulating folk concepts about what ethnic groups are and what they do. Many anthropologists, American and non-American, whose business it is to understand other cultures, have also incorporated American folk notions about ethnicity into their definitions and theories. For example, Abner Cohen, a British anthropologist, defines an ethnic group as

a collectivity of people who (a) share some patterns of normative behaviour and (b) form a part of a larger population, interacting with people from other collectivities within the framework of a social system. The term ethnicity refers to the degree of conformity by members of the collectivity to these shared norms in the course of social interaction [1974:ix–x].

He means this to be an analytic concept. He is also well aware that his definition would allow for some collectivities not normally considered "ethnic" to be included. For example, he contends that the City of London men are "as 'ethnic' as any ethnic group can be" (A. Cohen 1974:xxi). What he is really talking about is interest groups. For him, one of the primary functions of ethnicity is to organize "informal" interest groups – those lacking formal organization – however inefficiently.

In the terms of his definition, of course, Cohen can legitimately claim the City men as "ethnics," but to do so is to violate in a thoroughgoing way the native categories of thought in Britain. I doubt that many "natives" would agree to the proposition that City men are, taken together, an ethnic group. I suspect that more often these men would be referred to in class terms rather than ethnic ones, and to obliterate altogether any consideration of native categories is not only bad description, it promotes misleading analysis. For Cohen, however, "what matters sociologically is what people actually do, not what they subjectively think or what they think they think" (1974:x). Presumably, he would not worry over the question of whether it is meaningful to treat the analysis of City men as if it were the same as an analysis of, say, West Indians in London and/or in Britain.

Cohen also wants ethnicity to be a variable: "the constraint that custom exercises on the individual varies from case to case" (1974:xiv). Here Cohen is not interested in individuals' options, but in degrees of ethnicity present or absent in a society. We are offered what amounts to a scale of ethnicity – perhaps from "very ethnic" or "heavily ethnic" to "not very ethnic" or "slightly ethnic" – based on how many members of a group abide by the norms as well as how "constraining" the norms are. This says nothing at all of the quality of involvement, and how the quantity is to be ascertained is, Cohen admits, difficult to conceive.

In his "Introduction" to *Ethnic Groups and Boundaries,* Fredrik

Barth, a British-trained Norwegian anthropologist, has suggested a far more elaborate and extensive definition of ethnic groups. He begins with the notion that ethnic groups "are categories of ascription and identification by the actors themselves, and thus have the characteristic of organizing interaction between people" (1969a:10). Ethnic categories classify the individual "in terms of his basic, most general identity, presumptively determined by his origin and background" (1969a:13). Definitionally, then, ethnic identity is ascribed. Yet the same volume of articles, including one by Barth himself, contains examples of individuals who, it is claimed, have changed their ethnic identity (Barth 1969b, Haaland 1969). Barth claims that along the Afghanistan–Pakistan border, although non-Pathans may not become Pathans, Pathans living among the Baluch lose their Pathan identity (Barth 1969b:124–5). But Barth states elsewhere, "I have heard members of Baluch tribal sections explain that they are 'really Pathan'" (1969a:29).

One reason the Pathans who are living as members of the Baluch community present a problem for Barth is that, disclaimers aside, ethnic categories are "good for acting" rather than, in Lévi-Straussian terms, "good for thinking." Despite the fact that he seems to draw a distinction between ethnic "identification" and the role expectations normally associated with such an "identification," in fact, he assumes that the two should be congruent. Those who identify themselves as Pathans should act like Pathans, and if they do not, but do act like Baluch, they must not *be* Pathans. Perhaps, in one context, they consider themselves and are considered by their neighbors to be non-Pathan; in another, Pathan. But because Barth does not deal with the possibility of "identification" (let alone "identity") being dependent upon context and because he ignores the possibility that a closer look at Pathan and Baluch notions of their own and each other's identities might be illuminating, we are left with an unresolved anomaly.

If anything, Barth overdefines ethnicity, attempting to include many aspects of behavior in a peculiarly rigid way. Ethnic group membership entails, for him, shared criteria for evaluation and judgment within the group and a stringent limit on shared understandings outside it, a situation contradicted by Lee Drummond's (1975) account of Guyana. Drummond states that members of various "ethnic" groups – European, African, East Indian, Chinese, and Amerindian – use obviously distinctive symbols and myths to differentiate themselves, and that one ethnic group's knowledge of the attitudes and values of another is extensive. This knowledge about the differences among themselves is then employed to facilitate and smooth interaction between members of two or more groups. In the Guyanese case, it may be that the obviously distinctive symbols representing each group's identity act to minimize ambiguity in communication between groups and to encourage the recognition of significant differences among them.

The apparently sophisticated Guyanese folk recognition of widespread cultural differences and the use of this recognition in facilitating communication contrasts vividly with the spotty and often inaccurate knowledge of one Robeson County group about another, despite their speaking only English and their living in close proximity for more than 200 years. It may be that the more publicly, insistently, and explicitly Indians and Blacks assert their notions of who they are, where they came from, and what it was like along the way, the more each group – Black, White, and Indian – will come to understand and respect ("appreciate" in the Southern idiom) the reactions and feelings of the others, if not always to commend them.

For Barth, ethnicity is also a status superordinate to most other statuses, one which "cannot be disregarded and temporarily set aside by other definitions of the situation." The resultant constraints on individuals' behavior "tend to be absolute" and "quite comprehensive" (Barth 1969a:17). This notion fits the race consciousness of the Southern (and much of the Northern) United States, but not that of many ethnics in, for example, urban centers in the Northern United States. Barth also notes that ethnicity can be employed as a stratagem to maximize the individual's (if not, in the Pathan case, the group's) self-interest, as he demonstrates in his analysis of the Pathans (1969b). Here again, elements of the extremes of an American situation seem to be present – a stringent code for behavior, origins, background, limited understandings between groups, ubiquitousness.

Whereas British-trained anthropologists have tended to be concerned with behavioral features, which they incorporate into a theory or definition of ethnicity, American-trained anthropologists have tended to stress the cognitive aspects of ethnicity. For example, George De Vos has stated that an ethnic group is one that is "self-consciously united around particular cultural traditions" (1975:9). He goes on to try to make further generalizations, but notes that "usually" must modify all of them. He claims that exceptions do not "render invalid a definition based on those features shared by a group which combine to create a sense of ethnicity for those who include themselves in the group" (De Vos 1975:9). In other words, whatever works, works. Among the things that "usually" work to create a sense of ethnicity are cultural traditions not shared by others with whom a group is in contact, "racial" uniqueness, common territory, stable economic base, religion, "aesthetic cultural patterns," and language (De Vos 1975:9–16). He concludes:

In brief, the ethnic identity of a group of people consists of their subjective symbolic or emblematic use of any aspect of culture, in order to differentiate themselves from other groups [De Vos 1975:16].

Just what it is that sets "ethnic" groups apart from other symbolically differentiated groups with a strong sense of unity (e.g., a "town," a religious sect, a fraternal organization) is not clear.

Some challenges

What light can a few strategically selected and geographically scattered cases shed on such attempts at universal definitions? Regarding the limiting and encompassing nature of ethnic distinctions, evidence on Morocco, where the major "ethnic" divisions are Arab–Berber–Jew, suggests that such distinctions do not "determine" relations in any very limiting way.

What knowledge of another's ethnic background seems to indicate, then, is the ties someone of such a background already is most likely to possess, the ways he is most used to forming them with others, and the common bases upon which a dyadic, contractual, consociate tie may now be formed with this person. Ethnic identities do not, therefore, constitute all-embracing stereotypes which define the ways in which persons of different backgrounds must view and relate to one another in virtually all circumstances. Rather, such an identification gives one some of the basic information in terms of which particular kinds of personal relationships can be formed, relationships which will be influenced but in no sense fully determined by this or any other single component of one's social identity [L. Rosen 1972:443].

As to the point that ethnic groups are either potentially or primarily interest groups, it cannot be denied that what have been called ethnic groups often operate as interest groups. But the definitions offered fail effectively to distinguish between any interest group and ethnic groups. Such interest groups as the American Medical Association, for example, share many norms and values, and possibly affective ties if not "primordial sentiments." A second difficulty occurs with groups referred to as "ethnic" that only under extraordinary circumstances operate as interest groups, such as the Semai of Malaysia, as described by R. K. Dentan (1975).

The Semai appear to have a notion of the individual as surrounded by potentially threatening others, the least threatening of whom are consanguineal kin. They only very reluctantly and extremely rarely cooperate in large numbers. When they do, they apparently use organizational models derived from outsiders:

Indeed, one old Semai man who has tried to bring some sort of political unity to the Semai since he worked with the late anthropologist H. D. Noone, has finally given up trying, because the pervasive suspicion of outsiders and manipulators is so great that Semai distrust each other. What unity the Semai feel they have seems to come from their constant contrast of how they live with how Malays live [Dentan 1975:54].

. . . Malaysian security forces reported that in 1953, at the height of the Emergency . . . the Semai borrowed from the Temiar an organization, based on the population of a[n] entire watershed, which would put into effect a six point program . . . designed to frustrate both the government and the terrorists. . . . Only fear of outsiders, *mai,* could have united them [Dentan 1975:60–1].

What are we to understand about such people from Cohen's point of view if they so reluctantly and seldom act as interest groups, and then defensively? Are they then not ethnic, or only weakly so?

More challenging still, it appears that one of the most taken-for-granted aspects of ethnicity – its being an ascribed status – is not strictly the case in some areas of the world. Dentan, at the end of an article on the Semai, suggests:

Western anthropologists therefore tend to concentrate on the sociocentric aspects of ethnicity, which can lead to the idea of a fixed and immutable group membership. In Malaysia such an attitude can lead to counsels of despair, unallayed by an appreciation of people's wiliness and creativity.[1975:62].

The immutability of ethnic identity was, of course, long ago challenged by Edmund Leach's (1954) accounts of Burmese Kachins changing gradually into Shans. And if the more recent accounts of Barth (1965b) concerning the Pathan/Baluch on the Afghanistan—Pakistan border and of Gunnar Haaland (1969) on sedentary Fur cultivators becoming nomadic Baggara in Western Sudan are correct, ethnicity cannot even be considered a universally ascribed status.[15]

None of the features offered as defining characteristics of ethnicity or ethnic groups seems to be universally the case. And if ethnicity is "a variable," as Cohen suggests, is it a meaningful one if it sometimes mobilizes people as an interest group and sometimes not, sometimes is highly limiting and confining and sometimes not?

Added to the difficulties of universal definitions and the cases that challenge them is the fact that so many different kinds of groups are being designated as "ethnics" because they fit under one definition or another. It is beginning to be argued that religious sects can be considered ethnic groups. Gwen K. Neville maintains that the "core community" of Southern Presbyterians qualify as an ethnic group because they possess a shared meaning system, or world view, and are heavily endogamous, and thereby "encapsulated" (1975:260). That this core community might be considered "ethnic" by most Americans on the grounds of its members' descent from lowland Scots is likely. But most American laymen, including members of this sect, would regard this core community not as an ethnic group but as a religious group. Yet, the *Harvard Encyclopedia of American Ethnic Groups* has been planned to include groups usually counted as sects, such as the Amish and the Mormons. Instead of redefining religious groups as ethnic groups, it might be more useful to determine which qualities they share and where they differ and are seen to differ by the natives.

If one can speak of the ethnicization of caste in India, as Marguerite R. Barnett and Steve Barnett (1974) and Owen Lynch (1976) have done, and of the ethnicization of race in the United States, as I have done, do we understand anything substantial about either case or about ethnicity? If caste distinctions in India, religious distinctions in Lebanon, "tribal" distinctions in Africa and Asia, and national-racial-religious distinctions in the United States are all being called ethnicity, what do we understand about what is happening in these places, or, indeed, what can any of them be presumed to have in common except social differentiation of some sort?

To use ethnicity as it is so often used, to include exceedingly diverse phenomena under a "universal" definition or to refer in passing to some unspecified kind of social diversity as "ethnic," is to trivialize and disguise the real ways in which different peoples distinguish themselves. If "ethnicity" variously implies status seeking among Mossi immigrants in Ghana (Schildkrout 1978), oppressed status for the Nahuatl-speaking Hueyapeños of Mexico (Friedlander 1975), and an attempt to avoid another status among the Lue of Thailand (Moerman 1968), do we know all we want to know about these situations, and have we exhausted the meaning of these ethnic distinctions? Deciphering, decoding, or "unpacking" meaning involves more than finding a social structural referent; it requires an elucidation of the conceptual and affective life in which a particular ethnicity exists as well.

Too few analyses provide detailed descriptions of "ethnic" categories, their meanings, and the social actions associated with whatever kind of social differentiation is taking or has taken place (but see Eickelman 1976 on religious distinctions in Morocco; Geertz 1965 on divisions based on "primordial sentiments" in an Indonesian setting; L. Rosen 1972, 1973 on social diversity in Morocco; and Tobias 1977 on Chinese "ethnicity" in one part of Thailand). It is time, too, for more studies to trace changes in the categories of social differentiation, their meanings, and their impact (such as Deshen 1974, 1976 on changes experienced by Tunisian Jewish immigrants to Israel; Foner 1978 on the changed meaning of Blackness among Jamaican immigrants in England; Schildkrout 1978 on the changing structural implications of ethnicity for Mossi immigrants in Ghana; and Sutton and Makiesky 1975 on changes in concepts of race and ethnicity among Barbadians).

Ideally, the term ethnicity should be dropped altogether as a cross-culturally useful analytic term. Rather, it should be restricted to describing and analyzing what it does best, namely, an important form of social differentiation in the United States. But because that is about as likely to happen as our ceasing to use the term race except in a strict genetic sense, some other solution will have to be found. Certainly no use of the terms "ethnic" or "ethnicity" should occur without extensive and detailed description of the situation to which it refers in *both* sociological and cultural terms. "Ethnicity" requires at least as much caution, qualification, and amplification as the term "lineage" does in kinship studies. We must know the particulars of each case, what the interplay is between the categories and concepts people use on the one hand and the way they use them and how they act upon them on the other. Only then can we begin to understand the impact on the larger society of a particular way of viewing and being in the world. It is in understanding the complexities of these interrelationships and of the changes that occur in them that the interest lies, not in trying to find a universally applicable definition.

Toward understanding

Having ranged rather widely over the world, I now want to return, briefly, to the Lumbee.[16] I have tried to present a concept of group identity as Lumbees conceive it, of its complicated connection with notions and events of history, and of its impact over a period of time. I have addressed myself throughout to the question of collective or group identity, not to the separate problem of individual psychological structure. Because the kind of collective identity Lumbees possess has come to be considered "ethnic identity," I have discussed American notions of ethnic groups and race and have examined the relation of American folk notions of ethnicity to social scientific definitions that are meant to have application in other societies.

The most common social scientific approach to ethnicity has been to look for its social structural properties, so that symbols are reduced to being merely or primarily emblematic of group differences, and ethnic identity is based on those organizational features that set one group apart from another, be they racial, regional, religious, or linguistic. Thus, this kind of ethnicity is said to be "structured" along these lines of difference. For some theorists, ethnicity has to do with minority status and/or differential access to power; for others it provides a "unit" (the ethnic group) for social analysis, the membership, boundaries, and maintenance of which are of greatest concern. Ethnicity has been treated as a "factor" in situational analysis and as an "adaptation" to a changing socio-cultural environment.[17] With this focus on social organizational features, ethnicity is seen as (1) analytically separable and definable, however difficult it may be to fix upon a definition, and (2) instrumental, a means to political or economic ends for the individuals or groups in question.

Of course we all want to know how ethnicity functions in various situations. And most of us also want to know "why" it works as it does. Some have argued that it works as it does because ultimately the people involved are exemplifying or succumbing to the forces of one or another form of determinism – psychological, economic, historical, or whatever. Others maintain that people are working out the structured principles embedded in their heads or are following the dictates of narrowly defined self-interest. Still others are concerned, as I have been here, to uncover the motivations and intentions of the people involved, on the assumption that motivations are rarely simple and are most often deeply and complexly rooted. Understanding motivation and intention here means finding what in people's shared assumptions, world view, or interpretational framework shapes the way they initiate or respond to events. It is concerned with individuals as members of a group, not with individuals per se. For example, I have tried to show that Lumbees often respond violently to what they perceive as overt threats to their group integrity in part because they see themselves as a "mean" and "proud" people who "stick together" against Whites and who should act upon this image of themselves if they are to be "really" Indian.

If such understanding is our goal, then ethnic identity is a crucial area of inquiry in any study of ethnicity. Furthermore, ethnic identity must be conceived as something more than a simple reflex of the "reality" of group organization. It must consist in more than rules for group membership, the rights and duties associated with it, the roles and expectations attendant upon it, and symbols whose meanings are only these things. What is this "something more"?

Edward Spicer (1971) offers a clue in his discussion of what he calls "persistent identity systems."[18] He maintains that when a collectivity of people and their notions about their identity as a group persist over a long period of time, despite changes in the form of the governing state, they become significantly (though unspecifiedly) different from those that do not endure. They may be said to flourish in a particular type of situation – one in which there is opposition to them as a group. They must maintain themselves in the face of this opposition, and their ideas about themselves are embodied in shared symbols that are well-defined and that are taken from a common language. These symbols fit into an emotional and intellectual world view, and it is only in these unobvious terms that their "logic" becomes manifest. The symbols inevitably link the group to its perceived past and are connected in some form to political organization. The meanings of the symbols must be tied to institutions, although the ways in which the ideas are institutionalized vary (Spicer 1971).

Even though Spicer does not use the term "ethnic groups," he has outlined a model that the Lumbee situation closely approximates. There are, however, one or two problems. First, the implicit distinction between long-lasting and shorter-term "peoples" is unsatisfying, partly because it is difficult to see how the shorter-term peoples would differ significantly (except in their longevity) in either "characteristics" or "processes." Second, although it seems undeniable that opposition and conflict influence the formulation of a group's identity, that identity can also simultaneously influence substantially the nature and outcome of conflicts, as I have argued in the Lumbee case. Third, the notion that a group identity is embodied in symbols is a rather widely accepted notion, but how well-defined the symbols must be is, or should be, an open question. At the same time that he embeds the symbols in world view, Spicer also insists that the meanings of the symbols be tied to institutions, have historical reference, and be given political expression. A major difficulty with Spicer's model is its comprehensiveness. It has too many parts that are tied together in too rigid a manner to allow us to account for, say, long periods of political quiescence or symbols that identify but do not importantly refer to the past.

This kind of difficulty in models has been described by David M. Schneider (1965b) in his argument that too many kinship models weave together descent ideology, residence rules, group organization, and the like into a seamless cloth. Instead of seeking to make a seamless cloth, he suggests that we should be teasing apart the strands from which the cloth is woven in order to see how the strands are integrated first into one pattern, then into another. An analysis based on the separation of strands is useful for certain problems, such as those presented by many kinship models, and for tracing out the logic of the relationship between American ideas of race and ethnic group. At that level of analysis, the single-strand approach has proved valuable. It has been less useful in addressing problems of ethnic identity, as it tends to reduce the phenomenon to a catalogue of possible elements, such as those detailed by Isaacs (1974) and De Vos (1975).

Spicer does provide a clue to a more useful way of addressing the problems in his insistence on the importance of symbols, their meanings, and their being embedded in world view. However, we should not expect all symbols to be well-defined, nor all notions to be fully articulated. Indeed, the following passage from Freud suggests that feelings about ethnic identity may be stronger precisely when they are not fully articulated. Freud remarked on his feelings about his Jewishness,

But plenty of other things [besides faith and national pride] remained over to make the attraction of Jewry and Jews irresistible – many obscure emotional forces [*dunkle Gefühlsmächte*], which were the more powerful the less they could be expressed in words, as well as a clear consciousness of inner reality, the safe privacy of a common mental construction [*die Heimlichkeit der inneren Konstruktion; The Standard Edition,* London, 1959:273, as quoted in Erikson 1966:148].

The key here is the phrase "the more powerful the less they could be expressed in words." In the Lumbee case, the deliberately constructed accounts of Indian origins are, as conscious formulations, rather more easily altered and less deeply felt than the incompletely articulated but more emotionally compelling concepts I have called "behavioral characteristics."

Clifford Geertz (1963), too, has stressed the emotional power of an incompletely articulated sense of "collective selfhood" that is based on "primordial attachments." In his elaboration of Shils's term, he states:

By a primordial attachment is meant one that stems from the "givens" – or, more precisely, as culture is inevitably involved in such matters, the assumed "givens" – of social existence: immediate contiguity and kin connection mainly, but beyond them the givenness that stems from being born into a particular religious community, speaking a particular language, or even a dialect of a language, and following particular social practices. *These congruities of blood, speech, custom, and so on, are seen to have an ineffable, and at times overpowering, coerciveness in and of themselves* [emphasis mine. Geertz 1963:109].

Such primordial loyalties bind people, "as the result not merely of personal affection, practical necessity, common interest, or incurred obligation, but at least in great part by virtue of some unaccountable absolute import attributed to the very tie itself" (Geertz 1963:109). The ties provide the individual with an "unreflective sense of collective selfhood," and their power is seen as "rooted in the nonrational foundations of personality" (1963: 128).[19]

The kinds of ties people feel to be primordial are those that stem from commonalities of blood ties, race, language, region, religion, and custom (Geertz 1963:111–13). These can easily become foci for political activity, but this activity is not required for their maintenance. Such ties do, of course, become particularly visible if they are politicized, when they can make those they bind "candidates for nationhood" (1963:111).

Geertz's formulation differs from Spicer's in several respects. First, by focusing on the potentially motivating power such ties have for the people bound by them rather than on the particular kinds of ties, Geertz shifts concern away from the positing of invariant symbolic connections. Second, the matter of time depth is less important than intensity of feeling, so that recently formed groups may have as strong attachments to one or another of the "givens" as those constituted long ago. Furthermore, a particular set of people may at one time in their experience emphasize ties that are different from the ties they emphasize at another time. Finally, Geertz's formulation neither over-intellectualizes commitment to the ties that provide such an important sense of identity to so many, nor overestimates the self-consciousness with which the ties are regarded. For him, the sense of collective identity is to some extent "unreflective," unselfconscious. Ideas about it need not always be "well-defined," nor need its symbols be unambiguous.

Both Freud and Geertz are dealing with collective identity as it is *felt*. The unreflectiveness, partial inarticulateness, and felt basicness of such identity points to a different kind of approach to the problem of ethnic identity – an approach centered on the meaning of that identity, particularly to those who have it. In the explication of meaning, there is always a tension or a "dialectic" between the way the actors in question see what they are doing and the way we see what they are doing. There must be a translation of their way of seeing into ours based at least implicity on comparison of the two (Geertz 1977). Unless we can gain this kind of understanding based on meaning, we cannot make sense of what they do in either their terms or ours, and we therefore cannot identify with them, so attenuated do they seem. We know our own universe of meaning to be rich and nuanced, our motivations to be complicated, our moods to be many, and our feelings to be complex. If translation fails, we are left with a world of people who are lesser beings than we know ourselves to be because they are presented as less complex, diminished, reduced to primal urges or simpleminded self-maximization, the pawns of economy, society, or history.

Meaning cannot be reduced to a reflection of the social order nor can it be equated with a catalogue of symbols, however logically interconnected they are. Rather, meaning stresses the intimate interconnection of what people think, how they feel, and what they do. The meaning of group identity to the Lumbee cannot usefully be approached by neatly laying out the factors in a scheme of group self-definition, thereby attempting to get at some "more basic structure." A "teasing apart" kind of analysis that yields strands of a formerly whole cloth in this case destroys the object of study by reducing it to the sum of its parts. Lumbee group identity is simply not reducible below the level at which they conceive themselves. It is more than the sum of its parts.

Perhaps the kind of identity the Lumbee, and many others termed "ethnics," have is better envisioned as a tangle, an irreducible, unorderly, intricate intertwining of strands.[20] If the strands were separated and laid out, the tangle would disappear and could not be replicated by reweaving because it is not orderly, as is cloth. One cannot describe a tangle as the sum of its separate strands. However, one could draw out from the tangle, without undoing it entirely, now one thread and now another for brief examination, though each must be tucked back into place before the next is plucked out so that the deformation of the whole is minimal.

The danger in using a "tangle" metaphor is that it has negative connotations in English, as something messy, disordered, improperly formed, and waiting to be untangled in such a way that it cannot revert to its former undesirable state. In English, the orderly is good, the disorderly, bad.[21] But I do not mean the term to carry negative connotations. Whether a tangle is a positive virtue or a misbegotten nuisance depends very much upon one's point of view. From the viewpoint of the hunter, tangled undergrowth is a troublesome mass that obscures the game he seeks. From the perspective of the rabbit that is the object of the hunt, tangled undergrowth is a comfortable place to rest in peace and safety, a secure hideaway, a well-protected area in which to rear its young. When I say that the kind of ethnic identity the Lumbee have is best thought of as a tangle, I refer only to the form that identity takes. I do *not* mean to imply that either the Lumbee or their group identity is a mess, that Lumbees lead disordered lives or are confused people. The image is meant to illustrate the character of their identity, not the character of the people, the state of their reason, or the nature of their social organization.

Why do I find this an appropriate metaphor for characterizing Lumbee group identity? First because the irreducible core of Lumbee identity is a conviction of the overwhelming importance of that identity, and that core is surrounded by a jumble of largely unarticulated feelings, some of which pull in opposite directions (pride and insecurity, love and hate, hope and despair or cynicism). They are all wrapped up together and resist being laid out in some logical or mechanically situational fashion. So, too, are the "behavioral characteristics" I have discussed. They are intricately ensnarled with one another, sometimes double-edged in impact, centered loosely around pride, but otherwise not all obviously connected to one another in a logically tidy structure. Thus, pride, when acted upon, leads to sticking up for oneself and one's people ("acting mean"), which reinforces pride when Whites are involved but reduces it when Indian turns against Indian. Then again, pride in the form of "acting proud" among one's own is "egotistical" and probably a contributing factor to factionalism. Further, the relationship between "pride" and "keeping one's word" might be explicated with reference to Henry Berry Lowry (who is known for keeping his word and of whom Lumbees are proud), or with respect to religion (the virtue of honesty), or even with regard to widespread Southern notions of honor (a man's word is his bond).

"Logically" these are somewhat incompatible in that religion is never (or never that I heard) mentioned in relation to Henry Berry Lowry, probably because most people who consider themselves Christians would have a difficult time maintaining that his was a life of Christian virtue (which is not to say that he did not have some Christian virtues). But religion is a matter of pride and so is Henry Berry and so is going the White man one better at his own game of honor, each in slightly different ways, each with rather different emotional nuances. The aim is not to select the "best" of these possibilities, or to order them according to a set of priorities, but to appreciate how a tangled identity manages to suggest them all, providing a welter of associations, feelings, potential take-off points.

Because it is not a fully conscious, fully articulated notion, Lumbee group identity can, for them, spontaneously and genuinely "come from the heart" rather than coldly and calculatingly from the head (which is not to be confused with "state of mind"), even if some parts of that identity are rather deliberately manipulated from time to time. Such a "tangled" form of identity can, then, encompass contradictions, ambiguities, and fuzziness. New aspects can be added without apparent difficulty, just as alterations in the ideas about origins have been rather readily absorbed into the tangle, whereas they might have challenged or even destroyed the fabric of a tightly structured and explicitly defined identity. So too, various tactics developed through the years are added to their storehouse of possibilities without threatening Lumbee notions of who they are and how they ought to behave. This flexibility in their identity allows Lumbees a wide latitude in innovating or selecting from an already established repertoire when they express that identity in various situations.

In this sense, Lumbee group identity is situational. But it should not be supposed, as some outside investigators apparently have, that any single expression of identity is the essential or summary one. Brewton Berry (1963) and Guy B. Johnson (1939, 1964) have unfortunately assumed that being "not Black" (or, in their terms, not Negro) is the cornerstone of Lumbee identity, when it is only one expression of it, and one particularly likely to occur in the presence of Whites. In other situations and more recently, the Lumbee have expressed a "not-White" aspect of their identity as well (to both Blacks and Whites). It is significant, I think, that although I never heard a Lumbee use any kind of "we" expression that includes Whites and Indians, the phrase "we non-Whites" was very much in evidence. The not-White and not-Black expressions of Lumbee identity embody only two facets of their multifaceted sense of collective selfhood.

The tangled form of Lumbee identity with its situational quality has definite advantages in an environment over which Lumbees have minimal control. The positive features of such an identity are that it allows for flexibility, easy adjustment to innovations, and the perpetuation of a repertoire of multiple possibilities at the same time that a strong sense of continuity is maintained. In this sense, a tangled type of identity can be said to have helped the Indians to adapt to changes as well as to have spurred them to initiate changes. In using the term "adapt," I do not mean to imply that the Lumbee have the collective identity they do because it is adaptive or that adaptiveness of their identity in any way adequately "explains" its existence or form. To take either of these positions would be reductionistic.

Collective identities that can be seen as irreducible tangles of concepts, emotions, and motivations can be found in many areas of the world, but it is far from clear that all of what have been labeled "ethnic groups" have the same kind of identity. Some or even much of what has been designated in the literature as ethnicity might better be considered as varieties of politicized self-identification akin to what is happening in the United States among women and the aged. The budding ethnicity of WASPs is so far mostly politicized self-identification, the ramifications of which are far more limited than those of a tangled collective identity. But some such politicized self-identification may be on its way to becoming a tangled collective identity.

It is perhaps not too surprising that the central ineffableness and primacy of their group identity has been noted by a number of Native Americans, peoples who have at various points in the last 200 years been pressed to give up their distinctive identities by the assimilationist policies of federal and state governments and whose genuineness is constantly called into question by "culture loss" accusations and "blood quantum" arguments. Louis W. Ballard, a Cherokee-Quapaw, remarks:

That same Shawnee who said, "We may use it, but it is not in the Indian heart," at the same time drives a Chevrolet truck, eats out of Melmac plates, and watches television. So it seems somewhat strange when Indians say they don't want to be white people, when at the same time they are fond of using modern day conveniences. However, one of the characteristics of the Indian, and I suppose, of many cultures like that of the Indian, is to select what he can use – and make it "Indian," in the use of it [1969:6].

In response to the question "What is an American Indian?" N. Scott Momaday, a Kiowa poet and novelist, states:

> The answer of course is that an Indian is an idea which a given man has of himself. And it is a moral idea, for it accounts for the way in which he reacts to other men and to the world in general. And that idea, in order to be realized completely, has to be expressed [*Indian Voices* 1970:49].

As an extreme case of a people lacking any remembrance or records of "traditional" Indian lifeways and any encompassing and exclusively Indian formal organizations, Lumbees are particularly conscious of both the ineffableness and the primacy of their identity. As a young Indian man put it in an interview at the second annual Lumbee Homecoming celebration in 1971:

> "Indian is a state of mind," he said, "you don't really need beads or f[e]athers.
> "It's something you can't define, but you can ride down a street and see somebody and say I bet he's from Pembroke and he will be," said [Horace] Locklear [Mikeal 1971].

The tangle of Lumbee identity has at its core an intrinsic "state of mind" that is indefinable in itself, but identifiable in its expressions, which is why one could "see somebody and say I bet he's from Pembroke and he will be." In a living situation permeated with racial inequalities, their tangled form of group identity has aided the Lumbee in their struggle for survival and betterment through the strength, vitality, flexibility, direction, and emphasis on action it provides. Their identity has done more than allow the Lumbee to survive; it has been an active, motivating force enabling them to flourish.

Appendix: Events in Lumbee political history

1835	Indians disenfranchised as "free persons of color."
1864–74	Henry Berry Lowry band active.
1885	Legal recognition of Indians as "Croatan Indians" by North Carolina General Assembly; separate schools granted.
1887	General Assembly appropriation for Croatan Indian Normal School; marriages between Indians and Blacks illegal.
1888	Croatan petition for school aid to federal government.
1911	Indians' name changed to "Indians of Robeson County" by General Assembly; separate facilities for Indians provided in state asylum for the insane and county jail and home for the aged.
1912	U.S. Senate hearings on schools for Indians.
1913	U.S. House hearings on schools for Indians; Indians' name changed to "Cherokee Indians of Robeson County" by General Assembly.
1915	U.S. Senate inquiry on status and condition of Robeson Indians, who seek recognition as Cherokees ("McPherson Report").
1921	General Assembly provides Indians with a racial screening committee for schools.
1933–34	Congress considers bill to recognize Robeson Indians as "Siouan Indians of the Lumber River"; bill fails to pass.
1938	Twenty-two Indians enrolled under IRA; Red Banks Mutual Association begun; "Longhouse Movement."
1940	Deloria pageant, "The Life-Story of a People," performed for first time.
1941	General Assembly changes name of Normal School to Pembroke State College for Indians (PSC).
1945	PSC opened to federally recognized Indians.
1947	Election of first Indian mayor of Pembroke.
1951	PSC fully accredited by Southern Association of Colleges and Secondary Schools.
1953	First Whites admitted to PSC; General Assembly changes Indians' name to "Lumbee Indians."
1954	Supreme Court decision in *Brown* v. *Board of Education;* PSC opened to Blacks; election of first Indian judge.
1956	Congress legally recognizes Lumbee Indians, excluding them from benefits for Indians.
1958	Routing of Ku Klux Klan by Indians.
1965	Passage of federal Voting Rights Act.

1966–68   Intensive voter registration campaign among non-Whites in Robeson County; formation of Black–Indian coalition movement for 1968 elections.

1968   Regional Development Association formed, later renamed Lumbee Regional Development Association (LRDA); Red Banks cooperative ends.

1969   LRDA receives first small grant to combat adult illiteracy; Lumbee Indian appointed to Indian Claims Commission; PSC becomes Pembroke State University, a branch of state university system.

1970   First annual Lumbee Homecoming Day; "Tuscaroras" form to protest loss of all-Indian schools ("Prospect Suit" filed).

1971   North Carolina Commission on Indian Affairs formed with Lumbee director; LRDA receives 1.5 million dollars in federal funds; bill to remove exclusionary clause from Congressional Lumbee Act introduced; first Lumbee bank chartered.

1972   Some Tuscaroras join American Indian Movement in "Trail of Broken Treaties," demonstrate in Washington, D.C., at BIA; Coalition of Eastern Native Americans (CENA) founded.

1973   A few Indians tried for activities in Washington and acquitted; "Tuscarora" demonstrations, sit-ins, and march to Raleigh; "Double-Voting Suit" filed.

1976   "Double-Voting Suit" won by Indians; first performance of Lumbee drama about Henry Berry Lowry, "Strike at the Wind."

1977   First Indian cooperative tobacco warehouse opens for business.

1978   "Prospect Suit" dismissed for failure to prosecute.

1979   Lumbee River Legal Services, a program designed to provide legal aid to the poor of Robeson and four surrounding North Carolina counties, opens headquarters in Pembroke.

Notes

1. Why the Lumbee?

1 The 1970 U.S. census subject report on American Indians (U.S. Bureau of the Census–Population 1973b) records a total of 27,520 Lumbee Indians. This appears to be much too low a figure, because 26,486 Indians are reported in the 1970 U.S. census for Robeson County alone (more Lumbees live in neighboring counties). There are several possible explanations. One is that the 1970 census was self-enumerating, so that people wrote down the name of their group as they chose. Not all the Indians from Robeson County agree to call themselves "Lumbees," and some persist in using names under which the group either sought or gained recognition at an earlier period, such as "Cherokee" or "Siouan." Indeed, in a list of names by which Indians identified themselves in 1970 provided to Dr. Sam Stanley, Department of Anthropology, Smithsonian Institution, by the U.S. Bureau of the Census, there are indications that many who are legally designated Lumbee called themselves Cherokee or Siouan (Stanley 1970). Another possibility is that the sampling techniques used for the Indian census (it was based on a 20 percent sample) went awry in Robeson County, where Indians are sometimes difficult to identify, prying strangers are not particularly welcome, and bureaucratic forms are viewed with suspicion.

2 In 1957, at least one Lumbee reportedly asked a visiting anthropologist, "Why do Cherokees talk Cherokee?" At that time, the anthropologist asserts, he heard no talk about the Lumbee having "lost our culture."

3 "Once upon a time (a long time ago, it now seems) I desperately wanted to make sure that I was doing the respectable and approved thing, the most 'scientific' thing possible; and now I have learned, chiefly I believe from these people in this book, that it is enough of a challenge to spend some years with them and come out of it all with some observations and considerations that keep coming up, over and over again – until, I swear, they seem to have the ring of truth to them" (Coles 1971:42)

4 Much of this research was conducted during a year at the Smithsonian Institution, Department of Anthropology, under a National Endowment for the Humanities Postdoctoral Research Fellowship in American Indian Studies, 1971–72.

5 Area from U.S. Bureau of the Census–Population (1973a:Table 9). The next largest county is Sampson County, with 945 square miles, another county with a substantial Indian population (770 in 1970, 893 in 1960). In

238

U.S. Bureau of the Census–Population (1961), Robeson County is listed as being 944 square miles in area. See also Table 1.

6   For 1970, U.S. Bureau of the Census–Population (1973a) records a density for Robeson County of 89.4 persons per square mile and a population that was 72.7 percent (61,671) rural – i.e., living in places with populations under 2,500 (Table 9). In 1960, density was greater (94.4 persons per square mile), and the population 79.7 percent rural (71,030 persons) (U.S. Bureau of the Census–Population 1961:Table 6).

7   American Indian Policy Review Commission 1976:165. The commission also reported that, in 1970, 33 percent of all employed Indians were operatives, 20 percent agricultural workers, and 5 percent professionals (1976:166). There are no comparable figures for 1960.

8   American Indian Policy Review Commission 1976:166. Comparable figures for Blacks are not available.

9   The Conservatives adopted the name "Democratic Party" in 1876 and the Radicals were Republicans. Northerners who had moved into the South after the Civil War, particularly those who had moved into positions of power, were often derogatorily referred to as "carpetbaggers" by White Southerners, especially Conservatives. Conservatives used the term "scalawags" as a term of opprobrium for Radical Republicans.

10   At that time there were no motels in Pembroke, and no conveniently located Indian-run motels.

11   See also Gossett (1963:5) and W. Jordan (1968:17–18, 36, 41).

12   See Cash's discussion of what he terms "the rape complex," which centers around the Southern White woman as a sacred symbol of the old South and as the bearer of White sons in a legitimate line (Cash 1941:115–17).

13   White blood in sufficient quantities and over a number of generations used to be able to erase a person's Blackness, at least legally. An 1835 North Carolina law disfranchising "free colored" people reads, in part, "no free negro, free mulatto, or free person of mixed blood, descended from negro ancestors to the fourth generation, inclusive (though one ancestor of each generation may have been a white person), shall vote for members of the senate or house of commons" (McPherson 1915:223). Presumably, if a person had a distant enough "negro ancestor," he would no longer be considered "free colored" and thereby would have to be "free white."

14   A Black view of the power of Black blood, a deliberately twisted version of White notions, is recorded by Piri Thomas, a Puerto Rican, whose Black friend asserted:

> ". . . places like Georgia and Mississippi and Alabama. All them places, that end in i's an' e's an' a whole lotta a's. A black man's so important that a drop of Negro blood can make a black man out of a pink-asshole, blue-eyed white man. Powerful stuff, that thar white skin, but it don't mean a shit hill of beans alongside a Negro's blood" [P. Thomas, 1967:122].

15   Jordan reports that between 1550 and 1700, American colonists "developed no image of the Indian as a potential rapist. . . . In fact the entire interracial sexual complex did not pertain to the Indian" (W. Jordan 1968:163).

16   Perhaps if a very dark child were born to a White mother, it would be likely either that the child would be given away or that the mother and child would leave the area.

17 This incident took place after the Nixon desegregation guidelines of 1970 had resulted in actual widespread desegregation in many county schools. Before that time, most teachers were segregated, as were nearly all students.

18 The Indian's wife had left him, taking the children. The woman was requesting that the court compel her husband to pay child support, which he owed. The judge sentenced the Indian to eight months in prison, suspended on the condition that he pay twenty-five dollars a week in child support. He would be on probation for eighteen months. The Indian explained to the judge that he was a farmer and simply did not make that kind of money. The judge said he realized that, but the man could get a job in a factory. As a matter of fact, the judge continued, "Bill Smith" [a White], who runs a factory over in Lumberton had recently called the judge to tell him that he needs workers, so the Indian could get the money that way. Many Indians said that the factory at issue has the worst reputation of any in the area for mistreating its workers.

19 Jewish-Americans and Greek-Americans are the two White minority ethnic groups with which Robesonians are most familiar.

20 For more material on the Baltimore Lumbees, see Amanullah 1969 Makofsky 1971, and Makofsky and Makofsky 1973.

2. Where did they come from and what were they like before?

1 After Hamilton McMillan's (1888, republished 1898) treatise tracing the Robeson Indians' origins to the lost colony, many other historians and writers echoed his premise, some without crediting McMillan for the idea: Weeks 1891 (a North Carolina historian who does cite sources and who was in personal contact with McMillan), Baxter 1895, Melton 1895, Ford 1907, Fitch 1913, Terry 1931, and McPherson 1915. Anthropologist John Swanton (1934) wrote a report at the request of the Senate Committee on Indian Affairs stating that the "probable" identity of the group was "Siouan." The Indians themselves have also written about their origins. The writings of Robeson Indians tend to reflect the political claims for origins made by Indians at the time of their writings: Oxendine 1934, Brewington n.d., Lowry 1952, Lowrey 1960, L. Barton 1967, Chavers 1971–72, and Dial and Eliades 1975 (of these two, Dial is the Indian). In addition, there is a pamphlet by Butler (1916), apparently a Sampson County Indian, who points to intermarriages between Robeson and Sampson Indians as evidence of their common heritage.

2 Because orthography in the middle of the nineteenth century was more flexible and changeable than it currently is, several major family names among the Indians are spelled differently at one period than another, or are spelled differently in different sources. In making reference to these family names in the text, I have, except where quoting directly, followed the most common form of spelling today. Thus, most descendants of Henry Berry spell their name "Lowry" today, although the variant spelling "Lowrey" is maintained in other families. A list of the most common variants found in the literature follows, with the form I have used italicized:
Chaves, Chavoes, Chavers, *Chavis*
Dyal, *Dial*
Lockileer, Lockleer, Locklaer, Lockee, *Locklear*

Lowrie, Lowery, Lowrey, *Lowry*
Mainor, *Maynor*
Revil, Revells, *Revels*

3 Meyer notes that a tradition has grown up that suggests the Highlanders were forced into exile after the Battle of Culloden, and that many of these highland families and friends settled in North Carolina, particularly in the Cape Fear area. He argues strongly against this traditional view: "In the light of present available evidence, this historical tradition is without foundation. . . . Contemporary American and British documents . . . contradict [it]" (Meyer 1961:23).

4 Historian Stephen B. Weeks, who was in touch with McMillan about these matters, notes, "The deeds for these grants are still extant and are in the possession of Hon. D. P. McEachin, of Robeson County, North Carolina" (Weeks 1891:130n). By "these grants," he means the Henry Berry and the first James Lowrie grants. Weeks repeats McMillan's assertions about what the early White settlers found, adding, "The universal tradition among the descendants of these settlers is that their ancestors found a large tribe of Indians located on the Lumber river . . ." (Weeks 1891:138). McMillan, in a letter dated August 2, 1914, claimed:

> The oldest deed in Robeson County is one made by George II to Henry Berry and James Lowrie in 1732. This deed was lost through carelessness of a surveyor. I have seen and handled that deed, which called for 100 acres of land in upper Robeson, now Hoke, at present owned by Hon. D. P. McEachern, of Red Springs [McPherson 1915:242].

5 This report is also reprinted under "Miscellaneous" (North Carolina 1907b). There are differences between the two versions (the earlier printed in 1887) which suggest to me, at least, that the earlier may be the more accurate. For example, a former name for the Lumber River was "Drowning Creek," as reported in the earlier version, not "Drowner's (?) Creek" as reported in the later one. Further, there is suspiciously more punctuation in the second. Nonetheless, I record the second version in its entirety so that it can be compared with the first. I am indebted to Wesley White, Jr., for pointing out the discrepancies.

> Bladen Troop, Will'm Davys, Capt'n, with officers, 33 men. The Troops wants _____, with Blew Caps & mountings, fring'd Pellats, _____ Carbines, Broad Swords or hangers, with which they want to be furnished. No Indians [North Carolina 1907b:311].

> Col: Rutherford's Regim't of Troop in Bladen County, 441; a Troop of horse, 36. A new Company necessary to be made at Waggomas. James Row recommended for Capt'n. Drowner's (?) Creek on the Head of Little Pedee, 50, furnishes a mixt crew, a lawless people filleth the Lands without patent or paying quit rente. Shot a Survey'r for coming to view _____ (?) Lands, being inclosed in great Swamps. Quakers to attend musters or Pay as in the Northern Counties. Fines not high Enough to oblige the Militia to attend musters. No arms, stores or Indians in the County [North Carolina 1907b:314].

6 Lefler and Newsome state that the Tuscarora had been granted 227 acres per person by North Carolina and the Catawba had been allocated 2,500 acres per person in South Carolina (1963:151).

7 This last possibility was suggested to me by W. McKee Evans.

8 The Lumber or Lumbee River has a widespread reputation in Robeson County for being dangerous, full of whirlpools, and a place to be very careful when swimming. Indeed, Haynes reported in 1918 that he had been told similar tales about the river and that, in navigating it, he found it winding, but smooth and uneventful except for brushfalls across it in some places (Haynes 1918). Because Robeson County is flat, and the river slow moving, it is difficult to imagine what might be responsible for the genesis of these stories.

9 W. McKee Evans possesses a copy of the original manuscript, which I have not seen. There is a heavily edited typescript version in the North Carolina Collection of the University of North Carolina Library at Chapel Hill, and that is the source I have used.

10 Less useful are accounts based on similar material but lacking a sense of the place and the people, such as Magdol 1973, which presents an oddly distorted picture to anyone familiar with the county. For an account immersed in Robeson County lore, see G. Barton 1979, which provides a contemporary Indian version of the Henry Berry Lowry saga using a variety of published and unpublished materials.

11 Franklin notes that an 1839 North Carolina law provided that after an insolvent person had been convicted and fined for a crime and remained in jail for twenty days, he should be discharged. This applied equally to everyone in 1839, but in 1841 the law was amended to exclude free Negroes (Franklin 1943:90).

12 Evans describes a "Breton Brigman" as a "poor white" and states that he was sought "as late as March, 1866, with a capias charging him with harboring a Confederate deserter" (Evans 1971:72). This man is probably "Britton Brigman" listed in U.S. Census Enumerators' Reports (1850) as a forty-four year-old "mulatto" farmer with a White wife and children, and real estate valued at $300. It is possible that he was a member of the Indian (then, according to Whites, the "mulatto") community. If he was, he provides another case in which one of the more prosperous members of the community ran afoul of the law as Conservative Whites were enforcing it.

13 This same position was apparently expressed to Adjutant General John C. Gorman, who had been sent to quell the band with federal troops:

> Before leaving them [the outlaws], they assured me that they would not ambush or shoot any of the troops under my command, except they should be "cornered," in which event they intended to die game. They also promised that they would not physically injure any citizen except in defense of themselves, but said they were bound to eat, and as they were not allowed to work, they would be forced to make requisitions upon the farmers for supplies . . . [letter dated October 16, 1871, Gorman to *Daily Journal,* Wilmington, N.C., as quoted in Evans 1971:218].

14 It is difficult to know at this period whether the ancestors of the Lumbee generally referred to themselves specifically as "Indians," which after all

is a White term for the aboriginal peoples whom Europeans encountered in America, which they mistook for the Indies. The ancestors may well have claimed autochthonous status, but have referred to themselves as "we people," or something of the sort. It should be borne in mind that the terms used to denote one's own group in many North American Indian languages translate into the English "people" or "human beings."

15 Compare this with Townsend's report:

> Perhaps the solution of the white race, which blended originally with the Tuscaroras – a subject on which the learned Judge Leech [Leitch?], of Lumberton, has spent much inquiry – might be solved by the gypsy suggestion [Townsend's notion]. The Judge mentioned Portuguese (a truly piratical race since the days of Tolsnois), Spanish and several other races to account for the blood which others attributed in the Lowerys to negro infusion [Townsend 1872:20, 22].

16 Evans points out that each of these political stances included a wide range of opinion, sometimes overlapping (Evans 1971:56–7).

17 Evans notes that, in 1866, the governor of North Carolina offered a reward of $300 for Lowry, which was more than an Indian day laborer could earn in four years. The 1870–71 state legislature offered a reward of $2,000, which the following legislative session raised by $10,000 (1971:73, 154–5). In the end, Lowry simply disappeared and no one was ever able to claim the reward. It is variously reported that he left the county, that he was accidentally killed by his own hand, that one of his band killed him, and that he drowned (see Evans 1971:242–57).

18 That school was important before the Civil War is seen in the number of "free Negroes" reported by their families to be students in the 1850 census. Of twenty-five counties reporting free Negro students, Robeson (47), Wake (52), and Craven (46) are the only ones with more than 12 students (as reported in Franklin 1943:169, n 28).

19 Election figures reproduced by Evans (1966:285–6) show that the Robeson County Republican vote for governor decreased by 93 and the Democratic vote increased by 462 between 1884 and 1888. The Democrats had increased their "winning" margin from 369 in 1884 to 924 in 1888. The difficulty is, of course, that these figures cannot be broken down by race.

3. What changed and how?

1 That such offices need not necessarily be arenas for the working out of factional conflict is demonstrated by Loretta Fowler (1978) for the Wind River Arapahoe, who handle conflict by absorbing new leaders into "traditional" roles, or by creating new roles with traditional justifications. Open conflict over leadership has thus so far been avoided.

2 From an obituary "written for the *Robesonian*," newspaper clipping in the possession of Adolph Dial, Pembroke, N.C.; thermofax copy in possession of author. No newspaper head, no date, no page. Date of January, 1931, inferred from a neighboring legal advertisement.

3 NCAI supported the Lumbee with this small grant ($4,300) in 1969, but by 1976, after it became obvious that LRDA was highly successful in obtaining federal funds, some of which were channeled through the "Indian

desks" of various federal agencies, NCAI voted to end the long-standing membership of the Lumbee. This act by NCAI outraged many Lumbees.

4   Significantly, Oxendine (1945:28) maintains that no work of normal school level was taught until 1926, except during summer schools.

5   Wesley White, Jr., reports from his study of Sumter County, S.C., records that between 1906 and 1925 a group of people in Sumter County sold their land to outsiders and moved away (1975a).

6   A bill changing the group's name to "Cheraw Indians" had also failed to pass Congress in 1932 (U.S. Senate Reports 1934:2).

7   The Indians of Robeson County could be enrolled under the IRA if they met the criteria for Indianness. In that act, the definition of who could be Indian was, as the Assistant Commissioner of Indian Affairs reminded a representative of the Siouan faction in 1935,

> "The term 'Indian' as used in this Act shall include all persons of Indian descent who are members of any recognized Indian tribe now under Federal jurisdiction, and all persons who are descendants of such members who were, on June 1, 1934, residing within the present boundaries of any Indian reservation, and shall further include all other persons of one-half or more Indian blood."
>
> In order to share in the benefits of this act, your people must fall within the third class [letter, Robeson County Collection 1935–42].

This definition provides that all those previously recognized as Indians and their descendants shall be Indians. For those not previously recognized, like the Lumbee, the difficulties are greater, for how is one to "prove" that he has "one-half or more Indian blood" if one has never had any governmentally recognized Indians in his family? One must first "prove" how much Indian blood his parents had, which means that he must also prove how much his grandparents had, and so on in infinite regress.

Among the Lumbee, this problem of blood was "solved" in the 1930s by a physical anthropologist who used anthropometry, a method no longer employed by physical anthropologists, to "determine" that 22 of 209 people he examined were "one-half or more Indian blood." Blood is used as a measure of Indianness by the BIA and by many other organizations and individuals who are concerned with Indians. As William C. Sturtevant and Samuel Stanley have pointed out, using such a pseudo-biological criterion for Indianness is both arbitrary and misleading:

> Legal and cultural criteria here [in defining Indianness] as elsewhere are supposedly biological ("racial") but the fact that the actual criteria are social (caste-like and in terms of self-identification) is made very obvious by the complex modern situation in the Eastern states [1968:15]. . . . Furthermore, it would be dangerous and unfair to use biological Indianness as a main criterion for eligibility for extra assistance, since the problems involved in the special situation of these groups are cultural and social and should be recognized as such.
> It would be most unfortunate to strengthen the popular American definition of social caste membership as based on biological criteria; what should be attempted is to increase the recognition that such criteria are either false, or harmful and antidemocratic [1968:16].

8   BIA staff members urged the "Tuscaroras" to incorporate as the ECIO in order to make it easier to deal with government agencies at all levels, to

avoid confusion with the New York State Tuscaroras, and to allow the possibility of including other eastern Carolina Indian groups. Nevertheless, the name "Tuscarora" is still very much in use among Robesonians.

9   MSS, Robeson County Collection 1935–42. Among these papers is a report written by Fred A. Baker, superintendent of the Sisseton Sioux Agency, who had been instructed by the Commissioner of Indian Affairs to survey conditions among the Indians of Robeson County in order to determine the feasibility of purchasing land and setting up a work relief program. A copy of Baker's July 9, 1935, report indicates that the Indians were very enthusiastic about the possibility of such a project. Other papers in the collection, such as the letters mentioned here, reveal increasing disillusionment among the Indians.

10 Although many Indians referred to the Indian Normal School as "the college," it remained a lower school for many years. The first diploma for the completion of the school's scientific course was awarded in 1905, and the first high school diploma was awarded in 1912. By 1922, only four high school diplomas had been issued. The school was given a standard normal school rating by the state in 1928, and by 1935, two years of college work was available in addition to the normal course. In 1940, the first five degrees were awarded for the completion of a four-year college course (Oxendine 1945:26–30).

11 W. Evans notes that this was mistakenly reported in the national press as having involved an Indian woman and a White man (1971:255, n 26).

4. What are they trying to do now?

1   The linking of Communist sympathies with racial liberalism is not an uncommon one among White Southerners. One of the mottoes of the Ku Klux Klan in the late 1960s was "Fight Communism and Integration."

2   Until 1966, the districts of the North Carolina House of Representatives were the 100 counties. However, in 1964, the U.S. Supreme Court declared, in *Reynolds* v. *Sims,* that representation in two houses of a state legislature must be based on roughly equal divisions of population. This caused a 300-year-old custom of separate legislative representation for each county in North Carolina to change (Fleer 1968:3). The North Carolina constitution had already provided for revising senate districts according to population, but, as Fleer (1968:3) points out, there were no changes made between 1941 and 1963. Even then, however, the 1963 changes did not accord with the standards set down in the 1964 Supreme Court decision, so further alterations occurred in 1966.

3   It should be recalled that the term "Croatan" today is to Indians the derogatory equivalent of "nigger" to Blacks, hence very insulting when used by Whites.

4   There were several kinds of bootlegging activities in Robeson County in 1967–68. The income from this "industry" is, of course, unknown because it is illegal. Both the makers and the sellers of illegal "spirits" are called bootleggers. Bootleggers who are distillers are unlicensed, hence illegal, and they produce what is known locally as "white lightning," "stumphole," or "jimmy john." Bootleggers are also sellers of untaxed alcoholic beverages – whether those made by unlicensed distillers, or liquor and beer made by legal distillers and brewers but illegally imported and sold in the county. Before 1968 Robeson County was completely

"dry" because beer, wine, and liquor could not be sold there legally. Since that time, voters have decided to allow state-regulated liquor stores and state-licensed beer outlets in some but not all areas. Not until 1978 did North Carolina bars and restaurants begin to serve alcoholic beverages.

The bootleggers in Robeson County are segregated by race, as are the patrons, generally. Some bootleggers who sell whiskey and beer are simply pick-up stores for their clients, who drive up, make their purchase, and drive away. Other bootleg sellers maintain places of entertainment for socializing and dancing, often with a "piccolo" (juke box). Although their business has no doubt been hurt by the legalization of liquor and beer sales within the county, bootleggers still remain important sources for beer after hours, for illegally manufactured whiskey, and for untaxed whiskey purchased after hours and/or by those who do not wish to be seen buying alcoholic beverages publicly. There is a social stigma attached to drinking alcoholic beverages by those who are rigorous fundamentalist Protestants.

5   Genovese (1974) and Harding (1969) argue convincingly that before emancipation, at least, Black churches and ministers were often loci of political activism, however discreetly carried on. Most often, of course, the activism was concerned with the politics of the possible.

6   From an account given to the editor of *The Lumbee* (1967:1) by the Indian youth.

7   Perhaps one indicator of changing attitudes among Indians is the apparent readiness with which some younger middle-class Indians now (in the late 1970s) attend graduate schools and even undergraduate schools in Black as well as White universities and colleges. In 1967–68, middle-class Indian students attended White institutions, not Black ones, but that pattern began to change pronouncedly in the early 1970s. One graduate student at a Black institution, a young, middle-class Indian who could easily have "passed" for White and with whom I spoke at length in 1978, evinced an unselfconscious and apparently thoroughgoing lack of prejudice against Blacks. In addition, he seemed completely at ease with himself on this score. Most other adult Lumbees that I have encountered, almost all of whom are by now at least a few years older than this young man in his mid-twenties, have been quite self-conscious about fighting prejudice against Blacks, and many were tense and uneasy with the whole subject of Black–Indian relations. Of those his age that I had known in 1967–68, none was so relaxedly unprejudiced. To me, the contrast seems great, but it is difficult to tell whether the young man with whom I talked in 1978 is simply an extraordinary person or, as I would like to think, representative of at least some younger Lumbees who are benefiting from the dramatic changes that began in the 1960s.

8   See also Powdermaker (1939:223–85) for brotherhood imagery among Mississippi Blacks in the 1930s.

5. Who do they say they are?

1   Figures from U.S. Bureau of the Census–Population (1973b:Table 11) suggest that the Lumbee rank behind many other Indian groups, both reservation and nonreservation, in median years of school completed (8.2) and in percentage of high school graduates (19.0). However, these statistics appear to be based on seriously underreported population figures.

2 Many of the spelling peculiarities of proper names in this passage result from its having been transcribed from tapes made at the conference.

3 See G. Johnson 1939:519: "They [the Indians] evidently fell back on a sort of pragmatic definition, viz.: an Indian is a person called an Indian by other Indians."

4 On such "'tied mule' incidents," cf. Sider (1971:36).

5 Stories of Henry Berry Lowry circulate in the White community, too (Evans 1971 and personal communication), although they are rarely cited in public contexts. Nor are such stories confined to Robeson County Whites. Several years after I moved away from Robeson County, I interviewed a White man who had been reared in Richmond County, two counties west of Robeson. When he was growing up, he said, Henry Berry Lowry was understood to be an Indian, a Robin Hood. Henry Berry was an important part of the legend of wild violence Whites associated with the Indians. During the time he worked in Robeson County around 1950, the Indians were not very assertive, but they had a reputation among Whites for violence – "you didn't dare insult them." He had believed this reputation enough to hasten through Pembroke whenever he had occasion to drive westward from Lumberton. "Early on, about as early as anything," he remembered hearing about the lost-colony origins of the Indians, who were called "Croatans" in his county, and about Henry Berry Lowry. There were a few people in Richmond County who were also called Croatans. When I asked whether people would call the Indians "Croatans" to their faces, he said that he could not recall, but that he knew he never did because his mother, "who was a liberal and strong-minded," would never have allowed the use of that kind of word. "She was ahead of her time."

This man had married a woman from Scotland County, the first county west of Robeson. Her father, a man in his seventies in the late 1940s, used to say that on a trip to Florida he had met an old friend from fifty or sixty years ago. They had not seen one another in all that time. His friend told him, "Henry Berry Lowry gave me twenty-four hours to get out of the county, and I took him at his word." The man I interviewed remarked, "I don't know whether the story is true, but I believed it at the time."

6 *Life* reported that there were only about 350 Indians and fewer than 100 Klansmen (1958a:27). The *New York Times Index* (1959:509) mentions 500 Indians. Indians generally set the figures for both considerably higher – Indians, at least 500; Klansmen, 300–400.

7 Whether linguists would classify the Indian mode of speech as a separate dialect, I am not qualified to say. There have been no technical studies of the matter, but I can say that by the time I left Robeson County, after seventeen months of fieldwork, I could hear differences between most Indian and non-Indian speakers, which helped me to identify Indians. And Indians themselves can often identify the precise area of the county from which another Indian comes simply from his speech.

6. What difference does who they say they are make?

1 For the purposes of this argument, "Lumbees" are not distinguished from "Tuscaroras."

2 Recent research by Thomas Johnson (1975) on the Wind River Shoshone

and by Raymond J. DeMallie (personal communication) on the Dakota indicates that when individuals were initially enrolled on some reservations, a few "full-blooded" Whites were enrolled as "full-blooded Indians," presumably because they were living in an Indian style and were fully participating members of the Indian group. The Indians apparently raised no objections.

3   Raymond D. Fogelson found a somewhat similar phenomenon among the Eastern Cherokee in western North Carolina. He was told that the "real Indians" were in the next settlement but, upon reaching that settlement, was told the "real Indians" were in yet the next settlement. He eventually came full circle without ever finding anyone who claimed to be a "real Indian" (personal communication).

4   These dates were provided by Wesley White, Jr.'s research (1975a). He notes that the Sumter County group sold their land to outsiders between these two dates and moved from the area. This is also about the time they are reported to have appeared in Robeson County (Dial and Eliades 1975:98–9).

5   Frazier notes, "from the two principal families in the communities came two of the three men responsible for the well-known business enterprises in Durham" (1939:237). In 1968, a Lumbee pointed out an adult son of the current president of one of these large Black enterprises and explained that the son's grandmother was an Indian.

6   In studying the symbols of social differentiation, attention must be paid to symbols that apparently could be used for the expression of "ethnicity" (or race, or whatever) but *are not* as well as to those that *are* so used. Further, one must look at the range of uses to which a symbol representative of ethnic identity is put in other contexts. The fact that Robeson Indians do not use symbols of physical appearance to represent their group identity is as important as the fact that they do use origins, progressiveness, and behavioral imagery in characterizing themselves.

In using a behavioral-historical kind of group definition, the Lumbee may be closer in a general way to defining themselves in the way their Indian ancestors delineated themselves than are many reservation Indians today. Many Eastern Indians of the colonial period adopted members freely and apparently counted the adoptees as full members so long as they behaved in an appropriate manner and accepted their new group's customs and values. This is a far cry from the adoption of White standards of "blood" as a criterion for membership, which has become very common on reservations as a result of BIA regulations.

7. Where does the Lumbee problem lead?

1   This analysis was first developed in Blu 1979a.

2   For changes that have taken place in racial ideology, see Gossett (1963) and W. Jordon (1968).

3   Schneider (1969) has noted that in the United States the symbolic relationships among kinship, nationality, and religion can be seen as permutations and combinations of the same set of concepts. It might be useful to explore the relations of these factors to language and race. See also T. Parsons (1975).

4   In the early modern period, "ethnic" meant "heathen," "non-Christian" (Latin, *ethnicus*). It was used, for example, to describe "pagan"

philosophers such as Plato and Aristotle, who were said to have correct morals, despite their ignorance of Christianity. I am obliged to Quentin Skinner for pointing this out.

5   Thernstrom comments:

> Not only did the Yankee City investigators display an uncritical acceptance of the opinions of informants living in the community at the time; they tended to accept the opinion of informants from a particular social group with very special biases – Yankee City's "upper uppers" [1964:231].

6   For a discussion of symbolic dominance related to religious, rather than racial or ethnic, ideas, see Rabinow (1975); for a discussion of the perpetuation of the symbolic dominance of the French elite through education and an elaboration of a theory of dominance and reproduction, see Bourdieu and Passeron (1977).

7   This point was suggested to me by Martin Trow.

8   There is some evidence that Blacks and Jews, at least in New York, were each using the other in the 1960s as a model for exhorting their own people to concerted action (Draper 1970:92–3, 116; Glazer 1972; Terry Haywoode, personal communication).

9   This is what Gramsci (1971) calls "direct dominance" of the state.

10 Although "hegemony" and "direct domination" often go hand in hand (that is, one group is both hegemonic and directly dominant), the one may be seen to exist without the other in times of change. When a group that was formerly hegemonic and dominant loses the consent of those led, but continues to rule through force, there is a crisis of authority that must be resolved (Gramsci 1971:275). On the other hand, before a group can dominate, particularly in democracies, it must exercise leadership, thereby establishing hegemony (Gramsci 1971:57–9). See also Raymond Williams's provocative discussion of hegemony (1977:108–14).

11 For example, there are Black clubs that confer high prestige upon their members and that, at least in certain areas of the country, have required light skin as an informal criterion for membership.

12 There have been similar demands from women, some of whom have attempted to constitute themselves as a "group" patterned on an ethnic model.

13 Interview with Bess Meyerson on "A Woman Is . . .", February 4, 1977.

14 This point was suggested to me by Sam Stanley and Robert Thomas.

15 For economic reasons, some Fur become nomads and eventually become incorporated into Baggara communities, where they behave like Baggara and are judged by Baggara standards. In changing their mode of living, he argues, they change their ethnic identity (Haaland 1969:71). There are, however, some perplexing features of this "change." It seems that at least some nomadized Fur speak Fur and not Arabic in everyday conversation and that when they are asked what tribe they belong to, they identify themselves as Fur. That they are also identified by others as Fur seems clear from Haaland's informant, who asked whether Haaland wanted to visit "Fur people who live as nomads" (Haaland 1969:68).

16 I am deeply indebted to Lawrence Rosen for his penetrating comments on this section. Its formulation owes much to his insights.

17 In addition to the works already cited, see Ronald Cohen (1978) for a summary of some of the recent ethnicity literature.

18 By "persistent," Spicer means long-lasting, preferably through at least two kinds of state organizations into which a people has been incorporated. His concern is with collective, not individual, identity. As to "system,"

> What makes a system out of the identity symbols is not any logical, in the sense of rational, relationship among them. The meaning that they have fit into a complex that is significant to the people concerned. The meanings amount to a self-definition and an image of themselves as they have performed in the course of their history. . . . The essential basis for its study is the full and clear determination of the cultural "logic," or consistency, of a particular identity system at a given time; in short, sound ethnographic research [Spicer 1971:798].

In this discussion, Spicer is concerned to create a framework for analysis that can be used in many areas of the world.

19 Burgess mistakenly takes "primordial" to mean "innate, or 'instinctive' predisposition" (1978:266). "Primordialness" does not refer to biological or physiological givens, but to cultural ones, which by definition are learned.

20 This "tangle" metaphor was suggested to me by Lawrence Rosen, who was more apt than I at extending my cloth-and-strands analogy.

21 The only nonpejorative word similar to tangle that I could uncover in a quick survey of fluent speakers of German, Spanish, Italian, and French was the Italian *intrecciatura,* meaning a plait or braid (order intertwining), a tangle (disordered intertwining), things entwined or twisted together, and tiara. Albert Hirschman was kind enough to unearth this for me.

Bibliography

Akwesasne Notes. 1971. "They Work Here But Their Ties Are Elsewhere; The Lumbees: What Place Is Home?" *Evening Sun,* Baltimore, Oct. 1, 1970; reprinted in *Akwesasne Notes,* Rooseveltown, N.Y., 3 (2):34 (March).

Allen, Irving Lewis. 1975. "WASP – From Sociological Concept to Epithet." *Ethnicity* 2 (2):153–62.

Amanullah, Mohammod. 1969. "The Lumbee Indians: Patterns of Adjustment." In *Toward Economic Development for Native American Communities,* Sub-committee on Economy in Government, Joint Economic Committee, U.S. Congress. Washington, D.C.: U.S. Government Printing Office, pp. 277–98.

American Indian Policy Review Commission. 1976. Final Report on Terminated and Nonfederally Recognized Indians. Task Force Ten, Final Report to the American Indian Policy Review Commission. Washington, D.C.: U.S. Government Printing Office.

Ballard, Louis W. 1969. "Cultural Differences: A Major Theme in Cultural Enrichment." *Indian Historian* 2(1):4–7.

Baltzell, E. Digby. 1964. *The Protestant Establishment: Aristocracy and Caste in America.* New York: Vintage.

Barnett, Marguerite Ross, and Steve Barnett. 1974. "Contemporary Peasant and Postpeasant Alternatives in South India: The Ideals of a Militant Untouchable." *Annals of the New York Academy of Sciences,* vol. 220, art. 6:385–410.

Barth, Fredrik. 1969a. "Introduction." In *Ethnic Groups and Boundaries,* Fredrik Barth, ed., Bergen-Oslo: Universitets Forlaget and London: George Allen and Unwin, pp. 9–38.

1969b. "Pathan Identity and Its Maintenance." In *Ethnic Groups and Boundaries,* Fredrik Barth, ed., Bergen-Oslo: Universitets Forlaget and London: George Allen and Unwin, pp. 117–34.

Barton, Bruce. 1976. "As I See It: A Letter of Brandi." *Carolina Indian Voice,* Pembroke, N.C.: Oct. 28, p. 2.

Barton, Garry Lewis. 1979. *The Life and Times of Henry Berry Lowry.* Pembroke, N.C.: Lumbee Publishing Co.

Barton, Lew. 1967. *The Most Ironic Story in American History.* Charlotte, N.C.: Associated Printing Corporation.

Bass, Jack, and Walter DeVries. 1977. *The Transformation of Southern Politics: Social Change and Political Consequence Since 1945.* New York: New American Library.

Baxter, James Phinney. 1895. "Raleigh's Lost Colony." *New England Magazine,* n.s. 11(5):565–87.
Beale, Calvin L. 1957. "American Triracial Isolates: Their Status and Pertinence to Genetic Research." *Eugenics Quarterly* 4(4):187–96.
  1958. "Census Problems of Racial Enumeration." In *Race: Individual and Collective Behavior,* Edgar T. Thompson and E. C. Hughes, eds., Glencoe, Ill.: Free Press, pp. 537–40.
Bell, Daniel. 1975. "Ethnicity and Social Change." In *Ethnicity: Theory and Experience,* Nathan Glazer and Daniel P. Moynihan, eds., Cambridge, Mass.: Harvard University Press, pp. 141–74.
Bellamy, John D. 1900. "Remarks of Hon. John D. Bellamy, of North Carolina, in the House of Representatives." Thursday, Feb. 1. Washington, D.C.: n.p. North Carolina Collection, University of North Carolina Library, Chapel Hill (Cp970.03B43).
Berlin, Ira. 1974. *Slaves Without Masters: The Free Negro in the Antebellum South.* Reprinted 1976, New York: Vintage.
Berry, Brewton. 1945. "The Mestizos of South Carolina." *American Journal of Sociology* 51(1):34–41.
  1963. *Almost White.* New York: Macmillan.
Blu, Karen I. 1972. "We People: Understanding Lumbee Indian Identity in a Tri-racial Situation." Ph.D. dissertation, Department of Anthropology, University of Chicago.
  1977. "Varieties of Ethnic Identity: Anglo-Saxons, Blacks, Indians, and Jews in a Southern County." *Ethnicity* 4:263–86.
  1979a. "Race and Ethnicity – Changing Symbols of Dominance and Hierarchy." *Anthropological Quarterly* 52(2):77–85.
  1979b. "The Uses of History for Ethnic Identity: The Lumbee Case." In *Currents in Anthropology: Essays in Honor of Sol Tax.* Robert Hinshaw, ed., The Hague: Mouton, pp. 271–85.
  n.d. "Problems Posed by Local Isolated Ethnic Groups." MS.
Bourdieu, Pierre, and Jean-Claude Passeron. 1977. *Reproduction in Education, Society and Culture.* Tr. by Richard Nice. London: Sage Publications.
Braroe, Niels Winther. 1975. *Indian and White: Self-Image and Interaction in a Canadian Plains Community.* Stanford, Calif.: Stanford University Press.
Brewington, C. D. n.d. *The Five Civilized Indian Tribes of Eastern North Carolina.* Clinton, N.C.: Bass Publishing Co. (ca. 1953).
Brooks, Dexter. 1972. MS of speech given at "Save Old Main" rally in Pembroke, N.C., Feb. 4, 6 pp. (xerox copy in possession of author).
Buettner-Janusch, John. 1973. *Physical Anthropology: A Perspective.* New York: Wiley.
Burgess, M. Elaine. 1978. "The Resurgence of Ethnicity: Myth or Reality?" *Ethnic and Racial Studies* 1(3):265–85.
Butler, George E. 1916. *The Croatan Indians of Sampson County, N.C.: Their Origin and Racial Status.* Durham, N.C.: Seeman Printery.
The Carolina Indian Voice. 1975. "Lumbee Homecoming Will Include Awards Banquet." *The Carolina Indian Voice,* Pembroke, N.C., May 29, p. 3.
  1976a. "Editorial Viewpoint – An Indian Manifesto." *The Carolina Indian Voice,* Pembroke, N.C., Oct. 7, p. 2.

1976b. "Who Are the Voters in Robeson?" *The Carolina Indian Voice,* Pembroke, N.C., Oct. 28, p. 12.

1977. "Detroit *News* Article Provokes Ire of Lumbee Indians." *The Carolina Indian Voice,* Pembroke, N.C., Jan. 20, p. 6.

Cash, W. J. 1941. *The Mind of the South.* Reprinted, n.d., New York: Vintage.

Chavers, Dean. 1971–72. "The Lumbee Story, Part I – Origin of the Tribe." *Indian Voice* 1(10):11–12, 24.

Clancy, Thomas H. 1971. "Ethnic Consciousness I." *America* 124(1):10–11 (Jan. 9).

Cohen, Abner. 1974. "Introduction: The Lesson of Ethnicity." In *Urban Ethnicity,* Abner Cohen, ed., A.S.A. Monograph No. 12, London: Tavistock, pp. ix–xxiv.

Cohen, Robert Carl. 1972. *Black Crusader: A Biography of Robert Franklin Williams.* Secaucus, N.J.: Lyle Stuart.

Cohen, Ronald. 1978. "Ethnicity: Problem and Focus in Anthropology." In *Annual Review of Anthropology,* vol. 7, Palo Alto, Calif.: Annual Reviews, pp. 379–403.

Coles, Robert. 1971. *Migrants, Sharecroppers, Mountaineers (Children of Crisis,* vol. 2). Boston: Atlantic-Little, Brown.

Daniels, Robert. 1970. "Cultural Identities Among the Oglala Sioux." In *The Modern Sioux,* Ethel Nurge, ed., Lincoln: University of Nebraska Press, pp. 198–245.

Davis, Allison, Burleigh B. Gardner, and Mary R. Gardner. 1941. *Deep South.* Chicago: University of Chicago Press.

Deloria, Ella C. 1940. Letters to Franz Boas from Pembroke, N.C., Aug. 7 and Sept. 9. Boas Collection, American Philosophical Society. Freeman Guide No. 822.

Deloria, Vine, Jr. 1969. *Custer Died for Your Sins: An Indian Manifesto.* New York: Macmillan.

DeMallie, Raymond J. in press. "The Tutelo and Their Congeners." In *The Southeast,* Raymond D. Fogelson, ed., vol. 13, *Handbook of North American Indians,* William C. Sturtevant, ed., Washington, D.C.: Smithsonian Institution.

Dentan, R. K. 1975. "If There Were No Malays, Who Would the Semai Be?" *Contributions to Asian Studies* 7:50–64.

Deshen, Shlomo. 1974. "Political Ethnicity and Cultural Ethnicity in Israel during the 1960s." In *Urban Ethnicity,* Abner Coher, ed., London: Tavistock, pp. 281–309.

1976. "Ethnic Boundaries and Cultural Paradigms: The Case of Southern Tunisian Immigrants in Israel." *Ethos* 4:271–94.

De Vos, George. 1975. "Ethnic Pluralism: Conflict and Accommodation." In *Ethnic Identity: Cultural Continuities and Change,* George De Vos and Lola Romanucci-Ross, eds., Palo Alto, Calif.: Mayfield, pp. 5–41.

Dial, Adolph L., and David K. Eliades. 1975. *The Only Land I Know: A History of the Lumbee Indians.* San Francisco: Indian Historian Press.

Dinnerstein, Leonard, and Mary Dale Palsson, eds. 1973. *Jews in the South.* Baton Rouge: Louisiana State University Press.

Dobzhansky, Theodosius. 1962. *Mankind Evolving.* New Haven, Conn.: Yale University Press.

Dollard, John. 1937. *Caste and Class in a Southern Town.* Third ed., 1957, Garden City, N.Y.: Doubleday Anchor.

Draper, Theodore. 1970. *The Rediscovery of Black Nationalism.* New York: Viking Press.

Drummond Lee. 1975. "Making a Difference: A Symbolic Analysis of Intergroup Relations in Guyana." Paper read at 74th Annual Meeting, American Anthropological Association, San Francisco.

1977. "Structure and Process in the Interpretation of South American Myth: The Arawak Dog Spirit People." *American Anthropologist* 79(4) 842–68.

Dumont, Louis. 1970. *Homo Hierarchicus: An Essay on the Caste System.* Tr. by Mark Sainsbury. Chicago: University of Chicago Press.

Eickelman, Dale F. 1976. "Moroccan Islam: Tradition and Society in a Pilgrimage Center." Austin: University of Texas Press.

Erikson, Erik H. 1966. "The Concept of Identity in Race Relations: Notes and Queries." *Daedalus* 95(1):145–71.

1968. *Identity: Youth and Crisis.* New York: Norton.

Evans, W. McKee. 1966. *Ballots and Fence Rails: Reconstruction on the Lower Cape Fear.* Chapel Hill: University of North Carolina Press.

1971. *To Die Game: The Story of the Lowry Band, Indian Guerrillas of Reconstruction.* Baton Rouge: Louisiana State University Press.

Fallers, Lloyd A. 1973. "Introduction." In *Inequality: Social Stratification Reconsidered,* Chicago: University of Chicago Press, pp. 3–20.

1974. *The Social Anthropology of the Nation-State.* Chicago: Aldine.

Fischer, Ann. 1970. "History and Current Status of the Houma Indians." In *The American Indian Today,* Stuart Levine and Nancy O. Lurie, eds., Baltimore: Penguin, pp. 212–35. Originally published 1968.

Fitch, William Edwards. 1913. "First Founders in America, with facts to prove that Sir Walter Raleigh's Lost Colony was not lost." An address before the New York Society of the Order of the Founders and Patriots of America, New York City, Oct. 29. New York: The Society.

Fleer, Jack D. 1968. *North Carolina Politics: An Introduction.* Chapel Hill: University of North Carolina Press.

Foner, Nancy. 1978. *Jamaica Farewell: Jamaican Migrants in London.* Berkeley: University of California Press.

Ford, Alexander Hume. 1907. "The Finding of Raleigh's Lost Colony." *Appleton's Magazine,* July, pp. 22–31.

Fowler, Loretta. 1978. "Wind River Reservation Political Process: An Analysis of the Symbols of Consensus." *American Ethnologist* 5(4):748–69.

Franklin, John Hope. 1943. *The Free Negro in North Carolina 1790–1860.* Chapel Hill: University of North Carolina Press.

Frazier, E. Franklin. 1939. *The Negro Family in the United States.* Chicago: University of Chicago Press.

Friedlander, Judith. 1975. *Being an Indian in Hueyapan: A Study of Forced Identity in Contemporary Mexico.* New York: St. Martin's Press.

Gaillard, Frye. 1971a. "Indians, Blacks Eye Possible Coalition." *Akwesasne Notes,* Rooseveltown, N.Y., 3 (8):35 (late autumn).

1971b. "Lumbee Indians." *South Today* 3(2):4–5 (Sept.).

Galush, William. 1974. "American Poles and the New Poland: An Example of Change in Ethnic Orientation." *Ethnicity* 1 (3):209–21.

Garn, Stanley M., ed. 1960. *Readings on Race.* Springfield, Ill.: Charles C. Thomas.

Garrow, Patrick H. 1975. *The Mattamuskeet Documents: A Study in Social History.* Raleigh, N.C.: Archaeology Section, Division of Archives and History, Department of Cultural Resources.

Geertz, Clifford. 1963. "The Integrative Revolution: Primordial Sentiments and Civil Politics in the New States." In *Old Societies and New States,* Clifford Geertz, ed., New York: Free Press, pp. 105–57.

1965. *The Social History of an Indonesian Town.* Cambridge, Mass.: MIT Press.

1973. *The Interpretation of Cultures.* New York: Basic Books.

1977. "Found in Translation: On the Social History of the Moral Imagination." *Georgia Review* 31(4):788–810.

Genovese, Eugene D. 1974. *Roll, Jordan, Roll: The World the Slaves Made.* New York: Pantheon.

Gildemeister, Enrique Eugene. 1977. "Local Complexities of Race in the Rural South: Racially Mixed People in South Carolina." B.A. Thesis, State University of New York College at Purchase.

Glazer, Nathan. 1972. "Interethnic Conflict." *Social Work* 17(3):3–9.

Glazer, Nathan, and Daniel P. Moynihan. 1975. "Introduction." In *Ethnicity: Theory and Experience,* Nathan Glazer and D. P. Moynihan, eds., Cambridge, Mass.: Harvard University Press, pp. 1–26.

Goodyear, Toni. 1972. "Republican Briefly Heads County Election Board, But Democrats Oust Him." *The Robesonian,* Lumberton, N.C., March 7, pp. 1, 2.

Gossett, Thomas F. 1963. *Race: The History of an Idea in America.* Dallas: Southern Methodist University Press.

Gramsci, Antonio. 1971. *Selections from the Prison Notebooks.* Tr. and ed. by Quintin Hoare and Geoffrey Nowell Smith. New York: International Publishers.

Haaland, Gunnar. 1969. "Economic Determinants in Ethnic Processes." In *Ethnic Groups and Boundaries,* Fredrik Barth, ed., Bergen-Oslo: Universitets Forlaget and London: George Allen and Unwin, pp. 58–73.

Haley, Alex. 1976. *Roots.* New York: Doubleday.

Hannerz, Ulf. 1969. *Soulside.* New York: Columbia University Press.

Harding, Vincent. 1969. "Religion and Resistance Among Antebellum Negroes, 1800–1860." In *The Making of Black America,* August Meier and Elliot Rudwick, eds., New York: Atheneum, vol. 1, pp. 179–97.

Harper, Roland M. 1937. "A Statistical Study of the Croatans," *Rural Sociology* 2(4):444–56.

1938. "The Most Prolific People in the United States." *Eugenical News* 23(2):29–31.

Haynes, Williams. 1918. "Down the Old Lumbee." *Field and Stream,* 23rd year, no. 1, pp. 5–7, 48.

Hobsbawm, Eric. 1969. *Bandits.* Reprinted 1971, New York: Dell.

Hodge, Frederick Webb, ed. 1907. *Handbook of American Indians North of Mexico,* part 1. Bulletin 30, Bureau of American Ethnology. Washington, D.C.: U.S. Government Printing Office.

Hulse, Frederick S. 1963. *The Human Species.* New York: Random House.

Indian Voices. 1970. *Indian Voices: The First Convocation of American Indian Scholars.* San Francisco: Indian Historian Press.

Isaacs, Harold R. 1974. "Basic Group Identity: The Idols of the Tribe." *Ethnicity* 1:15–41.

Jensen, Arthur, R. 1969. "How Much Can We Boost IQ and Scholastic Achievement?" In "Environment, Heredity, and Intelligence." *Harvard Educational Review* 39(1):1–123.

——— 1971. "Can We and Should We Study Race Differences?" In *Race and Intelligence*, C. L. Brace, et al., eds., Anthropological Studies No. 8, American Anthropological Association, pp. 10–31.

Johnson, Guy B. 1939. "Personality in a White-Indian-Negro Community." *American Sociological Review* 4(4):516–23.

——— 1964. Review of *Almost White* by Brewton Berry. *American Anthropologist* 66(1):168–9.

Johnson, Joy J. n.d. *From Poverty to Power: An Autobiography of Dr. Joy Joseph Johnson.* Fairmont, N.C.: Joy J. Johnson (ca. 1975).

Johnson, Thomas Hoevet. 1975. "The Enos Family and Wind River Shoshone Society: A Historical Analysis." Ph.D. dissertation, University of Illinois, Champaign-Urbana.

Jordan, B. Everett. 1971. Remarks. *Congressional Record,* Senate, vol. 117, no. 161, Oct. 28. 92nd Congress, 2nd Session. Washington, D.C.: U.S. Government Printing Office.

Jordan, Winthrop D. 1968. *White Over Black: American Attitudes Toward the Negro, 1550–1812.* Chapel Hill: University of North Carolina Press. Reprinted 1969, Baltimore: Penguin.

Kaye, Ira. 1963. "The Turks." *New South* 18(16):9–14.

Keil, Charles. 1966. *Urban Blues.* Chicago: University of Chicago Press.

Key, V. O., Jr. 1949. *Southern Politics in State and Nation.* New York: Knopf. Reprinted n.d., New York: Vintage.

Kilson, Martin. 1975. "Blacks and Neo-Ethnicity in American Political Life." In *Ethnicity: Theory and Experience,* Nathan Glazer and D. P. Moynihan, eds., Cambridge, Mass.: Harvard University Press, pp. 236–66.

Kim, Choong Soon. 1977. *An Asian Anthropologist in the South: Field Experiences with Blacks, Indians, and Whites.* Knoxville: University of Tennessee Press.

Lawrence, Robert C. 1939. *The State of Robeson.* Lumberton, N.C.: Little and Ives.

Lawson, John. 1714. *History of North Carolina.* Reprinted as *Lawson's History of North Carolina,* 3rd ed., 1960, Frances L. Harriss, ed., Richmond, Va.: Garrett and Massie.

Leach, E. R. 1954. *Political Systems of Highland Burma: A Study of Kachin Social Structure.* Cambridge, Mass.: Harvard University Press. Reprinted 1965, Boston: Beacon Press.

Lefler, Hugh Talmage, and Albert Ray Newsome. 1963. *North Carolina: The History of a Southern State,* rev. ed. Chapel Hill: University of North Carolina Press.

LeVine, Robert A., and Donald T. Campbell. 1972. *Ethnocentrism: Theories of Conflict, Ethnic Attitudes, and Group Behavior.* New York: Wiley.

Lévi-Strauss, Claude. 1963. *Totemism.* Tr. by Rodney Needham. Boston: Beacon Press.

Life. 1958a. "Bad Medicine for the Klan; Robeson County, N.C." *Life* magazine 44:26–8 (Jan. 27).

1958b. "Indians Back at Peace and the Klan at Bay." *Life* magazine 44:36–36A (Feb. 3).

Loewen, James W. 1971. *The Mississippi Chinese: Between Black and White.* Harvard East Asian Series, no. 63. Cambridge, Mass.: Harvard University Press.

Lorinskas, Robert A. 1974. "The Political Impact of Anglo-Saxon Ethnicity." *Ethnicity* 1(4):417–21.

Lowrey, Clarence E. 1960. *The Lumbee Indians of North Carolina.* Lumberton, N.C.: n.p.

Lowry, D. F. 1952. "No Mystery (Lumbee Indians)." *The State* (N.C.) 20(29):24.

Lucas, John Paul, Jr., and Bailey T. Groome. 1940. *The King of Scuffletoun: A Croatan Romance.* Richmond, Va: Garrett and Massie.

Lynch, Owen M. 1976. "Some Aspects of Political Mobilization Among Adi-Dravidas in Bombay City." In *Aspects of Political Mobilization in South Asia,* Robert I. Crane, ed., Foreign and Comparative Studies/South Asian Series, no. 1, Syracuse, N.Y.: Maxwell School of Citizenship and Public Affairs, Syracuse University, pp. 7–33.

McMillan, Hamilton. 1888. *Sir Walter Raleigh's Lost Colony.* Wilson, N.C.: Advance Presses.

　1890. Letter to Stephen B. Weeks, bound in Weeks Collection copy of McMillan 1888, Dec. 11. Stephen B. Weeks Collection, University of North Carolina Library, Chapel Hill.

　1898. *The Lost Colony Found* (reprint of *Sir Walter Raleigh's Lost Colony,* 1888, including "Their Advance Movement" by J. J. Blanks). Lumberton, N.C.: Robesonian Job Print.

McPherson, O. M. 1915. *Indians of North Carolina: A Report on the Condition and Tribal Rights of the Indians of Robeson and Adjoining Counties of North Carolina.* U.S. Senate Document 677, 63rd Congress, 3rd Session. Washington, D.C.: U.S. Government Printing Office.

Magdol, Edward. 1973. "Against the Gentry: An Inquiry into a Southern Lower-Class Community and Culture, 1865–1870." *Journal of Social History* 6(3):259–83.

Makofsky, Abraham. 1971. "Tradition and Change in the Lumbee Indian Community of Baltimore." Ph.D. dissertation, Catholic University, Washington, D.C.

Makofsky, Abraham, and David Makofsky. 1973. "Class Consciousness and Culture: Class Identification in the Lumbee Indian Community of Baltimore." *Anthropological Quarterly* 46(4):261–77.

Manasse, Ernst Mortiz. 1947. "Max Weber on Race." *Social Research* 14(2):191–221.

Maruyama, Magoroh. 1974. "The Development of Ethnic Identification Among Third-generation Japanese Americans." In *The Rediscovery of Ethnicity,* S. TeSelle, ed., New York: Harper & Row, pp. 98–116.

Marx, Gary T. 1967. *Protest and Prejudice: A Study of Belief in the Black Community.* New York: Harper & Row.

Mayr, Ernst. 1963. *Animal Species and Evolution.* Cambridge, Mass.: Harvard University Press.

Melton, Frances J. 1895. "Croatans: The Lost Colony of America." *Mid-Continent Magazine* 6(3):195–202.

Meyer, Duane. 1961. *The Highland Scots of North Carolina 1732–1776*. Chapel Hill: University of North Carolina Press.

Mikeal, Roger. 1971. "Being Indian: 'State of Mind,' Say Still-Proud Lumbees." *Observer,* Charlotte, N.C., July 5, no pp. Xerox in possession of author.

Milling, Chapman J. 1940. *Red Carolinians*. Chapel Hill: University of North Carolina Press.

Moerman, Michael. 1968. "Being Lue: Uses and Abuses of Ethnic Identification." In *Essays on the Problem of Tribe,* June Helm, ed., Proceedings of the 1967 Annual Spring Meeting of the American Ethnological Society, Seattle and London: University of Washington Press, pp. 153–69.

Molnar, Stephen. 1975. *Races, Types, and Ethnic Groups*. Englewood Cliffs, N.J.: Prentice-Hall.

Montagu, Ashley, ed. 1964. *The Concept of Race*. New York: Free Press.

Moody, Anne. 1968. *Coming of Age in Mississippi: An Autobiography*. New York: Dial Press.

Mooney, James. 1894. *the Siouan Tribes of the East*. Bulletin 22, Bureau of American Ethnology. Washington, D.C.: U.S. Government Printing Office.

Moreland, John Kenneth. 1958. *Millways of Kent*. Chapel Hill: University of North Carolina Press.

Neville, Gwen K. 1975. "Kinfolks and the Covenant: Ethnic Community among Southern Presbyterians." In *The New Ethnicity: Perspectives from Ethnology,* John W. Bennett, ed., 1973 Proceedings of the American Ethnological Society. St. Paul, Minn.: West Publishing Co., pp. 258–74.

NA. 1868. National Archives, Record Group 393 (Records of U.S. Army Continental Commands 1821–1920), Second Military District, Letters Received 1868, Box no. 9, Letters R-10 and R-17.

News and Observer. 1968. "U.S. Stakes Lumbees to New Future." *News and Observer,* Raleigh, N.C., July 7, section 3, p. 8.

New York Times. 1959. Ku Klux Klan. *New York Times Index for the Published News of 1958,* vol. 46, p. 509. New York: New York Times.

Norment, Mary C. 1875. *The Lowrie History*. Wilmington, N.C.: Daily Journal Print.

   1909. *The Lowrie History* (4th ed., with an appendix by Col. F. A. Olds of Raleigh). Lumberton, N.C.: Lumbee Publishing Co.

North Carolina. 1887. *The Colonial Records of North Carolina,* vol. 5. William L. Saunders, ed. Raleigh, N.C.: Josephus Daniels.

   1890. *The Colonial Records of North Carolina,* vol. 9. William L. Saunders, ed. Raleigh, N.C.: Josephus Daniels.

   1907a. *The State Records of North Carolina,* vol. 20. Walter Clark, ed. Goldsboro, N.C.: Nash Brothers.

   1907b. *The State Records of North Carolina,* vol. 22. Walter Clark, ed. Goldsboro, N .C.: Nash Brothers.

Novak, Michael. 1971. *The Rise of the Unmeltable Ethics*. New York: Macmillan.

   1974. "How American Are You If Your Grandfather Came From Serbia in 1888?" In *The Rediscovery of Ethnicity,* S. TeSelle, ed., New York: Harper & Row, pp. 1–20.

Nunn, Louise V. 1937. "A Comparison of the Social Situation of Two Isolated

Indian Groups in Northern North Carolina." M.A. Thesis, Department of Sociology, Columbia University.

Oxendine, Clifton. 1934. "A Social and Economic History of the Indians of Robeson County, N.C." M.A. thesis, George Peabody College for Teachers, Nashville.

    1945. "Pembroke State College for Indians: Historical Sketch." *North Carolina Historical Review* 22(1):22–33.

Parsons, Elsie Clews. 1919. "Folk-lore of the Cherokee of Robeson County, North Carolina." *Journal of American Folklore* 32:384–93.

Parsons, Talcott. 1975. "Some Theoretical Considerations on the Nature and Trends of Change of Ethnicity." In *Ethnicity: Theory and Experience,* Nathan Glazer and Daniel P. Moynihan, eds., Cambridge, Mass.: Harvard University Press, pp. 53–83.

Peck, John Gregory. 1972. "Urban Station: Migration of the Lumbee Indians." Ph.D. dissertation, Department of Anthropology, University of North Carolina, Chapel Hill.

Pollitzer, William S., R. M. Menegaz-Bock, and J. C. Herion. 1966. "Factors in the Microevolution of a Triracial Isolate." *American Journal of Human Genetics* 18(1):26–38.

Powdermaker, Hortense. 1939. *After Freedom: A Cultural Study in the Deep South.* Reprinted 1969, New York: Atheneum.

    1966. *Stranger and Friend: The Way of an Anthropologist.* New York: Norton.

Price, Edward Thomas, Jr. 1950. "Mixed-Blood Populations of Eastern United States as to Origins, Localizations, and Persistence." Ph.D. dissertation, Department of Geography, University of California, Berkeley.

    1951. "The Melungeons: A Mixed-Blood Strain of the Southern Appalachians." *Geographical Review* 41:256–71.

Rabinow, Paul. 1975. *Symbolic Domination: Cultural Form and Historical Change in Morocco.* Chicago: University of Chicago Press.

Radzialowski, Thaddeus. 1974. "The View From a Polish Ghetto: Some Observations on the First One Hundred Years in Detroit." *Ethnicity* 1(2):125–50.

Robeson County Collection. 1935–42. Collection of typewritten drafts, handwritten drafts, and carbon copies of letters, mostly from various Robeson County Indians to officials of the Department of Interior, Washington, D.C. Includes a report by Fred A. Baker (1935) on conditions in Robeson regarding Indians. Xerox copies in possession of author.

Rosen, Gerald. 1974. "The Chicano Movement and the Politicization of Culture." *Ethnicity* 1(3):279–93.

Rosen, Lawrence. 1972. "Muslim–Jewish Relations in a Moroccan City." *International Journal of Middle East Studies* 3:435–49.

    1973. "The Social and Conceptual Framework of Arab–Berber Relations in Central Morocco." In *Arabs and Berbers,* Ernest Gellner and Charles Micaud, eds., London: Duckworth, pp. 155–73.

Schildkrout, Enid. 1978. *People of the Zongo: The Transformation of Ethnic Identities in Ghana.* Cambridge: Cambridge University Press.

Schneider, David M. 1965a. "Kinship and Biology." In *Aspects of the Analysis of Kinship Structure,* A. J. Coale, et al., Princeton, N.J.: Princeton University Press, pp. 83–101.

1965b. "Some Muddles in the Models, or, How the System Really Works." In *The Relevance of Models for Social Anthropology,* Michael Banton, ed., Association of Social Anthropologists Monographs, no. 1, London: Tavistock, pp. 25–85.

1968. *American Kinship: A Cultural Account.* Englewood Cliffs, N.J.: Prentice-Hall.

1969. "Kinship, Nationality, and Religion in American Culture: Toward a Definition of Kinship." In *Forms of Symbolic Action,* R. F. Spencer, ed., Proceedings of the 1969 Annual Spring Meeting of the American Ethnological Society, Seattle: University of Washington Press, pp. 116–25.

Schneider, David M., and Raymond T. Smith. 1973. *Class Differences and Sex Roles in American Kinship and Family Structure.* Englewood Cliffs, N.J.: Prentice-Hall.

Schockley, William. 1972. "Dysgenics, Geneticity, Raceology: A Challenge to the Intellectual Responsibility of Educators." *Phi Delta Kappan* 53(5):297–307.

Shils, Edward. 1957. "Primordial, Personal, Sacred, and Civil Ties." *British Journal of Sociology* 8:130–45.

Sider, Gerald M. 1971. "The Political History of the Lumbee Indians of Robeson County, North Carolina: A Case Study of Political Affiliations." Ph.D. dissertation, New School for Social Research, New York.

1976. "Lumbee Indian Cultural Nationalism and Ethnogenesis." *Dialectical Anthropology* 1:161–72.

Skinner, Quentin. 1972. " 'Social Meaning' and the Explanation of Social Action." In *Philosophy, Politics, and Society,* Peter Laslett, W. G. Runciman, and Quentin Skinner, eds., New York: Barnes and Noble, pp. 136–57.

Spicer, Edward. 1971. "Persistent Cultural Systems: A Comparative Study of Identity Systems that Can Adapt to Contrasting Environments." *Science* 174:795–800.

Stanley, Sam. 1970. Compilation of special statistics on American Indians from U.S. Bureau of the Census, *1970 Census of Population.* Breakdown by group affiliation. Copy of MS for North Carolina, South Carolina, and Virginia in possession of author.

Stanton, Max E. 1971. "A Remnant Indian Community: The Houma of Southern Louisiana." In *The Not So Solid South,* J. Kenneth Moreland, ed., Southern Anthropological Society Proceedings no. 4, Athens, Ga.: University of Georgia Press, pp. 82–92.

Sturtevant, William C., and Samuel Stanley. 1968. "Indian Communities in the Eastern States." *Indian Historian* 1(3):15–19.

Sutton, Constance R., and Susan R. Makiesky. 1975. "Migration and West Indian Racial and Ethnic Consciousness." In *Migration and Development,* Helen I. Safa and Brian DuToit, eds., The Hague: Mouton, pp. 113–44.

Swanton, John R. 1934. "Probable Identity of the 'Croatan' Indians." In *U.S. Senate Reports, Siouan Indians of Lumber River,* report no. 204, 73rd Congress, 2nd Session, Washington, D.C.: U.S. Government Printing Office, pp. 3–6.

Terry, G. Cunningham. 1913. "Sir Walter Raleigh's Lost Colony of Roanoke." *Blackwood's Magazine* 194(1175):320–8.

The Lumbee. 1967. "Crippled Youth Charges Councilman with Assault." *The Lumbee,* Pembroke, N.C., June 29, p. 1.

    1969. "An Exclusive Interview with Sen. Hector MacLean." *The Lumbee,* Pembroke, N.C., March 13, p. 2.

The Robesonian. n.d. "Life of Rev. W. L. Moore . . ." Written for *The Robesonian,* Lumberton, N.C., (ca. Jan. 1931). Copy of clipping in possession of author.

    1970a. "Celebration Revived." *The Robesonian,* Lumberton, N.C., July 5, p. 8A.

    1970b. "Lumbee Indian Exemption From HEW Order Sought." *The Robesonian,* Lumberton, N.C., Sept. 2, pp. 1, 2.

    1972. "Jones Is Elected Bd. Head." *The Robesonian,* Lumberton, N.C., May 2, p. 1.

The State. 1951. "The Indians of Robeson County." *The State* (N.C.) 18 (47):3, 22.

Thernstrom, Stephan. 1964. *Poverty and Progress: Social Mobility in a Nineteenth Century City.* Cambridge, Mass.: Harvard University Press.

Thomas, Piri. 1967. *Down These Mean Streets.* New York: Signet Books.

Thomas, Robert K. N.d. "Dominated and Enclaved Peoples." MS (ca. 1977).

Tobias, Stephen F. 1977. "Buddhism, Belonging and Detachment – Some Paradoxes of Chinese Ethnicity in Thailand." *Journal of Asian Studies* 36(2):303–26.

Townsend, George Alfred, comp. 1872. *The Swamp Outlaws.* New York: Robert M. De Witt.

Trillin, Calvin. 1969. "U.S. Journal: Sumter County, S.C. – Turks." *New Yorker* 45(3):104–10 (Mar. 8).

U.S. Bureau of the Census–Agriculture. 1972. *Census of Agriculture: 1969.* Vol. 1: Area Reports, Part 26: North Carolina; Section I: Summary Data; Section II: County Data. Washington, D.C.: U.S. Government Printing Office.

U.S. Bureau of the Census–Population. 1908. *The First Census of the U.S.: 1790.* Heads of Families at the First Census of the United States: North Carolina. Washington, D.C.: U.S. Government Printing Office.

    1961. *Census of Population: 1960.* Final Report (Characteristics of the Population) PC(1)-35 A, B, C, and D. Washington, D.C.: U.S. Government Printing Office.

    1973a. *Census of the Population: 1970.* Vol. 1, Characteristics of the Population. Part 35, North Carolina. Washington, D.C.: U.S. Government Printing Office.

    1973b. *Census of Population: 1970.* Subject Reports. Final Report PC(2)-1F. American Indians. Washington, D.C.: U.S. Government Printing Office.

U.S. Census Enumerators' Reports. 1800, 1810, 1820, 1840. U.S. Bureau of the Census, *Population Schedules, North Carolina.* Enumerators' Reports, microfilm.

    1850. U.S. Bureau of the Census, *Population Schedules, North Carolina.* Original Enumerators' Reports. State Archives, Raleigh, N.C.

U.S. House of Representatives. 1913. *Hearings before the Committee on Indian Affairs on S.3258 to acquire a site and erect buildings for a school for the Indians of Robeson County, N.C., and for other purposes,* Feb. 14. 62nd Congress, 2nd Session. Washington, D.C.: U.S. Government Printing Office. (Offprint in North Carolina Collection, University of North Carolina Library, Chapel Hill.)

U.S. Senate. 1912. *Hearings before the Senate Committee on Indian Affairs on S.3258 to acquire a site and erect buildings for a school for the Indians of Robeson County, N.C., and for other purposes,* April 4. 62nd Congress, 2nd Session. Washington, D.C.: U.S. Government Printing Office.

U.S. Senate reports. 1872. *Report on inquiry into the condition of affairs in the late insurrectionary states (North Carolina),* vol. 2, part 2. Report no. 41, part 2. 42nd Congress, 2nd Session. Washington, D.C.: U.S. Government Printing Office.

    1934. *Siouan Indians of Lumber River.* Report no. 204, vol. 1. 73rd Congress, 2nd Session. Washington, D.C.: U.S. Government Printing Office.

Van Alstyne, Carol. 1967. *The State We're In . . . : A Candid Appraisal of Manpower and Economic Development in North Carolina.* Committee on Manpower and Economic Development. Durham, N.C.: North Carolina Fund.

Vecoli, Rudolph J. 1974. "Born Italian: Color Me Red, White, and Green." In *The Rediscovery of Ethnicity,* S. TeSelle, ed. New York: Harper & Row, pp. 117–23.

Wallace, A. F. C., and Raymond D. Fogelson. 1965. "The Identity Struggle." In *Intensive Family Therapy,* I. Boszormenyi-Nagy and J. L. Framo, eds., New York: Harper & Row, pp. 365–406.

Warner, W. Lloyd, and Paul S. Lunt. 1941. *The Social Life of a Modern Community.* Yankee City Series, vol. 1. New Haven, Conn.: Yale University Press.

Warner, W. Lloyd, and Leo Srole. 1945. *The Social Systems of American Ethnic Groups.* Yankee City Series, vol. 3. New Haven, Conn.: Yale University Press.

Weber, Max. 1956. *Wirtschaft und Gesellschaft: Grundriss der Verstehenden Soziologie,* 2 vols. Johannes Winckelmann, ed., Tübingen: J. C. B. Mohr (Paul Siebeck).

    1968. *Economy and Society: An Outline of Interpretive Sociology,* 3 vols. Tr. by Ephraim Fischoff, et al.; Guenther Roth and Claus Wittich, eds. New York: Bedminster Press.

Weeks, Stephen B. 1891. "The Lost Colony of Roanoke: Its Fate and Survival." *Papers of the American Historical Association* 5(4):107–46.

White, Wesley, Jr. 1975a. "Report to Dr. Sam Stanley, Center for the Study of Man," Smithsonian Institution, Washington, D.C., May 27. Typed MS, 108 pp. (on various enclaves in South Carolina).

    1975b. "A History of the Turks Who Live in Sumter County, South Carolina, From 1805 to 1972." Report to Dr. Sam Stanley, Center for the Study of Man, Smithsonian Institution, Washington, D.C., July 27. Typed MS, unpaginated.

Williams, Raymond. 1977. *Marxism and Literature.* Oxford: Oxford University Press.

Williams, Robert F. 1962. *Negroes With Guns.* Marc Schleifer, ed. New York: Marzani and Munsell.

Willis, William, S. 1963. "Divide and Rule: Red, White, and Black in the Southeast." *Journal of Negro History* 48:157–76.

Wishart, Francis Marion. 1864–72. "Diary of F. M. Wishart, Commander of Action Against the Lowery Outlaws of Robeson County, N.C. 1864–

1872.'' Typewritten MS edited and with comments by William Clifton Wishart, 1966. North Carolina Collection, University of North Carolina Library, Chapel Hill.

Wood, Peter H. 1974. *Black Majority: Negroes in Colonial South Carolina from 1670 Through the Stono Rebellion*. Reprinted 1975, New York: Norton.

Woods, Frances Jerome. 1972. *Marginality and Identity: A Colored Creole Family Through Ten Generations*. Baton Rouge: Louisiana State University Press.

Index

Both first and last names of all Robesonians and Indians elsewhere are listed, where known. All other persons are designated by first initial and last name, unless these are the same, in which case, both names are spelled out.

Magdol, E., 242n10
Mainor, John, 47, 48
Makofsky, A., and D. Makofsky, 240n20
Manasse, E. M., 206
Mandan-Hidatsa, 141
Manteo, 40, 85, 136
Manuel, William, 46, 49
manufacturing, 14, 15 (Table 2), 16, 20, 240n18
marriage, 2, 50, 58, 77, 123, 124, 127, 131, 141, 171–7, 180, 184, 240n1
Martin (surname), 48
Marx, G., 129
Mattamuskeet, 41
Maxton, N. C., 13 (Table 1), 89, 96, 156, 157
Maynor (surname), 241n2
Maynor, Lacy, 73, 74
meanness, 25, 34, 35, 124, 143, 144–7, 148, 154, 159, 160, 161, 199, 228, 232
Meherrin River, 44
Melton, F. J., 240n1
"Melungeons," 43, 182
Mesquakie, 141, 142
Meyer, D., 37, 38, 241n3
Meyerson, B., 249n13
migration, 33–4, 110, 112, 113, 164
Mikeal, R., 235
Mingo River, 174
models, 228, 229, 249n12
Moerman, M., 226
Momaday, N. Scott, 235
Monroe, N.C., 124, 125, 126
Moody, A., 28–9
Mooney, J., 41, 77, 78
Moore, William Luther, 71, 72, 78, 120, 243n2
morality: Indian views of, 120, 121, 122, 128, 129, 130, 197, 198, 210
Moroccans, 224, 226
Moss Neck, 150, 151
motivations, 203, 228, 231, 235
Mohawk, 86
Moynihan, D. P., 212, 220
"mulattoes," 32, 39, 40, 49, 50, 53, 55, 56–65, 71, 78, 173, 181, 239n13,

242n12; *see also* "free Negroes," "free persons of color"
murders, 45, 51, 52, 53, 54, 55, 56, 59, 61, 146, 150
Murphey (surname), 42

name changes, *see* legislation
Nanticokes, 181
National Association for the Advancement of Colored People (NAACP), 124, 125, 126, 132
National Congress of American Indians (NCAI), 4, 72, 73, 243–4n3
Native Americans, *see* American Indians
"naturalness," 186, 187, 188, 192, 195, 197
Navajo, 140
Neuse River, 41, 47, 174
Neville, G. K., 225
Newburyport, Mass., *see* Yankee City
Newsom, Elijah, 47, 49
Normal School, 62, 71, 72, 78, 79, 81, 86, 87, 120, 137, 138, 139, 176, 236, 244n4, 245n10; *see also* Pembroke State College, Pembroke State University
Norment, Mary, 37, 40, 42, 45, 51, 54, 55, 58, 59, 60, 61, 67, 68, 146, 147, 152, 163, 173, 182
North Carolina Colonial Records, 38, 39, 241n5
North Carolina Commission on Indian Affairs, 4, 237
North Carolina-South Carolina border dispute, 43–4
Novak, M., 209, 218

Occaneechi, 43
Office of Indian Affairs, 71; *see also* Bureau of Indian Affairs
Olds, F. A., 146, 147
oral traditions: of Indians about Henry Berry Lowry and band, 149–56; of Indians about Ku Klux Klan rally, 156–60; of Indians about origins,